Situated Cognition

Social, Semiotic, and
Psychological Perspectives

Situated Cognition

Social, Semiotic, and Psychological Perspectives

Edited by

David Kirshner
James A. Whitson

 LAWRENCE ERLBAUM ASSOCIATES, PUBLISHERS
1997   Mahwah, New Jersey   London

Lawrence Erlbaum Associates, Inc., Publishers
10 Industrial Avenue
Mahwah, New Jersey 07430

Library of Congress Cataloging-in-Publication Data

Situated cognition : social, semiotic, and psychological perspectives
   / edited by David Kirshner and James A. Whitson.
      p.   cm.
   Includes bibliographical references and index.
   ISBN 0-8058-2037-X (cloth. : alk. paper). — ISBN 0-8058-2038-8
(pbk. : alk. paper).
   1. Cognition. 2. Cognitive learning theory. 3. Cognition and
culture. 4. Learning, Psychology of. I. Kirshner. David 1950–
II. Whitson, James A.
BF311.S5686 1997
153—dc20   96-34120
                                                                  CIP

Books published by Lawrence Erlbaum Associates are printed on acid-free paper,
and their bindings are chosen for strength and durability.

Printed in the United States of America
10 9 8 7 6 5 4 3 2 1

Contents

Preface

The shift within cognitive science to situated cognition theory embraced by some psychologists (Brown, Collins, & Duguid, 1989; Greeno, 1993) and endorsed by many others (see edited volumes by Resnick, 1989; Resnick, Levine, & Teasley, 1991; Salomon, 1993) is at least as profound, philosophically and methodologically, as was the shift to cognitivism from behaviorism some 35 years prior. In the earlier shift, the exclusive focus on measurable stimuli and responses, connected only by reflex or operant conditioning, was (largely) abandoned in favor of rich descriptions of mental processes. The payoff in terms of much subtler and more variegated models of human behavior is widely accepted and applauded today.

The obvious differences between these approaches mask some of their deep commonalities. Cognitivism, like behaviorism, understands knowledge and learning as resulting from experience within a stable, objective world. Community and culture can enter into cognitivist theory only insofar as they are decomposable into discrete elements that can participate in the stable, objective realm of experience. Thus, the opportunity to explore learning and knowledge as processes that occur in a local, subjective, and socially constructed world is severely limited by both behaviorist and cognitivist paradigms. Dissatisfaction with this limitation by educators, anthropologists, psychologists, and social theorists provides the main impetus for situated cognition theory.

Most situated cognitionists also are motivated by practical concerns for education. By admitting into the psychological discourse such obvious educational interests as thoughts, schemas, and motivations, cognitive science delivered a vital service to education, enabling a constructivist mission of teaching to each student's particular conceptions and misconceptions. What situated cognition theory promises as a next step is a model for dealing with knowledge and learning as fundamentally social and cultural, rather than as artifacts of an individual's journey through an impersonal and objective world.

Within situated cognition theory, the investigation of trade apprenticeships has served as a powerful platform for analyzing the pressing problems and possibilities of schooling and schools (Lave, chapter 2, this volume; Lave & Wenger, 1991). But such research has subsequently been co-opted to argue for literal apprenticeships in the United States (Bailey, 1993; Kvale, 1995), and to advocate market-driven microvouchers as a way to eliminate public education (Perelman, 1992).

Although a theory surely is not responsible for its misuses, we believe that this tendency to locate learning entirely within the lived world of daily experience, sacrificing the opportunities that schools provide for abstractive and reflective activity, exposes certain insufficiencies in the anthropological and socioculturral traditions that currently underpin situated cognition theory.

As we discuss in the Introduction, both of these traditions have tended to invert cognitive science's traditional focus on the individual's mind/brain as the site for learning to an exclusive focus on the community of practice. As attention is redirected to the social and cultural dimensions of knowledge and learning (to the neglect of neurological, psychoanalytic, and other intrapersonal dimensions), situated cognition theory loses part of its potential to inspire education, and more broadly runs the risk of being relegated to the status of a social supplement to a still-dominant individualistic psychology.

Although situated cognitionists have long recognized the need for an integrative account of social and individual perspectives (Forman, Minick, & Stone, 1993; Lave, 1988), it seems that further theoretical resources are needed to achieve it. For this reason, the contributors to this volume address the problems of situated cognition using conceptual resources from a broader range of social theory and using analytical tools from such diverse fields as semiotics, neurology, and psychoanalytic theory.

We began addressing these issues for a symposium at the 1992 annual meeting of the American Educational Research Association that brought together Jean Lave, Valerie Walkerdine, and some of the other chapter authors to discuss the problems and challenges that situated cognition theory presents. The enormous interest in the session foreshadowed the willingness of other strong scholars to contribute to the discussion with chapters of their own. A principal strength of the book is that from its inception to the last submission, each author has developed his or her contribution in response to the existing chapters. Thus, the volume has a distinct intertextuality, revisiting the unfamiliar concepts in one chapter with new interpretations and enquiries in the next. We invite you to enter the labyrinth of ideas that constitute *Situated Cognition: Social, Semiotic, and Psychological Perspectives.*

ACKNOWLEDGMENTS

We are indebted to many colleagues and students who have supported this project through discussion, information, and critique, including the faculty and students at Louisiana State University, who provided a rich intellectual environment during the initial conception of the project; the contributors to the XMCA listserve (formerly XLCHC), who maintain a constant (and often overwhelming) discussion of Mind, Culture, and Activity; and Marcy Driscoll, whose detailed and insightful prepublication review helped us to polish and refine the book. Finally, the help of Naomi Silverman, Linda Henigin, Teresa Horton, and, previously, Hollis Heimbouch at Lawrence Erlbaum Associates has been most appreciated.

—*David Kirshner*
—*James A.Whitson*

REFERENCES

Bailey, T. (1993). Can youth apprenticeship thrive in the United States? *Educational Researcher,* *22*(3), 4–10.

Brown, J. S., Collins, A., & Duguid, P. (1989). Situated cognition and the culture of learning. *Educational Researcher, 18*(1), 32–42.

Forman, E., Minick, N., & Stone, C. A. (Eds.). (1993). *Contexts for learning: Sociocultural dynamics in children's development.* New York: Oxford University Press.

Greeno, J. G. (1993). For research to reform education and cognitive science. In L. A. Penner, G. M. Batsche, H. M. Knoff, & D. L. Nelson (Eds.), *The challenges in mathematics and science education: Psychology's response* (pp. 153–192). Washington, DC: American Psychological Association.

Kvale, S. (1995, April). *An educational rehabilitation of apprenticeship learning?* Paper presented to the American Educational Research Association, San Francisco.

Lave, J. (1988). *Cognition in practice.* Cambridge, MA: Cambridge University Press.

Lave, J., & Wenger, E. (1991). *Situated learning: Legitimate peripheral participation.* Cambridge, MA: Cambridge University Press.

Perelman, L. J. (1992). *School's out: Hyperlearning, the new technology, and the end of education.* New York: Avon.

Resnick, L. B. (Ed.). (1989). *Knowing, learning, and instruction.* Hillsdale, NJ: Lawrence Erlbaum Associates.

Resnick, L. B., Levine, J. M., & Teasley, S. D. (Eds.). (1991) *Perspectives on socially shared cognition.* Washington, DC: American Psychological Association.

Salomon, G. (Ed.). (1993). *Distributed cognitions: Psychological and educational considerations.* Cambridge, UK: Cambridge University Press.

CHAPTER ONE

Editors' Introduction to
Situated Cognition: Social, Semiotic, and Psychological Perspectives

David Kirshner
Louisiana State University

James A. Whitson
University of Delaware

As James Greeno (1993) noted, the tradition of individual psychology has exerted enormous influence on education:

> It is widely believed, I think mistakenly, that the educational impact of research in cognitive psychology has been small. It seems to me that it has been pervasive and profound. Educational practice in the United States is shaped fundamentally by the view of cognition and learning that has dominated American psychological research—a view that focusses on individual knowers and learners who acquire knowledge and cognitive skill by adding small pieces incrementally to what they have learned previously. This view has been developed in great detail in the psychological research literature. It provides basic assumptions that underlie the organization of our school curriculum, our assessments of student achievement, and important aspects of teachers' classroom practices. . . . (p. 154)

Even as Greeno noted the importance of educational psychology in maintaining traditional educational practices, his own defection, together with other leading educational psychologists (e.g., Brown, Collins, & Duguid, 1989), to situativity theory, situated cognition theory, or other positions that seek to better reflect the fundamentally social nature of learning and cognition, are providing a dramatic new opportunity to reorient education (see also Resnick, Levine, & Teasley, 1991; Salomon, 1993). This influence is most obvious in mathematics, where the National Council of Teachers of Mathematics (NCTM) has taken a proactive role through its three-volume

Standards (NCTM, 1989, 1991, 1995) in promoting a vision of mathematics learning that is fundamentally at odds with the incremental, individual accretion to which Greeno alluded. But even for mathematics education, the pervasive influence of individual psychology contributes to an educational setting in which the majority of teachers, administrators, policymakers, and students remain unable to grasp and act on the new reform initiatives (Cohen, McLaughlin, & Talbert, 1993). For instance, 73% of secondary school mathematics teachers responding to a national survey agreed or strongly agreed that "activity-based experiences aren't worth the time and expense for what students learn" (Weiss, 1995, p. 5). Situated cognition theory needs to become more widely accessible in order to extend its influence in education.

As an entrenched academic position, individual psychology has certain inherent advantages over its newly emerging rivals. First, its individualistic and dualistic orientation accords well with commonsense assumptions about thinking and being that have emerged from centuries of philosophical debate in the Western tradition (Chaiklin, 1993; Lave, 1988). Thus, challenges to individual psychology need to problematize aspects of the relationship between the individual and the collective that generally are taken as unproblematic. Second, the practitioners of individual psychology are organized into a recognized scientific community with established procedures for accepting and disseminating research. Thus, individual psychology is able to claim a unified and coherent vision of its subject matter that its competitors may lack.

In attacking the cultural common sense about knowing and being, situated cognitionists are aided and abetted by currents of postmodernist thought that are percolating through the academy. Postmodern influences serve to intervene in the automatic assumptions of modernism, creating a more receptive intellectual environment for nontraditional theorizing. Indeed, a broad cross section of educational theorists accept that there are basic problems of approach in education, and are eager for new directions.

The more pressing strategic need for situated cognitionists is to develop a cohesive and coherent theoretical approach, an approach for comprehending the complex interrelationships of all aspects of our human cognitive engagement with our worlds. We are engaged not just as individuals, but as *socii*, and we are engaged in the worlds of each other and of ourselves and of things that surround us in concrete social and material situations: worlds that necessarily include us and are in formation with us as we form ourselves in part through cognitive/transformative engagement with each other, our surroundings, and ourselves.

Current initiatives of situated cognition theory blend traditions of anthropology and critical theory (e.g., Lave, 1988, 1991) with Vygotskian sociocultural theory (e.g., Forman, Minick, & Stone, 1993; Newman, Griffin, & Cole, 1989; Rogoff, 1990). As happens in this kind of rapid progress, developments may lead to new and sometimes conflicting possibilities, creating the need to link to more broadly related initiatives that can help to orient the new theory. For instance, Chaiklin and Lave (1993) "brought together psychologists, sociologists, and anthropologists with backgrounds in activity theory, critical psychology, Barker's ecological psychology, cognitive anthropology, and ethnomethodology" (p. 4) to grapple with the "problem of context" (p. 4) that involves relations between persons acting, the social world, and activity. These disciplines are especially helpful in providing conceptual and methodological resources for investigating the fundamental processes of cognition as social and situated activity, processes that have been neglected in a traditional cognitive science that presumes cognition to be a matter of individuals acquiring "knowledge" viewed as something more abstract and situation-independent.

The turn to critical anthropology and other critical social disciplines has been necessary for recognition of the essentially social and situated nature of human cognition, but exclusive reliance on those disciplines alone would run the risk of neglecting other aspects that are needed for a comprehensive view of cognition. Instead of offering a comprehensive alternative to the traditional approach, this would serve only to provide another partial approach to cognition: a socially oriented supplement to the individually oriented approach that is destined to remain influential unless and until a true alternative appears—an alternative that, for example, explicates the nature and participation of individuals within the social processes of cognitive activity. Accordingly, the current volume continues the quest for a more adequate approach to cognition by drawing from a broader range of disciplines—including psychoanalysis, neurology, and semiotics. This reflects our belief that the nature of the phenomena themselves requires a reconceptualization so fundamental as to demand a repositioning within the broader supporting disciplines.

The book grows out of a symposium at the 1992 annual meeting of the American Educational Research Association that explored these foundational issues. Preparation for the symposium was accompanied by much crossfertilization of ideas, as the speakers (many of whom are chapter authors) read drafts of each other's papers, incorporating their responses into subsequent drafts of their own papers. This core of papers was shared with each new author subsequently invited to contribute to the book. In most cases, the new chapters are explicitly responsive to the originals. Thus, there is a distinctive intertextuality to the volume that distinguishes it from the (relatively) disconnected contributions of many edited volumes. This intertextuality is intended as a strength of the book, facilitating the integration of the diverse theoretical perspectives presented. This introduction further eases access by providing a selective overview of situated cognition theory (see Rogoff & Chavajay, 1995, for a more comprehensive discussion), followed by a preview of the general problems that the authors address herein.

AN OVERVIEW OF SITUATED COGNITION THEORY

The first point to make about situated cognition theory is that, although they celebrate its accomplishments, its principal proponents fully understand it as a work in progress. The problematics of contesting the central under-standings of one's culture are relentlessly challenging. Every response, every new insight must be subjected to intense scrutiny against the bulwark of existing theory. There is never reliance on the comforting familiarity of common sense, never an easy victory. The exacting vocabulary and syntax of much situated cognition literature, which novice readers often mistake for affectation or obscurantism, are necessary cautions against appropriation to traditional ways of thinking. As Wertsch, Tulviste, and Hagstrom (1993) noted (following Joravsky, 1989), situated cognitionists do not have the luxury of mainstream psychologists to "gloss over many issues . . . that were once at the center of inquiries into human nature [though never adequately resolved]" (p. 336).

The central philosophical assumption against which situated cognition theories struggle is the functionalist belief in mind–body dualism (Lave, 1988). Viewing the world of a person's ideas, beliefs, and (intellectual) knowledge as autonomous—essentially disconnected from their bodily (i.e., lived) expe-rience, and hence from their sociocultural context—provides broadly for a devaluing of lived experience in favor of "higher" (abstracted) contemplative activity. Because this dualist hierarchy denies the means to abstraction (through experience), it is highly corrosive to educational enterprises (St. Julien, 1994, chapter 10, this volume). Despite the pragmatic realization that knowledge entails lived practices and not just accumulated information, putting into operation educational plans that seriously consider students' experience remains a mysterious assignment for many educators. Indeed, ideas, socially reified, are enormously effective determinants of activity.

One source of inspiration for situated cognitionists is the robust expertise that ordinary folks regularly display in ordinary situations. Against the back-drop of an educational enterprise that too often fails to engage students and develop their competencies are the multifaceted ways in which people suc-ceed and learn in all sorts of out-of-school settings. Anthropologists have contributed importantly to situated cognition theory by observing such pro-ductive settings in minute detail, providing an empirical base for theorizing about situated cognition. Thus, Nunes, Schliemann, and Carraher (1993) studied street mathematics, Lave (1988) studied grocery shopping, and so forth. These studies provide a reminder of the immense human capacity for effective learning and a rich data source for theoretical reconceptualizations of learning.

The most obvious type of activity in the everyday world to look to for insights into possibilities for schooling is apprenticeship. Apprenticeship, too, is concerned overtly with the development of expert practices, but in a setting that may reflect the more successful modes of learning in everyday situations. As Lave (1991) noted, effectively structured apprenticeships do not result in the inert knowledge, negative self-images, and high failure rates that are characteristic of schooling. Indeed, apprenticeship has come to figure importantly in theories of situated learning and into alternative models for schooling practices (Bailey, 1993; Collins, Brown, & Newman, 1989; Kvale, 1995; Lave, Smith, & Butler, 1988; Lave & Wenger, 1991; Perelman, 1992).

Since the early 1980s, analyses of situated learning and thinking have drawn heavily on the Soviet sociohistorical (or sociocultural) theories of Lev Vygotsky and his collaborators and students. The sociohistorical school takes, as its central problem, the processes whereby cultures reproduce themselves across generational boundaries. This program provides a useful contrast to the behaviorist focus on low-level behavioral responses on the one hand (Vygotsky's interests were toward higher cognitive capabilities, like scientific thinking), and to Piagetian individualism on the other (see Valsiner, 1988, to understand Vygotsky in the context of contemporaneous theories).

Vygotsky's collaborator, Leont'ev, has directed concern in sociocultural theory to the appropriation of cultural tools, like language and material artifacts, into the productive sphere of the novice's activity. Appropriation in sociocultural theory is an important alternative to the intrapsychological notion of internalization in cognitive science (where something external is taken into the novice's sphere). Rather, it is an aspect of interpsychological relations in which tools, linguistic or material, in the social environment are used by the novice adaptively in experimental imitation of the larger culture's usage. Paradoxically, it is the misconstrual by a responsive social milieu of the novice's incorrect usage that provides a crucial opportunity for the novice to reconfigure his or her understanding; alternatively, the culture may acquire new meanings and methods from the individual's variations. In responsive teaching/learning, mutual appropriation is of central importance (Newman, Griffin, & Cole, 1989; Rogoff, 1990). (See Arievitch & van der Veer, 1995, for a discussion of differences between Soviet theorists on the questions of internalization and appropriation.)

THE UNIT OF ANALYSIS

The critical strategic requirement for situated cognition theory is to shift the focus from the individual as the unit of analysis toward the sociocultural setting in which activities are embedded. Traditional cognitive psychology conceives of cognition intrapsychically. To the extent that social context is considered in such analyses, it must be decomposed into discrete facts or rules that can be entered into the individual's cognitive system. The increasing sophistication with which this is being done (Minsky, 1975; Rumelhart, 1980; Schank & Abelson, 1977) should not be mistaken for a fundamental change in the cognitivist agenda (Lave, 1988; St. Julien, 1994).

Situated cognitionists have developed complementary means for breaking out of the focus on individuals: by focusing on the structures and interrelations within activity systems; and by linking the community of practice to broader categories of social and political analysis. Sociocultural theory pursues this first agenda by examining appropriation of knowledge within the *zone of proximal development* (ZPD). The ZPD "refers to an interactive system within which people work on a problem which at least one of them could not, alone, work on effectively. . . . [T]he zone is considered both in terms of an individual's developmental history and in terms of the support structure created by the other people and cultural tools in the setting" (Newman, Griffin, & Cole, 1989, p. 61). The second agenda is pursued in Lave's (1988) critical anthropology, as informed by Bourdieu (1977, 1984). Here activity (locally conceived) is linked to broader social and political institutions by distinguishing *arenas* from *settings* and by relating these to each other:

> The supermarket [for example] as arena is the product of patterns of capital formation and political economy. It is not negotiable directly by the individual. It is outside of, yet encompasses the individual, providing a higher-order institutional framework within which setting is constituted. At the same time, for individual shoppers, the supermarket is a repeatedly experienced, personally ordered and edited version of the arena. In this aspect it may be termed a "setting" for activity. (Lave, 1988, p. 151)

Both of these strategies signal important attempts to break from the hegemony of individual psychology.

Problems With the Unit of Analysis

Several recent works indicate that the problems of the move from the exclusive focus on the individual as the unit of analysis have not been adequately resolved. The crux of the matter is the possibility of a simplistic solution that increasingly is eschewed by situated cognitionists: Merely adopt the community of practice as a new unifocal unit of analysis. But as Lave (1988) pointed out, psychology (which traditionally focuses on individuals) and anthropology (which traditionally focuses on community and culture), despite their apparent tensions and disputes, are actually collaborators in maintaining the functionalist duality. Any genuine breach of the hegemony must adopt a more complex, multifocal strategy.

Lave (1988) attempted to accomplish a synthesis by framing the individual and the context as mutually coconstitutive (or dialectically related): "a dialectical relation is more than a declaration of reciprocal effects of two terms upon one another. . . . A dialectical relation exists when its component elements are created, are brought into being, only in conjunction with one another" (p. 146). But, as she noted, "it is exceptionally difficult to theorize about context, because the most relevant theoretical traditions do not take experience in the lived-in world as their analytic object" (p. 148).

Similar concerns are addressed in the sociocultural tradition. As Minick, Stone, and Forman (1993) observed in their introduction to *Contexts for Learning*, the one-dimensional view of the individual that results from adopting the activity or community as the unit of analysis needs to give way to the study of:

> real people who develop a variety of interpersonal relationships with one another in the course of their shared activity in a given institutional context. Within educational institutions, for example, the sometimes conflicting responsibilities of mentorship and evaluation can give rise to distinct interpersonal relationships between teacher and pupils that have important influences on learning. For example, appropriating the speech or actions of another person requires a degree of identification with that person and the cultural community he or she represents. (p. 6)

Both of these approaches face deep and subtle problems in theorizing a unit of analysis that recognizes individuals in all of their complexity, while simultaneously crediting the intrinsically social nature of cognition and learning. Lave's (1988) critical approach incorporating fields and settings draws from Bourdieu's (e.g., 1977, 1984) extensive efforts to rethink the subject–object dichotomies of classical and current social theory. As Collins (1993) pointed out, Bourdieu's constant leaning is toward a social determinism that undervalues the productive possibilities of everyday conflicts and contradictions:

> Bourdieu's formulation emphasizes and provides insight into the *pregivenness* of verbal situation, into the already-situatedness of situated encounters. We may still wonder, however, about an *immediate*, determinate relation between social structure and (verbal) interaction. . . . For Bourdieu, however, the actions between agents, or personal intersubjective relations, are not the social. The social is fundamentally defined by fields of relations. . . . As part of his critique of subjectivism, he rejects any attempt to "reduce social space to the conjunctural space of interactions" and argues that it is necessary to construct an objective social space, "a structure of objective relations which determines the possible form of interactions" (1984: 244). (Collins, 1993, p. 123)

Collins (1993) attributed this social determinism to the mutual interdependence (and hence, analytic intractability) of Bourdieu's central organizing principles of capital (accumulable social-symbolic resources), field (the arenas of social life and struggle), and habitus (embodied social structures). He concluded that in Bourdieu's dialectic, "the discursive always seems deducible from, reducible to, in a word, determined by, something else: class conditions, capital composition, habitus, field effects. There is a truth in this determinist argument, but it is one-sided" (p. 134).

The Vygotskyan tradition is similarly weighted toward a deterministic social plane. The source of this weighting is the central tenet that:

> Any function in the child's cultural development appears twice, or on two planes. First it appears on the social plane, and then on the psychological plane. First it appears between people as an interpsychological category, and then within the child as an intrapsychological category. . . . Social relations or relations among people genetically underlie all higher [mental] functions and their relationships. (Vygotsky, 1981, p. 163)

Of course, the determinism of the social plane is not a simplistic copying of structures to the psychological plane. But neither was Vygotsky just providing a generalized endorsement of the importance of socialization in intellectual development. "Instead of taking either position, Vygotsky argued that there is an inherent relationship between external and internal activity, but it is a *genetic* relationship in which the major issue is how internal mental processes are *created* as a result of the child's exposure to what Vygotsky called 'mature cultural forms of behavior'" (Wertsch, 1985, p. 63). Cobb, Wood, and Yackel (1993) set about to articulate a more even-handed, nondeterministic approach to constructivist (individual) and sociocultural foci by viewing the concerns as complementary but separable for the purposes of specific analyses. But as Hatano (1993) observed, such extensions "are so radical that some readers may doubt that the authors are still Vygotskians" (p. 159).

OVERVIEW OF THE BOOK

It is an overstatement to say that the current volume recommends some particular resolution to the problems of situated cognition theory we have sketched. Although written in relation to one other, the chapters reflect varying theoretical backgrounds and methods and were independently conceived. But the positions staked out, for the most part, do have a certain sense of fit with each other, and there is a story that can be told about the cumulative vision of the book. It is with this story that we launch the reader into the body of the text; recommending, however, that the chapters be individually considered and savored.

The theme of this story is that the notion of the individual in situated cognition theory needs to be fundamentally reformulated. No theoretical reconfiguration of the social world or of social practices can compensate for an individual cast in the dualist tradition. This reformulation probes the physiological, psychoanalytic, and semiotic constitution of persons.

Perhaps a good place to begin is with the notion of transfer of training that is so central to traditional cognitive psychology and to its applications in schooling. As Lave (1988) argued, traditional cognitive psychology has found precious little evidence of people's ability to apply knowledge gained in one context to problems encountered in another. Rather, psychology clings to the notion of transfer because it is the heart of the cognitivist explanation of how individuals function in a complex and diverse world: Cognitive abstraction (or analogical finesse) allows the core structure of some piece of knowledge to be shorn from its original home, to be applied in some other.

Conceived in these terms, the problem of transfer is irreconcilable. As long as contexts are seen as isolated units of sociophysical space, there is no adequate explanation for the human ability to move between them. This is the problem with both the anthropological and sociocultural approaches. Each of them begins by identifying a unitary community of practice that consists of persons and resources wherein to locate the analysis. Their analytic tools are designed to illuminate the relationships and activities within such literal communities. That communities may be understood to intersect (e.g., gender or racial groups within the community of practice of a classroom) provides a slight broadening of the confine; but even here, the peer group within the larger classroom community is defined by its sociophysical relations. The problem of transfer from context to context is alive and well within these traditions.

Lemke (1995, chapter 3, this volume) casts ecosocial systems as a new object of inquiry for situated cognition theory: "In an ecosocial systems model, the primary units of analysis are not things or people, but processes and practices. It is the processes/practices which are interdependent, linked, creating the emergent properties of the self-organizing system" (p. 47). The problem of transfer, so intractable in other approaches, is transformed into the problem of understanding how apparently discrete contexts are complexly interlinked, and how particular individuals, through multiple positionings in multiple communities, do or do not participate in those linkages.

Walkerdine (1988, chapter 4, this volume) pursues how linkages between discursive practices are manifested as a semiotic chaining of signifiers for individuals engaged in everyday activities at home or at school. Calculative rationality in, say, mathematics reflects a particular movement of signifiers away from metaphoric content toward metonymic form. For Walkerdine, this semiotic chaining is related to the psychoanalytic process of fantasizing, and she is deeply concerned with how subjects of different sorts ("woman," "the child," "mathematically talented," etc.) are produced within inscribed social and institutional practices. Agre (chapter 5, this volume) provides brief but very sharp summaries of Walkerdine (1988) and of Lave (1988) while systematically comparing and contrasting their approaches.

Kirshner (chapter 6, this volume) presents a case study of his son's logical development in infancy. In line with Walkerdine's focus on development of subjectivities, he argues that the ability to function in ways that are consistent with logic emerges not through reflective abstraction on actions (as Piaget proposed), but through an enhanced sense of agency as more responsible roles are adopted in daily life practices.

Whitson (chapter 7, this volume) also finds Walkerdine's results to be of great interest, but argues that a broader range of semiotic tools is needed for situated cognition theory. Walkerdine's semiotics draws on the Saussurean approach (through Lacan's reformulation) of signs as dyadic structures relating signifieds and signifiers. Whitson discusses how Greimas' semiotic squares can supplement her analyses by displaying the oppositions, contradictions, and presuppositions inherent in the terms she uses. But even taken together, Saussure's and Greimas' structural approaches provide only limited access to the full range of linkages envisioned in a reconceived situated cognition theory. Whitson recommends Peirce's triadic semiotics as better able to provide a comprehensive accounting of the interrelatedness of signs (although structures of binary oppositions can be important in the analysis of elements within the triadic relations). A virtue of Whitson's treatment of the complex semiotic lexicon is his clear exposition supported by revealing diagrams.

A central concern for situated cognitionists is the philosophical problem of *thought:* Thoughts are generally considered to be in the head, leading to the usual dualism of a world of mental representations separated from the real, outside-the-head world. In current situated cognition theory, the evolving applications of semiotics tend to be limited to "language as a multitide of distinct speech genres and semiotic devices" (Forman, Minick, & Stone, 1993, p. 6). In line with Peirce's dictum that we think only in signs, Whitson suggests that semiosis, the activity of signs, can be much more foundational to situated cognition by providing an analytic alternative to thought in which the constituent sign elements are distributed in the world.

Cobb, Gravemeijer, Yackel, McClain, and Whitenack (chapter 8, this volume) explore this possibility for semiosis in their observations of learning in a Grade 1 classroom. They set out to examine the development of mathematical competence within the classroom community in a way that balances the emphases on the individual and the community. They found that "a parallel can be observed between the process of constituting a chain of signification and the conceptual activity of the students who contribute to the process" (p. 220). But because signification is necessarily constituted in the social and material worlds, this focus on the individual does not entail the sense of internality that contributes to dualist thinking (as do some forms of distributed cognition theory).

Gee (chapter 9, this volume) also is interested in the mutual constitution of social and individual knowledge. Through a variety of accessible examples, he argues that familiar terms and concepts normally available through linguistic labels are cultural models, to be distinguished from the variegated and hidden midlevel meanings that reflect their situated usages in social activity. These situated usages spring from the correlation of features that situated activity and experience bring together. Using this framework, Gee explains how two social ills are interrelated: When cultural models are not integrated with their midlevel constituents through relevant practices and experiences, they form a kind of inert knowledge, unavailable for creative personal uses. At the same time, they are a vehicle for colonization, in that their use fulfills others' meaningful, situated life experience.

St. Julien (chapter 10, this volume) addresses himself to the material (neurological) substrate through which cultural models and midlevel meanings emerge. Part of the appeal of traditional cognitive psychology, he argues, is the metaphor of information coursing through the brain via the electrical circuitry of neurons, dendrites, and the like—much as it does in a serial digital computer. It is instructive, therefore, that the physiology of the brain does not support such metaphors, and that a renegade branch of psychology has devised a different kind of operating system to model learning on the computer in a way that is more neurologically plausible. Even as the serial digital computer has been a wonderful (if flawed) source of inspiration for traditional cognitive psychology, the parallel distributed processor (PDP) has inspired a connectionist psychology with much to offer situated cognition theory.

What neurology tells us is that cognition occurs as patterns of activitation in the brain, not as linear sequences. New stimuli interrupt the temporary stasis of the brain, and patterns of activation spread out until a new equilibrium is gained. Parallel distributed systems are able to perform the sorts of tasks, like pattern recognition, that people do best and have more trouble with serial processes that only computers do well. Thus, PDP systems can model the kinds of responsive interaction that situated cognition explores. Indeed, St. Julien (chapter 10, this volume) describes an experimental study illustrating how learning environments can be structured to take advantage of the perceptual underpinnings of cognition.

Bereiter (chapter 11, this volume) takes up the materiality of cognition through his observation that nonhuman animals, too, have situated cognition. He cautions that theorists with educational interests need to address themselves to knowledge products that usually are conceived of as abstract and decontextualized. In an ingenious reversal of the cognitive science position that logic-based computers simulate human cognition, Bereiter argues that (situated) humans can simulate the logic of the computer. He notes that situated cognition theory usually has directed itself toward problems of educational process and ethics and urges a more direct interest in knowledge products.

We begin the book with a chapter of Jean Lave's (1990), reprinted from *Cultural Psychology: Essays on Comparative and Human Development* with permission of the publisher. The centrality of her work to the issues discussed in this book (and indeed to situated cognition theory in general) make an overview of her work an essential starting point.

EDUCATIONAL MOTIFS

As Lave (1988) observed, the problem of continuity of cognition across settings is crucially important for education. If abstract decontextualized knowledge is theorized to be the means by which people transfer learning from context to context, then schools will set their goal to provide as much of it as possible with the greatest possible efficiency. Thus, teaching becomes telling and learning becomes listening and memorizing.

By demonstrating the local character of knowledge, situated cognition theory has created a moment in education for entertaining new ideas about teaching and learning. The next step is to develop a sufficiently compelling view of situated learning and knowing to reanimate the educational project.

Current formulations of situated cognition have not provided sufficiently robust educational models. Apprenticeship, with its focus on authentic practice, seems to undermine the very possibility of schooling, as evidenced by a resurgent interest in literal apprenticeship (Bailey, 1993; Hamilton, 1993; Kvale, 1995). Or it may lead to a literalistic focus on realistic applications in school (Nunes, Schliemann, & Carraher, 1993). More promising approaches like cognitive apprenticeship (Collins, Brown, & Newman, 1989) compete well with these others, but with no stronger claim to theoretical legitimacy.

In a similar vein, sociocultural theory stands in danger of becoming educationally trivial:

> The zone of proximal development addresses how the child can alter his behavior by adopting my behavior to become more like me. As noted above and by others (Nelson, 1986, p. 237), its use can come perilously close to a description of learning as a neobehavioristic shaping of behavior. It is especially true when the adult's role is described as a series of carefully arranged steps and teaching skills . . . and when the child's contribution as *tabula rasa* is to absorb the language and structure from the adult input. (Litowitz, 1993, p. 190)

The recent tendency of sociocultural theorists in responding to problems of context is to sidestep the issues of generality and transfer and to focus on the analysis of particular educational settings and activities. As Goodnow (1993) noted, "specificity now seems to be taken for granted by scholars working from a Vygotskian base" (p. 375). But ignoring the problems of generality and transfer does not answer education's needs. It merely cedes the field to individual psychology.

In this volume, a clear motive in shifting situated cognition theory back toward the individual is to be able to respond to the educational challenge. All three chapters that directly deal with educational issues grapple with problems of academic knowledge domains. Cobb, Gravemeijer, Yackel, McClain, and Whitenack (chapter 8, this volume) examine learning of such prototypical school topics as place value, missing addend problems, and number lines. St. Julien (chapter 10, this volume) investigates microbiological distinctions usually taught in college courses. Bereiter (chapter 11, this volume) is interested in *knowledge products* that constitute the nonsituated knowledge objects to be addressed in students' situated school learning.

As Cobb et al. (chapter 8, this volume) note, a theoretical framework for cognitive analysis does not imply a unitary instructional approach. They chose to adopt Realistic Mathematics Education (RME) to ground the educational approaches taken in the Grade 1 classroom they studied because they found it generally congruous with their framework. But RME was developed independently from it, and presumably reflects a variety of other theoretical concerns and priorities.

Similarly, Bereiter (chapter 11, this volume) promotes *collaborative knowledge building* as an educational method that is generally compatible with his views on the situated nature of cognition. But collaborative knowledge building incorporates a variety of theoretical notions like *intentional learning* (Bereiter & Scardamalia, 1989) that are grounded in cognitive science theory. Intentional learning might also yield to the sorts of psychoanalytic approaches advanced in an emerging situated cognition paradigm, but this has not been attempted. In general, instructional programs that respond to the full range of concerns of educational practice provide too complex a starting point for situated cognition theory.

In this respect, St. Julien's (chapter 10, this volume) investigation of learning in an experimentally contrived and controlled environment may be more tractable. St. Julien developed a computer microworld that instantiates his theoretical observations about the need for distinctions to arise from perceptual experience in situated activity prior to the usual semiotic mediation of intellectual discourse. His results provide strong corroboration for this principle. **Perception before mentation:** certainly not a theory of instruction, but perhaps a building block for a situated educational practice that truly integrates individual and social dimensions.

REFERENCES

Arievitch, I., & van der Veer, R. (1995). Furthering the internalization debate: Gal'perin's contribution. *Human Development, 38*, 113–126.

Bailey, T. (1993). Can youth apprenticeship thrive in the United States? *Educational Researcher, 22*(3), 4–10.

Bereiter, C., & Scardamalia, M. (1989). Intentional learning as a goal of instruction. In L. B. Resnick (Ed.), *Knowing, learning, and instruction* (pp. 361–392). Hillsdale, NJ: Lawrence Erlbaum Associates.

Bourdieu, P. (1977). *Outline of a theory of practice.* Cambridge, UK: Cambridge University Press.

Bourdieu, P. (1984). *Distinction: A social critique of the judgement of taste.* Cambridge, MA: Harvard University Press.

Brown, J. S., Collins, A., & Duguid, P. (1989). Situated cognition and the culture of learning. *Educational Researcher, 18*(1), 32–42.

Chaiklin, S. (1993). Understanding the social scientific practice of *Understanding Practice.* In S. Chaiklin & J. Lave (Eds.), *Understanding practice: Perspectives on activity and context* (pp. 377–401). Cambridge, UK: Cambridge University Press.

Chaiklin, S., & Lave, J. (Eds.). (1993). *Understanding practice: Perspectives on activity and context.* Cambridge, UK: Cambridge University Press.

Cobb, P. (1994). Where is the mind? Constructivist and sociocultural perspectives on mathematical development. *Educational Researcher, 23*, 13–20.

Cobb, P., Wood, T., & Yackel, E. (1993). Discourse, mathematical thinking, and classroom practice. In E. Forman, N. Minick, & C. A. Stone (Eds.), *Contexts for learning: Sociocultural dynamics in children's development* (pp. 91–119). New York: Oxford University Press.

Cohen, D. K., McLaughlin, M. W., & Talbert, J. E. (Eds.). (1993). *Teaching for understanding.* San Francisco: Jossey-Bass.

Collins, A., Brown, J. S., & Newman, S. (1989). Cognitive apprenticeship: Teaching the crafts of reading, writing, and mathematics. In L. B. Resnick (Ed.), *Knowing, learning, and instruction* (pp. 453–493). Hillsdale, NJ: Lawrence Erlbaum Associates.

Collins, J. (1993). Determination and contradiction: An appreciation of and critique of the work of Pierre Bourdieu on language and education. In C. Calhoun, E. LiPuma, & M. Postone (Eds.), *Bourdieu: Critical perspectives* (pp. 116–138). Chicago: University of Chicago Press.

Forman, E., Minick, N., & Stone, C. A. (Eds.). (1993). *Contexts for learning: Sociocultural dynamics in children's development.* New York: Oxford University Press.

Goodnow, J. J. (1993). Direction of post-Vygotskian research. In E. Forman, N. Minick, & C. A. Stone (Eds.), *Contexts for learning: Sociocultural dynamics in children's development* (pp. 369–381). New York: Oxford University Press.

Greeno, J. G. (1993). For research to reform education and cognitive science. In L. A. Penner, G. M. Batsche, H. M. Knoff, & D. L. Nelson (Eds.), *The challenges in mathematics and science education: Psychology's response* (pp. 153–192). Washington, DC: American Psychological Association.

Hatano, G. (1993). Time to merge Vygotskian and constructivist conceptions of knowledge acquisition. In E. Forman, N. Minick, & C. A. Stone (Eds.), *Contexts for learning: Sociocultural dynamics in children's development* (pp. 153–166). New York: Oxford University Press.

Hamilton, S. F. (1993). Prospects for an American-style youth apprenticeship system. *Educational Researcher, 22*(3), 11–16.

Joravsky, D. (1989). *Russian psychology: A critical history.* Oxford, UK: Basil Blackwell.

Kvale, S. (1995, April). *An educational rehabilitation of apprenticeship learning?* Paper presented to the American Educational Research Association, San Francisco.

Lave, J. (1988). *Cognition in practice.* Cambridge, UK: Cambridge University Press.

Lave, J. (1990). The culture of acquisition and the practice of understanding. In J. W. Stigler, R. A. Shweder, & G. Herdt (Eds.), *Cultural psychology: Essays on comparative and human development* (pp. 309–327). Cambridge, UK: Cambridge University Press.

Lave, J. (1991). Situated learning in communities of practice. In L. B. Resnick, J. M. Levine, & S. D. Teasley (Eds.), *Perspectives on socially shared cognition* (pp. 63–82). Washington, DC: American Psychological Association.

Lave, J., Smith, S., & Butler, M. (1988). Problem solving as everyday practice. In R. I. Charles & E. A. Silver (Eds.), *The teaching and assessing of mathematical problem solving* (pp. 61–81). Hillsdale, NJ: Lawrence Erlbaum Associates; Reston, VA: NCTM.

Lave, J., & Wenger, E. (1991). *Situated learning: Legitimate peripheral participation.* Cambridge, UK: Cambridge University Press.

Lemke, J. L. (1995). *Textual politics: Discourse and social dynamics.* London: Taylor & Francis.

Litowitz, B. E. (1993). Deconstruction in the zone of proximal development. In E. Forman, N. Minick, & C. A. Stone (Eds.), *Contexts for learning: Sociocultural dynamics in children's development* (pp. 184–196). New York: Oxford University Press.

Minick, N., Stone, C. A., & Forman, E. A. (1993). Integration of individual, social, and institutional process in accounts of children's learning and development. In E. Forman, N. Minick, & C. A. Stone (Eds.), *Contexts for learning: Sociocultural dynamics in children's development* (pp. 3–16). New York: Oxford University Press.

Minsky, M. (1975). A framework for representing knowledge. In P. H. Winston (Ed.), *The psychology of computer vision* (pp. 211–277). New York: McGraw-Hill.

National Council of Teachers of Mathematics. (1989). *Curriculum and evaluation standards for school mathematics.* Reston, VA: Author.

National Council of Teachers of Mathematics. (1991). *Professional standards for the teaching of school mathematics.* Reston, VA: Author.

National Council of Teachers of Mathematics. (1995). *Assessment standards for school mathematics.* Reston, VA: Author.

Nelson, K. (1986). *Event knowledge: Structure and function in development.* Hillsdale, NJ: Lawrence Erlbaum Associates.

Newman, D., Griffin, P., & Cole, M. (1989). *The construction zone.* Cambridge, UK: Cambridge University Press.

Nunes, T., Schliemann, A. D., & Carraher, D. W. (1993). *Street mathematics and school mathematics.* Cambridge, UK: Cambridge University Press.

Perelman, L. J. (1992). *School's out: Hyperlearning, the new technology, and the end of education.* New York: Avon.

Resnick, L. B., Levine, J. M., & Teasley S. D. (Eds.). (1991). *Perspectives on socially shared cognition.* Washington, DC: American Psychological Association.

Rogoff, B. (1990). *Apprenticeship in thinking.* New York: Oxford University Press.

Rogoff, B., & Chavajay, P. (1995). What's become of research on the cultural basis of cognitive development? *American Psychologist, 50*(10), 859–877.

Rumelhart, D. (1980). Schemata: The building blocks of cognition. In R. J. Spiro, B. C. Bruce, & W. F. Brewer (Eds.), *Theoretical issues in reading and comprehension* (pp. 33–58). Hillsdale, NJ: Lawrence Erlbaum Associates.

Salomon, G. (Ed.). (1993). *Distributed cognitions: Psychological and educational considerations.* Cambridge, UK: Cambridge University Press.

Schank, R. C., & Abelson, R. (1977). *Scripts, plans, goals, and understanding.* Hillsdale, NJ: Lawrence Erlbaum Associates.

St. Julien, J. (1994). *Cognition and learning: The implications of a situated connectionist perspective for theory and practice in education.* Unpublished doctoral dissertation, Louisiana State University, Baton Rouge.

Valsiner, J. (1988). *Developmental psychology in the Soviet Union.* Bloomington: Indiana University Press.

Vygotsky, L. S. (1981). The genesis of higher mental functions. In J. V. Wertsch (Ed.), *The concept of activity in Soviet psychology* (pp. 144–188). Armonk, NY: M. E. Sharpe.

Walkerdine, V. (1988). *The mastery of reason: Cognitive development and the production of rationality*. London: Routledge.

Weiss, I. R. (1995, April). *Mathematics teachers' response to the reform agenda*. Paper presented at the Annual Meeting of the American Educational Research Association, San Francisco.

Wertsch, J. V. (1985). *Vygotsky and the social formation of the mind*. Cambridge, MA: Harvard University Press.

Wertsch, J. V., Tulviste, P., & Hagstrom, F. (1993). A sociocultural approach to agency. In E. Forman, N. Minick, & C. A. Stone (Eds.), *Contexts for learning: Sociocultural dynamics in children's development* (pp. 336–356). New York: Oxford University Press.

CHAPTER TWO

The Culture of Acquisition and the Practice of Understanding[1]

Jean Lave
University of California at Berkeley

When I began research on craft apprenticeship among Vai and Gola tailors in Liberia 15 years ago, the community of scholars who worked on cross-cultural comparative studies of education and cognitive development had definite opinions about "informal education." Learning through apprenticeship was assumed to be concrete, context-embedded, intuitive, limited in the scope of its application, mechanical, rote, imitative, not creative or innovative—and out of date. Views have changed. There is considerable interest, currently, in situated learning, embodied knowledge, and the mutual constitution of the person and the lived-in world. The math-learning research community, which certainly claims a stake in debates about crucial forms of thinking and knowing, has begun to explore apprenticeship learning, or "the new cognitive apprenticeship." By this they mean that it might be possible to learn math by doing what mathematicians *do*, by engaging in the structure-finding activities and mathematical argumentation typical of good mathematical practice (e.g., Brown, Collins, & Newman, in press; Schoenfeld, 1985). They emphasize the situated character of problem-solving activity while focusing on learning in doing. There is agreement, then, about the situated character of learning and knowing in apprenticeship, while the significance of this fact has become subject to quite different valuation over time. Indeed, those same math-learning researchers are likely to describe conventional school math learning as the all too mechanical transmission of a collection of facts to be learned by rote, a process devoid of creative contributions by the learner. Current critical

---

[1]Reprinted from *Cultural Psychology: Essays on Comparative and Human Development* (1990) with permission of Cambridge University Press.

concerns about math learning in school sound very much like descriptions of informal learning some years ago.

There are several puzzles to be addressed here: How are we to account for the change over time in the significance attributed to apprenticeship, while no one disputes its situated character? Why talk about apprenticeship at all—after all, this is not the feudal era, and the typical contemporary child is not engaged in learning a craft. How can studies of apprenticeship and adult math practice help us understand what's wrong with the way children learn math in school?

The answers may be sought through discussion of two theories of learning, characterized as "the culture of acquisition" and "understanding in practice." The first theory proposes that learning is a naturally occurring, specific kind of cognitive functioning, quite separate from engagement in doing something. Educational institutions such as schools are assumed to function by specializing in learning. Teachers and curricula concentrated on teaching make it possible to intensify learning processes and to make explicit and specific the content to be learned. School students are considered to differ only by being better or worse at "getting it."

"The culture of acquisition" also refers to the practice of social scientists who think that culture *is* "something to be acquired." This view is based on contemporary assumptions about culture as an accumulation of factual knowledge (e.g., D'Andrade, 1981; Romney, Weller, & Batchelder, 1986). There is a further assumption that cognitive benefits follow only when the process of learning is removed from the fields in which what is learned is to be applied. This belief underlies standard distinctions between formal and informal learning, so-called context-free and context-embedded learning, or logical and intuitive understanding. Schooling is viewed as the institutional site for decontextualizing knowledge so that, abstracted, it may become general and hence generalizable, and therefore transferable to situations of use in the "real" world. Bartlett (1958) talks about freeing learners from the shackles of immediate time and place. This view is reflected in the removal of children's activities into the school, the transmission of information verbally and "from the top down," and tests as the measure of knowledge. Another major theme in this approach is the conception of the teaching/learning process as one of cultural *transmission*. This implies that culture *is* a body of knowledge to be transmitted, that there is no learning without teaching, and that what is taught is what will be learned (if it gets learned).

Recent research on learning has turned to apprenticeship for theoretical inspiration because it offers a shorthand way of "saying no" to the theoretical position of "the culture of acquisition." Those interested in an apprenticeship approach, or more generally in theories of learning-in-practice, assume that processes of learning and understanding are socially and culturally constituted, and that what is to be learned is integrally implicated in the forms in which it is appropriated, so that, for example, *how* math is learned depends on its being *math* that is learned, and how math is learned in school depends on its being learned *there*. Apprenticeship forms of learning are likely to be based on assumptions that knowing, thinking, and understanding are generated in practice, in situations whose specific characteristics are part of practice as it unfolds. The gulf in time, setting, and activity assumed to separate school learning from the life for which it is "preparation" is neither reflected nor generated in the process by which apprentices gradually come to be master practitioners. Apprentices learn to think, argue, act, and interact in increasingly knowledgeable ways, with people who do something well, by doing it with them as legitimate, peripheral participants.

None of the researchers who have explored this approach is suggesting that it would be a good idea, or even possible, to borrow some form of craft apprenticeship from China or medieval Europe, or for that matter from Liberia in the 1970s, and transplant it into contemporary school classrooms. Researchers who have recently taken up the idea of "apprenticeship learning" have either drawn on their common sense notions about what "apprenticeship" might mean (e.g., Brown, Collins, & Newman, in press), or on some particular, historically/culturally situated instance of craft apprenticeship that appears to have theoretically relevant characteristics (e.g., Lave, n.d.). They are interested in apprenticeship not because it offers a prize to capture, bring home, and install in schools, but because scenarios of apprenticeship learning are useful to "think with."

In sum, there is a theoretical tradition, part of Western history, institutionalized in Western schooling, in which teaching/transmission is considered to be primary and prior to learning/internalizing culture. What is transmitted is assumed to be received in an unproblematic fashion, while processes of instruction and learning are assumed to be general and independent of what is to be learned. Let's call this a functionalist theory and note that it offers explanations of how school works and of what is the matter when it doesn't work, and that it is embedded in a theory about relations between society and the individuals who pass through and are socialized into it. This theory also treats socialization or cultural transmission as the central mechanism for the reproduction of social systems.

There are comparable things to be said about learning, schooling, and sociocultural order subsumed in a theory of situated practice (Lave, 1988). But this is not a familiar theoretical position, and an extended example may provide opportunities to work out some of its concepts in immediate terms. A more general theoretical description appears later in the chapter. Suffice it for the moment to mention some of the theorists who have considered issues concerning the nature of practice—Marx ([1887] 1957), Bourdieu (1977), Giddens (1979, 1984), and Sahlins (1976), among others, and the new activity theorists (e.g., Engestrom, 1987; Davydov & Radzikhovskii,

1985). Their theories take as crucial the integral nature of relations between persons acting (including thinking and learning) and the social world, and between the form and content of learning-in-practice. The discussion that follows is focused on what learning-in-practice might mean. Analytic resources developed in the studies of craft apprenticeship and dieting cooks may then be brought to bear on the analysis of learning in school as an everyday practice.[2]

THE CURRICULUM OF TAILORS' APPRENTICESHIP

My field research with the tailors took place during five field trips to Monrovia between 1973 and 1978 (Lave, n.d.). At that time, a number of Vai and Gola tailors clustered their wood, dirt-floored, tin-roofed tailor shops along a narrow path at the edge of the river bordering the city's commercial district. Tailors' Alley sheltered 120 master tailors and as many treadle sewing machines in 20 shops. With apprentices, the shops had a working population of about 250 men. No women worked as tailors there. (However, women do tailor clothes for sale, learning and working in their homes.) There were several masters present in each shop, visibly doing what masters do—each ran a business, tailored clothes, and supervised apprentices. Apprenticeship, averaging five years, involved a sustained, rich structure of opportunities to observe masters, journeymen, and other apprentices at work; to observe frequently the full process of producing garments; and, of course, to observe the finished products.

The tailors made clothes for the poorest segment of the population, and their specialty was inexpensive, ready-to-wear men's trousers. But they made other kinds of garments as well. Indeed, in the course of research in Tailors'

---

[2]Before trying to describe a craft apprenticeship system and illustrate how such a study offers resources for thinking about learning in the context of schooling, I would like to amplify the notion that the research strategy employed here—"looking back" at the sociocultural form, schooling, from a viewpoint located in a different educational "world"—is useful. In my view, one of the hazards facing researchers on cognition, learning, and education is the densely interwoven history and contemporary relations among schooling, cognitive theory, the educational establishment, and the lives of school alumni. They share underlying beliefs about life, learning, and the pursuit of life-after-school. The everyday character of schooling, its social situatedness, and historical integration with academic theories of cognition and learning are mainly treated as if they did not exist, or worse, did not matter. For this reason, going straight to schools for empirical studies of processes of learning while at the same time trying to reexamine the prevailing theory, is fraught with pitfalls—it should be difficult to tell whether one universal process of learning is being articulated by the academy and instantiated in schools, or whether there is cultural/historical coordination of one set of beliefs about learning in the academy and in schools simultaneously. It seems helpful, in short, to try to understand how learning is organized and what people think about it elsewhere before addressing this question to schooling.

Alley I asked many times what an apprentice needed to learn in order to become a master tailor. Repeatedly the response was an inventory of garments: hats, children's underwear, short trousers, long trousers, Vai shirts, sport shirts, Muslim prayer gowns, women's dresses, and Higher Heights suits (the latter are two-piece men's suits with elaborately tailored, short-sleeved jackets). When I first discovered that this was to be the most common response to my inquiries, it appeared to be a ritualistic litany, a list without internal form. Gradually it became clear that the list of garment types in fact encoded complex, intertwined forms of order integral to the process of becoming a master tailor. The tailors engaged in dressing the major social identities of Liberian society. Apprentices first learn to make hats and drawers, informal and intimate garments for children. They move on to more external, formal garments, ending with the Higher Heights suit. Along the way they learn to create the material markers of gender, religion, age, and politics.

The organization of the process of apprenticeship is not confined to the level of whole garments. The earliest steps in the process involve learning to sew by hand, to sew with the treadle sewing machine, and to press clothes. Subtract these from the corpus of tailoring knowledge and the apprentice must learn how to cut out and sew each garment. Learning processes do not merely reproduce the sequence of production processes. In fact, production steps are reversed, as apprentices begin by learning the finishing stages of producing a garment, go on to learn to sew it, and only later learn to cut it out. This pattern regularly subdivides the learning process for each new type of garment. Reversing production steps has the effect of focusing the apprentices' attention first on the broad outlines of garment construction as they handle garments while attaching buttons and hemming cuffs. Next, sewing turns their attention to the logic (order, orientation) by which different pieces are sewn together, which in turn explains why they are cut out as they are. Each step offers the unstated opportunity to consider how the previous step contributes to the present one. In addition, this ordering minimizes experiences of failure and especially of serious failure (errors in sewing may be reversed; those made while cutting out are more often irrevocable).

There is one further level of organization to the curriculum of tailoring. The learning of each operation is subdivided into phases that I have dubbed "way in" and "practice." "Way in" refers to the period of observation and attempts to construct a first approximation of the garment. An apprentice watches masters and advanced apprentices until he thinks he understands how to sew (or cut out) a garment, then waits until the shop is closed and the masters have gone home before trying to make it. Once an apprentice produces a first garment that has all the parts correctly oriented in relation to each other, with all the necessary construction steps, he moves on to the phase of practice in which he makes many of the same item until he can do so at high speed, and well. The practice phase is carried out in a particular way: Apprentices reproduce a production segment from beginning to end (doing what masters do), although they might be more skilled at carrying out some steps in the process than others. Whole-activity practice is viewed as more important in long-term mastery than is the consistent, correct execution of decomposed parts of the process.

There are no formal tests in tailors' apprenticeship to screen out learners at any stage, and this reflects an assumption that equal accomplishment is possible and expected for all learners. Apprentices are rarely praised or blamed, yet they know when they have made mistakes, and they have rich means of gauging their own skill. They can decide for themselves whether the clothes they make are good enough to sell and what price to set, and they discover how much customers are willing to pay for their efforts compared with garments made by other tailors.

A high percentage of apprentices become masters (85% of those I observed over a period of years). Those who quit do so, with rare exceptions, for reasons extraneous to the process of learning. And, it might be added, masters do not distinguish greater or lesser mastery among themselves. To be a master tailor implies mastery of the curriculum of tailoring. This is no mechanical reproduction of a traditional repertoire—the tailors generate new styles and procedures for making clothes and expect innovation to be part of their "craft."

This form of craft apprenticeship has a greater rate of successful completion than does contemporary schooling, which is a good reason to give it closer study. But there are crucial differences between apprenticeship and schooling that argue against direct adoption of apprenticeship forms of learning in classrooms. One important feature of the tailors' apprenticeship is that the increasing skill of the apprentice is of direct value to masters as well as to their apprentices. Even hemming cuffs helps the master to produce trousers for sale more efficiently; by the time the apprentice can construct trousers skillfully he can contribute to the master's output in a much more substantial way. Apprentices have the privilege of learning from *masters*, in two senses—masters have truly mastered their craft, for one thing, and they are also highly respected, which gives value to the project of learning to be "like them." Apprentices know from the beginning that when they complete apprenticeship there will be a legitimate field for the practice of tailoring in which they are already peripheral participants.

In sum, the tailors' form of education seems remarkably successful—apprentices learn a substantial trade without being taught, in practice. This educational form does not involve separation of learning from practice. "Motivation" is not a problem. Rewards appear to be intrinsic. People spend a lot of time doing what they are learning and vice versa. The process has order to it—there is a multilevel curriculum. The order does not depend much on intentional pedagogical activities by teachers/masters. Learners know clearly what the curriculum is, and it organizes the basic outlines of their everyday practice but does not specify what they should do or precisely how to do it.

Two points may be made about this analysis in anticipation of the exploration of math-learning practice in a school setting. The curriculum of tailoring differs sharply in intentions and organization from school curricula. The curriculum of tailoring is more a set of landmarks *for* learners than specific procedures to be taught *to* learners. It shapes opportunities for tailoring activity and hence the processes of learning to tailor. We might consider the possibility that in school, the prescriptive curriculum embodied in teachers' teaching plans, specific lesson plans, and textbook assignments creates unintended opportunities to learn math in practice. Teaching may have powerful indirect effects on math learning through the ways it shapes possibilities for developing a math practice.

If there are systematic differences between the organization of what children are intended to learn and what in fact they learn, then the question of what motivates activity—what gives it meaning and impels people to act—looks increasingly important. The question rarely surfaces in discussions of learning in school where demands for compliance mask other means by which learners fashion meaning in action. It is difficult, indeed, to see *why* people do what they do in any situation (including craft apprenticeship) that is organized in multiple, pervasive ways to enable them to do it. In the supermarket and in the kitchen people have to generate math problems if they are going to "have a problem," and if they "have" problems it can be said that they "own" those problems themselves. It may be easier, then, to work out what is meant by problems and problem-solving activity, and what motivates problem solving in situations of everyday practice. The study of math learning in the kitchen, while new Weight Watchers learn how to manage a new diet, offers such an opportunity.

DILEMMAS AND PROBLEMS:
LEARNING MATH AS A WEIGHT WATCHER

The Weight Watchers study (de la Rocha, 1986) explored the activities of nine new members of the dieting program as they incorporated new measurement practices into meal preparation over a period of weeks. Because of its emphasis on meticulous control of portions of food consumed, this particular diet program promised to generate many opportunities for calculation in the kitchen, and we hoped to see new math skills coming into existence in a setting far removed from school (Lave, 1988). The Weight Watchers study involved intensive interviewing, including an exploration of the participants' biographies as dieters. The participants were observed repeatedly as they prepared meals in their kitchens, and at the end of the six-week observation period they took part in a variety of arithmetic-testing activities. The participants also kept diaries of all food items they consumed each day. We conducted interviews with the food diaries in hand about the process of dieting, how each person learned the Weight Watchers' system of food portion control, and the specific procedures used in weighing and measuring each item.

There was lots of measuring and calculating activity to be observed. All dieters calculated portion sizes for half the food items they prepared, on average, across the six weeks. But this pattern requires qualification in two respects. Some dieters calculated considerably more often than others. And there was much more measurement and calculation going on as the dieters began the new program than was to be observed after six weeks. I shall try to account for both of these points. Second, comparisons of individuals' in situ success in solving math problems with their success on mathematically isomorphic problems in a test situation produced the result that the same problems were solved consistently more successfully in other settings than scholastic ones. All of the participants demonstrated the level of success (65–70%) on formal arithmetic tests characteristic of market vendors, dairy workers, and grocery shoppers in closely related research studies (cited later in this chapter). Third, in general, the problematic quantitative relations that troubled the cooks were not as difficult arithmetically as the math at which they were successful on the math tests. Formal test results suggested that scholastic math "expertise" did not constrain the dieters' math activities in their kitchens. Fourth, having carefully coded the measuring and calculating activities involved in the preparation of the hundreds of food items by the dieting cooks, de la Rocha showed that none of the following factors that might plausibly account for differences between the cooks' measuring patterns was useful in doing so. Things that *didn't* explain their uses of arithmetic included their age, the number of children living at home, the dieters' years of education, the amount of weight they hoped to lose, the amount of weight they had already lost, and their scores on the arithmetic tests.

All of these factors that might have led to lower or higher incentives to employ school math in the kitchen had to be discarded. Further, the Weight Watchers organization did not treat the preparation of meals as a series of lessons, homework assignments, or occasions for formal arithmetic problem solving. We could not easily invoke school math knowledge, incentives to use it, nor formal demands for math problem solving in order to account for the observed patterns of variation. There was reason to wonder why the dieting cooks bothered to calculate at all, what led them to calculate on some occasions but not others, and what led them to view some events as involving math *problems*. These may be reduced to one central question: Wherein lies the motivation for generating and solving problems in settings where there are not set tasks imposed on the problem solver?

De la Rocha's analysis of the dieters' accounts of their lives and diets offers considerable insight into the dilemmas that impel dieters to engage in math problem solving. She found it possible to work out, in a series of steps, an answer to the question about why dieters engage in math in the kitchen. The analysis begins with Western culture writ large. The abundance of food products in the United States and Americans' fascination with the self-mastery reflected in a slim physique have provoked an obsession with body weight and its control. For most plagued by it, excessive weight is a blight on the image of the body and the self. Although it can be remediated by dieting, this is accomplished with great difficulty and often for only brief intervals. In translating the determination to lose weight into practical action, the dieter faces the dilemma of, on the one hand, a strong desire to alter the distortions of the body that come with being overweight, and on the other, cravings for the solace and pleasure of food. Dieting is a long process that requires not just one decision, but a continual struggle in which the question of self-denial arises many times each day over many months and even years. Inconsistent commitment leads to backsliding or the end of a diet cycle and resulting feelings of failure and depression. From interviews about their history as dieters, it appeared that participants in the project had relatively long-term, consistent resolutions to these dieting dilemmas. Some espoused the view that meticulous control of food portions was the way to control weight. Others expressed their approach as "so long as you feel hungry you must be losing weight." Each of them put their resolution to these dilemmas into practice: Long-term dieting styles clearly shaped measurement activity differently. Earlier I pointed out that as a group the dieters measured half of the food items they prepared. But methodical dieters used arithmetic measurement and calculation techniques on 61% of the food items they recorded in their food diaries, whereas the "go hungry" dieters measured only 26%.

Gaining control over food intake or over decisions not to eat is the central dilemma of dieting. But attempts to control food portions come into conflict with other concerns of the dieters: The more elaborate the steps to gain control of quantity, the greater the conflict with getting food efficiently on the table. While the dieter calculates, the family and the evening meal wait. The conflict between dieting rules and efficient food handling appeared most directly to generate the dieters' arithmetic "problems" and clearly shaped the long-term shift from more to less calculation over time.[3] All the

---

[3]A short round of definitions may be in order here. Thus, broad sociocultural *contradictions* (e.g., between eating for beauty and eating for pleasure) are experienced in conflict, as *dilemmas* in the lived-in world (e.g., to diet or to binge, thus to look different in the long run or feel better in the short run). They are embedded in social practice, of which the dieters' philosophies and activities surrounding food would be an example. A *problem* (e.g., calculating protein options while fixing lunch) is a closed-system puzzle. The motivation for problem-solving activity resides in the dilemmas that lead to such activity. Thus motivation (meaning- and action-impelling forces) must be specified to produce an adequate account of problem-solving activity. I shall come back to this in the analysis of math practice in the classroom.

dieters responded to this conflict in two ways, by generating reusable solutions to recurring math problems, and by finding ways to *enact* solutions
as part of ongoing activity. One simple example may illustrate both. Initially,
to find the correct serving size for a glass of milk, the dieter had to look up
the correct amount in the Weight Watchers' manual; get out a measuring
cup, a drinking glass, and the carton of milk; pour the milk into the measuring cup; pour the milk from the measuring cup into the glass; wash the
measuring cup and later the glass. This procedure was shortly transformed
into get out glass and milk and pour milk into the glass up to just below
the circle of blue flowers. This is one among a myriad of examples, for the
cooks invented literally hundreds of units of measurement and procedures
for generating accurate portions (de la Rocha, 1986). In the process they
made it possible to do less and less measurement and calculation over time.

There are two other points to be made briefly about the generation of
problems in conflict and their resolution in ongoing activity. First, it is the
specific character of action-impelling conflicts that generally determines
which of several problems lurking in a situation needs to be solved. Indeed,
the history and structure of particular activity-motivating conflicts gives shape
and meaning to what comes to constitute "the problem." Second, in school-
like settings, where closed-puzzle problem solving is common, the solution
to a problem is assumed to mark the endpoint of activity. But in other
activities (re)solutions to math problems generate conflict in ongoing activity
as often as they resolve it. There is a good example in which the dieters
were asked to make peanut butter sandwiches according to Weight Watchers'
guidelines. Having made the necessary calculation correctly (in nine unique
ways), the cooks discovered a new problem. As a result of their calculations
they now had a grossly overburdened slice of bread. Each responded with
a protest that it was too much peanut butter and promptly scraped some
off, in spite of knowing that the amount was (arithmetically) correct.

For the cooks, math problem solving is not an end in itself; procedures
involving quantitative relations in the kitchen are given shape and meaning
by the dilemmas that motivate activity; school math knowledge does not
constrain the structure of their quantitative activity, and it does not specify
what shall constitute math problems. It may serve as an initial resource but
not in its form as remembered-school-procedure so much as in an embodied
form in tables in kitchen manuals and in kitchen tools. (School algorithmic
math is more likely to circulate through the printed page and utensils than
through the heads of people cooking meals.) Algorithmic math gets in the
way when the person engaged in activity does not need a formal proxy for
quantities and their relations, because those quantities and relations are
directly at hand.

One reflection of the belief that it is crucial to separate learning from practice
and therefore schooling from the everyday world is a widespread assumption

that it is the responsibility of schooling to *replace* the (presumably) faulty and inefficient mathematical knowledge acquired by people in the real world. But research on everyday math, by Scribner (Scribner & Fahrmeier, 1982; Scribner, 1984), de la Rocha (1986), Carraher, Carraher, and Schliemann (1982, 1983), Carraher and Schliemann (1982), Acioly and Schliemann (1985), Murtaugh (1985a, 1985b), Lave, Murtaugh, and de la Rocha (1984) and Lave (1988) challenges the view that school is the central source of everyday math practice. In the situations explored here math is dilemma driven, as the study of Weight Watchers shows vividly. A prerequisite for working on a math problem is "owning" the problem—a felt dilemma and a ballpark sense of its solution. Otherwise it is not a problem but only a constraint. When people own problems about quantities and their relations, they act to relate them in ways that make sense within ongoing activity. They do not "pop out" to represent them in mathematical formulas, which furnish only an impoverished representation when the world is available as a "model" of itself. This research suggests that quantitative relations are assembled inventively and effectively in everyday situations, independently of problem solvers' past school biographies.

It is now possible to distinguish two conceptual developments from the particularities of apprenticeship and dieting. In both cases learners encounter opportunities to develop a practice derived from the multiple and varied (but not infinitely varied) circumstances of their activity day by day. These self-and-other, and activity-organized opportunities for activity might be called a learning curriculum (as opposed to a teaching curriculum). And second, activity is dilemma-motivated: Practice will be so shaped. It is important, therefore, to inquire into the activity-motivating aspects of situations as these are experienced by learners if we are to discover what they are coming to understand in practice.

In making these claims I am leading up to the assertion that what children engage in day by day in school *is* an everyday practice, like dieting for adults, and learning to tailor for apprentices in Tailors' Alley. Several questions follow. How is learning-in-practice given order in school? What is the learning curriculum for this practice? How does the teaching curriculum affect the learning curriculum? What motivates children, in both senses, to solve math problems in schools? Children's typical classroom math understanding has been described by math-learning researchers over the last 10 years in searching and penetrating ways. If we begin with these descriptions of what appears to be the effects of a common learning curriculum of primary school mathematics, perhaps we can account for faulty math learning in school *as* a matter of learning-in-practice.

As soon as we examine this body of math-learning research closely, the negative side of the "culture of acquisition" becomes apparent, for this work implicates the functional theory of learning-at-a-distance in children's learning difficulties. Thus, in spite of generally held beliefs that powerful learning must occur "out of context" for use in other situations, and that "out-of-context" learning should lead to abstraction, generalization, mental exercise, transferable knowledge, and cognitive efficacy in the rest of life, it is also the case that schooling is a compartmentalized and at the same time pervasive institutional setting of children's everyday lives. What is learned "out of context" is in danger of being suspended in vacuo. This danger is reflected in the concerns of learning researchers that everyday life provides too little relevant experience, or erroneous experience, or children actively construct erroneous concepts out of it, or the connection between what is taught and intuitive everyday experience is too weak (e.g., Schoenfeld, 1987, in press; Resnick, 1986; Brown et al., in press). School alumni also maintain a version of this diagnosis of their encounters with math in school. Whether discussing their uses of math in the supermarket (Lave et al., 1984), or discussing home heating use or electric bills (Kempton, personal communication) they inevitably deny that they engage in "real math" and disclaim the value of their everyday math practice in "real life." In sum, it appears that the academic and educational establishments are caught in a serious dilemma concerning the role of distance from experience in strengthening and at the same time weakening learning. And this in turn strongly shapes the sociocultural form of teaching and learning in school.

Resnick (1986) sums up the extensive body of research on what children do and don't learn about math in school in the following way. First, there is good evidence that learners learn actively, and through construction and invention of mathematical procedures. But there is no guarantee that in so doing learners will understand mathematical principles. In fact, by Resnick's assessment, school learners (a) have reasonably correct calculational rules; (b) they learn, in the classroom, rules for manipulating the syntax of symbolic notation systems; but (c) they fail to learn the meaning of symbols and the principles by which they represent quantity and its permissible constrained transformations. In other words, wrong answers are likely to look right, while at the same time conceptual errors betray a lack of mathematical understanding. I take this to be rough evidence of the learning curriculum of primary school math.

Schoenfeld (1985) has observed a high school geometry class where students display the same general characteristics as Resnick describes for elementary school arithmetic learners. He characterizes the students as naive empiricists who plunge into geometry problem solving with straight edge and compass in constant play, without planning, without making sure they understand the problem, believing that mathematical proof is irrelevant. They do not bring their mathematical resources to bear, have no control over the process and believe themselves unable to invent or discover procedures (because they are not mathematical geniuses). Schoenfeld addresses

the question of how the curriculum of teaching has unintended consequences for what children learn about math in classroom lessons (1985,
chap. 10; 1988). Well-taught lessons by well-meaning teachers aimed at
preparing students to successfully pass state and national standardized examinations lead to routinized procedures at the expense of understanding.
Lessons place emphasis on the form of presentation of results at the expense
of mathematical argumentation. Students expect problems to take less than
2 minutes to solve and they believe that if they can't solve a problem in
about 10 minutes they will never be able to do so. They believe that mathematics is to be received not discovered, and that it is a body of knowledge
rather than a form of activity, argumentation, and social discourse. Schoenfeld concludes that math is *taught* as what experts know to be true rather
than as a process of scientific inquiry (what mathematicians might be said
to do). The decomposition of skills—a major structuring device in math
curricula—strips problem-solving activity of any relation with mathematical
practice. And all this is done in the name of preparing students to do geometry constructions so automatically that they will be sure to pass the New
York state regency exams.

MATH PRACTICE IN SCHOOL CLASSROOMS

In an ethnographic study of math lessons in a bilingual Spanish/English
third-grade classroom it was possible to look closely at the process of development of faulty math practice in children's everyday classroom activity.
My collaborator, Michael Hass, focused on a group of 11 children, the "upper"
math group. The children brought to a three-week unit on multiplication
and division facts almost as much knowledge as when they finished. They
could solve, on average, half of the problems on a 40-problem test given
before and after the unit (Hass, n.d.). There were differences in pretest
scores between children in the group. But the performances of the less
successful converged over time with those of the more adept, so that all
finished with roughly the same level of performance on the final test. When
these findings are discussed with colleagues, this capsule summary provokes
a variety of diagnoses, typically, that the teacher must not be teaching effectively, or there is something wrong with the testing procedure, or individual children must have learning difficulties, be poorly motivated to learn,
or have insufficient mental capacity to advance more rapidly. In contrast to
these explanations, which focus on teaching/transmission and individual
motivation, we sought an explanation in the everyday practice of the children
(which includes the teacher's participation in and effects on learning activity
as well). Hass discovered, by following the children's activities closely, that
in the three-week period the children were deeply engaged in math work

during individual work time (about 75% of class time), but invested minimal attention and involvement in ongoing activity during the teacher's instruction sessions (about 25% of class time). During the three weeks the children gave no evidence of having adopted *any* of the specific strategies demonstrated by the teacher during periods of general instruction.

The children sat around a table for individual work and the teacher moved about between their table and two others helping children, or she sat at her desk checking workbook exercises as they finished their assignments. There was a great deal of interaction among the children at the table. (The three who interacted least were the least able in math. One improved sharply after being placed between two highly interactive students who drew him into much greater participation.) The children began their group work sessions by making sure they agreed on what they were supposed to do. They coordinated the timing of their activity so as to work on approximately the same problems at the same time. They asked each other for help and helped each other without being asked. They collaborated and invented procedures. They discovered that the multiplication table printed in their book could be used to solve division problems, an opportunity for mathematical discussion of which the teacher was unaware. Each of the 11 turned in nearly errorless daily practice assignments. On the rare occasions when one of the students consulted the teacher for individual help, the information gleaned in the interaction quickly spread around the table. Essentially all problems were solved using counting and regrouping strategies. These were not presented in lessons and were not supposed to be in use.

The children had unintended opportunities to practice the problem-solving methods they invented or brought with them to the classroom. But they employed them so as to produce the appearance of having used the teacher's procedures, for which she took a correct answer as evidence. The children produced correct answers to problems that had been designed to inculcate a particular way to carry out arithmetic operations that they did not use. Interviews with the teacher suggested that she was unaware of the interactive math activity of the children; the children when interviewed individually reported that they consulted the teacher when they had difficulty solving problems. In sum, the teacher, text, and exercise books prescribed in detail how the children should act—what their everyday practice of math should be—while the children produced a different practice. When the teacher prescribed specific new procedures for carrying out multiplication and division operations, the children did not adopt the prescribed practice. The children did not take the risk of failing to get the answer right, but engaged in familiar processes of arithmetic problem solving instead, developing their practice of learning math in the classroom cautiously, out of known quantities. This was aimed at success or at least survival in the classroom—a specialized collection of activities—rather than being focused on deep understanding of mathematics. The dilemmas that seemed to motivate this practice were ones about performance and blame avoidance. Further, by working out answers using their own techniques and then translating them into acceptable classroom form on their worksheets, the children generated a powerful categorical distinction for themselves between "real" and "other" math. It is not necessary to search beyond the classroom for the generation of this distinction.

Other research supports the claim that the classroom promotes a working repertory of mathematical practices that are not taught, but that are brought into play in order to produce proper appearances of successful problem solving. Brenner (1985) carried out research in Liberia on primer, first-, and fourth-grade arithmetic classes in Vai schools in Grand Cape Mount County. The Vai arithmetic procedures and number system (which tallies at 5, 10, and 20) are different from those taught in Vai schools, where English is the language of math instruction, old "new-math" textbooks are used, and a base-10 number system is taught. The children routinely develop a *syncretic* form of Vai and school-taught arithmetic, and become increasingly skilled in its use over time, although it is never taught. Presumably the urge to manufacture a successful performance in the classroom is important there as well. In short, the work of Schoenfeld, Hass, and Brenner, among others, suggests that the problems that genuinely engage even enthusiastic math learners in school classrooms are, at an important level, dilemmas about their performance rather than mathematical dilemmas. These give shape to learners' everyday mathematical activity in the classroom as they strive to succeed and in the process generate appearances of understanding.

I have argued that problem solving in general (and thus in school) is dilemma-motivated. Ongoing activity in school appears to be shaped by, and shapes in turn, whatever issues are lively and problematic for learners. Teachers cannot make math the central ongoing activity by decree (or lesson plan); math will be problematic in substantive ways only when the central dilemmas of ongoing activity are mathematical ones. Where mathematics learning is consistently the official activity but not the central dilemma, then learners in most U.S. schools should be expected to generate a veneer of accomplishment through activity of a dependable and effective kind, in ways teachers do not teach or intend.

CONCLUSIONS

It is time to sketch a more general theoretical description of understanding-in-practice. Ortner (1984) has pointed out that although 20 years ago socialization, or cultural transmission, was viewed as the central mechanism for the reproduction of social systems, today there is some consensus around the view that everyday practices "embody within themselves, the fundamental notions of temporal, spatial and social ordering that underlie and organize the [sociocultural] system as a whole" (1984:154). Understanding-in-practice looks like a more powerful source of enculturation than the pedagogical efforts of caregivers and teachers. Social practice theory argues that knowledge-in-practice, constituted in the settings of practice, based on rich expectations generated over time about its shape, is the site of the most powerful knowledgeability of people in the lived-in world. The encompassing, synthesizing intentions reflected in a theory of understanding-in-practice make it difficult to argue for the separation of cognition and the social world, the form and content of learning, or of learning and its "applications." Internalization is a less important vehicle for transmission of the experience the world has to offer, in this view, than activity in relation with the world.

This theoretical perspective and the research on everyday math practices in kitchens and schools together challenge the privilege accorded school settings as sites of universally applicable knowledge that alumni should expect to take out into the world and substitute for their everyday practices in order to improve them. School math at its best looks no less mathematically powerful from this vantage point, but it looks powerful in specialized ways, as a practice with conventions, occasions, organization, and concerns of its own. Further, the notion that school is not part of "real life" is inaccurate as well as pejorative in its connotations about the significance of schooling; so is the notion that everyday math should be replaced by "real" math. The latter assertion involves a misanalysis of the notable disjunctions between school math algorithms and the generative assembly and transformation of quantitative relations in everyday life. These misunderstandings and conflicting evaluations of social situations and knowledge-to-be-learned must surely cause students both apprehensions and misapprehensions, and contribute to the general sense that schools fail to educate children in meaningful ways.

There is a widespread belief that the more schools fail to educate children, the more learning should become the object of concentrated, specialized attention and standardized accountability. Curricula, textbooks, and lessons should make more explicit what is to be learned (cf. Apple, 1979). Improving teaching under these circumstances is a process of increasing the prescriptive and detailed character of the transmission of knowledge. The curriculum of school mathematics lessons should provide more detailed recipes for activity itself, for example, on placeholding algorithms, and on single arithmetic operations. Mathematics lessons should be organized as specifications of proper practice—algorithms for solving problems anywhere in the world, any time, taught so specifically that if applied correctly they are guaranteed to produce correct answers. The problem is that any curriculum intended to be a specification *of* practice, rather than an arrangement of opportunities *for* practice (for fashioning and resolving ownable dilemmas) is bound to result in the teaching of a misanalysis of practice (as in the third-grade math classroom) and the learning of still another. At best it can only induce a new and exotic kind of practice contextually bound to the "educational" setting (the syncretic Vai math, for instance). In the settings for which it is intended (in everyday transactions), it will appear out of order and will not in fact reproduce "good" practice.

On the other hand, the curriculum of tailoring names tasks without specifying procedures. "Learn to make garments!" would be the prescriptive message at the highest level. "Learn to sew them, then learn to cut them out" would be the prescription at the next level down. At the third level there are no instructions (only a summing up of my observations about what apprentices do). Apprentices observe and experiment until they achieve a first approximation; then they practice. This curriculum shapes opportunities for doing tailoring work. Master tailors spend a lot of time doing what apprentices want to learn to do, where apprentices can see them do it and can also assist their masters in increasingly central ways. It means no one is unclear about the goals of apprenticeship, and also that the process of getting there, one day at a time, has both well-defined goals and an improvisational character.

Learning in school, like all practice, is improvised, but there are two reasons why that practice may not be what the teacher intends to teach. When the teacher specifies the practice to be learned, children improvise on the production of that practice but not the practice itself. And it is not possible to resolve problems that are not, in some sense, their own. The more the teacher, the curriculum, the texts, and the lessons "own" the problems or decompose steps so as to push learners away from owning problems, the harder it may be for them to develop the practice.

"Owning problems" and "understanding" are closely related in a conception in which learners appropriate knowledge into their improvised everyday practice. But different theories of learning have different metaphors for relations between learners and what they are learning. In recent years much of that imagery—(micro)*worlds*, knowledge domains, and problem spaces—has made problems to be solved very large. Researchers have imagined learners moving around inside them, as if the problem contained the learner. The idea of apprenticeship, or learning in practice, reverses this relation by making central the encompassing significance and meaning—understanding—that children have the opportunity to develop *about* things they are learning. In the first of these views, the subject matter is supposed to be the environment of the child—it envelops the learner in a "world." In the latter, the child's understanding (giving significance to, and critical analysis of relations of the subject to other aspects of the life world) encompasses and gives meaning and value to the subject matter, the process of learning it, and its relations with the learner's life and activity more generally. This development seems to me a more interesting long-range goal of education than the acquisition of information. And it serves notice that a theory of learning in practice must expand to include more than one level of learning activity (see, e.g., Engestrom, 1987) at the same time that it includes more than one level of understanding of the subject to be learned in practice.

Given that the development of an understanding about learning and about what is being learned inevitably accompanies learning in the more conventional sense, it seems probable that learners whose understanding is deeply circumscribed and diminished through processes of explicit and intense "knowledge transmission" are likely to arrive at an understanding of themselves as "not understanding" or as "bad at what they are doing" even when they are not bad at it (such seems the fate of the vast majority of the alumni of school math classes). On the other hand, learners who understand what they are learning in terms that increasingly approach the breadth and depth of understanding of a master practitioner are likely to understand themselves to be active agents in the appropriation of knowledge, and hence may act as active agents on their own behalf. This is not a ruly process and it is sure to have unintended consequences different from the present unintended consequences of teaching, but perhaps less counterproductive ones than when the question of understanding is simply not addressed in classrooms, as is now generally the case. Such an improvised, opportunity- and dilemma-based learning process may even be a prerequisite for widespread, self-sustained learning.

ACKNOWLEDGMENTS

I want to thank Rick Shweder and Jim Stigler, the organizers of the Symposium on Children's Lives in Cultural Context (November 1987), for the opportunity to participate in the symposium and to write this essay. The essay was prepared during my stay as a visiting scholar at the Institute for Research on Learning, Palo Alto, CA.

This chapter was first published in *Cultural Psychology: Essays on Comparative Human Development*, James W. Stigler, Richard A. Shweder, and Gilbert Herdt (Eds.). Copyright © Cambridge University Press 1990. Reprinted with the permission of Cambridge University Press.

REFERENCES

Acioly, N., & A. D. Schliemann. 1985. Intuitive mathematics and schooling in understanding a lottery game. Unpublished paper. Recife, Brazil: Universidade Federal de Pernambuco.

Apple, M. 1979. *Ideology and curriculum.* London: Routledge & Kegan Paul.

Bartlett, F. C. 1958. *Thinking: An experimental and social study.* New York: Basic Books.

Bourdieu, P. 1977. *Outline of a theory of practice.* Cambridge: Cambridge University Press.

Brenner, M. 1985. Arithmetic and classroom interaction as cultural practices among the Vai of Liberia. Unpublished doctoral dissertation. University of California, Irvine.

Brown, J. S., A. Collins, & S. E. Newman. In press. Cognitive apprenticeship: Teaching the craft of reading, writing and mathematics. In L. B. Resnick (Ed.), *Knowing, learning and instruction: Essays in honor of Robert Glazer.* Hillsdale, NJ: Lawrence Erlbaum.

Carraher, T., D. Carraher, & A. Schliemann. 1982. Na vida dez, na escola, zero: Os contéxtos culturais da aprendizagem da matimatica. Sao Paulo, Brazil. *Caderna da pesquisa 42*:79–86.

Carraher, T., D. Carraher, & A. Schliemann. 1983. Mathematics in the streets and schools. Unpublished manuscript. Recife, Brazil. Universidade Federal de Pernambuco.

Carraher, T., & A. Schliemann. 1982. Computation routines prescribed by schools: Help or hindrance. Paper presented at NATO conference on the acquisition of symbolic skills. Keele, England.

D'Andrade, R. G. 1981. The cultural part of cognition. *Cognitive Science 5*:179–195.

Davydov, V. V., & L. A. Radzikhovskii. 1985. Vygotsky's theory and the activity-oriented approach to psychology. In J. V. Wertsch (Ed.), *Culture, communication, and cognition: Vygotskian perspectives* (pp. 66–93). Cambridge: Cambridge University Press.

de la Rocha, O. 1986. Problems of sense and problems of scale: An ethnographic study of arithmetic in everyday life. Unpublished doctoral dissertation. University of California, Irvine.

Engestrom, Y. 1987. *Learning by expanding.* Helsinki: Painettu Gummerus Oy.

Giddens, A. 1979. *Central problems in social theory: action, structure and contradiction in social analysis.* Berkeley: University of California Press.

Giddens, A. 1984. *The constitution of society.* Berkeley: University of California Press.

Hass, M. n.d. Cognition-in-context: The social nature of the transformation of mathematical knowledge in a third grade classroom. Social Relations. University of California, Irvine.

Lave, J. 1988. *Cognition in practice: Mind, mathematics and culture in everyday life.* Cambridge: Cambridge University Press.

Lave, J. n.d. Tailored learning: Apprenticeship and everyday practice among craftsmen in West Africa. Unpublished manuscript.

Lave, J., M. Murtaugh, & O. de la Rocha. 1984. The dialectic of arithmetic in grocery shopping. In B. Rogoff & J. Lave (Eds.), *Everyday cognition: Its development in social context.* Cambridge, MA: Harvard University Press.

Marx, K. 1957 (1887). *Capital.* (Dona Torr, Ed. and Transl.). London: Allen and Unwin.

Murtaugh, M. 1985a. A hierarchical decision process model of American grocery shopping. Unpublished doctoral dissertation. University of California, Irvine.

Murtaugh, M. 1985b. The practice of arithmetic by American grocery shoppers. *Anthropology and Education Quarterly 16*(3):186–192.

Ortner, S. B. 1984. Theory in anthropology since the sixties. *Comparative Studies in Society and History 26*(1):126–166.

Resnick, L. B. 1986. Constructing knowledge in school. In L. S. Liben and D. H. Feldman (Eds.), *Development and learning: Conflict or congruence?* Hillsdale, NJ: Lawrence Erlbaum.

Romney, A. K., S. Weller, & W. Batchelder, 1986. Culture as consensus: A theory of culture and informant accuracy. *American Anthropologist 88*(2):313–338.

Sahlins, M. 1976. *Culture and practical reasons.* Chicago: University of Chicago Press.

Schoenfeld, A. H. 1985. *Mathematical problem solving.* New York: Academic Press.

Schoenfeld, A. H. 1987. What's all the fuss about metacognition? In A. Schoenfeld (Ed.), *Cognitive science and mathematics education.* Hillsdale, NJ: Lawrence Erlbaum.

Schoenfeld, A. H. 1988. When good teaching leads to bad results: The disasters of "well taught" mathematics courses. *Educational Psychologist 23*(2):145–166.

Scribner, S. 1984. (Ed.). Cognitive studies of work. Special issue of the *Quarterly Newsletter of the Laboratory of Comparative Human Cognition 6*(1 & 2).

Scribner, S., & E. Fahrmeier. 1982. Practical and theoretical arithmetic: Some preliminary findings. Industrial Literacy Project, Working Paper No. 3. Graduate Center, CUNY.

CHAPTER THREE

Cognition, Context, and Learning: A Social Semiotic Perspective

Jay L. Lemke
City University of New York
Brooklyn College School of Education

SITUATING COGNITION

We blame the early Moderns of Rene Descartes' 17th-century Europe for cleaving Mind from Body and Society from Nature (e.g., Latour, 1993; Shapin & Schaffer, 1985). From them, we inherited a chain—cognition in the mind, mind "in" a material brain, brain in a mindless body, body in a natural environment separate from society, society made up of persons not bodies, persons defined by cultures, cultures created by minds—a chain that binds us still and runs us around and around in ever smaller circles.

We rebel, we transgress. We want the freedom to construct a materiality of mind, an intelligence of the body. We want meaning to arise from material processes and Culture to be once again a part of Nature. We want to resituate cognition in a larger meaning-making system of which our bodies and brains are only one part. We are willing to pay the price, to abdicate our Lordship over Creation, to become *part*-ners rather than *over*-seers. Creation, after all, has been getting pretty unruly anyway.

We are not the first rebels. Peirce (see Buchler, 1955; Houser & Kloesel, 1992; and Whitson, chapter 7, this volume) wanted to fuse Logic and Nature into a single system of meaning-making processes: a natural semiosis, a semiotic Nature. Bateson (1972) followed the chain of differences that make a difference outward from the mind–brain into the motor–body that wielded the cultural tool that engaged the material environment that reacted back on the tool, changing the dynamic state of nerves, muscles, heart rate, adrenalin, glucose, brain activity, meaning, choice, value, action, and activity. Where could you break this circuit? Where did cognition end and action begin? Cognition, information processesing, meaning-making, flowed through the circuit. The system of relevance in which to define and study cognition, now synonymous with meaningful activity, was not arbitrarily bounded by the brain or the body: It was the whole interacting "ecology," including body and brain and tool and environment, through which that circuit flowed.

Lave, in a series of classic studies (Lave, 1988; Lave & Wenger, 1991), observed people in the routine activities of their lives, engaged in what for us is problem solving, but which for them is simply a way of participating in immediate, concrete, specific, meaning-rich situations. They are functioning in microecologies, material environments endowed with cultural meanings; acting and being acted on directly or with the mediation of physical-cultural tools and cultural-material systems of words, signs, and other symbolic values. In these activities, "things" contribute to solutions every bit as much as "minds" do; information and meaning is coded into configurations of objects, material constraints, and possible environmental options, as well as in verbal routines and formulas or "mental" operations.

How we play our parts in these microecologies depends not just on what the other parts do to us, and us to them, but on what these doings mean for us. The characteristic meanings of things and happenings vary from person to person, from context to context, even from one run-through of an oft-repeated routine to another, but they do not vary so much, or in such capricious ways, that two-person ecologies cannot function, activities in different contexts become interdependent, or distinct instances of the same activity type be usefully compared. There are communities of practice. There are networks of interdependent practices and activities. There are continuities and trajectories of practice, development, and learning. Or, at least we can usefully make sense with such notions.

What does it mean to learn as a participant in such an ecology of people, meanings, and things? Lave gave us the beginnings of a model of learning as participation in a "community of practice" in which we join others in their ecological doings and their situated meaningful activities as a "legitimate peripheral participant." We come, in this way, to be able to do as they do. Our activity, our participation, our "cognition" is always bound up with, codependent with, the participation and activity of Others, be they persons, tools, symbols, processes, or things. How we participate, what practices we come to engage in, is a function of the whole community ecology, or at least of those parts of it we join in with.

As we participate, we change. Our identity-in-practice develops, for we are no longer autonomous Persons in this model, but Persons-in-Activity. We are somewhat different as persons from one activity to another, and as participants in one community of practice or another. Work must be done to construct continuities for our Selves across these contexts (cf. Bruner, 1990). Learning now becomes an aspect of this developmental process; it is as universal, persistent, and inevitable as change itself.

As with any promising model, in order to develop it further, we need to construct significant critical perspectives on it.

Walkerdine (chapter 4, this volume) wants to be sure we can critically analyze the construction of subjects and subjectivities in these ecologies and not leave Persons as still some mysterious melding of bodies and minds. She wants to know how contexts are made, how they are determined, and not leave them as unproblematically given environments. She doubts that the notion of activity by itself overcomes the Cartesian separation of the semiotic and the material; how are meanings made in material systems?

Whitson (chapter 7, this volume) and St. Julien (chapter 10, this volume) praise Lave's model for helping us see why abstract mental entities (ideas, concepts) need not automatically transfer from one context to another because there is now no purely mental cognition anymore, independent of the specificity of the present context. But they want to know how the same model can also account for the cases where we *can* usefully abstract across contexts, without subordinating situatedness to abstraction. And St. Julien wants to know what the material brain can tell us about how we link one situation to another, how we can combine the connectionist paradigm with situated cognition in general, as he learned to do in helping students see a new pattern.

My own recent work (Lemke, 1994a, 1995) has led me to pose some of these same questions; some of what I have done may suggest ways to extend and refine the model in order to respond to these critical concerns. How can systems and networks of activities be simultaneously material ecologies and semiotic makers of meaning? What kinds of learning can take place wholly within a single community of practice and its activities, and what kinds require journeys that must take us also into others? How are human subjects made and differentially valued by their participation in communities of practice, and how do the trajectories of individual lives remake the wider networks that conjoin and disjoin communities? How do biography, history, and culture act in the here-and-now of situated activity? What are the implications for our views of learning and schooling of extending the model in these ways?

THE SEMIOTICS OF MATTER

Whitson (chapter 7, this volume) provides a helpful introduction to the Saussurean and Peircean traditions of formal semiotics. *Semiosis* is meaning-making; it is taking one thing as a sign for another, construing a thing, event, process, or phenomenon in relation to one or more others. Semiosis is selective contextualization; it is making something meaningful by seeing it as a part of some wholes rather than others, as being an alternative to some options rather than others, as being in some particular relation to some things rather than others. Meaning is possible only where not all possible relations and combinations are equally likely in all possible contexts; deviation from this condition means that there is information, order, regularity, form, meaning, structure, system, semiosis.

Every act of semiosis, every occurrence of semiosis, every semiotic practice in a community is necessarily also a material process in some physical, perhaps also biological, perhaps also social and human system (cf. Walkerdine, chapter 4, this volume, that "all practices are . . . both material and discursive"). Meaningful, meaning-making practices are hybrid objects (Latour, 1987, 1993; Lemke, 1984, 1994a, 1995), they are both natural and cultural; they are part of material ecologies and they are part of cultural systems of meaning. They have physical, material, thermodynamic, ecological relationships and interdependencies with one another, and they have meaning relations of other kinds, including value relations to one another in the cultural system of a community.

An ecosystem is an example of a complex, self-organizing system (cf. Prigogine & Stengers, 1984). Matter, energy, and information in various forms flow through it along complex pathways that link air and water, soil and rock, trees and insects, predators and prey in multiple intersecting networks of interaction and interdependency. A human community is a special kind of ecosystem, if we define it to include not just persons, but all our tools and artifacts, the other species that we depend on and those that depend on us, the air we breathe, the water we drink, the waste we create. In fact, we should define it now as an *ecosocial system* (Lemke, 1994a, 1995). What is so special about ecosocial systems among all other possible ecosystems is not that they contain us and our things, but that our behavior within the system, and so the overall dynamics of the system as a whole, depends not just on the principles that govern the flow of matter and energy in all ecosystems, but also on what those flows mean for us. We cultivate some species and exterminate others, mine some ores and ignore others, dam some rivers in some places, produce goods of certain kinds in certain quantities, consume, wage war, and do all the other things we do to, in, and with the rest of the material ecosystem not just on the basis of nutrient chemistry or physical mass, but also because of all the other cultural meanings and values things have for us.

The dynamics of any ecosystem depends on the networks that link, couple, and connect this element with that and make this process interdependent with that. In an ecosocial system, there are additional links based on other principles of cultural meaning. You cannot analyze the behavior of an ecosocial system with just physics, chemistry, and biology; you also need to take into account economics, politics, and other sorts of cultural beliefs and values. If we are made by our participation in networks of microecologies of situated activities, the conditions of what we can become are determined by the global structure and dynamics of the ecosocial systems that these networks help constitute.

What does it mean to say that ecosystems, and therefore ecosocial systems, are self-organizing? Hurricanes and gas flames are self-organizing. They are defined by systems of processes, by exchanges of matter, energy, and information with their immediate environments, in such a way that from calm or randomly disorganized air currents, from turbulent gas and oxygen mixtures, emerges a spontaneous pattern, form, order, and organization. A circular vortex feeds on surrounding air currents and moisture and pressure gradients to grow itself; a synergy of convections draws oxygen and flammable gas together in perfect proportion and placement to replicate itself from millisecond to millisecond with hardly a flicker. Living systems are self-organizing in the same sense, although much more complexly. The Earth as a physical-biological totality is also such a system.

These systems are individuals, they have histories, in some cases even histories that matter to their present reactions, and sometimes histories that can matter to new systems of their kind not yet born. Such systems age, and some of them die. Electrons are not self-organizing systems (so far as we know), they do not age, they do not die; they are not individually distinguishable, they have no histories that matter to their behavior. Atoms are the same. Very large molecules or very numerous collections of atoms (even in a gas) begin to have some of these characteristics. Complex systems come in a whole hierarchy of types (Lemke, 1995; Salthe, 1985), each type with all the properties of those more general than itself but with new additional properties. The most specified kinds of systems, those with the most properties that matter, the most kinds of differences that make a difference, are ecosocial systems (not individual human organisms).

Ecosocial systems, and most living organisms, are also *developmental systems*; they have a relevant history, a trajectory of development in which each stage sets up conditions without which the next stage could not occur. Ecosocial systems and individual human organisms are also *epigenetic systems*: The course of their development depends in part on information laid down (or actively available) in their environments from prior (or contemporary) systems of their own kind (our DNA is a kind of interiorized environment of this sort; our families' and neighbors' speech and behavior, the tools and built environments around us, exterior). Such systems, as individuals, *develop* along an average trajectory typical of their kind, but also deviate from it depending on their unique histories; the average trajectory of the kind *evolves*.

All of this growth and development is part of the self-organization of the system or of the larger systems of which it is a part. None of it has a cause. None of it is predictable from a knowledge of the starting point of the system (except by comparison to the past trajectories of other similar systems). There is no master control program within the system that determines the form of the patterns it achieves. There are only regulating and constraining inputs to the total dynamics of the system. The nucleus does not control the cell, it is just part of the cell. DNA does not control development, it is one part of a developing system. The brain does not control the body or cognition; it is part of a body-in-environment system that makes order, meaning. All these systems generate order. They create information and pattern.

Yes, even the inanimate ones. Peirce (see Whitson, chapter 7, this volume) tried to say what was madness in his day, and still heresy in ours: that semiosis, meaning-making, is not solely the province of human minds. We do it a bit differently, but all matter is capable of semiosis, of intelligence if you wish, provided only that it is properly organized. Even hurricanes, bacteria, ecosystems, living planets. Perhaps even some possible computers; certainly the universe as a whole.

Now we can see learning, too, as an aspect of self-organization: not just of the human organism as a biological system, but of the ecosocial system in which that organism functions as a human being, a hybrid of both material body and social-cultural persona, a body-subject. And we can look to models of the mosaic (Lemke, 1994a, 1995) and network (Latour, 1987, 1993) organization of ecological and ecosocial systems to better understand how we participate in activities within and across different communities of practice, how we get constructed as body-subjects, and how we make an ecosocial difference as body-subjects through this participation.

PARTICIPATING IN ACTIVITY NETWORKS

Part of what it means to be a legitimate peripheral participant (LPP) in a community of practice (Lave, chapter 2, this volume) is that full membership in the community is the assumed consequence of increasing participation. Both Lave (chapter 2, this volume) and Walkerdine (chapter 4, this volume) point out that some communities have ways of denying women and members of other oppressed groups full membership no matter what their level of participation. This important fact alone invites more careful consideration of trajectories of participation.

In the simplest case, we might imagine, a small homogeneous community of practice differs from member to member only in the degree of mastery of particular practices. Newcomers can aspire to oldtimer status, the oldtimers welcome their increasing participation, and the newcomers become oldtimers in their turn. If a community of practice (CoP) is defined in relation to its practices, so that any real community consists of many communities of practice, and every community member very likely participates in several of these, then for some CoPs, the simplest model will be valid. But many CoPs are not like this. For one thing, many have hierarchically differentiated roles where there is no expected upward mobility for occupants. Teachers do not expect their students to become teachers with increasing participation in the classroom community. Do teachers and students then belong to different communities of practice? Not if the practice is defined in terms of activities in which both roles must be filled.

What if mastery of a practice is not to be had solely by participating in that practice? Then increasing participation in a particular CoP will never be enough by itself to achieve full membership. It may be that one must also participate in some other CoP or engage in some other practices in order to master or be counted as having mastered the practices of the first CoP. This, too, often happens in real communities, where participation in a ritual (even if allowed) by noninitiates never in itself reveals to them the keys to its esoteric meanings, which alone could enable them to be full participants. That can be had only by participating in some other activities, some other practices (initiation rites), perhaps even in a different community, certainly in a different CoP. It is not enough to hang around with lawyers or doctors or scientists, to assist them, to learn to speak part of their lingo, even to become very good at some of their visible practices to begin to be counted as one of them. You also have to have been schooled in their mysteries, taken certain (even functionally irrelevant) courses, bear certain credentials, have passed certain rituals. The CoP of schools and the CoP of practitioners are linked, but they are not identically the same CoP.

Because practices are not just performances, not just behaviors, not just material processes or operations, but meaningful actions, actions that have relations of meaning to one another in terms of some cultural system, one must learn not just what and how to perform, but also what the performance means in order to function and be accepted as a full member of a CoP. One must know the meaning in order to appropriately deploy the practice, to know when and in what context to perform how. Or one must know just because knowing is a condition of membership. For many practices, participation in the same activity in which the form is learned is sufficient to also learn its meaning, but for some practices in some, perhaps all, communities, this may not be so. In these other cases, there are underlying, prerequisite, assumed, linked, or just associated practices that can only be learned in some other CoP, in some other context, some other activity, perhaps by explicit initiatory or schooled instruction.

To understand these more complex cases, we need a model of networks of linked or interdependent activities and CoPs within a complex ecosocial system. The trajectories of individuals' participation in the community as a whole, in the ecosocial system, trace out these networks, from activity to activity, from CoP to CoP, partly constrained by existing networks (opportunities, policing) and partly fashioning in their very biographies new connections and links that others may or may not recapitulate. Individual identities are constructed across the whole trajectory of participations, but not necessarily equally in each activity or CoP.

In the science classroom, teachers do not expect their students to grow up to become either teachers or scientists, and most students do not long for either fate. Only some of them are potentially building, or having built for them, identities as future teachers or future scientists. Many, in fact, even resist the identity of student, although they have little choice except to not participate. But they are building *some* identities, grounded in the activities of some other CoPs, in the family, the peer group, after-school activity, and so forth. What are the links that can exist between those activities (and their institutional or *ad hoc* CoPs) and those of the school and the classroom? What are the possibilities for forging such links? Given the dynamics of the larger ecosocial system in which such bits of networks are embedded, what are the chances these links would last? Grow? Be traced again by other individuals?

Walkerdine (chapter 4, this volume), discussing mathematics, uses Lacan's semiotic chains of significations (see also Whitson, chapter 7, this volume) to discuss how very specific practices—naming, finger-reckoning, verbal counting, cardinal quantifying—are linked together within a single event that may or may not be a common cultural activity. This particular sequence of linked practices perhaps recapitulates, as part of the development of some individuals, its own sequence of historical formation. It represents a stable, available fragment of a very small-scale network that links different social practices and activities. Walkerdine offers it as an example of a common tendency in the practices of mathematics: to link and move toward progressively more abstract, less context-specific practices; to leave behind what it was we were counting (people, pebbles) and to make practices in which the salient participant is a pure number, pure cardinality. Insofar as mathematics does this consistently, it also leaves behind the identity links of many students. It constructs a discourse and repertory of practices to which they literally do not know how to relate; from which, to them, theirs and all human identities are excluded. There are, of course, ways to assume an identity within this network of practices, but they are not taught in most mathematics classes.

Neither mathematics nor the sciences aim to educate "the whole person" as do the humanities. They do not help students construct identities in relation to their practices, they simply display the practices. In this way, they actively discourage most students from identifying with them (cf. Lemke, 1990). Performing the practices (e.g., by young women in Walkerdine's study) does not count toward membership unless there is evidence that the practices are performed from the proper "motivation", that is, on the basis of the canonical, esoteric meaning assigned to those practices by (here, a predominantly male) standing membership. Similarly so for working-class students relative to the schooled practices of a predominantly middle-class, academic culture.

Some students' trajectories will eventually lead them into membership in scientific or mathematical communities of practice. They will have traced a path through the network of practices, activities, and CoPs that will have passed through all the right places to give them the keys to understand and participate fully in the activities of that community. They could not have acquired those keys solely through the activities of that final professional CoP itself; activities in that CoP presume prior learnings in other communities. They build on top of many sedimented layers of such prior learnings. In some cases, the links between their visible practices and the material contexts from which alone one could glean their meanings are so underdetermined that only explicit instruction, elsewhere, in the activities of some very different CoP can provide them. Not all systems of mutually interdependent practices are lumped together in the activities of a single CoP; some are distributed over more than one, sometimes many CoPs, linking them together into an ecosocial network.

PERSONS-IN-ACTIVITY: THEORIZING SUBJECTS AND TRAJECTORIES

If notions of cognition and mind must now be distributed beyond the boundaries of the human organism, then they can no longer define the human Subject for us in the traditional way. What units of organization and analysis are appropriate in our new model? How can we properly say in what ways we are the same and different as persons in different activities? How does the traditional notion of the human individual get remapped onto the now-separable notions of biological organism, social subject, personal identity, and person-in-activity?

Lave (chapter 2, this volume) begins from the notion of person-in-activity, the person as defined by their participation in an activity, by their roles in the social practices that constitute this activity, whether as agent or affected. The person-in-activity is therefore partly specific to that activity and captures the sense in which we are different selves (cf. Bruner, 1990, 1991) in different company or when we play different life roles. Lave also uses expressions like "children-becoming-adults" that try to capture the complementary sense of continuity along the trajectories of our lives, from one activity to another and from one age of life to another.

Walkerdine (chapter 4, this volume) uses the work of Foucault (e.g., 1966, 1969, 1980) to make another distinction, "the subject . . . is not the same thing as an actual person" (p. 63). The social subject here is the creation of discursive practices in a community (actions as well as representations) that define generic subject types (the child, the adolescent, the feminine woman, the masculine man, the working-class drunk, the upper class esthete, etc.) and do the social work of making particular actual persons be or seem to fit these types, for others and perhaps even for themselves.

Walkerdine (chapter 4, this volume) also provides several examples of how people's responses to situations and tasks, their participation in particular activities, is specific to the trajectory of their life history. What did *more/ no more* mean in their home, conceptually and affectively? What has happened in their lives to make seemingly neutral math problems more stressful for some people than for others, affecting their calculations? What kinds of subjects has their participation in social activities been trying to make them into? And how does this affect their present participation as persons in an activity like solving a math problem?

Walkerdine begins to formulate the important issue of the role of affect in situated, embodied cognition. Contrary to the rather ideologically lopsided tradition of rationalism, which pits affect against cognition and emotion and feeling against reason and logic (and, not accidentally, assigns the one it values more to males and the middle class, and the less valued one more to females and the working class), practitioners' identities load positive affect onto their typical forms of meaning-making practices: Reasoning *is* an affective state or process, and an enjoyable one for the mathematician. All cognition, because it is embodied, is necessarily also affective. We do not think without feeling. When a kind of thinking is a good-feeling, we tend to become good at doing it. And when it feels bad to us, we dither, defer, get distracted, and reject it. Meaning-making is a material process of bodies-in-context; feeling and affect are subjective construals of one aspect of this process. Feeling tone can be a guide to the quality of our cognition, or it can signal to us a conflict of identity.

The Foucauldian notion of subjectivation, that the social forces we are subjected to in activity make us Subjects of historically particular kinds, complements the more traditional notion of identity, whose formation may be social, but for which the person in question is granted a special right to define what his or her identity is. Identities are also more uniquely individual than subject types. But both identities and subject types extend over life trajectories, constructing continuities across participations in distinct events and different activities.

The most basic ground for the continuity of individuals across moments of interaction is that of their bodies. We construct a continuity for biological organisms across time and events by a complex set of semiotic-material practices, despite the fact that the molecules of which we are composed, and most of our cells, are constantly being replaced by others. But, as I have argued elsewhere (Lemke, 1988b, 1995) when analyzing the problem of individuals and subjects, these are very different practices from the ones by which we define the continuity of social persons. Culturally, these two sets of practices are linked: We conflate an organism and a social persona to make the hybrid notion of an individual. There are many cases, of course, where this fusion does not work so seamlessly, where we can see the joins and analyze them.

In an ecosocial systems model, the primary units of analysis are not things or people, but processes and practices. It is the processes and practices that are interdependent, linked, creating the emergent properties of the self-organizing system. Organisms are defined by the processes that constitute them, critically including the processes that transgress their boundaries, that exchange nutrients and wastes, information and entropy with their immediate environments. The social persona is likewise defined, on the semiotic side, by certain aspects of the meaning and value in a community of the still quite material behaviors and performances of an organism or other (e.g., video or holographic) embodiment.

Individuals, as organisms, as social subjects, as personal identities, are constructs and products of the activity of the larger self-organizing system, the community and its semiotic ecology; they are not pregiven, natural units of analysis or organization. In each case, they are also constructions of continuity along developmental trajectories from interaction/activity to interaction/activity (the moments when they are observed, when they make a difference). These trajectories are themselves defined by the extent to which events earlier along them create the conditions of possibility and shape the possible forms of participation of the trajectory-entity in events further along them (cf. Lemke, 1994a, 1995; Prigogine & Stengers, 1984; Salthe, 1985, 1993).

St. Julien (chapter 10, this volume) offers us a partly biological model of continuity of person across activity: the cases, as he says, where some kind of transfer does occur from one context to another. Part of what is the same across different contexts is the biological continuity of the human organism, a body-with-a-brain that has acquired certain habits of interacting with its perceptual-motor environment. Once we have learned to see a pattern of a certain kind, we tend to project this pattern onto a reasonably wide variety of new contexts. This, in turn, can be interpreted as a continuity of meaningful behavior and so of the social persona, and not just of the biological organism.

In this case, too, as St. Julien (chapter 10, this volume) notes, there is a social and cultural dimension. The pattern that was learned was a pattern made by others in the community (biologists' ways of seeing morphological differences between prokaryote and eukaryote cells), and it was learned through participation in cultural practices widespread in the community (genres of verbal-visual organization of information), with which the students were already familiar from activities earlier along their personal trajectories. Their learning of this pattern is an aspect of the self-organizing activity of the ecosocial system in which they participate.

How does this learning occur? Clearly, it is more than a matter of a brain entraining itself into some perceptual Gestalt. Perception is always an active process with an efferent, motor component. In Edelman's (e.g., 1992) model of neuronal group selection, in which the brain stimulates some groups of nerve cells by using them and leaves others to atrophy, the stimulation processes have a motor component, and, in order to get results that simulate cultural categorization, also a value component. The organism not only interacts with the environment, not only self-organizes only insofar as it is coupled into a larger system than itself, but it also requires some criteria of preferential salience of features to pick out a pattern. For some basic processes, these saliences may be built in by evolution, but for cases like the pattern acquisition in St. Julien's (chapter 10, this volume) experiment and many others, it is the cultural values of a community of practice that supply this needed element.

The meanings we make when participating in this activity now are a function of past participations, not only in similar activities, but also in different ones, and the network of connections that determines which past ones are taken to be more relevant to this present one (cf. the principle of general intertextuality; Lemke, 1985, 1988a) is an embodiment of our participation in the culture of a community. This notion of embodied dispositions accumulated along a trajectory of interactions in a community is expressed in Bourdieu's (1972, 1990) concept of a habitus. Like any developmental trajectory notion (see previous), it has both a type-specific component, which concerns Bourdieu more, and an individuated component. The type here is the subject type of Foucault and Walkerdine. People raised to be women, or working-class, or Catholic (or men, or middle-class, or Protestant) are subjected to forms of participation in activity and construals of the meaning of their participation that construct them as subjects of these types. Their trajectories of experience have an average similarity, their dispositions for further participations have an average resemblance, and the cumulative effect is to make their participation in any activity seem more alike.

What about individuation along trajectories? As Walkerdine's and many other examples show, how we participate in a particular activity, although always a function of our trajectory, also depends on relatively unique experiences along this trajectory. The ways in which we connect past events and present ones are always partly unique; our meaning systems have a biological ground, a cultural set of historically specific resources, and a socially shaped set of commonalities with others, but they also have a psychological individuality. That individuality can only be properly identified and analyzed after the other levels of commonality have been factored out. You cannot define how someone's reading of a text or affective reaction to a math problem is uniquely individual until you understand which aspects of their participation are typical of their social subject-positioning, of the use of the resources and common patterns of a particular culture or subculture, or a function of how brains and material environments couple together generally in processes of self-organization.

Individuation is important for social and cultural change. The trajectories of individuals to some extent always create rare or unique new connections among practices, activities, and communities of practice that are not already typical of those that define the prevailing subject types of a community. People with unusual histories will participate in activity in peculiar ways. Participation in activity is not just a means for reproducing practices and communities of practice. It is also the means for creating new connections, and, so, new possibilities of emergent patterns of self-organization in the system—provided that we look at more than just one activity or one CoP at a time. We must look at the networks of interdependencies among practices, activities, and CoPs to understand the dynamics of ecosocial systems.

HISTORY, CULTURE, AND BIOGRAPHY IN NETWORKED ACTIVITIES

How do biography, history, and culture act in the here-and-now of situated activity? Walkerdine (chapter 4, this volume) follows Foucault in distinguishing a method "that examines the historical conditions" (p. 62) in which subject types emerged, from linguistic and semiotic methods that may have great formal power in analyzing activity, but that neglect to situate activity in history and social relations.

The tradition of social semiotics on which I principally draw (e.g., Halliday, 1978; Hodge & Kress, 1988; Lemke, 1984, 1995; Thibault, 1991) began from an analysis of how we make meaning with the lexical and grammatical resouces of language in particular situated contexts. In this model, however, it is not only the context of situation that is relevant, but also the context of culture (cf. Firth, 1957; Hasan, 1985; Malinowski, 1923, 1935). How we interpret the meaning of a situation and how we participate in a situated activity depends on a wider system of cultural formations (discourses, genres, activity types, institutions, modes of representation) not fully available or wholly contained in the immediate situation itself. In my own work, this notion led to an analysis of how we use intertextuality to make meaning in particular situations (Lemke, 1985, 1988a, 1990, 1993). We interpret a text or a situation in part by connecting it to other texts and situations that our community or our individual history has made us see as relevant to the meaning of the present one. Our community, and each of us, creates networks of connections (and disconnections) among texts, situations, and activities.

This linking of text to text and situation to situation is not an entirely *ad hoc* process. There are a small number of systematic principles in our own culture that underlie the kinds of connections we are more or less likely to make. We make these in common with others who share typical trajectories with us, and we may differ in this way from those with other life experiences. In this way, culture, which extends across situations and activities and which characterizes communities without necessarily being the same for all castes or individuals within a community, finds its way through us into the activity of the moment. Of course, we are not the only participants in activity; our tools, our texts, our symbolic productions of many kinds also embody this wider context of culture. For them, too, there are networks of activities that lead to other sites, other events, that are relevant for here and now because what happened there and then is embodied in these present nonhuman participants.

These networks of connections that we make, and that are made in the self-organizing activity of the larger systems to which we belong, extend backwards in time as well outwards into the social-material world. The same principle that governs our developmental trajectories, namely that prior events created the conditions of possiblity for, or shape the possible forms of participation in, present events, applies also to networks with historical depth. Not only we, but our tools and technologies also have a history without which they would not exist or would not be as they are. So also do our symbolic resources (e.g., our language, our conventions for writing, drawing, graphing) and our cultural conventions of seeing one thing as relevant to the meaning of another. And so do the actual texts, symphonies, visual designs, and so forth in and through which we live as the meaning-making beings we are.

All these notions make sense only insofar as we see networks of connections among events, moments, practices, activities, communities of practice, historical periods, stages of life, texts, and so forth. These networks are not homogeneous; they do not connect only texts to texts, tools to tools, persons-in-activity to persons-in-activity. They are also fundamentally heterogeneous (Latour, 1987, 1993); they make visible the interdependencies, at once material and meaning-based, of texts and tools, tools and people, events and texts, and so forth.

Ecosocial systems, ecologies of and with meaning-based connections, have a complex topology (Lemke, 1993, 1995, and references therein). Viewed in the three-dimensional space they create, they have a fractal topology: subsystems within systems within supersystems, across many scales and orders of magnitude. And they also have a mosaic topology: Side by side on the same scale are diverse, variant local systems, of different ages, different compositions, and different internal networks of connections. These topologies are mainly a function of local connections, local interactions linking nearby systems.

Ecosocial systems, however, also have, superimposed on these local connectivities and in part coinciding with them, more extended networks of connections that have smaller dimension, or codimension. There are layer systems (of codimension two) in which points in the same layer, even far apart, interact more strongly with one another than they do with nearby points in a different layer. And there are networks themselves, of codimension one, along which points or events interact strongly even at great distances from one another, but do not necessarily interact equally strongly with points not in the network but that may be at comparable distances, or even much closer.

All networks are locally three-dimensional. They all consist of events and interactions in the immediate ecosocial system of the points that belong to the network. But globally, they are one-dimensional, linking distant points selectively, irrespective of the total ecosocial systems on those scales of distance (but within them, of course, and made possible by them). Think of networks of tunnels, networks of power grids, networks of communication lines, the dedicated communication and supply lines of armies or multinational corporations. Think of your own personal social network of contacts, of people you interact with more often and more intensely even though they are far away, when you may have little interaction with other people who are much closer, who are coparticipants in your local ecosocial system (your building, your neighborhood, your city).

Networks of lower codimension can intersect in more ways than can subsystems of full dimension (i.e., three-dimensional ones). Three-dimensional local systems can only interact with and intersect with their local neighbors at their margins, can only abut them or overlap them. They have two- and three-dimensional boundary zones, borderlands between them. They tend to exclude one another. But one-dimensional extended networks can freely interpenetrate one another and the local networks of local three-dimensional systems. They can interact and intersect at the center, or anywhere inside, and not just at the boundary or the margin. This is why you can be part working-class and part middle-class, part Christian and part Jewish, part masculine and part feminine, part Hispanic and part African, part child and part adult, part straight and part gay, a farmer, a church-goer, a Mason, and a mother all at once and without occupying more than a metaphorically marginalized borderland.

Yes, some networks do also exclude other networks, but they must do work at more sites to accomplish this feat, and they frequently fail. There is far more interpenetration of networks of different genders, sexual orientations, classes, ages, cultures, ethnicities, and so forth in our ecosocial systems than our prevailing discourses and ideologies might like us to believe (see Heath, 1994; Lamphere, 1992). Individual trajectories that move between these networks also knit them together, also open them up to change due to one another's influences. We need these more topologically complex models and metaphors to understand how history, biography, and culture become present in situated activity.

LEARNING AND SCHOOLING

Yes, we learn in activity, and in a community of practice, but we also learn many things across activities and communities of practice. Yes, learning is an aspect of identity formation, but we form and incompletely integrate many identities for our Selves, and not every activity or every practice we learn matters equally to us or equally shapes our identities.

What we have already learned and experienced influences our future learning, in individual and idiosyncratic ways, but also in ways that mark us as more or less typical products of cultures, communities, and histories. Our trajectories are each unique and individual, but they are also molded by the social systems around us to conform to prevailing social types by age, gender, class, and caste.

We learn in activities, but more fully in networks of activities that are interdependent on one another, that facilitate and enable one another, that are marked out as being relevant to understanding each other's meanings. These networks are constructed differently by different groups, and to some extent also by different individuals, not only in what we say are relevant connections, but in what we make to be relevant connections by how we act and what we do, and sometimes by the very fact of our lives' bridging these networks together.

We always perceive, act, and learn by participating in the self-organization of systems that are larger than our own organism (see the many examples in Smith & Thelen, 1993). The meaning-making, the meaningful activity, whether we call it semiosis or cognition, is taking place in that larger system, and not solely in our organism or its brain. We embody our past, as our environment embodies its (and so our collective) past, and in our interaction, not only memory but culture and historical and sociological processes are renewed and continued, diverted and changed.

Schools are communities of practice that do not preach what they practice. They teach about practices of other communities, for example, about the practices of science and mathematics, but they say very little about the practices of schooling. The practices of science and mathematics that they display have their fully contextualized meanings only when resituated in the activities that gave rise to them historically and in which they enact their present social functions. These same practices, however, cannot be learned solely from participation in these primary contexts because there they are too deeply embedded in other practices, too thoroughly presuppose intertextual connections to practices in other contexts, and depend on meanings underdetermined by their connections to visible and material actions in the primary contexts.

Schools and communities of professional, specialized practice are joined together by networks of interdependency among their activities and by the trajectories of those individuals who pass back and forth between them. Unfortunately, these individuals are rarely students, few of whom and only long after may make this crossing. I have argued elsewhere (Lemke, 1994b, 1994c) that we need a substantial clinical component in science education (the field I know best), in which we strengthen the network connections between school activities and professional activities and allow students to pass more readily along these networks, integrating them into their personal trajectories on the scale of weeks or months rather than decades or life stages. If these connections were strengthened, not only would the abstract content of the school curriculum make more sense in relation to its primary contexts of use, but that content would tend to change insofar as it might be actually out-of-step with or useless in these further contexts. For this to happen, not only students but teachers need to travel along the connections between the networks of school and professional practices. And perhaps professional scientists and technologists should make the return journey more often, as well; especially before presuming to prescribe what schools should be doing.

Much of the creative capacity of our society is vested in the capability of individuals to connect networks not usually connected. That capability is greater among the young insofar as they have not yet been as thoroughly subjectified into dispositions that will tend to make them willingly confine themselves within certain networks of activities. It is greater among the old to the extent that they have acquired the tools available within some networks to do the work of making connections to others (if they have not by then lost all desire to do so). Why do we place such obstacles in the way of the young to hinder them from crossing the boundaries of the existing networks? Why do we refuse to let them explore all knowledge, as in the model of the library, and instead restrict them to a curriculum shaped entirely within specific subcommunities? Why do we exclude them from most communities of adult professional practice and confine them to schools?

I believe we do these things to minimize the overall rate of social and political change (Lemke, 1995), and at the cost of alienating students who do not find congenial identities within the limited parts of these networks that include the practices of schooling. We construe this alienation as failure, and use the failure to justify the great disparities of resource provision that characterize our present social and economic order. We justify these restrictions on young adults with a belief in their inherent incapacity, a belief whose consequences, as with any ideology, seem to support the belief. Perhaps, for at least some students, the networks being created by new information technologies will allow them to escape or bypass these restrictions to a greater degree, unless, in the name of protecting them from themselves, we again oppressively restrict their freedom to do so (Lemke, 1994c, 1995, 1996).

Even this small potential loophole (the new information technologies and our practices in using them) is itself made possible by practices that belong to particular communities and particular networks, and our culture is fast at work defining some Subjects (male, middle-class, English-speaking, technophiles) as those who will feel comfortable with these new technologies, and subtly excluding others or putting them at a disadvantage. This is work that seeks to extend existing imbalances of power and privilege to a new domain. It is a normal part of the processes of ongoing self-organization in our ecosocial system, but so are the processes that directly oppose it and those that can unpredictably shift the balance of power by making new and unexpected connections.

We need to extend the networks of the classroom and the school. To extend them into professional communities of practice. To extend them into the sphere of private life. To extend them into the sphere of direct political activity. To extend them into libraries and information worlds where there are no preferential barriers to crossing from one domain to another at will. To extend them into the productive activities of our ecosocial system: industrial, agricultural, financial, informational. Most of all, we need to extend them outside the networks that define only masculine, heterosexual, middle-class, northwest European cultural values and historical traditions as normative and that seek to deny the already pervasive interpenetration of Other networks and practices in our ecosocial systems.

REFERENCES

Bateson, G. (1972). *Steps to an ecology of mind*. New York: Ballantine.
Bourdieu, P. (1972). *Outline of a theory of practice*. Cambridge, UK: Cambridge University Press.
Bourdieu, P. (1990). *The logic of practice*. Stanford, CA: Stanford University Press.
Bruner, J. (1990). *Acts of meaning*. Cambridge, MA: Harvard University Press.
Bruner, J. (1991). The invention of self: Autobiography and its forms. In D.R. Olson & N. Torrance (Eds.), *Literacy and orality* (pp. 129–148). Cambridge, UK: Cambridge University Press.
Buchler, J. (Ed.). (1955). *Philosophical writings of Peirce*. New York: Dover.
Edelman, G. (1992). *Bright air, brilliant fire*. New York: Basic Books.
Firth, J. R. (1957). *Papers in linguistics 1934–1951*. London: Oxford University Press.

Foucault, M. (1966). *The order of things.* New York: Random House.

Foucault, M. (1969). *The archeology of knowledge.* New York: Random House.

Foucault, M. (1980). *The history of sexuality* (Vol. 1). New York: Random House.

Halliday, M. A. K. (1978). *Language as social semiotic.* London: Edward Arnold.

Hasan, R. (1985). Meaning, context, and text: Fifty years after Malinowski. In J. D. Benson, & W. S. Greaves (Eds.), *Systemic perspectives on discourse* (pp. 16–49). Norwood, NJ: Ablex.

Heath, S. B. (1994, April). Cracks in the mirror: Class, gender, and ethnicity in multicultural education. Paper presented at the Annual Meeting of the American Educational Research Association, New Orleans, LA.

Hodge, R., & Kress, G. (1988). *Social semiotics.* Ithaca, NY: Cornell University Press.

Houser, N., & Kloesel, C. (1992). *The essential Peirce.* Bloomington: Indiana University Press.

Lamphere, L. (1992). *Structuring diversity.* Chicago: University of Chicago Press.

Latour, B. (1987). *Science in action.* Cambridge, MA: Harvard University Press.

Latour, B. (1993). *We have never been modern.* Cambridge, MA: Harvard University Press.

Lave, J. (1988). *Cognition in practice.* Cambridge, UK: Cambridge University Press.

Lave, J., & Wenger, E. (1991). *Situated learning: Legitimate peripheral participation.* New York: Cambridge University Press.

Lemke, J. (1984). *Semiotics and education* (Toronto Semiotic Circle Monographs, 1984, No. 2). Toronto: Victoria College.

Lemke, J. (1985). Ideology, intertextuality, and the notion of register. In J. D. Benson & W. S. Greaves (Eds.), *Systemic perspectives on discourse* (pp. 275–294). Norwood, NJ: Ablex.

Lemke, J. (1988a). Discourses in conflict: Heteroglossia and text semantics. In J. D. Benson & W. S. Greaves (Eds.), *Functional perspectives on discourse* (pp. 29–50). Norwood, NJ: Ablex.

Lemke, J. (1988b). Towards a social semiotics of the material subject. *SASSC Working Papers,* *2*(1), 1–17.

Lemke, J. (1990). *Talking science: Language, learning, and values.* Norwood, NJ: Ablex.

Lemke, J. (1993). Intertextuality and educational research. *Linguistics and education, 4*(3–4), 257–268.

Lemke, J. (1994a). Discourse, dynamics, and social change. *Cultural dynamics, 6*(1), 243–275.

Lemke, J. (1994b, April). The missing context in science education: Science. Paper presented at American Educational Research Association annual meeting, Atlanta. (ERIC Documents Service ED 363 511)

Lemke, J. (1994c). The coming paradigm wars in education: Curriculum vs. information access. In *Cyberspace superhighways: access, ethics, and control* (pp. 76–85). Chicago: John Marshall Law School.

Lemke, J. (1995). *Textual politics: discourse and social dynamics.* London: Taylor & Francis.

Lemke, J. (1996). Hypermedia and higher education. In T. M. Harrison & T. D. Stephen (Eds.), *Computer networking and scholarship in the 21st century university* (pp. 215–232). Albany: State University of New York Press.

Malinowski, B. (1923). The problem of meaning in primitive languages. Supplement I to C. K. Ogden & I. A. Richards (Eds.), *The meaning of meaning* (pp. 296–336). New York: Harcourt Brace.

Malinowski, B. (1935). An ethnographic theory of language. Part 4 of *Coral Gardens and their Magic, Vol. 2* (pp. 4–78). London: Allen & Unwin.

Prigogine, I., & Stengers, I. (1984). *Order out of chaos.* New York: Bantam.

Salthe, S. (1985). *Evolving hierarchical systems.* New York: Columbia University Press.

Salthe, S. (1993). *Development and evolution.* Cambridge, MA: MIT Press.

Shapin, S., & Shaffer, S. (1985). *Leviathan and the air-pump: Hobbes, Boyle, and the experimental life.* Princeton, NJ: Princeton University Press.

Smith, L. B., & Thelen, E. (Eds.). (1993). *A dynamic systems approach to development.* Cambridge, MA: MIT Press.

Thibault, P. (1991). *Social semiotics as praxis.* Minneapolis: University of Minnesota Press.

CHAPTER FOUR

Redefining the Subject in Situated Cognition Theory

Valerie Walkerdine
Goldsmiths College
University of London

CALCULATING AS IF YOUR LIFE DEPENDED ON IT

To be thought of as calculating is not complementary. Calculating is often what the other is: women; scheming, wheeling, and dealing bargainers. The refined mind reasons, but does not calculate. Indeed, witness the oft-told joke that mathematicians cannot add up. Modern theories of cognition have taken their central plank to be that reasoning is a centralized process, occurring on the basis of a naturalistic path of development, itself guaranteed by a structural model of thinking and of the world. This view, taking some of its impetus from Descartes and some from Kant, has become an almost commonsense wisdom.

I want to draw attention to several features of our understanding of cognition that deserve greater scrutiny:

- Calculation is understood as secondary with the transition from mercantile to industrial capitalism.

- Reason is understood as the other to unreason and those others—women, colonial peoples, the proletariat, children, the insane—are seen as lacking reason. The irrational and emotional are understood as antithetical to reason.

- Reason becomes naturalized as a feature of the most civilized and evolved human beings: by the 19th century, these are White European bourgeois and upper class men.

I want to argue that moves made within psychology and elsewhere over the past 15 or so years to challenge the notion of a central processor model of cognition (Cole, 1981; Lave, 1988; Scribner & Fahrmeier, 1982) need to take on this whole historical baggage. Why? Because attempts to demonstrate that cognition is produced in practices and not in an abstract way always hit up against the theoretical edifice on which cognition theories are built and the fears, phobias, and fetishes that are inscribed in them.[1] In my view, it is not enough to demonstrate that people's everyday calculations are different without thoroughly challenging the basis on which others can turn around and immediately argue that cognition, real cognition, is abstract reasoning that occurs only through schooling. It is necessary to challenge the ideas of proof, abstraction, calculation, low level, and so forth.

It is also necessary to challenge this view because, as we all know, those who are seen as able to make their way on the street, with a calculated cunning and a quickness of purpose but who lack real rationality are, generally speaking, the oppressed and exploited of this world. In my view, a poststructuralist historical analysis provides a good basis from which to begin. I think that it is also necessary to specify more clearly the discursive and semiotic, as well as unconscious, aspects of the regulation of practices through which calculation is produced. In this chapter, I wish to discuss and relate to Lave's important work with reference to some of my own.

COGNITION IN PRACTICES

If thinking is produced in practices, we need to understand what practices are and how it is that they produce cognitive processes. Lave (1988, chapter 2, this volume) presented us with what, in my view, is the most sustained analysis of this issue so far available. She outlined a number of problems with existing formulations of cognition: the separation of cognition from the social world, the separation of form and content, and, therefore, the dissociation of cognition from context. She presented us with a clear analysis of the rise of the stress on reason and rationality and the stress within psychology on the clear differentiation between scientific reasoning and everyday thinking. As Lave pointed out, although the concern with the savage mind is a phenomenon of the 19th century, lately, the savages have simply been transported into our midst as opposed to being in far-flung colonies. The postcolonial natives are still restless. She quoted Bartlett (1958), who made

---

[1]These are terms borrowed from Bhabha's (1984) use of the work of Fanon (1967) in his analysis of the way in which the regulation of colonial peoples depends on stories about colonial peoples—the lazy Black, for example—that have to be endlessly retold as if to make them true. Bhabha suggested that such stories are filled with deep fears, phobias, and fetishes about the colonial population, such that these stories help both to exploit these fantasies and to keep the fears at bay.

the distinction between closed (puzzle-solving) thinking and open-ended (adventurous) thinking to encapsulate the difference between routine thinking and that of the civilized mind.

In my view, this distinction enters current work in a variety of guises. All those characterized as outside of reason (colonial peoples, women, the proletariat, the mad, children) within 19th-century thinking have been targeted within modern psychology. The idea of children's thinking being concrete, the 1960s arguments about Black intelligence as low level, and the current arguments about girls' mathematical performance all point to the tenacity of this model. For example, boys are said to make conceptual leaps whereas girls remain firmly rooted in everyday calculation.

Lave asked why the central processor model of mind and transfer theory have held sway for so long, and argued that this has to do with social stratification and the division of labor. However, I would like to suggest that the understanding of this distinction and its tenacity with respect to current theories has to be understood within a wider framework.

In this chapter, I want to discuss this wider framework and attempt to put forward an analysis of the production of thinking in practices that builds on poststructuralism, semiotics, and psychoanalysis. I do this because, although Lave's account was extremely suggestive, I do not think that she got to grips with an account of how practices in which thinking is inscribed are produced. She made reference to the concept of activity, but apart from the clear demonstration of the route taken by shoppers and weight watchers in making their calculations, she did not really theorize how subjects are produced in practices.

My own work has attempted to examine the same issue of context and transfer, but with reference to debates about children's cognitive development and thus their mathematical performance in and out of school. This debate, in Britain at least, is dominated not by cognitive psychology, but by Piagetian structuralism or critiques of his work (e.g., Donaldson, 1978). In the work of Piaget, an evolutionary model was used in which scientific and mathematical reasoning were understood as the pinnacle of an evolutionary process of adaptation. This model viewed the physical world as governed by logicomathematical laws, which came to form the basis of children's development of rationality through their action on and adaptation of their mental structures to the structures describing the physical world. It was an extremely powerful theory and one that attempted to counter a Darwinian evolutionary pessimism. For Piaget, it was love, cooperation and reason that were the natural order of things, not competition, aggression and war.

Such a model, emerging as it did, between the two World Wars, acted as a powerful force for the hope for peace and democracy that was generated in that political climate. An analysis of the historical production of the importance of Piaget's work for education is far too complex to attempt here.[2] However, it is perhaps important to note that Piaget built on an idea of rational man that far preceded him.

Ever since the Enlightenment, the idea of man as emerging through scientific thinking, controlling the forces of nature, which stood as the irrational to be kept in check, has been a potent image. Those others of unreason, as Foucault called them, were set up as challenging and threatening the power of scientific rationality, a power clearly related to the rise of the bourgeoisie and central in republican and progressive bourgeois forms of thinking. What I am suggesting therefore, is that there was a great deal invested in rationality and a huge sense of threat to the forces of reason from the dark forces of unreason, the feminine, the mob, the proletariat, the animal, the savage. Such threats were extremely strong in political terms, both in relation to fears of mass uprising, but also, later, fears of fascism.

There was, I am suggesting, a great deal, psychically as well as socially, invested in the production of reasoning beings. It is therefore not tangential that the just plain folks that Lave referred to are those who are least schooled, those who have not, it seems, transferred the lessons of reason learned at school. Such people present a considerable threat, a threat easily exemplified by the concern expressed when poor children appear to possess advanced calculating skills—indeed, sometimes not only more advanced than their school performance would suggest, but actually more advanced than that of some of their higher class peers.

Such children, like those Third World adults presented to us in some of the earlier work of Lave and others like Cole, present us with something advanced when, by rights, they should be underdeveloped; underdeveloped precisely because they fail to display those characteristics associated with civilized rationality. In my own research, teachers tend to understand such children as underdeveloped and overmature. They present a threat to an idea of childhood and appear as adults before their time. Thus, the story goes, they may not have been able to develop properly, and this could be a danger signal, a signal of something bad to come, something that threatens the smooth running of the social order.

The postwar mathematics education literature is full of the importance of reason over calculation, a distinction that is stated in a number of different ways: procedural and propositional knowledge, having concepts versus hard work or rote learning, and so forth. I believe that it is not at all tangential that those children taken to display procedural knowledge or rote learning are taken to have demonstrated an apparent maturity that hides their lack of appropriate conceptual development. Their performance is counted as a kind of false evidence because it signals something produced through the wrong means.

---

[2]However, I have discussed this at length elsewhere. See Henriques et al. (1984).

In the literature on girls and mathematics, this debate reached huge proportions (see Walkerdine, 1989, for a review). Considerable efforts are made to discount girls' performance as low-level calculation and to downplay the threat represented by female success in a domain taken to be produced through a rationality considered male. Indeed, although girls' and women's hard work may be deemed pathological and abnormal when it comes to ideas of proper performance, their reasoning is just as threatening to the idea of femininity, which, in the 19th century, was seen as necessary to ensure the reproduction of an imperial race that was threatened by the fecundity of the degenerate lower orders. Reasoning women, it was argued, might not mother (Walkerdine, 1989).

In attempting to understand this, I have found Foucault's work more useful than anything else. This is because Foucault examined the historical production of scientific knowledge about the population and understood them as part of modern strategies of government. Modern populations, he argued, are not forced so much as covertly policed. Scientific ideas become truths by which to measure the normal citizen. Government can then be ensured through a range of technologies and practices that regulate the production of the correct kind of subject. People who do not fit can then be understood to be abnormal, and a whole range of corrective and, indeed, humane and therapeutic measures can be brought into play to help the individual adjust.

For Foucault, the individual is a specifically historical form of the human subject, not a universal and transhistorical category. In my view, Foucault presented us with the basis of an account of the historical production and importance of the idea of reason as formal, abstract, and so forth, and of the idea of transfer. In addition, he allowed us to understand this as part of a strategy of government, of regulation that renders calculation not only abnormal but deeply politically threatening.

In understanding the critique of the transfer debate, I have therefore found this kind of work enormously helpful because it can allow the possibility of theorizing a subject that is historically and socially produced— produced, furthermore, not through natural processes and behaviors, but in and through discourses and practices. In the rest of this chapter, I should like to elaborate how these ideas might help to extend the position that Lave put forward in moving toward an account of cognition in practices.

SUBJECT POSITIONS AND SUBJECTIVITY

The position that I am putting forward draws on earlier work published in *Changing the Subject* (Henriques, Hollway, Urwin, Venn, & Walkerdine, 1984) and the *Mastery of Reason* (Walkerdine, 1988), respectively. In the former volume, the authors draw on the work of Foucault to explore the historical constitution of the subject. For Foucault, the subject was a fictional construct produced in those regimes of truth that claim to describe 'him.' The subject is not coterminous with subjectivity, the condition of being a subject, and an important issue is how to understand this relation.

Foucault avoided the problem altogether. Therefore, it is necessary to go beyond his work in order to completely deal with the terrain presented to us by developmental and cognitive psychology's model of a subject who knows or comes to know because of some psychological apparatus that can then be applied in contexts. I would like to use this example to demonstrate how we might approach the issue of the relation of the subject to subjectivity.

Using a Foucauldian analysis, we can specify the way in which the specific form of the subject is created in discourse, but this method is unlike linguistic approaches to discourse because it examines the historical conditions in which certain subject forms emerged. Without doing that historical work, I cannot specify the conditions of emergence for cognitive psychology's subject, although I have pointed to the importance of the man of reason. Nevertheless, I have done some work on the emergence of developmental psychology's 'child' (Henriques et al., 1984).

Child study began in Britain after a number of people, including Darwin, had made evolutionary studies of infants. Child Study Societies were set up to calibrate the ages and stages of childhood. This did not happen out of the blue. It happened in a historical period in the early decades of the 20th century in which children and the future of the nation had become a key issue, an issue in which the management and government of the population, especially the relatively new urban population, had become a real problem.

Problems of crime and poverty were laid at the door of the poor and criminal themselves, who were taken to have not developed the correct habits of industriousness and displayed frightening signs of degeneracy. One of the cures for this social ill was seen as the introduction of compulsory schooling, so that children could be withdrawn from the workforce and inculcated with good habits. An account of childhood was therefore understood as necessary.

I am here necessarily glossing over a huge amount of vital historical detail, but the point I wish to make is that a history of ideas cannot sufficiently explain the emergence of certain theories and approaches to developmental psychology, neither can a sense of a disinterested search for truth. The emergence of new ideas is intimately connected with the emergence of technologies for the administration of the population (Rose, 1985, 1990).

The ideas become inscribed, that is, written into practices of administration and regulation. I demonstrated that they are in elementary education with respect to developmental psychology (Henriques et al., 1984). It is in these practices that we can locate the production of children as developmental psychology's 'child.' In other words, the issue is not simply about the production of scientific concepts, but the complex intertwining of these with certain conditions that allow them to emerge, and certain practices in which they are used and have their meaning. These practices can be described as discursive because they do not and cannot operate outside of the 'truths' that are produced in discourse.

The relation of these discursive practices to 'the real' and 'material' is therefore quite complex. It is here that I part company with Lave's formulation of practices. For Lave, practices were activities and people acting in a setting, specified by a dialectical relationship. I do not think that this is at all clear and carries the danger that neither the person nor the setting is theorized. Thus, we are left rather too close to traditional individual–society dualism than I presume that Lave would like. In this analysis, the discursive practice is the place in which the subject is produced. This, note, is not the same thing as an actual person.

What I mean here is that 'the child' is a sign created within discursive practices. This is what Foucault meant by *subject*. What is important, therefore, is how actual children become 'the child'; in other words, the relation between the subject and subjectification. All practices are produced through the exchange of signs and are both material and discursive. They are not simply created in language. I am suggesting that actual practices are created through their embodiment of the truths of child development, the way, for example, in post-Plowden British primary school—the whole architecture of the school, the seating arrangements, the timetable, and so forth—all embodied the idea of the child developing in a facilitating environment. Ideas of children developing at their own pace and learning through playful activity became the truths embodied in the classroom, the parameters through which the practices were produced and regulated.

For example, guides for teaching around the time of the Plowden report in 1967 advocated the transformation of the space of the classroom, usually from rows into groups of desks. Such new arrangements designated a different kind of learning in which a new conception of what the child is was constituted. In one version of the new classroom, for example, there is a designated area, an "uncommitted area for the sudden, unpredictable interest that requires space" (Nuffield Mathematics Project, 1967 p. 31). Thus, there are interests. These can be unpredictable, but must be pedagogically catered for by the assignment of space. In the old version of the classroom, such interests, spaces, or indeed—in a conceptual sense—children having such interests and needing such space did not exist.

Such arrangements and the practices they enshrined defined what 'the child' is and is expected to be. In the child-centered pedagogy, 'the child' is defined in relation to certain developmental accomplishments. These are what are sought and looked for. The very practices that claim to discover them actually produce them. Each child in the classroom is classified according to the record card. The records take on the status of truth. 'The child' is inscribed. How, then, do actual children become embodiments of 'the child'?

If the methods of regulation that I have exemplified define the truth of the child, it is clear that not each child will be judged to be the same. Some will be fast developers, some slow, and so forth. The regulation of those others—girls, Black children, working-class children, and so forth—that I mentioned at the beginning will take the form of their categorization and sometimes pathologization within the truths of child development.

They are too slow or overmature and underdeveloped. In other words, the regulation of the practice contains subject positions through which the truth about each child is produced. The practice, therefore, contains not only modes of regulation, but actual ways of understanding and describing the children in the classroom, those who are developing well, those who are working when play is the evidence that would prove that their development is genuine, and so on. The pathologized children are, in my view, the very 'just plain folks' that Lave talked about.

SUBJECTIVITY AND CALCULATION

How, then, do classrooms and other practices produce forms of calculation or calculating subjects?

In order to understand this, it is necessary to examine more closely the detail of the regulation of practices. The aim of this section is to attempt to flesh out how subjects in practices might be understood, because although Lave gave us one analysis, it still retains the dualism of which I spoke earlier.

I also suggest that the concept of activity is not enough to deal with the complexity of the relation of subject to material to discursive. What I am concerned to specify here is the way in which the subject is a relation of signification, and the idea of subjectivity itself is not something that preexists signification, but that is produced within practices. In this analysis, school practices and other practices are analyzable in terms of their relations of signification and their functioning in terms of 'truth effects.'[3]

What is particularly important here is the relation between signifier and sign. I want to argue that each practice is regulated in and through discourse,

---

[3]Although it is true that other studies, especially the work of Cole and his colleagues (Cole, Hood, & McDermott, 1980), have already applied techniques of ethnography and conversational analysis to classroom practices, demonstrating how, for example, children's abilities are collectively produced in the classroom, this does not carry the detailed analysis of subjectivity that I am proposing.

such that the relation Piaget specified as between action and object is actually about the subject as a relation. Each action and each object is made to signify within a discursive relationship.

Schooling practices are no less practices than any other, but operate with their own relations of signification and modes of regulation. The difference comes in the truth effects of the statements produced within each practice. Let me explore what I mean by examining certain relations in practices outside schooling and then specifying what transformations have to be accomplished to make these into school mathematics practices. One of the assumptions that I am criticizing here is the idea that logicomathematical structures are inherent across contexts so that any kind of sorting task, for example, in any practice is the same as any other, whether it involves laying the table, tidying the cutlery drawer, or sorting blue, green, and red blocks at school.

However, if we examine these relations as relations of signification, it becomes clear that each practice is different although we can specify relations between them. Situated cognition, in this instance, then, is not people thinking in different contexts, but subjects produced differently in different practices, in which certain transformations are necessary to turn, for example, nonschool mathematical into school mathematical practices.

These transformations are in the relations of signification that produce different subject positions and different truth conditions. For example, in Walkerdine (1988), I examined practices involving the comparison of quantities. In primary school mathematics lessons, it was very common to get children to carry out tasks that focused on the comparison of quantities. In textbooks for teachers, notes suggested that teachers pay attention to the terms of *more* and *less* as ways of representing this comparison. Theories of cognitive development assume that if children fail such comparison tasks, they lack the requisite logicomathematical structures, whereas theories of semantic development assume that they have not yet acquired appropriate word meanings. Such approaches treat both the cognitive and semantic relations as though they were fixed and immutable.

Whereas I attempted to demonstrate that these terms, *more* and *less*, were produced as relations of signification within specific practices and that although they might be the same signifiers, the actual signs, the specific relation with signifieds, was made in specific practices. I undertook an analysis of a corpus of recordings of mothers and their 4-year-old daughters at home. These demonstrated that although comparison of quantities was undertaken, the terms *more* and *less* were not used to describe those relations and that although *more* was used, it was in quite different circumstances. Comparison of quantities tended to use terms such as *a lot* and *a little*.

The terms *more* and *less* were not used once to describe comparison of quantities in home practices. Where the term *more* was used was in the regulation by mothers of their daughters' consumption of commodities. Conversations of the following type were typical:

C: I want some more.
M: No, you can't have any more.

Sometimes, the mother might add some explanation about there being uneaten food on a plate, greed, unused paper to draw on, and so forth, followed by further explanations that the commodity in question was expensive. In this way, the mother appeared to be the source of the regulation of consumption, but my argument is that she is positioned as the moral regulator as well as the guardian of the domestic economy. That her daughter may experience her as the source of regulation does not detract from the fact that we could historically chart the truth of her positioning as both moral and domestic guardian.

Within the particular practice of the regulation of children's consumption, the term *more* does not function as an expression of a comparison of quantity. Its opposite is not less, but something like *no more* or *no*. In other words, it may be the same signifier, but it is certainly not the same sign as more when used in a primary school math lesson. Moreover, the strong moral regulative content of 'more' in the domestic practice suggests another layer to the analysis of signification. The term *more* was used more frequently in a negative sense in working-class than middle-class homes—homes in which resources were scarcer and therefore regulation had to be more obvious and frequent. I want to suggest that this means that the mother in such cases may be positioned as more punitive, less facilitating, and indeed more pathological than the truth of mothering discourse tells us.

French psychoanalyst Lacan (1977) suggested that the unconscious 'is structured like a language' and that what Freud saw as chains of association could be understood as chains of signification held within the unconscious. The signification of *more* in these instances then could be presented as relating to deep issues of desire, longing, need, nurturance, and the ways that this is made to signify in terms of the position of the mother.

In my view, this aspect of subjectivity within practices is vital and yet it is an area that is totally ignored within the rather cognitivistic approach that Lave adopted. Indeed, the intrusion of emotionality points to the dreaded irrational or unreason, as Foucault put it, lurking beneath the surface of rational discourse.

My arguments that people are positioned as subjects within practices therefore also relate to the way in which relations of signification, the fusion of the material and the discursive, that produce them also produce the unconscious.

Evans (1993) gave some very interesting examples of adults' discussions about standard numeracy test items in which certain practices have strong emotional connotations. For example, a woman who was asked to calculate an appropriate tip after a restaurant meal was conscious that she usually did not pay for meals out, but "did not want to be a burden." She produced errors in calculation although she managed more complex percentages in other items. A middle-class young man making simple errors in a best buy problem remembered his mother's anger after shopping expeditions in which she had been shortchanged by shop assistants for amounts often no greater than a penny.

That therefore produces the possibility of what is referred to as *transfer across practices* if we do not use a model of in-the-head cognition. I think that the transformation is produced in the relations of signification themselves.

I do not suggest that nonschool practices are really mathematics, but that certain semiotic chains may so transform the relations of signification that a new fusion of signifier and signified is produced. As Lave demonstrated, not only do calculations within shopping and other practices exist in a different way than in school, but the calculation is often not the purpose of the exercise. In my work examining home and school practices involving calculation, the significant transformation occurred to make the task mathematical only when calculation became the target of the exercise. In home practices, this was rarely the case. Cooking practices at home had a cooking product as their aim.

When a calculation became the focus, certain semiotic shifts occurred. In several examples of exchanges between mothers and daughters that I analyzed, the mothers made certain discursive shifts when the focus of the task moved from cooking to calculation as a product. These shifts reoriented the focus of the task so that, as in school, the making of cakes or some other practical task was no longer the product.

The product is the production of the counting string, an addition sum, or whatever. To accomplish this shift, in the examples that I analyzed, the mothers helped their daughters produce the move by the use of semiotic chains in which new signs were constantly formed. For example, one mother got her daughter to name people they were pouring drinks for and to work out how many drinks by holding up one finger to correspond with each name. This is the first relation of signifier to signified. In this case, we might describe the names as signifiers that are attached to signifieds, the people to which they refer. But here they have dropped to the level of signifieds to be united with new signifiers, in this case iconic signifiers, the fingers.

The next stage, which is not reached by this mother–daughter pair but is by another, is for the fingers to drop to the level of signifieds to be united with new signifiers, in this case spoken numerals. By this time, any reference to people outside the counting string no longer exists within the statement. In this case, the mother goes on to get the daughter to unite fingers and numerals in small addition tasks of the form: "Five and one more is . . ."

I argued that discursive shifts such as this were central to the accomplishment of the discursive transformation and to the repositioning of the subject
it entails. Statements of the form of "five and one more is . . ." can refer to
anything. All external reference and metaphoric relations are excluded from
the string. They create a discourse in which there is no *I*, except an omniscient
one (the God of mathematics) which can describe the world as a book
written in mathematics. I therefore argued that discursive shifts, basic as
they are in this case, produce the possibility of huge shifts of subjectification
and the production of the man of reason, because for Lacan at least, semiotic
chains are carried along the metaphoric axis, and this no longer exists in
school mathematics discourse.

In Lacan's analysis of unconscious processes, a signifier can drop to the
level of the signified and a new signifier/signified pair can be formed. This
is what Lacan meant by a semiotic chain. In examples such as these, such
chains form a bridge between one practice and another.

However, mathematical strings have certain characteristics. The articulation of a counting string that can refer to anything has the external reference;
the metaphoric content, removed or suppressed; and the counting string
becomes the product rather than cakes, for example. This is a peculiarity
of mathematical discourse and is what has given it the properties that made
Rotman (1980) describe it as "Reason's Dream," a discourse in which things
once proved true stayed true forever. Nevertheless, the semiotic shifts are
fairly precise and the use of the fingers to unite signifier and signified and
the move for the fingers to take the place of the signified itself is the central
constituent of the discursive transformation that I have signaled.

I am suggesting, therefore, that nonmathematical practices, although they
may have some forms of calculation contained within them, are not the
same as academic mathematical practices because the product of each practice is different—a calculation in one case and not in the other, the relations
of signification are different, the regulation of the practice and the positioning
of the subjects is different, and the emotional signification is different. (In
academic mathematical practices, I argued that this emotional content is
suppressed. See the arguments in Walkerdine, 1988.)

Mathematical practices may, however, be dressed up to look like nonmathematical ones. For example, school mathematics practices often present
practical examples, aiming to draw on children's experience of nonschool
practices in the hope that this meaningfulness will aid transfer. I think that
this idea is quite spurious because it is easy to demonstrate that the supposed
meaningful transfer is based on a fallacy. Indeed, in one example of a
shopping game that I observed in an infant school-mathematics lesson, the
fact that the rules of the game did not correspond with actual shopping
practices provided the basis for failure of at least one of the participating
children.

The product of the game was a subtraction calculation. The children were given 10 pence and asked to select an item on a card from a pack, such as a yacht for 8 pence. The children had to work out the change and record the subtraction sum on paper. One child made a mistake because he did not realize that he got a fresh 10 pence each turn. Others had to translate between *change* and *taking away*. The product was not an item to be bought, but a calculation. There was no exchange and the prices were completely unrealistic. This latter point was the focus of considerable fantasy play in the group, where they imagined they were rich shoppers because of the juxtaposition of normally expensive goods and very low prices.

Indeed, the sophistication of the young children with respect to the rules of shopping practices far outweighed the sense that they could only handle the small numbers and concrete objects that were at the heart of their mathematics education. Far from aiding any 'transfer,' the shopping game positively hindered them from making a transition that demanded that they suppress their inscription into those familiar everyday practices to become subjected in academic mathematics.[4]

PATHOLOGIZED CALCULATORS

Such children as the shopping game group easily become understood as the children who are conceptually poor, the ones who are over-mature and underdeveloped, those who are not being given a proper childhood, and so on. What I am suggesting is that the inscription of these children within shopping and their failure to recognize the difference in the practices renders them understood as 'slow learners' or as not having mastered appropriate mathematical concepts.

In my research on girls and mathematics (Walkerdine et al., 1989), the regulation of school mathematics practices depended not on the production of effective calculation, but precisely on understanding effective calculation as a problem. What was necessary was to ensure that the calculation had been produced through conceptual understanding and propositional knowledge, not effective procedures or following rules. Those children who worked hard were not categorized as playful; active children were deemed

---

[4]Indeed, in Walkerdine (1988), I argued that subjectification in academic mathematics did not mean a greater grasp of the real world, but a deeper inscription in fantasy, a different fantasy than the imaginary wish-fulfillment conveyed in the *more* example, where more love as well as more food might lie in the semiotic chain. The distinction Lacan made is between the imaginary order, the order of wish fulfillment and the symbolic order, which he took to be the patriarchal order of signification where mathematization constantly covers over the pain and desire that form the subject. In this analysis, academic mathematics was not a greater grasp of the real world at all, but an expression in discourse of a desire for absolute control.

not to be producing concepts but were instead simply low-level calculators. Indeed, the whole debate about girls and mathematics is bedeviled by an insistence that 'real' mathematical performance is produced through abstract conceptualization. Girls who did well faced having their performance down-graded even when they come to the top of the class.

The 'truth' about mathematical performance contains the fears and fantasies about those calculating others who threaten the very dominance of the government of reason. Time and time again, girls are accused of being good only at calculation. And school mathematics practices are treated as though they were not practices at all, as though they were not as regulated as other practices. I hope that I have begun to take this 'truth,' this fiction apart and to demonstrate how we might analyze practices to show how the truth of calculation is produced and how human beings are produced as subjects within them.

REFERENCES

Bartlett, B. (1958). *Thinking: An experimental and social study*. New York: Basic Books.

Bhabha, H. (1984). The other question: The stereotype and the colonial discourse. *Screen, 24*(6), 18–36.

Cole, M. (1981). *Society, mind and development*. Paper delivered at the Houston Symposium IV on Psychology and Society: The Child and Other Cultural Conventions, Houston, TX.

Cole, M., Hood, L., & McDermott, R. (1980). *Ecological niche picking*. New York: Laboratory for Comparative Human Cognition, Rochello University.

Donaldson, M. (1978). *Children's minds*. London: Fontana.

Evans, J. (1993). Unpublished PhD thesis, Institute of Education, University of London, England.

Faron, F. (1967). *Black skin, white masks*. New York: Grove.

Henriques, J., Hollway, W., Urwin, C., Venn, C., & Walkerdine, V. (1984). *Changing the subject*. London: Methuen.

Holzman, L., & Newman, F. (1994). *Vygotsky: Revolutionary scientist*. London: Routledge.

Lacan, J. (1977). *Ecrits: A selection*. London: Tavistock.

Lave, J. (1988). *Cognition in practice*. Cambridge, UK: Cambridge University Press.

Nuffield Mathematics Project. (1967). *I do and I understand*. London: W. R. Charbes and John Murray.

Rose, N. (1985). *The psychological complex*. London: Routledge.

Rose, N. (1990). *Governing the soul*. London: Routledge.

Rotman, B. (1980). *Mathematics: An essay in semiotics*. Unpublished monograph.

Scribner, S., & Fahrmeier, E. (1982). *Practical and theoretical arithmetic: Some preliminary findings*. Industrial Literacy Project, Working Paper Number 3, Graduate Center, City University of New York.

Walkerdine, V. (1988). *The mastery of reason*. London: Routledge.

Walkerdine, V. (1989). *Counting girls out*. London: Virago.

CHAPTER FIVE

Living Math:
Lave and Walkerdine on the
Meaning of Everyday Arithmetic

Philip E. Agre
University of California, San Diego

In the last several years, Jean Lave and Valerie Walkerdine have developed searching analyses and critiques of mathematics education, particularly in their books *Cognition in Practice* (Lave, 1988) and *The Mastery of Reason* (Walkerdine, 1988). Despite their many differences, they share a compelling view of mathematics not as an abstract cognitive task but as something deeply bound up in socially organized activities and systems of meaning. The influence of their analyses has been growing steadily as educational researchers have looked for conceptions of cognition and learning that locate knowledge in particular forms of situated activity and not simply in mental contents (Brown, Collins, & Duguid, 1989). Their work has also been part of an increasing interest in the ethnographic study of everyday mathematics (Leap, 1988; Saxe, 1991), the shared construction of mathematical knowledge in school (Newman, Griffin, & Cole, 1989), and the relationship between school activities and the rest of life (Carraher, Carraher, & Schliemann, 1985; Resnick, 1987; Scribner, 1986). Their sociological understanding of mathematics is a striking turn, holding out the hope for an analysis of math—and perhaps of schooling and learning in general—that includes homes, workplaces, and aspects of social relations that structure knowledge and learning across the whole of an individual's life.

The promise of Lave and Walkerdine's sociological analyses of mathematics, then, is considerable. But the very sophistication of their theories puts up equally considerable obstacles. Not only are their respective sociological methods unfamiliar to many readers, but the application of these methods to mathematical activities is demanding even as social-scientific research goes. As a result, future research in this area may benefit from a complex understanding of their conceptual frameworks. In this chapter, I propose simply to draw some distinctions and pose some questions within the shared horizons of their research. Lave's (1988) *Cognition in Practice* and Walkerdine's (1989) *The Mastery of Reason* are challenging on their own for the scope of their intellectual ambition and for the powerful theoretical frameworks on which they draw in analyzing their materials. And they are particularly challenging to read in conjunction, given that despite their broad commonality of purpose and subject matter, they get ahold of their materials in remarkably different, and indeed often almost incommensurable, ways.

LAVE ON MATHEMATICAL ACTIVITY

First, though, let me summarize Lave and Walkerdine's respective theories in just enough detail to motivate the deliberations that follow. Lave was concerned to refute the view of mathematics as the kind of abstract thinking that a long tradition of research in cognitive psychology has called "problem solving." The salient feature of this process is that it unfolds in three distinct steps: life situations are translated into formal cognitive structures or "problems"; these structures are then manipulated through mental processes whose outcomes are called "solutions"; and these outcomes are finally interpreted within the larger life situation as actions to take or answers to give.

Mathematical calculation is often held to reflect this theory of cognition. In particular, Lave suggested that word problems presuppose certain ideas about mathematics and cognition: that occasions for mathematical reasoning present themselves as clear-cut problems, that these problems can be solved by extracting mathematical information from a situation and then setting up the necessary calculations, that the outcomes of these calculations can be interpreted as solutions to these problems, and so on.

Lave took particular issue with a theory of mathematical learning that she called *transfer*. Educationalists have used this word in a variety of ways, but Lave had something specific in mind. She associated the problem-solving theory of cognition with a particular view of knowledge, according to which the contents of knowledge can be specified in abstract, formal terms independent of the larger social organization of the activities within which this knowledge is used. Learning is held to consist in the construction of this kind of knowledge, in large part through the discovery of structural analogies between one situation and another.

In contrast to this theory, Lave argued that mathematical reasoning must be viewed as deeply bound up with the activities within which it takes place. Her argument had several steps, which I can only briefly indicate here. Her central conclusion was that ordinary life activities do not present clear-cut problems in the sense required by the problem-solving theory of cognition. She argued this point ethnographically, by exhibiting some of the properties of naturally occurring mathematical reasoning in particular settings. For example, she showed people bringing such a complex variety of considerations to bear on their decisions that one cannot find clear boundaries among the different phases of problem solving. In particular, one does find clear "solutions" but simply "resolutions" that keep things moving along, subject to later revision; things are not so much solved as usefully transformed. Even when the people are set to performing school-like calculations, for example in scientific diet programs, the activity quickly evolves and the boundaries between calculation and the rest of the activity steadily blur.

Lave concluded from this that the natural unit of analysis is not abstract knowledge but structured activity. People certainly do know things, but this knowledge is to be understood as an attribute of the varieties of structured activity that the people are capable of engaging in while pursuing particular socially organized ends in organized settings. Most importantly, knowledge is to be understood relationally—that is, as something located in the evolving relationships between people and the settings in which they conduct their activities.

This is a tremendously difficult idea and it helps to understand the kind of motivation that Lave offered for it. Her project was ethnographic: She and her students hung out with some people, documented their activities, intervened in them to some extent, and searched for language that adequately described the things they saw. The language of problems and transfer, they argued, does not allow us to formulate adequate descriptions of what the people did, and this can be demonstrated by telling an orderly sequence of representative stories about their field informants and pointing to the difficulty or impossibility of describing the action in those stories using the conventional vocabulary. The point is not that the problem-solving theory makes the wrong predictions, but that the theory cannot even be applied. If the problem-solving theory can be applied to laboratory situations or even to some classrooms, she would argue, that is because the social and physical structures of those places have specifically provided for its applicability. It then stands to reason that forms of activity that arise in those settings may have little consequence, whether scientific or educational, for the quite different forms of activity found elsewhere.

Having found the problem-solving theory inapplicable to describing the activity she found in ordinary activities, Lave proceeded to develop her own descriptive vocabulary in relational terms. This descriptive vocabulary has two properties: It is dialectical and it operates on several levels. For example, when a person is engaged in cooking dinner, one would provide a series of descriptions of the relationship between the cook and the kitchen, each of which would be framed in dialectical terms.

For Lave, two entities (e.g., a person engaged in an activity and the setting in which that activity takes place) are related dialectically when three conditions obtain: The entities interact with one another, the entities are changed over time through their interactions, and the cumulative changes are sufficiently extensive or complicated that it is difficult or impossible to give an account of either one except in terms of their unfolding relationship to one another. These changes need not be equal in magnitude—for example, supermarkets have changed me more than I have ever changed them—but the reciprocal influences should not be neglected.

The descriptive levels on which activities are described dialectically are:

1. How various activities fit together, for example when someone is simultaneously preparing dinner, putting the groceries away, minding the children, and listening to the news.
2. The interaction between the person engaged in the activity and the setting of that activity; for example, the evolving arrangements of various tools and materials on countertops and stoves and the guidance that these arrangements provide to the cook.
3. The interaction between the person considered as a social agent in a much larger sense and the socially organized *arena* within which the activity takes place; for example, the cook who was brought up to regard food and cooking in a certain way, working in a kitchen that was designed by the efficiency and marketing experts of a particular era.
4. The political economy and the cultural meanings of these things, as historically coevolving systems.

This is a complex story, and Lave would not claim to have proven its necessity or adequacy in any complete way. It does, however, do justice to her central observations about the actual nature of everyday mathematical reasoning.

WALKERDINE ON MATHEMATICAL ACTIVITY

Before assessing Lave's story any further, let us turn to a brief account of Walkerdine's (1988) theory. Whereas Lave drew on the dialectical tradition of social thought, Walkerdine drew on a more recent tradition of French poststructuralist theory, specifically a synthesis of certain ideas of Michel Foucault (1977, 1979) and Jacques Lacan (1977). Although it is impossible to give a brief account of these thinkers' views, Walkerdine's use of them in *The Mastery of Reason* can be summarized briefly.

Walkerdine also viewed mathematical reasoning as deeply bound up with the larger activity within which it takes place; she furthermore understood activity itself in relational terms. Nonetheless, her analysis of these propositions was significantly different. Walkerdine was centrally concerned with processes by which something called "the child" is produced in various social settings, particularly the classroom. This, too, is a tremendously difficult idea. Its core intuition is that people with authority over children—teachers, parents, school administrators, and others—orchestrate classroom and home activities in elaborate ways that allow them to "see" something that they can understand as a proper child. In doing so, they are guided by complicated and historically specific discourses about child development. That is, they actually put these discourses into practice, going to tremendous lengths to arrange their relationships with children in ways that make their "truth" evident in the visible details of the various joint activities that make up an average day in a school or other institution.

Walkerdine developed a set of conceptual tools for analyzing the activities within which authoritative adults manage to discover the child they are looking for. She fashioned these tools out of materials provided by the tradition of semiotic analysis. The child that is produced in a classroom is specifically a *sign*. But Walkerdine's notion of a sign is distinctive and requires careful attention. For Saussure (1974), a given language distinguishes a set of meanings, called signifieds, that are organized as a field of differences. Put in another vocabulary, languages divide the world into different categories, perhaps distinguishing different types of cheeses, boats, or sexualities. The signifieds are defined by nothing more than these relationships of being-different-from-one-another. Each sign, then, comprises one of these signifieds and the particular signifier ("cheddar," "yacht," "straight") that names it.

Walkerdine, although retaining the vocabulary of semiotics, had a different understanding of what signifieds are and how they go together with signifiers to make signs. For her, a signified was not an abstract meaning but rather a form of activity, and specifically a form of joint or shared activity among a number of people. To produce the child as a sign, then, is to orchestrate a form of joint activity that can be recognized as exhibiting the signified that goes together with a particular signifier, namely "the child." More generally, this activity will exhibit the whole interconnected system of signs organized by a particular discourse about childhood, development, learning, motivation, and so forth.

Let me remark in passing that these ideas combine themes from Foucault and Lacan in a complex way. Walkerdine's semiotic ideas, and particularly the emphasis on the connections and interrelations among signifiers that are central to her theory of mathematics, derive from Lacan. Her ideas about historically specific discourses and their role in organizing activities and producing particular kinds of people derived from Foucault. Her principal goal was to develop concepts to analyze particular kinds of empirical materials, but it should be noted that she made little effort to develop the wider consequences for Foucault's and Lacan's larger philosophies of the particular synthesis she has developed. Indeed, Foucault regarded psychoanalysis as one more discourse aiming at producing a historically specific "truth" about people, and Lacan had next to nothing to say about the organization of material activity. Nonetheless, Walkerdine's synthesis is not obviously incoherent, and further conceptual analysis would probably be rewarding.

Be this as it may, Walkerdine's theory of discourses and signs provides an exceptionally sharp instrument for the analysis of everyday mathematics. Numbers for her are signifiers that signify forms of activity. For example, a child's counting forms a series of signs through the verbalization of a sequence of signifiers in synchrony with a sequence of pointing motions. Mathematical activity, then, is activity whose forms are orchestrated so as to exhibit specifically mathematical signs. This is where the distinction between signifiers and signs becomes crucial. Walkerdine demonstrated that a mathematical signifier such as "more" can be embedded in wholly different signs in different settings. In the homes of the people she studied, for example, children and adults employed the signifier "more" in the context of contests over the consumption of food and other things. (As in, "A: Can I have more? B: No, you cannot have more.") This "more" has quite a different discursive logic than the "more" of classroom mathematics assignments, and it is no wonder if children stumble in their acquisition of the pairing of signifiers and signifieds that is specific to mathematical activity.

Mathematical signs, as we have seen, are produced in a series of operations by which objects, images, fingers, heads, and so forth are made visible as participants in mathematical signifieds. What is specifically mathematical about these signs is the ending point of the series: a signifier such as "three" that has become effectively shorn of any empirical signification. Submitted to a mathematical operation such as counting, arrays of real-world things such as three bears, three fingers, three books, and three knocks on a door all yield the same signifier, "three." Having no inherent attachment to particular signifieds, mathematical signifiers become universally applicable. As signifiers go, they are uniquely self-sufficient; whereas most signifiers are more or less inconsequential unless bound up in signs within the complex and contingent world of activity, mathematics offers a closed system whose relations, consequences, outcomes are not contingent at all. And when read back onto material activities to form signs, mathematical signifiers promise to represent the world in a uniquely transparent way. For example, when the "seven" that results from a calculation might then be formed into a sign denoting "seven apples," we feel confident that everything we wish to know about those apples is already present in "seven." Of course, this is not true in reality; the application of numbers to real-life situations is fraught with numerous problems of interpretation. But this is an easy point to miss when the situation is only presented through a fantasy story.

In an altogether remarkable sequence of chapters, Walkerdine argued that the detachability of mathematical signifiers from empirical signification affords a particular kind of emotional investment. The process by which arithmetic yields useful signifiers is—at least given conventional algorithmic means of teaching arithmetic—pretty magical to begin with. And people who proceed to treat these signifiers as transparent representations of the world are engaged in a fantasy—the fantasy in which the differences between signifiers and signifieds no longer matter. Of course, all fantasy suspends the complex link between thought and reality. But mathematical fantasy is supported by an elaborate system of prestigious social institutions. These institutions effectively encourage children in the idea that they can comprehend and control the world by encoding and manipulating it symbolically.

Of course, many children never develop or consolidate this fantasy life or the formal skills that support it. Walkerdine suggested that one reason for this lies in the nature of mathematical story problems themselves. Story problems are frequently unrealistic, for example in the prices they assign to desirable objects. As a result, children regularly become involved in playing out the wrong fantasies. Perhaps, she suggested, the children who find these fantasies appealing are distracted from taking on the deeper and more formidable fantasies of symbolic control. This may help to explain the tendency of mathematical skill to become gendered: Inasmuch as fantasy is part of the development of personal identity, the many encouragements and discouragements that shape gender identity will also tend to shape a child's choice of fantasies—and thus his or her affinity to mathematics.

VIEWS OF ACTIVITY

These brief accounts of Lave's and Walkerdine's positions neglect many points and risk oversimplification of the points that remain, but they are perhaps sufficient to begin exploring the complex relationships between them. To begin with, the tremendous differences in their vocabularies should not blind us to several points of convergence. They are both concerned with math education, and they both wish to describe math education against the broad background of the production of ordinary activities. They both understand activity in relational terms; that is, as something that can only be described through the socially organized relationships into which people enter. They both recognize that mathematical reasoning occurs, but they are also both critical of the abstraction and formality of mathematical reason.

The similarities between Lave's and Walkerdine's work extend to the level of institutions as well. Both of them argued that school and nonschool activities organize mathematical reason differently, and their critiques begin with those differences. Although neither presented a detailed analysis of school institutions (see, however, Henriques, Hollway, Urwin, Venn, & Walkerdine, 1984; Lave & Wenger, 1991), they both regarded school activities as historically specific. School activities interconnect with much else in society, and must be understood in those terms. The organization of school activities is influenced to a substantial degree by complex systems of ideas; these in turn are historically specific and should not be accepted uncritically. To the contrary, the ideas themselves are very much part of the larger phenomenon requiring explanation.

These vaguely expressed commonalities provide starting points for the more difficult analysis of the two authors' differences. To begin with, despite their shared interest in mathematical activity, they understood both mathematics and activity in quite different ways. Specifically, they understood mathematics differently as a vehicle by which forms of reasoning can be abstracted from concrete situations. For Lave, abstraction is prototypically something that happens in school. It is part of the practice of problem solving and proceeds by formalization, calculation, and the formal derivation of conclusions. For Walkerdine, abstraction is a feature of discourse; it is part of the practice of incremental recoding that proceeds from nonmathematical discourses to mathematical discourses, and from signs that have empirical references within concrete activities to signs that do not. Lave believed that mathematics can occur without abstraction, for example in the everyday practice of cooks and grocery shoppers. Walkerdine, on the other hand, believed that mathematical discourse can be found produced in a wide variety of milieux, provided only that the necessary practices of resignification are present. In other words, Walkerdine found mathematical abstraction in places where Lave did not.

As a result, the authors provided different accounts of school and its effects. Although both recognize that school varies historically, they were both concerned with particular kinds of contemporary schooling. And each of them analyzed school in terms of a set of ideas about children. But whereas for Lave, these ideas related learning to cognition, for Walkerdine they related learning to emotion. In Walkerdine's view, schools are centrally concerned with arranging for students to develop emotional investments in the forms of activity and of subjectivity within which the normative "child" can be discursively produced. Lave did not analyze this aspect of schooling at all, instead analyzing in greater detail than Walkerdine the whole system of ideas around problems, transfer, and knowledge.

They did converge, however, in accusing school-based activity of being organized in such a way that children are encouraged in an unfortunate kind of relationship to reality. In each case, this occurs through the construction of artificial problems that are amenable to wholly abstract treatment. But they differed markedly in their view of the outcome of this process—the problem-solving model of activity versus fantasies of control—and especially in how successful they viewed school as being in bringing these things about. For her part, Lave viewed schools as failures, inasmuch as the problem-solving methods they teach have little application to everyday life. Walkerdine, on the other hand, viewed schools as only too successful in inculcating a particular kind of fantasy life and a particular connection between these fantasies and the child's gendered identity.

More generally, Lave and Walkerdine differed significantly in their analysis of activity as such. For Lave, activity is dialectical engagement; it is the self-organizing interaction and reciprocal influence of socially constituted persons and socially constituted settings of activity. Activity for Lave can be analyzed on several levels, bringing into focus the sociology and history of particular arenas of activity, such as schools and grocery stores. For Walkerdine, activity is produced discursively. Discourse, for Walkerdine, is not simply verbal or simply symbolic. Although books and speeches might arrange clouds of signifiers into complex formal relationships, the signifieds with which they form signs are precisely human interactions; school activity can be interpreted as producing the sign "counting to five" or the sign "a child who is ready to begin work with fractions."

These vocabularies of dialectical activity and discourse are very different in their surface forms and it is not a simple matter to reconcile them. One point of comparison is their respective treatments of educational theory itself. Lave understood the effectivity of the concept of transfer, for example, within the vocabulary of ideology and consciousness. Transfer and its embracing functionalist framework are held to be ideologies in the sense, among other things, that they are wrong. They can be disproven by exhibiting their inapplicability to ethnographically observed activities; they can be demonstrated to be absent in their proponents' data through a reanalysis of their experiments; and they can be viewed as mystifications in relation to some different, deeper, and more accurate story about activity, in which they play a part—for example, as apology or rationalization—but that they do not totally constitute.

As such, Lave's theory leads to a complicated story about the understandings of mathematics that people take away from school; these understandings are precisely ideologies. As such, they can be compared and contrasted to the understandings of things that people actually have—that is, in more precise language, the consciousness of their world with which they live their lives. The ideas of ideology and consciousness both require more analysis than we have any need for here. Suffice it to say that they are not, for example, simply propositional statements or beliefs. Rather, like everything else in Lave's theory, they are aspects of people's relationships to the arenas in which they conduct their activities. She observed, for example, that the cultural prestige of mathematics regularly combines with the frustration of problem solving to produce the harmful experience of oneself as being "bad at math." Lave was willing to argue that this idea is simply mistaken and can be disproven by carefully observing actual arithmetic calculations in super-markets and kitchens and working up a schoolish score for them.

This dialectical approach is to be contrasted with Walkerdine's Foucauldian approach, which has no concept of ideology at all. In place of ideology, Foucault employed concepts like discourses, disciplines, and the laborious production of both subjects and signs. Again, activities on this view are constituted by discourses; on this view, school itself is one big discourse. What makes school different from any other site of activity is simply which particular discursive formation it is. It is important to understand that a discourse, in Foucault's sense, is not right or wrong; it is simply what the people in a given institution are producing. This is the controversial sense in which Foucault spoke of disciplinary practices as producing "truth," or "truths," with quotation marks. This is troubling to many people, for whom it sounds like relativism. Although it is not entirely unproblematic, it is not any simple kind of relativism. Neither Foucault nor Walkerdine would ever argue that institutions can produce anything at all; their concern, rather, was to describe the historical processes and the practical means by which particular "truths" *are* produced, in classrooms or anywhere else.

The contrast between Lave's and Walkerdine's theories seems so irrec-oncilable in part because of the contrasting details of their case studies. Lave focused on adults in their largely solitary and self-directed activities; she wants to provide a vocabulary in which we can describe the structure of those activities and the history through which they acquired that kind of structure. In particular, it is we, the investigators and readers, who are finding significance in the individuals' activities, which assume their special forms without our influence. (But this is not quite true, because the fieldworker necessarily shapes, to some degree, the activities in which she participates by observing; Lave remarked on this, but only in passing.)

Walkerdine, for her part, focused on interactions between adults and children; within these relationships, particular signs are produced that are held to be predicative of the children on their own. These signs "are produced," in the passive voice, in that they are not necessarily consciously or deliberately negotiated but rather are manifestations of the anonymous power relations within which the very social beings of the adult and child are organized. Walkerdine's theory, like Foucault's, has a certain ambiguity on this point: To what extent should we view the children as putty that is being passively shaped into the discursive "child," and to what extent should we view the children as active participants in the process? This is, to be sure, a point of instability in many theories of development. Each theory offers an explanation for the negative labels that are applied to children who fail to conform to norms. But what is missing in each case is a substantive account of the children's active noncooperation with the adults' plans for them.

To put the contrast crudely, whereas Lave's is a two-level model describing contradictions within subjectivities and between ideologies and realities, Walkerdine's is a one-level model in which the social order constitutes the activities as such. Put in simpler words, Lave contrasted the falsehood of cognitivist psychology, which she treats as an ideology, to the (provisional, approximate) accuracy of her own description of activity, whereas Walkerdine simply described a discourse that is part-and-parcel of particular kinds of activity, judgments of truth and falsehood being beside the point. Whereas Lave's negative assessment of cognitivism was both empirical (it fails to explain the phenomena) and ethical (it distracts people from the reality and causes them to discount their own abilities), Walkerdine's negative assessment of school discourse is wholly ethical (it marginalizes whole categories of students and it inculcates regrettable fantasies of control).

CONCLUSION

I will not attempt to reconcile these differences. Instead, I see them as organizing a horizon of new research topics. The best way to proceed, in my view, is not to generate a list of contrasting predictions by which we might perform some kind of differential diagnosis. Instead, we should take these projects in the spirit in which they were intended, as provisional ethnographic accounts of enormously complicated things. The descriptive vocabularies that each author has proposed will be thoroughly tested, and presumably extended and transformed, as ethnographic research begins to fill out the picture of institutional and social relationships that surround the practices of school and of mathematics.

One crucial direction for further development of Lave and Walkerdine's ideas is in critical studies of educational institutions. Teachers, for example, are not simply passive transmitters of discourses and ideologies passed down from on high. Each theory would also benefit from an encounter with the practices of classroom discipline that are prerequisites of mathematical activities—and that should probably be viewed as part of those activities.

Given that both authors are concerned with the relationship between school and nonschool activities, both of their theories would benefit from more extensive analyses of the cultural and practical resources that children carry with them in each direction. The processes of discursive recoding that Walkerdine regarded as defining mathematics also apply, for example, to the semiotics of the Teenage Mutant Ninja Turtles. These television sign systems, as well as those from shopping, have been omnipresent in my exposure to elementary school mathematics. Such investigations would help us ask more carefully what mathematics and mathematics education should be like.

REFERENCES

Brown, J. S., Collins, A., & Duguid, P. (1989). Situated cognition and the culture of learning. *Educational Researcher, 18*(1), 32–42.

Carraher, T. N., Carraher, D. W., & Schliemann, A. D. (1985). Mathematics in the streets and in schools. *British Journal of Developmental Psychology, 3*, 21–29.

Foucault, M. (1977). *Discipline and punish: The birth of the prison* (A. Sheridan, Trans.). New York: Pantheon.

Foucault, M. (1979). On governmentality. *Ideology and Consciousness, 6*(1), 5–21.

Lacan, J. (1977). *Ecrits: A selection* (A. Sheridan, Trans.). New York: Norton.

Henriques, J., Hollway, W., Urwin, C., Venn, C., & Walkerdine, V. (1984). *Changing the subject: Psychology, social regulation, and subjectivity.* London: Methuen.

Lave, J. (1988). *Cognition in practice: Mind, mathematics, and culture in everyday life.* Cambridge, UK: Cambridge University Press.

Lave, J., & Wenger, E. (1991). *Situated learning: Legitimate peripheral participation.* Cambridge, UK: Cambridge University Press.

Leap, W. K. (1988). Assumptions and strategies guiding mathematics problem solving by Ute Indian students. In R. R. Cocking & J. P. Mestre (Eds.), *Linguistic and cultural influences on learning mathematics* (pp. 161–186). Hillsdale, NJ: Lawrence Erlbaum Associates.

Newman, D., Griffin, P., & Cole, M. (1989). *The construction zone: Working for cognitive change in school.* Cambridge, UK: Cambridge University Press.

Resnick, L. B. (1987). Learning in school and out. *Educational Researcher, 16*, 13–20.

de Saussure, F. (1974). *Course in general linguistics* (C. Bally & A. Sechehaye, Eds., W. Baskin, Trans.; rev. ed.). London: Fontana.

Saxe, G. B. (1991). *Culture and cognitive development: Studies in mathematical understanding.* Hillsdale, NJ: Lawrence Erlbaum Associates.

Scribner, S. (1986). Thinking in action: Some characteristics of practical thought. In R. J. Sternberg & R. K. Wagner (Eds.), *Practical intelligence: Nature and origins of competence in the everyday world* (pp. 13–30). Cambridge, UK: Cambridge University Press.

Walkerdine, V. (1988). *The mastery of reason: Cognitive development and the production of rationality.* London: Routledge.

CHAPTER SIX

The Situated Development of Logic in Infancy: A Case Study

David Kirshner
Louisiana State University

One cannot speak of the child without asking whether logic is a social thing and in what sense. I have been bothered by this question; I have sought to put it aside; it has always returned.
—Piaget (1927/1977, p. 204; in Rogoff, 1990, p. 33)

As I see it, the body is a classy chassis to carry your mind around in.
—Sylvester Stallone

I think, therefore I was.

—not Descartes

This chapter contributes to the critique of the grand tradition of modernism that Descartes helped to launch some 350 years ago. What is compelling about that tradition is its love for the individual conceived as an autonomous intellectual entity: "But what am I? A thing that thinks. What is that? A thing that doubts, understands, affirms, denies, wills, refuses, and which also imagines and senses" (Descartes, 1641/1979, p. 19). To the less scrutinizing, we might think ourselves more than Descartes allows; perhaps also a thing that belongs, a thing that intuits, a thing that despairs. But under such intense intellectual examination, we are bound to see ourselves reflected only in our consciousness. Jaynes (1976) was eloquent in his assessment:

Consciousness is a much smaller part of our mental life than we are conscious of, because we cannot be conscious of what we are not conscious of. How simple that is to say; how difficult to appreciate. It is like asking a flashlight

83

in a dark room to search around for something that does not have any light
shining upon it. The flashlight, since there is light in whatever direction it
turns, would have to conclude that there is light everywhere. And so consciousness can seem to pervade all mentality when actually it does not. (p. 23)

The mantle of modernism is carried in our day by the tradition of mainstream cognitive science, which understands the mind according to the
model of the serial digital computer (the computational metaphor). As
Haugland (1985) noted, there are three philosophical dilemmas that have
stood in the way of Descartes' mind–body dualism and now are resolved:

(i) the metaphysical problem of mind interacting with matter;
(ii) the theoretical problem of explaining the relevance of meanings, without
appealing to a question-begging homunculus; and
(iii) the methodological issue over the empirical testability . . . of "mentalistic"
explanations. The computational idea can be seen as slicing through all three
dilemmas at a stroke; and this is what gives it [cognitive science], I think, the
bulk of its tremendous gut-level appeal. (p. 2)

In addition to explaining how minds separated from bodies can cooperate
productively in the world, modernism also needs to account for the development of such capacities over the human life span. We begin as helpless
infants, manifestly incapable of reason, reflection, language, or any of the
other defining mental capacities of modern man. How is it that we come
to acquire them? One obvious approach is to assume that they emerge
naturally as the child matures; that they are contained within the genetic
program of the species. This nativist position is argued most forcefully in
the present era by Chomsky (e.g., 1980, 1986) and Fodor (1975, 1980), who
challenged that no viable alternative explanations have been proffered, and
questioned the possibility of ever finding any. But as Reber (1993) cautioned,
such negative motivations should be eschewed in that they serve to block
investigation far beyond their merit:

I find myself drawn to the conclusion that the rationalist, mentalist program
of the content-specific nativist is a homolog of the extreme environmentalism
of the behaviorist. They would take us to the same point by different routes.
Each would block off psychology, bound the field by affiliation with one
particular domain and denial of . . . the role of other domains. Both, in their
idiosyncratic ways, would actually extend the perceived boundaries of explication beyond what can be conveniently subsumed within their spheres. (p.
157)

The alternative approach is to attribute the development of modern man's
characteristic intellectual capacities to the influence of experience. The extreme empiricist position of John Locke's *tabula rasa*—blank slate—view

of the child is not espoused in our day (Gardner, 1987). Rather, it is recognized that the organism is uniquely endowed to benefit from experience. Reber's (1993) distinction between content-specific nativism and process-specific nativism (following Slobin, 1966) is useful here. Nativists of a Chomskyan persuasion believe that the basic content structures of knowledge are inborn, with environmental stimulation serving merely to trigger their unfolding. For process-specific nativists like Piaget, it is the functioning of intelligence, not its particular contents, that is predetermined by heredity. Content structures become constructed by the organism in its adaptive give-and-take with the environment:

> Fifty years of experience have taught us that knowledge does not result from a mere recording of observations without a structuring activity on the part of the subject. Nor do any a priori or innate cognitive structures exist in man; the functioning of intelligence alone is hereditary and creates structures only through an organization of successive actions performed on objects. Consequently, an epistemology conforming to the data of psychogenesis could be neither empiricist nor preformationist, but could consist only of a constructivism, with a continual elaboration of new operations and structures. (Piaget, 1980, p. 23)

Piaget's contributions to educational thought and practice are as complex and multifaceted as they are pervasive. There can be no attempt here to untangle this diverse legacy. Rather, I am narrowly interested in the connections between his work and the great philosophical problems of dualism; and, in that, in the nature of the "child" whose development he has studied. As Glick (1983) noted:

> The conceptual problem that Piaget set out to solve has deep roots in the Western philosophical tradition. . . . The particular conceptual problem was to solve the issue posed by Plato and Aristotle over the relationship between experience and ideas. As Plato posed the problem "how can we gain stable (eternal/necessary) ideas from experience which is contingent, changeable, and distorted." As Aristotle posed the issue "Accepting that Plato has identified the characteristics of ideas (eternal/necessary) how can we form a relationship between rather than just draw a line between, these ideas and experience." (p. 39)

In particular, Piaget was intrigued by the achievement in adults of the characteristic forms of rational thought, consistent with logic:

> The main problem with which we have been concerned stems from our interest in genetic epistemology. . . . We want to know why the organization of behaviour in classification and seriation takes the forms that it does. In particular we want to know why later forms tend to approximate more and more closely to logico-mathematical structures. (Inhelder & Piaget, 1964, p. 281)

The basic outline of his solution to the problem is well known: Logico-mathematical structures are abstracted not from objects in the world, but from reflection on one's actions on such objects. As Glick (1983) noted, this is a brilliant solution to Plato's problem of obtaining eternal, necessary structures (like logic) from contingent experience: "Since action can be the same while the contents differ, it has the required characteristic of being something that is engaged with the world of experience and yet importantly goes beyond it" (p. 41).

But there is a price tag associated with Piaget's solution: Not all aspects of the world are equally fertile ground for actions that yield the regularities from which logical structure can be abstracted. In particular, Piaget's world is predominantly a material world. Experience is physical rather than cultural or emotional.

In accordance with this world, Piaget staked out a particular subject for observation and study. Eschewing the *psychological subject* who has a particular history and individual nature, Piaget opted for the *epistemic subject* that "is of a common nature and makes up the basis for mathematical knowledge" (Skovsmose, 1993, p. 167). As Glick (1983) expressed it:

> The child is, in a theory of this sort . . . a *site* wherein the conceptual problems are located, rather than a topic of inquiry in its own right. The child is the natural object within which the conceptual object [the process of development] is located. We should not conflate the two. It may very well be the case that the conceptual problem may be brilliantly solved chez l'enfant, without at all informing us very much about the nature of the child that the conceptual problem is visiting. (p. 40)

This chapter reports a study of situated logical development in infancy. By "situated logical development," I intend to signal two departures from Piaget's classical studies. First, there is no a priori assumption that the logical competencies to be achieved are indicative of abstract logicomathematical structures. Rather, it is assumed only that infants come to function more successfully in the world in ways that are compatible with logic. The actual nature of the evolving competence is an open question to be resolved through the research itself. Second, to cast the broadest net for competence, the world in which the infant develops is not restricted to its physical dimensions. The social, physical, cultural, and emotional rhythms of life are the presumed world of the child's development.

THE PACIFIER DILEMMA

The single subject for the study was my infant son, Nathan, during the first year or so of his life. Nathan was born on November 25, 1993. It was during a feeding episode in his third month that I first noticed the *pacifier dilemma*.

The pacifier dilemma occurred when I presented Nathan with his bottle at the same time that he happened to be sucking on his pacifier. Rather than spitting out the pacifier or knocking it away with his hand (both of which he already was capable of doing), an intriguing sequence of responses ensued. First, perhaps in excitement and anticipation of the bottle, he began to suck harder on his pacifier. Next (because that is their function), sucking on the pacifier relaxed and calmed him, markedly reducing the rate of his sucking activity. But moments later he observed that sucking was not satisfying his hunger, and that there was a bottle in front of him. This led to a renewal of the intense sucking, followed again by a more relaxed and calm period, followed again by a renewal of the intense sucking. . . . After four or five iterations, Nathan's frustration level had risen to the point of the onset of crying. As he opened his mouth to begin crying, the pacifier fell out and I quickly inserted the bottle. Each phase of this episode took 20 to 30 seconds, with the whole experience taking 2 to 3 minutes.

Over the next few days, I observed this same sequence of responses on several more occasions. Without any clear expectation or hypothesis, I decided to systematically observe and study the progress of Nathan's response to the pacifier dilemma. Many months later, Nathan achieved competence in reliably removing the pacifier when presented with his bottle. About 350 observations of the pacifier dilemma during that period form the basis for this report.

Theoretical Framework

Research by Piaget and others based on systematic observations of infants during the sensorimotor period of the first 2 years of life provides a set of explanatory principles and a timetable to anticipate the successful resolution of the pacifier dilemma. To begin with, the sucking reflex becomes operative in utero and continues throughout infancy (Field, 1990). But starting at birth, the infant shows increasing control and discrimination in sucking activity, clearly distinguishing the situations in which sucking can satisfy her or his needs.

> It is very interesting, in the second case [after a few days experience], to see how the reflex, excited by each contact with the breast, stops functioning as soon as the child perceives that sucking is not followed by any satisfaction, as is the taking of nourishment, and to see how the search [for the breast] goes on until swallowing begins. (Piaget, 1963, p. 31)

For roughly the first month of life, the infant's interactions with the world are dominated by the refinement of reflexive responses. From here, development progresses through increasingly decentered stages of circular reaction (Piaget, 1963). Circular reactions are based on the infants' propensity to repeat actions that lead to interesting or pleasurable results (Ginsburg & Opper, 1969). In primary circular reactions (1–4 months), the infant's body is the locus for activity. Thus, coordination is developed by placing fingers in the mouth during this period. Or time may be spent in focusing the eye on interesting visual textures (Piaget, 1963). In secondary circular reactions (4–10 months), the locus extends to external objects. For instance, the infant may continue to push a ball to see it roll, or she may repeatedly hit toys that are dangling within reach to watch them shake. In months 10 to 12, the child becomes more goal oriented, and increasingly is able to coordinate secondary circular reactions. Thus, if the child has a scheme for grabbing things to bring them to himself, and another for striking things to see them move, he may coordinate these by striking the hand that blocks his access to a toy, which he then may grab (Piaget, 1963). In tertiary circular reactions (12–18 months), external objects and properties become interesting to the child in their own right. Thus, whereas the child at the stage of secondary circular reactions may repeatedly drop an object to delight in the control this action affords, at this new stage, the child will systematically vary the height from which the object is released to observe the influence of height on bouncing characteristics. At this same time, the child can begin to use new means to achieve a goal. For instance, Piaget set up a box around a pivot and observed his daughter Lucienne's attempts to get an object at the far end of the box. Previously she had solved similar problems by pulling the supporting item toward her, but this method was unsuccessful because the box was anchored. Then she hit the box and noticed it pivot a little. Lucienne quickly apprehended that pivoting could be used as a new means to obtain the object (Piaget, 1963).

From these vignettes of cognitive development, it might be supposed that by the time tertiary circular reactions are available, the child would be able to resolve the pacifier dilemma. But through the tertiary circular reactions, there is a crucial aspect of the child's competence that Piaget stressed repeatedly: The child's method of discovery is accidental. Thus whereas the 10- to 12-month-old child is goal oriented and able to coordinate schemes for action, it is only by accident that the child can discover that some method will be effective. Similarly, Lucienne discovered the pivoting action of the box by accident. The child has no capacity to anticipate what a new action will do. This latter capacity must await the development of symbolic reasoning skills, which emerge in the final stage of the sensorimotor period (18–24 months).

The final sensorimotor stage is distinguished by the child's ability to anticipate the results of actions mentally. Piaget (1963) described a characteristic incident in which Lucienne was presented with a matchbox containing a chain. In previous episodes, the box had been opened sufficiently for her to retrieve the chain directly, but now it is nearly completely closed:

> She only possesses two preceding schemes: turning the box over to empty it of its contents, and sliding her fingers into the slit to make the chain come

out. It is of course this last procedure that she tries first: she puts her finger inside and gropes to reach the chain, but fails completely. A pause follows during which Lucienne manifests a very curious reaction. . . .

She looks at the slit with great attention; then, several times in succession, she opens and shuts her mouth, at first slightly, then wider and wider! Apparently Lucienne understands the existence of a cavity subjacent to the slit and wishes to enlarge that cavity. The attempt at representation which she thus furnishes is expressed plastically, that is to say, due to inability to think out the situation in words or clear visual images she uses a simple motor indication as "signifier" or symbol. . . .

Soon after this phase of plastic reflection, Lucienne unhesitatingly puts her finger in the slit, and instead of trying as before to reach the chain, she pulls so as to enlarge the opening. She succeeds and grasps the chain. (pp. 337–338)

The pacifier dilemma is inscrutable precisely because it affords so little opportunity for experimentation and trial and error. Unlike the episodes of play described earlier, the pacifier dilemma occurred within the child's life practices of feeding. Within these practices there are established roles for participants: Caregiver presents bottle, baby sucks formula. There is little room for deviation. Importantly, from Nathan's first experience of the pacifier dilemma until his final resolution of it by removing the pacifier manually, there was no evidence of experimentation or happenstance. Thus, it seems reasonable to conclude that successful resolution of the pacifier dilemma must involve rudimentary mental representation of the removal-of-the-pacifier scheme, which can occur only in the final sensorimotor stage. These considerations provide a framework through which to begin to analyze Nathan's resolution of the pacifier dilemma. To the extent that they are insufficient, other theoretical approaches are introduced in the discussion section.

Methodology

Observations of Nathan were begun in February 1994, and concluded in December 1994. During that period, the researcher was a secondary caregiver for Nathan, responsible for about 40% of his feedings. The pacifier dilemma was induced by the researcher only when Nathan happened to be sucking his pacifier at feeding time. With rare exceptions, Nathan was not set up with the pacifier prior to feeding in order to obtain more data. The researcher was the only caregiver to induce the pacifier dilemma. Other caregivers removed the pacifier from Nathan's mouth prior to presenting the bottle.

There was a slight decline in Nathan's pacifier use over the 11-month study, from about 70% to about 60% of the feedings. This is one small factor contributing to a steady decline in the opportunities to observe the pacifier dilemma. The major factors in this decline were the reduction in the number of feedings per day (from about 8 to about 4 during the course of the study), and the gradual introduction of solid food. In all, Nathan's bottle use decreased from about 8 times to about 3 times per day. As a consequence, observations of the pacifier dilemma decreased from once or twice per day at the start of the study to about twice per week at its finish. But until Nathan's final mastery of the pacifier dilemma (by removing it from his mouth), the characteristic sequence of responses described earlier was observed on each possible occasion.

The following protocols were more or less strictly adhered to throughout the course of the study. I would show Nathan the bottle and gently push it against the tip of the extruding pacifier. I would then carefully observe his sequence of responses, including the alternation between intense and subdued sucking and the onset of crying. Occasionally, I would retouch the protruding end of the pacifier with the bottle, or I would touch his cheek with the bottle. As soon as the onset of crying occurred (usually within 2 minutes) and the pacifier fell from Nathan's mouth, the bottle was inserted. On some occasions when his saliva made the pacifier adhere to his open mouth, I removed the pacifier manually to make room for the bottle, but I was reluctant to do this very often.

My reluctance to remove the pacifier myself is central to my construction of the study. The world in which I wanted to test Nathan's development was a Piagetian world of physical objects and actional regularities. My own removal of the pacifier might have constructed for him a Vygotskyan world of knowledgeable others to learn from. This would have weakened my ability to assess the viability of Piaget's views of logical development.

Ethical Considerations

The ethics of participant observer research in which there is potential harm to subjects (e.g., through personal humiliation or loss of interpersonal trust) have been debated for decades (Cassell, 1982). In this study, the pacifier dilemma initially was observed by happenstance, when my expectation that Nathan would spit out the pacifier was not met. There was certainly some degree of anxiety that the procedure entailed for Nathan. But it was a self-regulating process, because the onset of crying terminated the procedure. Judged in relation to other frustrations that an infant boy faces in the day-to-day activities of living, the pacifier dilemma was extremely mild. For instance, holding his arms to direct them into his shirt sleeves frequently resulted in major pushing and screaming sessions.

Results and Analysis

Nathan's physical, social, and cognitive development were normal. When slightly less than 2 months old, he had grasped the bells that ornament his changing table. Around that time, he was grabbing clumsily for his pacifier and lunging his head toward it to get it in his mouth. At 4 months of age, he first put the pacifier in his own mouth. By the end of his sixth month, Nathan could remove the pacifier from his mouth and reinsert it in a never-ending (although belabored) cycle. In Piaget's terms, the scheme for removing the pacifier had become well established. At around this same time, he could clearly discriminate the pacifier from the nipple of the bottle, as evidenced by the deliberateness of his selection when presented with both.

Despite the presence of these component capabilities, it took a further 5 months before Nathan resolved the pacifier dilemma by removing it from his mouth to make room for the bottle. As these months progressed, the pacifier dilemma became a ritual part of our relationship. Gradually the acuteness of the various stages of Nathan's response subsided. He still alternated between the intense and the more relaxed sucking, but the difference between these phases became less discernible. The onset of crying was often just a peep as the pacifier fell out of his mouth and the bottle was inserted. But other than the dulling of this response pattern, he made virtually no progress in utilizing his perceptual and motor skills to deal with the obstructing pacifier.

About 3 weeks into the study, an event transpired that suggested some hypotheses for me concerning the nature of his eventual mastery. On this occasion, I was startled by the temporary cessation of Nathan's struggles with the pacifier dilemma as he stared unblinking at me for about 2 full, uninterrupted minutes. Eventually, this response was overcome by new bouts of hunger, and the characteristic responses of the pacifier dilemma were resumed. But I could not escape the strong impression that Nathan's developing awareness centered not on objects and locations, but on a sense of the roles of the different participants in feeding practices. His intent stare seemed to signal his understanding that it was the caregiver's role to make sure that the bottle was placed in his mouth. This led me to hypothesize that no amount of decontextualized logical development would suffice to overcome the pacifier dilemma. It would require a change in Nathan's perspectives on the roles of the participants in feeding practices. I speculated that this change in perspective would be tied to his development of the motor control needed to direct the bottle to his own mouth, and to the altered sense of agency that would emerge from these new feeding practices. The lengthy staring interlude was not repeated during the course of the study. But staring at me, rather than at the bottle, became a new feature of his response to the pacifier dilemma from this point on.

Resolution of the Pacifier Dilemma

Nathan's manual skills increased steadily toward the end of his first year. Early in his 10th month (September 4, 1994), Nathan could support the bottle in his own mouth as he lay back against the floor or a pillow. A few days later, he could remove and insert the bottle in his own mouth using both hands. A week into his 11th month (September 30), Nathan was sitting on my leg holding his own bottle as I was pushing it against the pacifier in his mouth. On this occasion, Nathan pulled the pacifier from his mouth and opened his mouth for the bottle. On October 12 at about 6:00 a.m., Nathan resolved the pacifier dilemma unassisted by removing the pacifier from his own mouth when presented with the bottle. But by this time, he had the manual coordination needed to take full control of his own feeding. He could hold the bottle with one hand and insert the bottle into his mouth. A few moments later, I reinserted the pacifier into his mouth, and he removed it with one hand while holding the bottle with the other.

That night, Nathan came down with a severe fever that kept him on antibiotics for a week. At the next observation, on October 18, he had lost the ability to handle the bottle with one hand. Also, his competence to resolve the pacifier dilemma was lost. It took nearly a full month before he began to recover these competencies. His November 13 feeding began with the pacifier dilemma, which was quickly terminated by the onset of crying. Then he inserted the pacifier into his own mouth and himself removed it to make way for the bottle. On December 6, he again removed the pacifier with one hand while inserting the bottle with the other hand (see Fig. 6.1). By this time, the pacifier dilemma was reliably resolved. On December 22, Nathan was seen to remove the pacifier from his mouth in order to insert a Cheerio.

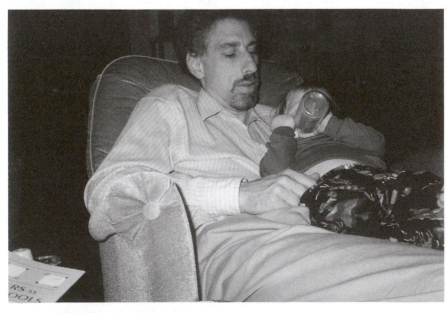

FIG. 6.1. Nathan removes the pacifier from his own mouth and inserts the bottle, as Dad looks on.

Discussion

Piaget (1963) was careful to stress that in the stages through tertiary circular reactions, the timetable for development is quite fluid, whereas the onset of symbolic processes emerges distinctly and tardily:

> The facts remain so complicated and their sequence can be so rapid that it would be dangerous to separate these stages [through tertiary circular reactions] too much. On the other hand, with the behavior patterns, which we are now going to describe, begins a new period [of invention through deduction or mental combination] which everyone will concur in considering as appearing tardily, much later than the preceding behavior patterns. (p. 331)

Why was Nathan able to resolve the pacifier dilemma at 13 months of age—5 months prior to the age which Piagetian research predicts (Ginsburg & Opper, 1969)? As special as he is to his father, Nathan certainly is not a prodigy. According to his pediatrician, his linguistic development at the time of this writing (21 months) is normal or slightly delayed in comparison to his age cohort (not uncommon for young boys). There is no evidence of developmental advantage to explain the results. To understand his accomplishment it will be necessary to reassess the connections and discontinuities between this study and the Piagetian framework for analysis.

Superficially, this study appears to be in the Piagetian tradition. Naturalistic observation is the primary data source, with informal experimental manipulations used to observe a wider range of response. But these similarities mask profound differences in approach. Piaget's informal experiments concern the activities of the child at play. Indeed, at this age level, the play is solitary. The clear methodological assumption is that cognitive development is uniform across contexts of activity. Thus what is observed in solitary play would be equally present in life practices of feeding, interacting, and so forth, and vice versa (see Wolf, 1982). Development is linear and unitary.

To see this more clearly, let us briefly examine a discussion of Inhelder and Piaget (1964) about the ability to classify and seriate:

> If we try to analyse the course of behaviour and thinking at stage I, we are inevitably struck by the fact that the child is taking each step as he comes to it, forgetting what went before, and not foreseeing what must follow. One example . . . is the collective object, or the complex object, when the child is simply putting elements together without any consistent plan (indeed, he may actually say half way through "I'm going to build a house," but although in a sense this is a plan, it means that he has now forgotten the original intention, which was to classify, because he has drifted into a play attitude). (pp. 285–286)

The drift that Inhelder and Piaget observed is taken to indicate a certain incapacity. But does such an incapacity extend beyond the context of clinical examinations to other life practices?

For Piaget, the answer is yes. *Décalage* (the uneven evolution of the indicators of a particular stage) was always treated as a technical problem due to the "friction" of the task (Piaget, 1971). But there is now ample evidence from cross-cultural studies that differences in cultural values and social expectations produce vastly different patterns of developmental competence in children (Rogoff, in press). Interpolating these results within a given culture reveals the central importance of "the immediate practical goals being sought and the enveloping sociocultural goals into which they fit" (Rogoff, 1990, p. 139).

Indeed, this study owes more to the anthropological tradition of Scribner (1977), Cole (1977), and Lave (1988) in which ecological validity is addressed than to Piagetian methodology. Nathan was observed involved in the life practices of feeding—negotiating a recurrent dilemma of daily life. From the data, it appears that the cognitive ability Nathan could express was constrained by his role within feeding practices, particularly by his sense of agency within those practices. It was only as he began to assume responsibility for self-administering his bottle that he could express the ability to think his way out of the pacifier dilemma. Prior to that, he merely submitted to the experience, waiting for the bottle to be put in his mouth and staring quizzically at his dad concerning the delay.

Thus, we are led to speculate that cognitive development is not the child's cumulative experience with physical objects and actions, but a culturally modulated expression of evolving control and power within established social practices. To Walkerdine's poststructural approach (1990, chapter 4, this volume) we owe the further insight that agency develops not along a uniform continuum demarcated by fixed social positions. Rather diverse subject positions emerge at the interstices of multiple and conflicting practices.

CONCLUSION

On the face of it, removing a pacifier from one's mouth to make room for a bottle is a rational behavior. When adults (or computers) solve problems by such means, we ordinarily ascribe some kind of logical process to them. In mainstream cognitive science, Terry Winograd's (1976) famous SHRDLU program was able, using blocks in a block world, to solve problems of a similar sort to that which Nathan's pacifier presented. Part of the strength of SHRDLU was that it could respond to questions and commands given in ordinary English. But for our purposes, the important observations concern its reasoning processes. SHRDLU uses means–end analysis, backward search, and other heuristics frequently observed in human problem solvers (Newell & Simon, 1972). Thus, if one block rests upon another and SHRDLU is requested to get the lower one, it establishes as a subgoal the removal of the upper one. In a similar vein, it is possible to ascribe logical processes to the solving of the pacifier dilemma: When presented with the bottle, a plan is formulated to make one's mouth available for the bottle, the presence of the pacifier is realized as an obstacle to that plan, and a subplan is formulated to expel the pacifier.

Whereas humans can learn to simulate this kind of reasoning program (Bereiter, chapter 11, this volume), St. Julien (chapter 10, this volume) argues that the human brain is not configured for it. Cognition is holistic, based on dynamic pattern-matching and pattern-generating capacities rather than on linear programs. Cognition evolves in situated practices, from which it is inseparable (Lave, 1988, 1992). Linkages across practices are manifestations of semiosic chaining (Whitson, chapter 7, this volume) not of logic. The conditions for such linkage are the interpenetration of ecosocial systems (Lemke, chapter 3, this volume), not individual autonomy.

What do such postmodern perspectives contribute to educational theory? As Bereiter (chapter 11, this volume) points out: That logic and rationality are not native to the human biological system does not imply that education should eschew them. Indeed, logic and rational thinking provide humankind with essential recombinative possibilities that otherwise are impossible. But this logic is post hoc and reconstructive, not a primary mode of engagement to be imputed to any participants who happen to be involved in sociocultural practices that have identifiable form and structure (Gee, 1992, chapter 9, this volume). This is true equally of infants with pacifier skills and secondary school students with algebra skills (Kirshner, 1989). Educationally, this entails engaging in rational discourse as a social activity of justification, not as a primary mode of production. It is to reflect this reconstructive function of rationality that Descartes' famous epigram is reworked in the final epigraph to this chapter.

REFERENCES

Cassell, J. (1982). Harm, benefits, wrongs, and rights in fieldwork. In J. Seiber (Ed.), *The ethics of social research* (pp. 7–32). New York: Springer-Verlag.

Chomsky, N. (1980). *Rules and representations*. New York: Columbia University Press.

Chomsky, N. (1986). *Knowledge of language: Its nature, origin, and use*. New York: Praeger.

Cole, M. (1977). An ethnographic psychology of cognition. In P. N. Johnson-Laird & P. C. Wason (Eds.), *Thinking: Readings in cognitive science* (pp. 468–482). Cambridge, UK: Cambridge University Press.

Descartes, R. (1979). *Meditations on first philosophy in which the existence of God and the distinction of the soul from the body are demonstrated* (D. A. Cress, Trans.). Indianapolis, IN: Hackett. (Original work published 1641)

Field, T. (1990). *Infancy.* Cambridge, MA: Harvard University Press.

Fodor, J. A. (1975). *The language of thought.* Cambridge, UK: Cambridge University Press.

Fodor, J. A. (1980). On the impossibility of acquiring "more powerful" structures. In M. Piatelli-Palmarini (Ed.), *Language and learning: The debate between Jean Piaget and Noam Chomsky* (pp. 142–162). Cambridge, MA: Harvard University Press.

Gardner, H. (1987). *The mind's new science* (2nd ed.). New York: Basic Books.

Gee, J. P. (1992). *The social mind: Language, ideology, and social practice.* New York: Bergin & Garvey.

Ginsburg, H., & Opper, S. (1969). *Piaget's theory of intellectual development: An introduction.* Englewood Cliffs, NJ: Prentice-Hall.

Glick, J. A. (1983). Piaget, Vygotsky, and Werner. In S. Wapner & B. Kaplan (Eds.), *Toward a holistic developmental psychology* (pp. 35–52). Hillsdale, NJ: Lawrence Erlbaum Associates.

Haugland, J. (1985) Semantic engines: An introduction to mind design. In J. Haugland (Ed.), *Mind design* (pp. 1–34). Cambridge, MA: MIT Press.

Inhelder, B., & Piaget, J. (1964). *The early growth of logic in the child.* New York: Routledge & Kegan Paul.

Jaynes, J. (1976). *The origin of consciousness in the breakdown of the bicameral mind.* Toronto: University of Toronto Press.

Kirshner, D. (1989). The visual syntax of algebra. *Journal for Research in Mathematics Education, 20*(3), 274–287.

Lave, J. (1988). *Cognition in practice.* Cambridge, MA: Cambridge University Press.

Lave, J. (1992, April). *Learning as participation in communities of practice.* Paper presented at the annual meeting of the American Educational Research Association, San Francisco.

Newell, A., & Simon, H. A. (1972). *Human problem solving.* Englewood Cliffs, NJ: Prentice-Hall.

Piaget, J. (1963). *The origins of intelligence in children.* New York: Norton.

Piaget, J. (1971). The theory of stages in cognitive development. In D. R. Green, M. P. Ford, & G. P. Flamer (Eds.), *Measurement and Piaget* (pp. 1–11). New York: McGraw-Hill.

Piaget, J. (1980). The psychogenesis of knowledge and its epistemological significance. In M. Piatelli-Palmarini (Ed.), *Language and learning: The debate between Jean Piaget and Noam Chomsky* (pp. 23–34). Cambridge, MA: Harvard University Press.

Reber, A. S. (1993). *Implicit learning and tacit knowledge: An essay on the cognitive unconscious* (Oxford Psychology Series No. 19). Oxford, UK: Oxford University Press; New York: Clarendon Press.

Rogoff, B. (1990). *Apprenticeship in thinking.* New York: Oxford University Press.

Rogoff, B. (in press). Developmental transitions in children's participation in sociocultural activities. In A. Sameroff & M. Haith (Eds.), *Reason and responsibility: The passage through childhood.* Chicago: University of Chicago Press.

Scribner, S. (1977). Modes of thinking and ways of speaking: Culture and logic reconsidered. In P. N. Johnson-Laird & P. C. Wason (Eds.), *Thinking: Readings in cognitive science* (pp. 483–500). Cambridge, UK: Cambridge University Press.

Skovsmose, O. (1993). The dialogical nature of reflective knowledge. In S. Restivo, J. P. Van Bendegem, & R. Fisher (Eds.), *Math worlds* (pp. 162–181). Albany: State University of New York Press.

Slobin, D. (1966). Comments on McNeill's "Developmental Psycholinguistics." In F. Smith & G. A. Miller (Eds.), *The genesis of language* (pp. 129–148). Cambridge, MA: Harvard University Press.

Walkerdine, V. (1990). *The mastery of reason: Cognitive development and the production of rationality.* London: Routledge.

Winograd, T. (1976). *Understanding natural language.* New York: Academic Press.

Wolf, D. (1982). Understanding others: A longitudinal case study of the concept of independent agency. In G. E. Forman (Ed.), *Action and thought: From sensorimotor to symbolic operations* (pp. 297–327). New York: Academic Press.

CHAPTER SEVEN

Cognition as a Semiosic Process: From Situated Mediation to Critical Reflective Transcendence

James A. Whitson
University of Delaware

My purpose in this chapter is parallel, in some respects, to that of Bereiter in his article on "Implications of connectionism for thinking about rules" (1991). Bereiter noted that connectionism is but one of the significant recent departures from classical, rule-based views of cognition and learning, and he identified situated cognition (citing Brown, Collins, & Duguid, 1989a) and embodied cognition (citing Johnson, 1987; Lakoff, 1987) as other examples deserving particular attention from educational researchers (Bereiter, 1991). Bereiter stipulated that he was not presenting connectionism as a competing theoretical alternative, but rather "as a way of conceiving a whole class of alternatives in computational terms" (p. 14).

It is not clear to me that situated cognition and embodied cognition should be seen as rival or competing theoretical alternatives, for that matter, rather than as potentially complementary aspects of an emerging class of alternatives to the classical rule-based theories. Also, it seems to me that various forms of constructivism and constructionism should be included (whether as competing theoretical alternatives or as aspects of more comprehensive theories).

Bereiter's presentation of connectionism is put forward as an explanation of how computational tasks are performed by the brain in ways that are consistent with the alternative views of cognition as situated or embodied, as opposed to the more classical rule-based approaches. In a somewhat similar spirit, I am presenting semiotics as a way of accounting for the cognitive functioning of sign activity, or *semiosis*, that I see as relevant to the whole class of theoretical alternatives. The semiotic perspective might, in fact, provide conceptual resources for observing crucial relationships among situated, embodied, connectionist, constructivist, and other aspects within emergent understandings of cognition. In this connection, I must emphasize, I do not see semiotics in itself as providing a more comprehensive theory of cognition, subsuming all those other aspects; rather, I see semiotics as offering an elemental conceptual vocabulary for tracing the interrelationships through which those aspects of cognition actually do work together in the real world, and as offering a nondualistic perspective in which cognition, understood as one function of semiosis (i.e., the activity of signs), takes place within the world and not in "minds" construed as somehow separate from or outside of the world.

PEIRCE AND SAUSSURE: SOURCES AND TRADITIONS OF SEMIOTIC INQUIRY

In her chapter in this volume, Walkerdine introduces one kind of semiotic analysis in her critical investigation of problems in current approaches to understanding situated cognition. Her semiotic vocabulary and approach are derived from the European tradition in semiotics that was proposed (under the name *semiology*) by the Swiss linguist Ferdinand de Saussure.

My own point of entry into the discussion of situated cognition will be my response to problems raised by Clancey and Roschelle (1991), in which I draw primarily from the semiotic tradition inaugurated earlier by the American philosopher Peirce. I believe that both traditions have something to offer toward the understanding of cognition as a situated social process, and that these potential contributions will be enhanced by an inclusive framework that recognizes the articulations among semiotic structures and relationships examined by the followers of Peirce and of Saussure. After discussing implications of each of these traditions, I venture my own suggestions toward such an inclusive, articulated framework.

Others have generally avoided trying to reconcile the two traditions. Those favoring a Peircean approach (e.g., Merrell, 1992) are often dismissive (if not contemptuous) of Saussurean semiotic structuralism, whereas European structuralists (e.g., Greimas) have often seemed oblivious to the Peircean approach.

As explained by Deledalle (1992), who is highly respected as a translator of Peirce for French readers more familiar with Saussure:

> Everybody knows that Peirce defines a sign as a triad made of three inde-composable elements: a representamen, an object and an interpretant.
>   For Saussure, a sign is an indissoluble pair or couple composed of a signifier and a signified.

> Can we translate Peirce's definition into Saussure's? . . . My opinion is that the two theories are untranslatable into one another, because their underlying philosophies and logics are incompatible. (pp. 289–290)

I do not believe that Deledalle is overstating the difference between Peircean and Saussurean approaches. The inclusive framework that I suggest later in this chapter is not one that attempts to translate the terms of one definition into terms of the other. Instead, I suggest that each approach captures some aspects of the structures and relationships involved in all semiosic processes—including cognitive processes.

Deledalle (1992) commented: "If I were permitted to give some advice to readers of Peirce, I would say: If you want to understand Peirce's theory of signs, never read 'sign' when you see the word, but translate it either by 'representamen' or by 'semiosis.' And leave the word 'sign' to Saussure's terminology"[1] (p. 300). The Peircean tradition emphasizes semiosis as the continuously dynamic and productive activity of signs. Saussure was more concerned with relatively stable structures, such as the phonemic or syntactic structures of a language. I take these not as rival theoretical approaches to the same phenomena but as complementary traditions exploring different aspects of phenomena that are not exhaustively accounted for within either approach.

TRIADIC SIGN RELATIONS AND THE PROBLEM OF REPRESENTATION

One perennial problem for theories of cognition has been how to account for the nature of representation. Clancey and Roschelle (1991) addressed this problem in a way that is extremely relevant to an appreciation of cognition as a situated social process, arguing that "cognitive science research has distorted the nature of representations, and hence at its heart distorted

---

[1] *Semiosis* refers to the activity of signs whereas *semiotics* properly refers to the study of semiosis (although *semiotics* is often used for both). *Representamen* will be defined and discussed at length later. Peirce was constantly reformulating his analysis and revising his usage throughout his life, so there is no usage that is consistent with all of his writings. (Deledalle, 1992, provides an excellent discussion of such problems in reading Peirce.) I agree that Peirce's view is best understood in terms of Peirce's definition (quoted from Deledalle, 1992, p. 289) of a sign as "a triad made of three indecomposable elements: a representamen, an object and an interpretant" (discussed later). From this, it follows that we should read "representamen" in place of "*sign*" when Peirce referred to that *one element* within the triad (as Deledalle advised); but the word "sign" should still be used for the *triad* constituted by those three elements (provided that we do not confuse this Peircean "sign" with the "sign" defined differently by Saussure). "Semiosis" is not really a substitute for "sign", as a word referring to the triad; "semiosis" refers, rather, to the continuous activity of mediated and mediating relations in which the elements function together as networks, webs, or relays of triadic signs.

the nature of cognition" (p. 9). Roschelle and Clancey (1992) observed that "cognitive science has most frequently taken a correspondence view of representation, a retrieval view of memory, and an individualistic view of meaning," and that "these views minimize the need to consider social and neurological processes jointly" (p. 14).

Although these researchers have embraced situated cognition theory and expressed appreciation for the work of Lave and others who have begun to recognize cognition as a social process, they have insisted that we need to account for cognition as a process that is both social and neurological, one in which "representations are created and given meaning in a process that integrates social and perceptual levels of organization" (Clancey & Roschelle, 1991, p. 4):

> To make progress now, cognitive scientists, AI researchers, and educators cannot continue to live in a representational flatland. Neither social nor neural science can be simply left to other researchers, as if they are merely levels of application and implementation for psychology. . . . The time is right for relating these perspectives, for creating a kind of neural-sociology of knowledge that will constitute a new cognitive science, which is neither individual nor social, but does justice to both. (p. 5)

The rule and schema-based models are said to portray a "representational flatland" because they omit "the vast variety of materials and physical forms that people claim to be representations" (p. 7).

The Peircean model of sign activity is one that does recognize the unlimited variety of forms and substances that can participate as elements of dynamic signifying relationships, but without regarding representations as being limited to things that people consciously recognize or claim to be representations. Peirce's approach obviates the problems of voluntarism and subjectivism found in Clancey and Roschelle's (1991) formulations while revealing greater importance to some of their formulations than even they are likely to have realized. As they have explained the matter, for example, "something becomes a representation by virtue of someone claiming that it stands for something. Meaning is not inherent in the form, but attributed by further representations about the form. That is, representational status is attributed by an observer" (p. 9).

In Peircean terms (see Fig. 7.1), something becomes a representamen (r), in relation to an object (o), by virtue of the possibility that an interpretant (i) will be produced; that is, a singular event, or an habitual or regular response, that responds to the representamen as signifying an object (something other than itself) in some respect. This model recognizes even more far-reaching implications of the principle that signification (including representational signification) is a matter of further significations, but without the

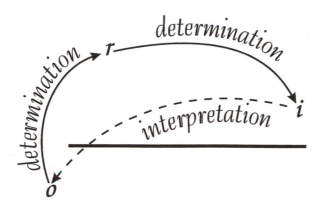

FIG. 7.1. Triadic sign relations (Peirce).

suggestion that it is a matter of subjective, conscious, or even voluntary attribution. In one of Peirce's (1909) own notoriously dense formulations:

> I define a sign [here, "representamen"] as anything—be it an existent thing or actual fact, or be it, like what we call a "word," a mere possible form to which an audible sound, visible shape, or other sensible object may conform to [sic], or be it a property or habit of behaviour of something either experienced or imagined,—which is on the one hand so determined (i.e. affected either by causation or through the medium of a mind) by an object other than itself and on the other hand, in its turn so affects some mind, or is capable of doing so, that this mind is thereby itself mediately determined by the same object. (3:233 [1909])[2]

The object is interpreted, in some respect, in the interpretant—not directly or im-mediately, but only through the mediating representamen. (In Fig. 7.1, the horizontal bar and broken line indicate that the object is not immediately present to the interpretant.) The representamen is related to the object in some way (e.g., symbolically, indexically, or iconically) so that the object "determines" the representamen as something having a potential to "determine" something else, in turn, as an interpretant, which is indirectly "determined" as a mediated interpretation of the object.

An example might be helpful at this point:

> Suppose I look at a barometer, say "Let's go," pick up my umbrella, and start for the door. You pick up your umbrella and follow. The barometer reading

---

[2]Unless noted otherwise, quotations from Peirce will be referenced in the standard manner to the volume and paragraph numbers in the *Collected Papers* (1931–1935), along with the original year for the quotation. On terminological shifting in Peirce, see Deledalle (1992) and footnote 1 of this chapter.

is being interpreted as a sign of rain (the object represented). It is functioning as a sign when it produces as its interpretant the event (me picking up my umbrella) in which the reading is interpreted as a sign of rain. That interpretant can, in turn, function as a sign of rain producing a subsequent interpretant (for example, you taking your umbrella). The two of us both leaving with umbrellas can function as a sign producing (as an interpretant) a co-worker's decision not to go out for lunch. [Cf. Fig. 7.2.]

My barometric "reading" is actually already an interpretant which takes the needle position as a sign of atmospheric pressure, and hence a mediated sign of rain. But what, exactly, is "atmospheric pressure," and how does it come to function as a sign of rain? If the rain is not yet (presently) falling, then [it is clear that] it didn't dynamically cause the needle position on the barometer, which can in any case function as a fallibly interpretable sign even if it's not functioning mechanically at all. Peirce's basic idea is that the efficacy of the triadic (object–sign–interpretant) functioning of semiosis is not reducible to the dyadic (cause and effect) functioning of mechanics. In this sense, my use of barometric pressure is mediated semiotically by elementary school science classes, TV weather reports, and (by extension) my situation within the society and culture generally. (Whitson, 1991a, pp. 245–246)

First, it should be noted that this model of continuously productive triadic sign relations can accommodate relations among the most diverse elements even within a single triadic sign. A verbal utterance or a cultural norm can occur as an interpretant—as can an institutional policy, a connectionist pattern of neurological activity, a sound, a shape, a color, a physical movement, or a social practice. Of course, any of these (or other kinds or combinations) can also function semiosically as an object or as a representamen within other triadic signs; moreover, a single triadic sign might be comprised of widely disparate elements, ranging across physiological, linguistic, and social levels. This model would support Clancey and Roschelle's movement beyond

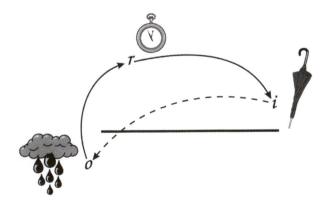

FIG. 7.2. Triadic signification: Barometer example.

"representational flatland": It would include not only "the vast variety of materials and physical forms that people claim to be representations," but also the even broader variety of things that can participate as elements of triadic signification within the continuous activity of semiosis.

Recognition that the most diverse elements can operate within a triadic sign also has implications for the kind of interdisciplinary work needed to account for cognition and other semiosic processes. Instead of seeking linkages, or ways of bridging gaps between social, economic, cultural, linguistic, psychological, neurological, or other "levels" of organization, this approach first shows the need to account for processes that actively and intricately cut across such levels (so that it cannot be assumed that order is established first on each of those respective levels, which might then be seen to "interact"), and second, provides a conceptual and notational vocabulary for investigating such processes.

Finally, Peirce's use of the term *mind* in the previous quotation demands some comment. Peirce sometimes spoke of the interpretant as being produced by a mind or by a person who is interpreting the representamen; but he himself referred to this usage as a compromise he made in "despair of making my own broader conception understood" (Letter to Lady Welby, December 14, 1908, in Hardwick, 1977, pp. 80–81). A more adequate expression of Peirce's broader conception can be seen in his references to signs as being used not only consciously by human persons, but used as well by any kind of "'scientific' intelligence, that is to say, by an intelligence capable of learning by experience" (2.227 [c. 1987]).[3]

---

[3] *Experience* is used here in the broad sense of being affected by the results of past interpretive responses; it need not involve all of what Dewey and others have described as aspects of human experience. Thus, Peirce's usage here would include the evolution of a species' semiosic capabilities (e.g., the instinctive responses of some species to the shapes, colors, or other signs of their predators—responses that (in the species, if not in the individual) can be adapted for responding more successfully to deal with such things as camouflage by predators and mimicry by other species) as a kind of learning from experience, and the system capable of such learning could be regarded as a "scientific" intelligence, in that sense. For Peirce, even a plant species exhibited a rudimentary intelligence in the evolution of its heliotropic response to sunlight. Note that the plant's leaves are not dynamically caused to move by any mechanical force from the sunlight; instead, the plant has its own mechanism for triadically responding to the sunlight as a sign of the energy to be absorbed by its leaves. A single specific instance of such movement could be described as a series of dyadic (cause and effect) events. But that description does not account for the existence of the phenomenon, which is actually (although somewhat "degenerately"—see this footnote) triadic. Because the culture of positivistic analysis trains us to think that we have not understood something "scientifically" until we understand it exclusively in terms of dyadic causation, it is not surprising if the description of the plant's movement as an interpretant, or as an event in which the plant responds to the sunlight as a sign (or, more precisely, as a representamen) of nutrient energy, strikes us as unwarranted and unscientific pre- (or post-) modern anthropomorphizing mysticism.

However, the scientific justification for Peirce's view is demonstrated easily enough (and we should remember that Peirce made his career as a practicing laboratory scientist, as well

As a matter of existential fact, there must always be some kind of intelligent interpreter (i.e., some system or processes capable of being modified on the basis of past results) that produces the interpretant in responding to the representamen as a representamen standing for an object other than itself in some respect. However, as a matter of logic (and we must remember

---

as a philosopher of logic and mathematics), in the familiar principles from which a biologist could hypothesize that a plant species would adaptively come to discriminate in responding to different kinds of light (e.g., based on color or other qualities), signifying differences in the energy available for photosynthesis. The process does comprise a complex of mechanical (dyadically caused) events, but the process itself occurs and the outcome of the complex of mechanical events is determined on the basis of a triadic relation in which the leaves respond to light not as a simple cause or stimulus, and not for the energy which *that* light made available for photosynthesis, but as a representamen; that is, as something signifying the energy available from the light to be absorbed later, after stems and leaves have moved. This triadicity can be seen in the corrigibility of the process, by which the response to light can be corrected, modified, or lost as the species "learns" from its "experience" in responding to the source of nonpresent (future) energy through the mediation of the present light.

In the present light of this discussion, we can consider how the "scientific intelligence" of the botanists differs from that of the plants. The measurements, designs, constructs, models, and calculations developed and produced by the scientists would be included among the kinds of things that Clancey and Roschelle (1991) defined as representations. The botanists themselves are at least partially *aware* that they are interested in these things *as* representations of things other than the signs themselves, so the scientists (unlike the plants) are capable of deliberately and consciously changing their representational and interpretive practices to better serve their interests (including scientific, as well as budgetary, career, ideological, or other interests). Peirce would have accounted for this as an example of how triadicity is more fully realized in the semiosic activity of the botanists than in that of the plants. A false hypothesis or less than satisfactory model or instrument can be corrected or improved through critical symbolic reflection and does not depend on such a crude corrective mechanism as survival of the fittest. Although the plant species might also exhibit rudimentary triadic intelligence, its triadicity is relatively "degenerate" (i.e., in a sense analogous to that in which Peirce, as a mathematician, would recognize a circle as a degenerate ellipse, and a square as a degenerate rectangle. Peirce explored various kinds and degrees of degeneracy in the triadicity of signs, but the implications of this line of inquiry need not be explored here.).

We see that Peirce's notion of scientific intelligence extends beyond the traditional American psychologist's notion of intelligence in human individuals. It would include the social intelligence involved in situated cognition at the level of "interactions between people over the course of a few minutes," as discussed by Clancey and Roschelle (1991, p. 4; Roschelle & Clancey, 1992). Beyond this, it includes various kinds of intelligence in broader social processes. Peirce's faith in science as advancing through communally self-critical inquiry might have opened him to the kinds of criticism applied to Popper and his "critical realism," but Peirce's followers also include some of Popper's severest critics, such as Habermas. Although Toulmin (1972) would expect to find both Popper's and Kuhn's processes at work, Toulmin's own evolutionary model might suggest how the intelligence of peer review in determining survival of the fittest research programs more closely parallels the intelligence of heliotropic plants than some philosophers of science would like to think. Beyond that, of course, are the Foucauldian insights that Walkerdine brings to our present discussion, in light of which we need to understand that presumably scientific and cognitive activities at any level may be determined by the interested generation of new realities, rather than by "cognitive" or "scientific" interests per se.

that Peirce was a philosopher studying the logical aspects of semiosis), the interpreter was an external condition of the sign and not an essential internal constituent of the triad.

This irreducible triadicity has important implications for our understanding of representational signification and cognition. By showing how cognition operates on the atomic level through the action of signs that combine elements as diverse as social policies and neurological or even meteorological events into indecomposable signifying triads, this helps to demonstrate how knowledge is always situated in the world and how knowledge exists as something distributed across diverse aspects of our mental, physical, and social world. But this is not subjectivistic in the way suggested in the formulations of Clancey and Roschelle (1991), whose line of argument asserted that "knowledge is always subjective," because "the world ('reality') has no objective properties" (p. 6).

From the Peircean perspective, if it is true that the world has no properties that are objective (in the sense of being nonsubjective), this is because such a dichotomy between objective and subjective is false; so it does not follow that knowledge is always subjective (in the sense of being nonobjective). I believe that Peircean semiotics helps us to account for the specific ways in which representations and cognition are at once both objective and subjective (with those terms understood differently than in the Classical/Cartesian/Kantian frame of reference that has constrained mainstream and dissident cognitive scientists alike).

I believe a more adequate alternative is made possible by including aspects of existential phenomenology within the framework opened up by Peircean semiotics. This framework enables us to account for the specific ways that things appear within and against the particular horizons and backgrounds of specific phenomenological subjects (see Fig. 7.3).

For example, the representamen can be seen to appear within a horizon that does not include the object itself, and we can describe how the appearance

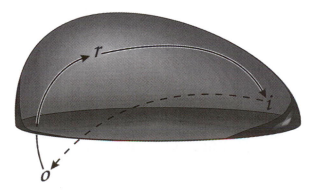

FIG. 7.3. Sign relations, background, and horizons.

of that representamen is conditioned by the background against which it appears—thus conditioning the kinds of interpretants that can be produced as mediated interpretive representations of the object. Such representations are subjective in important ways but without denying them their objectivity.

The existential phenomenology that informs this perspective has important implications for our understanding of the "practices" within which situated cognition takes place. Existentialists understand practices as being fundamentally determined by their phenomenological horizons. Lave, however, is developing an understanding of practices that is influenced by Bourdieu, who presented his subtle and complex work as a critique of both the phenomenological and structuralist traditions (see, e.g., Lave & Wenger, 1991, and Bourdieu, 1972/1977, 1980/1990). I agree with Bourdieu in rejecting either structuralism or phenomenology as providing the overall framework for explaining practices in general. On the other hand, I believe that phenomenological aspects such as backgrounds and horizons are of crucial importance for an understanding of many practices and particularly those practices that are more importantly concerned with cognitive interests and processes; and I believe that the tools of structuralist analysis are especially valuable for understanding backgrounds and horizons that can decisively enable and constrain the development of practices.

We can now turn to the tradition of structuralist semiotics to see how the insights and analytical devices from this tradition complement those from phenomenology and Peircean semiotics within a more comprehensive semiotic approach to human cognition.

THE STRUCTURAL/POSTSTRUCTURAL TRADITION

Saussure's Model of the Sign

As noted earlier, the use of semiotics in the discussion of situated cognition theory has been introduced by Walkerdine (chapter 4, this volume). Her discussion employs terminology derived from Lacan's radicalized variation on the model of *semiology* introduced by the Swiss linguist Saussure. Although Lacan's variation is certainly more capable of accounting for the dynamic and creative (i.e., not merely static and representative) character of sign activity, I believe that it neglects features of Saussurean, or structuralist, semiotics that make it possible to account for other aspects of semiosis in general, and of cognition in particular.

Without neglecting the important differences among semiotic theories, I can begin my introduction to Saussure with a central point on which all semiotic theorists agree: Semiotics begins with a rejection of the naive, commonsense understanding of the sign as something that simply denotes another object in the world. Saussure's definition of the sign, in general, is derived from his definition of the linguistic sign, in particular:

FIG. 7.4a. Constituents of the sign (Saussure).

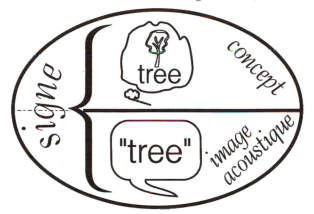

FIG. 7.4b. The <tree>/"tree" example (Saussure).

The linguistic sign is, then, a two-sided psychological entity, which may be represented by the following diagram [see Fig. 7.4a]. . . . In our terminology a *sign* is the combination of a concept and a sound pattern [*image acoustique*]. But in current usage the term *sign* generally refers to the sound pattern alone. . . . The ambiguity would be removed if the three notions in question were designated by terms which are related but contrast. We propose to keep the term *sign* to designate the whole, but to replace *concept* and *sound pattern* respectively by *signification* [*signifié*, the "signified"] and *signal* [*signifiant*, the "signifier"—see Fig. 7.4c].[4]

As Holdcroft (1991) explained,

In one fairly natural usage, if a word expresses an idea it might be said that it is a sign of an idea. But this usage is not Saussure's. For him, a sign does involve two things, an acoustic image and a concept, but he does not think

---

[4]Saussure (1916/1986, pp. 66–67). I have retained the original French terms in Figures 4a through 4c in view of difficulties translating them into English. In his careful translation, meticulously informed by the critical literature on Saussure's text, Harris used *signification* and *signal* as the English terms for *signifié* and *signifiant* (rather than the conventional *signified* and *signifier* (cf. Saussure, 1916/1959, 1916/1968), which will be used in this chapter except when quoting from the Harris translation). This is apparently his way of dealing with the terminological problem indicated here by Saussure, as well as Saussure's insistence that "A linguistic sign is not a link between a thing and a name, but between a concept and a sound pattern" (p. 66).

FIG. 7.4c. Constituents of the sign (revised).

of the former as a sign of the latter. On the contrary, the sign is the union of both of them, and can be represented as in [Fig. 7.4a]. (p. 50)

Saussure illustrated his definition with the example of the sign formed by the union of the concept <tree> with the sound pattern *"arbre"* (or *"tree"*). (See Fig. 7.4b). The sign is not a *sound* referring to a *tree*. The elements that comprise the sign are a structurally generalized or typical *pattern* of sound, together with a structurally generalized or typical *concept* of a tree. Of course, an infinite variety of sounds can be produced within the limits of the human vocal apparatus. But the only sounds that can be used in intelligible speech are those that will be understood as expressions of the general sound patterns that have *phonemic* value within the phonemic structure of the given language. Through their conjunction with concepts (which, in turn, are [similarly?] determined through structures of difference from related concepts), these sound patterns participate in determining the *semantic* values available to speakers of the language.

Harris characterized the expression *image acoustique* as "perhaps the most unhappy choice in the whole range of Saussurean terminology" (pp. xiv–xv), noting that in English translation, "'sound-image' unfortunately suggests some combination of the spoken and the written word (as if words were stored in the brain in quasi-graphic form)" (p. xv). As Harris explained:

> Insofar as it is clear exactly what is meant by *image acoustique*, it appears to refer to a unit which supposedly plays a part in our capacity to identify auditory impressions (e.g. of sounds, tunes) and to rehearse them mentally (as in interior monologue, humming a tune silently, etc.). It is thus an auditory generalisation which the mind is able to construct and retain, just as it is able to construct and retain visual images of things seen or imagined. The English expression which seems best to designate this is 'sound pattern'. (in Saussure, 1916/1986, pp. xiv–xv)

Ironically, it turns out that the insight into sound patterns of this kind might justify *image acoustique* as a happy choice, after all, in light of the connectionist discoveries discussed by St. Julien in chapter 10 of this volume.

Indeed, it turns out that "concept" (the counterpart of *image acoustique*) is in fact the more problematic term. Holdcroft (1991) cautioned against understanding "signified" as "a near-synonym for 'concept,' " in light of Saussure's efforts "to elucidate the notion of a signified in terms of the notion of value, albeit a very special kind of value arising from social usage," so that "the suggested identification of a signified with a concept, and not even a concept of a special kind, is, to say the least, unfortunate, since the dangers of lapsing into the sort of nomenclaturist theory that Saussure so objected to are clear" (p. 51).

For us, however, the problem of correctly understanding Saussure's theory is subordinate to our interest in an understanding of cognition as the achievements and processes of socially situated human activity. The semiotic account of cognition offered in this chapter suggests that concepts of the kind addressed in formal logic are in fact not the kind of things that thought (cognitive or otherwise) is made of. Implications of this difference include those observed by Walkerdine (chapter 4, this volume) in her discussion of ideologically differentiated attributions of "conceptual" versus "nonconceptual" achievements of students.

Saussure himself moved beyond the model of concepts united with sound patterns when he replaced that terminology with his more general definition of the sign as a combination of a signified together with its signifier (see Fig. 7.4c, and text at Footnote 4). Although Saussure explained this substitution as a way of indicating the relatedness of terms within the sign, it also generalized his definition of the sign beyond his initial reference to *linguistic* signs (with sound patterns as signifiers), so that he could propose a more extensive new science of "semiology":

> It is therefore possible to conceive of a science *which studies the role of signs as part of social life*. It would form part of social psychology, and hence of general psychology. We shall call it *semiology* (from the Greek *sēmeîon*, 'sign'). It would investigate the nature of signs and the laws governing them. . . . Linguistics is only one branch of this general science. The laws which semiology will discover will be laws applicable in linguistics, and linguistics will thus be assigned to a clearly defined place in the field of human knowledge. (Saussure, 1916/1986, pp. 15–16, italics in original)

From Saussure to Lacan

The anthropologist Lévi-Strauss provided the most influential example of how Saussure's structuralist approach could be generalized for diverse uses in the humanities and social sciences (see, e.g., Gardner, 1981). The influence of the psychoanalyst Lacan is more important for our purposes, however, because it is Lacan's departures from Saussure's model of the sign that paved the way for a recognition of the semiosic processes discussed by Walkerdine (chapter 4, this volume). At the risk of violently oversimplifying Lacan's notoriously subtle and complex formulations, we can identify two basic steps in the transformation of Saussure's semiotic model that have been adopted in a broad range of poststructuralist semiotic analysis.

First, Lacan inverted the priority of signified over signifier that was at least implicit in Saussure's model of the sign. Although Saussure did not overtly attribute any great significance to the vertical arrangement of the terms within his diagrams (see Figs. 4a–4c), Lacan pointed out that formulation of the sign as $\frac{\text{Signified}}{\text{Signifier}}$ does in fact tacitly preserve a kind of classical bias (cf. Plato) that accords some kind of priority to the signified—whether the signified is seen as a purely mental concept that can be "communicated" through expressions of a related sound-pattern, or whether the signified is seen (even more mistakenly, from a structuralist point of view) as a *referent* (i.e., an object that exists prior to the sign, and is *referred to* by the signifier). Lacan insisted on inverting this relationship, yielding his formulation of the sign as $\frac{\text{Signifier}}{\text{Signified}}$, and accordingly recognizing far-ranging autonomy for a dynamic and continuously productive play of signifiers that was not so easily recognized when it was assumed tacitly that a signifier was somehow constrained under domination by the signified. The more autonomous play of signifiers can be seen, for example, in a kind of "chaining" process, $\left\{\frac{\frac{\text{Signifier}_2}{\text{Signified}_2}}{\frac{\text{Signifier}_1}{\text{Signified}_1}}\right\}$, in which the signifying term (Signifier$_1$) in a preceding sign combination comes to serve also as a signified term (Signified$_2$) in a succeeding sign combination.

In such a "chaining of signifiers," the preceding signifieds and sign combinations are sometimes described as "sliding under" the succeeding signifiers (cf. Fig. 7.5a). Terms that may have originated in relation to certain needs and interests of the speakers (or of those engaged in practices using linguistic and/or nonlinguistic signs) become displaced from active use by terms of the succeeding signs. Succeeding signifiers may initially be admitted into use as substitutes for the preceding terms, as if the sense and import of those terms has been preserved through the succeeding links along the chain of signifiers. Ironically, it is the very ability of succeeding signifiers to appear as sense-preserving substitutes that allows preceding terms to disappear without notice as the use of succeeding terms gets taken over by the competing projects and practices in which they are introduced and deployed.

Common misunderstandings can be avoided by observing Walkerdine's (chapter 4, this volume) example from a dialogue in which "one mother gets her daughter to name people they are pouring drinks for and to work out how many drinks by holding up one finger to correspond with each

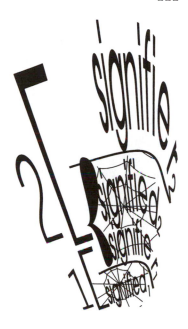

FIG. 7.5a. Chaining of signifiers
(Lacan).

name" (p. 67). Here (cf. Fig. 7.5b), we might begin with the people's names as signifiers$_1$, in conjunction with the signifieds$_1$ that somehow designate those other people within the conversational and mental discourse(s) of the mother and daughter. As Walkerdine observes, however, those names drop quickly to the level of signifieds$_2$ in relation to new signifiers$_2$—the fingers. Subsequently, spoken numerals might be used as signifiers$_3$ in relation to

FIG. 7.5b. Example of a chain of
signifiers.

the fingers, which are now signifieds$_3$. "By this time any reference to people or outside the counting string no longer exists within the statement." Walkerdine reports observing how, at this point, the combination of fingers and numerals starts being used in "small addition tasks of the form: 'five and one more is . . .' " (p. 67).

Walkerdine calls our attention to the "discursive shift" that has occurred when the numerals and fingers are used to deal with problems posed in forms that "can refer to anything." The same physical fingers and sound patterns might be used in either discourse, but these are merely the "sign vehicles": When they occur in discourses of abstract calculation, the signs in which the numerals serve as signifiers, and fingers serve as signifieds, are not the same signs (and those numerals and fingers are not the same signifiers and signifieds) as those that occur in other discourses (even when the same fingers and numerals are being used in either case). In such cases, the same sign vehicles are conveying different signs, with different semiotic values, when employed in different discourses. All of this might sound like a scholastic or sophistic quibble, except for all that we have learned from Walkerdine and others who have shown numerous and varied examples of how such differing discourses provide very different structural potentials for the positioning of subjects able to participate within those discourses—with dramatic consequences for formation of the very selves and subjectivities of the participants. Such examples help us avoid misunderstanding the chaining of signifiers as a process in which originally real and material signifieds are progressively concealed behind illusory or merely symbolic signifiers. Instead, we understand sites along the chain as sites of conflict among competing material practices—conflict in which the sign activity produces real and consequential practices even as those practices produce the signs by which they are themselves conducted.

Such uses of Lacanian semiotics by Walkerdine and other critical social scientists have impressively succeeded in escaping limitations of Saussure's structuralism. In doing so, however, I believe that they have overlooked aspects of structuralist semiotics that, when used within a less confining semiotic framework, can reveal semiosic structures that are important in supporting and constraining human cognitive activity. I believe that a more capacious framework can be developed by including elements of phenomenology as well as structuralist (e.g., Saussure and Greimas) and poststructuralist (e.g., Lacan and Walkerdine) semiotics along with the Peircean approach to signs and sign activity. After briefly introducing what I see as important aspects of structuralist semiotics, I briefly indicate how I think the elements from these disparate traditions need to be integrated within a more comprehensive framework. Finally, I review what I see as the major potential contributions of this semiotic approach in accounting for human cognition as a situated social process.

Structures of Semantic Difference

> It is my contention (following Henriques, Hollway, Urwin, & Walkerdine, 1984) that the signifier 'woman' does not describe or represent a unitary signified. Rather, any woman exists at the nexus of contradictory discourses, practices, and therefore positions. In this case, we could take the signifiers "child," "teacher" and "girl," or the dichotomies "active"/"passive," "rote-learning"/"real understanding," as examples. (Walkerdine, 1990, p. 74)

Again, Walkerdine's analysis provides examples that can be used to explain aspects of structuralist semiotics, and to illustrate the value this might have in advancing our critical understanding of the matters involved here.

Although Lacan's notion of a chaining of signifiers helps in explaining how signifiers can take on lives of their own, as it were, free from domination by any "true nature" of the "signifieds" that might be presupposed as a realistic basis for the signs in use, Lacan's focus on relations between signifieds and signifiers neglects the relationships of difference (as in the dichotomies noted by Walkerdine) that have been observed as the basic elements of semantic structures.

The semiotic structuralist Greimas has made the most elaborate study of such structural relationships, making particular use of what Greimas and Cortés (1979/1982) defined as a semiotic square (see Fig. 7.6). The square marks out four central positions related to each other by contradiction, opposition, or presupposition. Discursive practice makes use of verbal, conceptual, or other sign elements as they are invested in the structure of these relationships, thus generating a field of more extensive semiotic positions to be invested with related terms within the discourse.

The disparate uses of the word *more* discussed by Walkerdine (chapter 4, this volume, pp. 65, 66) can be used as an example. In school mathematics tasks, *more* is used for quantitative comparisons, in opposition to *less* (see

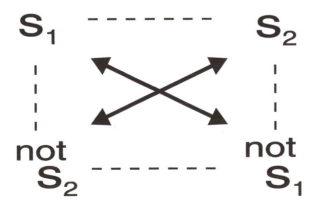

FIG. 7.6. General form of the semiotic square.

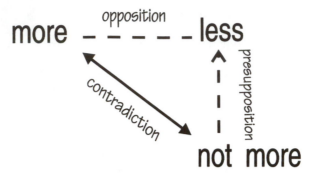

FIG. 7.7a. *More* as opposed to *less*.

Fig. 7.7a). *Less* is actually only one of the possible oppositions that would presuppose the negatively defined contradictory (not-more); but when *more* and *less* are used as antonyms in these discursive practices, then the practices within which *that* opposition is most relevant will pragmatically determine the semantic sense of both terms in their relation to each other. (This, by contrast with a positivistic understanding of meaning, in which words or concepts have their meanings *positively* (versus relatively), prior to their relationships and differences with other terms.)

Walkerdine demonstrates the kind of mistake that researchers can make when neglecting the differences between school mathematics tasks of this sort and other tasks in other situations in which particular students might be more consequentially familiar with the "same" words (such as *more*), but with very different meanings—as in the example where the opposite of *more* is not *less*, but *no more* (see Fig. 7.7b). As in this case, that difference can be even greater than one of differing conceptual opposition: Here, the conceptual or *semantic* opposition between *more* and *less* is contrasted with a *pragmatic* opposition between speech acts: "More (please)?" and "No more!"

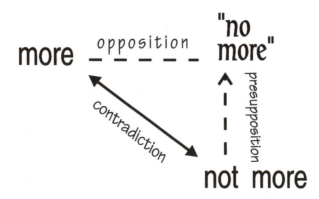

FIG. 7.7b. *More* as opposed to "no more."

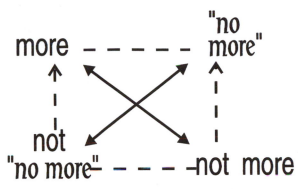

FIG. 7.7c. *More* vs. "no more" (semiotic square).

Filling in the central terms of the square (see Fig. 7.7c), we can begin to appreciate the value and continuing validity of principles that are neglected when Lacanian poststructuralism loses sight of its structuralist origins. Walkerdine (chapter 4, this volume) argues that "although [the terms *more* and *less*] might be the same signifiers as the actual signs, the specific relation with signifieds was made in specific practices" (p. 65). Although Lacan's chaining of signifiers would help in accounting for the flexibility of sign relations in accommodating certain social and cognitive requirements of the practices in question, it neglects other structural dimensions of those sign relations, and the ramifications that can both influence and transcend those practices.

One general form can be observed, first, in the example that we have already been dealing with. Figure 7.7d illustrates what Greimas would refer

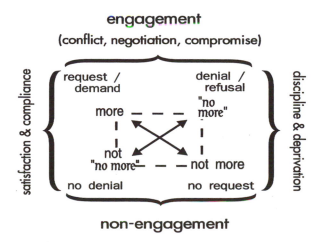

FIG. 7.7d. Elaborated square: *more* vs. "no more."

to as *secondary meta-terms* of the square generated by the opposition of "more" (as a demand or request) and "no more" (as refusal or denial). On this level, we find oppositions between engagement and nonengagement and between satisfaction or compliance and discipline or deprivation. The semiotic structures both incorporate and generate the semantic meaning and pragmatic force of terms within the discursive practice here, in sharp contrast to school mathematics or other discourses in which some of the same signifiers might occur.

Figure 7.8a illustrates a situation reported by Walkerdine (1990; 1992) and Walkerdine and The Girls and Mathematics Unit (1989) in which, paradoxically (at least from the standpoint of official rationales for schooling), school achievement by girls is disparaged, even as nonachievement by boys is regarded in a more positive light—and sometimes even treated as a sign of brilliance!

The structural coding of these attributions can be understood in relation to what Walkerdine (chapter 4, this volume) reports as "the concern expressed when poor children appear to possess advanced calculating skills, indeed, sometimes not only more advanced than their school performance would suggest, but actually more advanced than their higher class peers" (p. 60). Having observed that "teachers tend to understand such children as 'underdeveloped and over mature' " (cf. Fig. 7.8b), Walkerdine explains that "those children taken to display procedural knowledge or rote learning are taken to have demonstrated an apparent maturity that hides their lack of appropriate conceptual development" (p. 60).

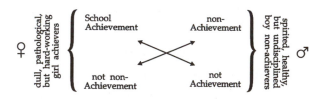

FIG. 7.8a. Differential characterizations of (pathological) girl achievers versus (healthy) boy nonachievers.

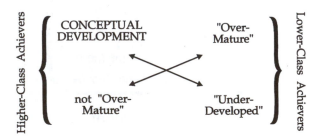

FIG. 7.8b. Class-differentiated coding of achievement.

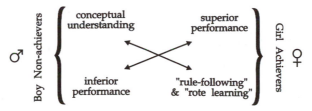

FIG. 7.8c. Performance and conceptual understanding.

As Walkerdine (1990) explained (cf. Fig. 7.8c):

Girls may be able to do mathematics, but good performance is not equated with proper reasoning. . . . On the other hand, boys tend to produce evidence of what is counted as "reason", even though their attainment may itself be relatively poor. . . . Throughout the age range, girls' good performance is downplayed while boys' often relatively poor attainment is taken as evidence of real understanding such that any counter-evidence (poor attainment, poor attention, and so forth) is explained as peripheral to the real (Walden & Walkerdine, 1983). It is interesting that in the case of girls (as in all judgments about attainment), attainment itself is not seen as a reliable indicator. (p. 66)

One aspect of this discourse addressed by Walkerdine (1990) is its articulation with the opposition between "production" and "reproduction" (see Fig. 7.8d). Achievement by girls is attributed to rote learning and rule following, which is invested with positive value as a kind of *reproduction*, even though this is not credited with the value attributed to the boys' achievement, which is marked, rather, as a *production* of real (i.e., conceptual) understanding. Walkerdine noted, in this connection, that the peculiar combination of (reproductive) attainment along with a purported lack of real (productive) cognitive development

. . . is precisely that combination which is required for the entry of girls into the "caring professions", in this case specifically the profession of teaching young children. Recruitment to elementary teacher training requires advanced qualifications, but usually a lower standard (poorer pass marks, for example) than that required for university entrance. (p. 72)

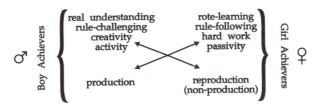

FIG. 7.8d. The production (and nonproduction) of real understanding.

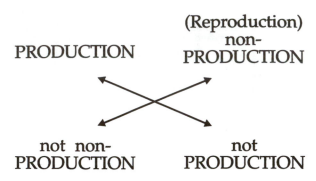

FIG. 7.8e. Production versus reproduction.

In this observation of discursive practice in specific homes and classrooms, we can begin to see how the structures in which terms (such as *achievement, development, maturity, conceptual,* etc.) take on their effective meanings in concrete social practices, do so in part by embedding the specific local practices within semiotic structures as far-reaching as the schemata generated by encodings of difference between "production" and its opposites and contradictories (see Fig. 7.8e).

The next step is to see how semiotic structures of this kind can be articulated with the triadic sign relations featured in the Peircean approach to semiosis.

AN INTEGRATED APPROACH

An Example: Signifying Motivation

To illustrate how structural and Peircean semiotics can be used together in the analysis of specific cases in education, I use an example in which student misunderstandings of a textbook lesson resulted from an assimilation of the textbook material into semiosic structures that were acutely meaningful to them in their life practices both in and out of school. The material in question was a chapter on motivation, which a few of the first-year college students interpreted in a sense that was more meaningful to them, but that prevented them from understanding the terminology and problematics of their textbook. The problem arose with students for whom motivation was a highly salient concern within their daily lives—but in a sense that educational psychology traditionally would describe as interfering with the students' ability to correctly understand a text that used the "same word" in an altogether incommensurable sense.

Such problems are traditionally addressed by providing more explicit definitions, along with examples and nonexamples from which students are to learn the defining characteristics of the concept to be learned (cf. chapter 10, this volume), as if this were a problem of providing enough information to identify a formal concept analytically defined in terms of intensional and extensional properties. But "motivation" functioned in the lives of these students, as well as in the program of behaviorist research presented by the textbook, not as a formally determined concept, but as a *sign* determined by a myriad of substantial signifying relations. We can begin, however, with the formal structure of relations between "motivation" and its opposites and contradictories (see Fig. 7.9a).

In a Consumer Science course taken primarily by first-year college students, a textbook on consumer behavior included a chapter on motivation. The chapter presented findings from a massive body of research on motivation, which was theoretically defined and experimentally operationalized in terms of changes in the human or nonhuman subjects' levels of physiological arousal and overt behaviors correlated with arousal. When used in the marketing and merchandising discourses of such textbooks, this construction forms the nucleus of categories relevant to purchasing behavior (see Fig. 7.9b). The primary positive term is addressed as a matter of how to stimulate the desired level of motivation. The opposing positive term is relaxation and its contradictory is arousal (which is presupposed by motivation, as nonarousal is presupposed by nonmotivation). A therapeutic discourse might be more concerned with a healthy integration of the positive terms (motivation and relaxation), as opposed to a pathological union of negatives (such as arousal without motivation); but the discourses and practices of marketing are more concerned with aroused and motivated directed (purchasing) behavior, as opposed to nonmotivated inactivity.

For some students in the class, however, the word "motivation" was engaged in a completely different set of discourses and practices. Their writing and comments in class revealed that for them, "motivation" was a highly charged and deeply significant term, one that was most often heard as an explanation for someone's academic or personal failures, as in: "I knew he would flunk out; he didn't have enough motivation." For them,

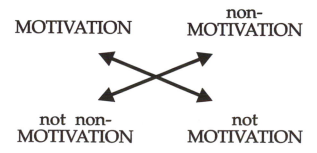

FIG. 7.9a. Schema form for motivation.

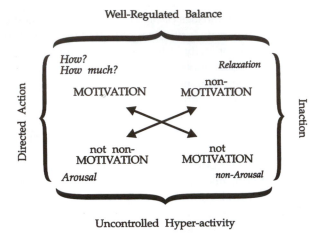

FIG. 7.9b. Motivation as a matter of behavioral psychology.

motivation was not a scientific matter of physiological arousal, to be manipulated for therapeutic or commercial purposes; instead, it was a matter
of morality and personal character (see Fig. 7.9c). With motivation signified
in terms of striving for achievement, its opposite was signified in terms of
positive distracting or competing pleasures and appetites (rather than relaxation, which had invested that structural position in the discourse of
physiological behavior). This moral discourse celebrates self-control and
discipline, in various forms, as the means, the outcome, and the signifying
evidence of successful reconciliation of the conflicting positive terms.

(Two variations of this moralizing discourse were actually observed: In
one, expressed by students from fundamentalist religious backgrounds, the
conflicting positive terms were signified more as a conflict between virtue

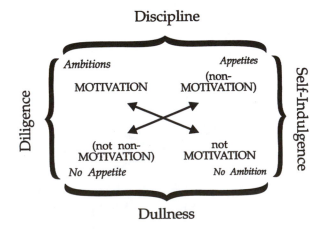

FIG. 7.9c. Motivation as a matter of personal or moral character.

and temptation to sin. The other discourse, expressed by students with quite secular agendas, signified both positive terms as competing virtues. In this discourse (unlike the fundamentalist), the successful reconciliation could be materialistic yuppies who take pride in partying as hard as they work, and the combination of negative terms could be embodied in the nerd.)

Although European structuralist semiotics is often regarded as being fundamentally incompatible with Peircean semiotics, I believe that semantic structures such as those illustrated previously can complement the analysis of triadic sign activity.

Figure 7.9d illustrates the kinds of triadic signifying relationships in everyday practices that both sustain and are sustained by such semantic structures. Here, such elements of the college student's everyday regimen as his or her use of alarm clocks and coffee can be understood as elements of triadic signification, in which practices that play a part in forming one's self-concept might also reinforce the semantic schema for "motivation" in a way that influences how one understands the motivation chapter in a textbook on psychology. In Fig. 7.9d, routines of self-regulation through the use of coffee and an alarm clock are represented as two interpretants, each signifying motivation, in some sense, through the mediation of a person's reflective thoughts of discipline and self-control. Of course, such practices may be determined in large part for the sake of their more direct effects (such as waking up and making it to school on time); but specific aspects of those practices, as well as their more general significance, can at the same time be determined partly by the overarching strategies and practices of self-formation within which they occur.

As Fig. 7.9e illustrates, coffee and alarm clocks can directly (or dyadically) cause physiological conditions such as sleep deprivation and stimulation

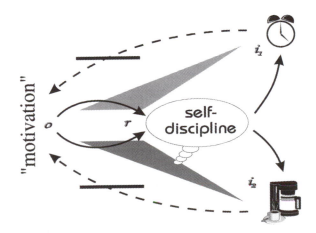

FIG. 7.9d. Practices of self-management as signs of motivation.

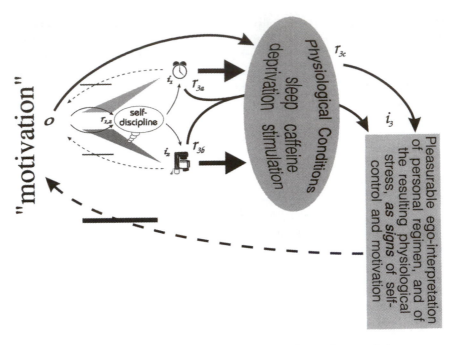

FIG. 7.9e. Psychological inscription of concepts within triadic sign relations.

from caffeine. But these conditions themselves might still be serving as representamena (r_{3c}) mediating the sense in which motivation will be signified through an interpretant (i_3). Here, we would not expect that the production of sleep deprivation and caffeine stimulation would have any intentional purpose of signifying motivation, so it may seem strange to think of these things as representing motivation in any sense. But they are related to the idea of motivation through the mediation of the two triads illustrated earlier, in which the alarm clock and the coffee served as interpretants ($i_{1,2}$). This mediated relationship between caffeinated sleep deprivation and the "motivation" idea provides the grounding for sign activity in which those physiological conditions can actually "stand for" motivation, insofar (for example) as a person can respond to feelings of such physiological stress, in part, by feeling pride in their self-disciplined program of accomplishment. That stressed-out physical condition can thus serve together with the clock use and coffee use as representamena ($r_{3a\text{-}3c}$) in relation to such feelings, which in turn serve as interpretants (i_3) mediately signifying motivation.

It might still seem that these physiological conditions, directly (dyadically) caused by sleep interruption and the pharmacological effects of caffeine, were not really produced as signs of motivation and do not really represent motivation unless someone believes or claims that they are representations. A close analogy might help. The sensation caused by muscle strain is unpleasant, if not painful; yet, the weightlifter is not bothered by this pain and may actually enjoy the sensation as a sign of progress in his strength training or body-building program: "No pain, no gain," as they say. That same sensation will become a painfully disturbing one, however, if he learns that it is a symptom of a degenerative disease syndrome. Likewise, if the stressed-out student learns that feelings of fatigue are caused by a chronic illness, she might change her daily practices to make sure she is better rested and abandon regimens that were previously reinforced, rather than discouraged, by the weariness attributed to a highly motivated self-regulation. This attribution need not be consciously entertained before it functions in triadic signification. This can be seen in the counterfactual: The sensations may be ones that would give rise to worry about one's health, except for the explanatory attribution, which might function only tacitly in such a way that no thought is even given to the stress and weariness. In this case, what occurs as an interpretant is the very absence of the worried interpretations that would have arisen in response to those same physiological conditions, had they not become triadically involved within signs signifying motivation and self-discipline.

Figure 7.10 illustrates how this interpretant can be endowed with semantic value by virtue of its position within the structure of semiological possibilities. The absence of worry can function as an interpretant even though it is not something that exists or occurs in a *positive* way, apart from its structurally significant relations with other things and events. Without raising the ontological question of whether there are any entities existing *positively* in this way, I would argue that any thing or event that participates in triadic signification—including, from this Peircean perspective, all cognitive processes—participates by virtue of its relative existence: that is, its existence as one term of its relationships with the things or events (including absences and nonoccurrences) that serve as the other terms of those relationships. As Saussure (1916/1986) learned from the exceptionally obvious example of phonemic value, semiotic value (*valeur*) derives from the relationships: A sound type does not have phonemic value in and of itself, for example, but only as a term within the structure of phonemic similarities and differences. Potentially significant value does not inhere in things or events as positive entities, but accrues to them as terms within relationships. These

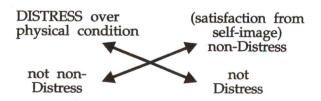

FIG. 7.10. Distress (semiotic square).

include both *syntagmatic* relationships (i.e., relationships of combination, with other co-occurring things or events within the context) as well as *paradigmatic* relationships (i.e., relationships of alternation or exclusion, with other things or events that could occur within the context, but to the mutual exclusion of each other).

Within a web of triads signifying motivation, we have used semiotic squares to identify self-image (as an interpretant) and motivation (as an object, elaborated more extensively in Figs. 7.9a to 7.9c) as terms that are also located within such structures of semiological constraints and possibilities. I believe that this could also be done with the mediating representamena, such as clock use and coffee use. Each element within the triadic sign relation is seen to be endowed, therefore, with semiological value that arises from the structure of its binary relations of similarity and difference with other terms. But even as such binary structural relations are in that sense internal to the constitution of each term in the triadic sign relations, so also are the triadic sign relations internal to the constitution of each semantic term that enters into binary or serial structural relationships with other semantic terms. Thus, each of these two kinds of semiotic relationships (the Peircean/triadic, and the Saussurean/binary) is internally constitutive of terms or elements within the other. This does defy the simple logic of positivistic analysis (in which anything can be analyzed into positively self-identical constituents); but that is not a flaw in this semiotic account if, in reality, cognition and other semiosic processes conform instead to principles of other logics, logics of reciprocally internal relationships among things and events.

This extended exploration began with an example of students interpreting the concept of motivation in a way that was fundamentally different from its use as a scientific construct in their psychology text. I believe that the example does show how contextual situations are pragmatically implicated in the very constitution of the sign. In this light we may consider the "contextualism" of Jenkins (1974) who was quoted by Clancey and Roschelle (1991) as he "describes the roots of situated cognition in American pragmatism, in the work of William James, C. S. Peirce, and John Dewey" (p. 2). Instead of focusing on the "pragmatist" criteria for truth, Jenkins (1974) chose for emphasis "the less familiar, but more descriptive, name *contextualism*":

> Contextualism holds that experience consists of *events*. Events have a *quality* as a whole. By quality is meant the total meaning of the event. The quality of the event is the resultant of the interaction of the organism and the physical relations that provide support for the experience. The relations can be thought of and analyzed into *textures*. A texture in turn consists of *strands* lying in a *context*. (p. 786)

An approach that integrates the semiotics of Peirce and Saussure enables us to identify very diverse strands and textures through which "contextual" structures are woven into the structures of the signs themselves, as within these structures signs give rise to other signs:

> Symbols grow. They come into being by development out of other signs, particularly from icons, or from mixed signs partaking of the nature of icons and symbols. We think only in signs. These mental signs are of mixed nature; the symbol-parts of them are called concepts. If a man makes a new symbol, it is by thoughts involving concepts. So it is only out of symbols that a new symbol can grow. *Omne symbolum de symbolo.* (Peirce, c. 1895, 2.302)

I have been trying to demonstrate how these strands and textures weave together elements of the most diverse kinds, including abstract verbally articulated concepts as well as habits, regimens, ideologies, emotions, and physiological states. Responding to Clancey and Roschelle's (1991) point that "a science of learning without the neural perspective is like agriculture without genetics" (p. 5), I have tried to demonstrate an approach in which the kinds of neurological phenomena described in the discussions of connectionism by Bereiter (1991), Gee (1992), and St. Julien (chapter 10, this volume) can be seen as elements that can participate triadically with other elements as diverse as social norms and public policies within the fundamental nuclei of sign activity.

Starting with the motivation example, however, I fear that my demonstration may have remained too close to the personal, psychological, and physiological, and not gone far enough toward demonstrating the participation of such elements in triads that also include social, economic, institutional, political, and cultural phenomena as other objects, representamena, and interpretants within the same triads, along with psychological and physiological elements. I have no doubt that this could be done with the motivation case itself (recall that some of the students were invoking discourses from their fundamentalist church backgrounds whereas others were pursuing Reagan-era dreams of being young, upwardly mobile professionals).

Representation, Concepts, and Perception

Referring more directly to the kinds of subject matter taught in schools, Toulmin (1972) proclaimed that "*Concepts are Micro-Institutions*" and "*Institutions are Macro-concepts*" (pp. 352–353, italics in original). Toulmin persuasively described social and historical institutions functioning as concepts; but I believe that our Peircean approach makes it even easier to understand in a more fundamental theoretical sense that concepts are comprised of triadic sign relations in which even the most macrolevel institutions can participate.

This raises the problem of how to understand concepts and conceptuality in relation to the situated nature of cognition. According to Brown, Collins, and Duguid (1989a):

> For centuries, the epistemology that has guided educational practice has concentrated primarily on conceptual representation and made its relation to objects in the world problematic by assuming that, cognitively, representation is prior to all else. A theory of situated cognition suggests that activity and perception are importantly and epistemologically prior—at a nonconceptual level—to conceptualization and that it is on them that more attention needs to be focused. An epistemology that begins with activity and perception, which are first and foremost embedded in the world, may simply bypass the classical problem of reference—of mediating conceptual representations. (p. 41)

Clancey and Roschelle (1991) agreed with the emphasis on perception; insisting that "it is by perceptual processes that representations are created and given meaning" (p. 3), however, they would not recognize representation as belonging to some nonperceptual conceptual level:

> Perception involves coordinating current processes of talking, seeing, and moving with the processes that have been constructed previously. The result is always novel, though composed of past coordinations. To the extent that environment is regular, stable behaviors will develop. Representations are created and given meaning in the course of this perceptual process. (pp. 21–22)

This seems to agree with Brown, Collins, and Duguid (1989a) when they claimed, "A concept . . . will continually evolve with each new occasion of use, because new situations, negotiations, and activities inevitably recast it in new, more densely textured form. So a concept, like the meaning of a word, is always under construction" (p. 33). Rather than excluding concepts from any important place in their accounts of cognitive activity, Brown et al. (1989a) were concerned with clarifying how concepts should be better understood, as when they argued that "to explore the idea that concepts are both situated and progressively developed through activity, we should abandon any notion that they are abstract, self-contained entities" (p. 33). It is still not altogether clear, however, how situated cognition theory would account for the attainment of conceptuality.

But first, it is not even clear what is being meant by "concept" or "conceptuality." Brown et al. (1989a) commented that "whatever the domain, explication often lifts implicit and possibly even nonconceptual constraints (Cussins, 1988 [cf. Cussins, 1990]) out of the embedding world and tries to make them explicit or conceptual" (p. 41). In Cussins and the other sources we might turn to (e.g., Johnson, 1987; Lakoff, 1987), we find extensive and sophisticated arguments against trying to understand cognition primarily or exclusively in terms of abstract, formal, decontextualized "concepts." Yet, whether these authors are making a case for the importance of "nonconceptual" elements or arguing for a less restrictive understanding of the "conceptual," it is never clearly stated what they take "concept" or "conceptuality" to mean.

I cannot assess competing descriptions of conceptuality until I have an idea of what it is that I mean to describe. Nor can I assess the merits of a plea for the nonconceptual until I know how that is being distinguished from the conceptual. In Cussins' usage (accurately reflected in the previous reference by Brown et al., 1989a), conceptuality seems to be defined partly on the basis of explicitness. Lakoff relied heavily on the formulation of "preconceptual experiences" discussed in more detail by Johnson (1987; see Lakoff, 1987, pp. 267–268); and again, although their structural descriptions of the levels referred to as conceptual and "preconceptual" are clear and persuasive, it is not clear how and why "conceptuality" itself is being understood in terms of abstractness and explicitness, almost as if by some unquestionable definition of the word. Brown et al. (1989a) argued against the ideology of teaching "abstract, decontextualized formal concepts," "the abstract concept alone," or imparting "abstracted concepts as fixed, well-defined, independent entities that can be explored in prototypical examples and textbook exercises," to students who will then be able to "manipulate algorithms, routines, and definitions," but without showing any real understanding or ability to make use of real knowledge in authentic situations (pp. 32–33).

Although I agree with those who challenge this ideology of abstract, rule-determined concepts, I would like to hear "conceptuality" itself defined so that we have some basis for considering how other characteristics may or may not pertain to "concepts." If conceptuality is understood as the capacity of an idea or sign to serve as "a general idea [or sign] derived or inferred from specific instances or occurrences" (First definition under "concept" in *The American Heritage Dictionary of the English Language*, Third Edition, 1992, p. 390); then we can see abstractness, analyticity, explicitness, and so forth as other characteristics that are not intrinsic to the sense or meaning of conceptuality as such, but that have become incorporated into established theories of how conceptuality occurs. These are not the only possible explanations of conceptuality, however, and I would argue that the Peircean approach explains how the generality of concepts as such can be achieved concretely (and not by abstraction) and in ways that are not necessarily analytically rule-governed or explicit.

I believe that this is an important problem for situated cognition, so I hope that it does not sound like pedantic quibbling over words ("merely" semantic, as they say). St. Julien (chapter 10, this volume) argues that any adequate theory of situated cognition must recognize that transfer of learning does sometimes occur, and must be able to account for how such transfer can take place. I am not sure that transfer is a good metaphor for what is happening, but certainly I do need to account for how learning can be generalized as meaningful and useful beyond the immediate situation in which it has originally occurred. Although I would not claim that the basic Peircean model of triadic signs, in itself, provides a sufficient theory of generalizable learning, I believe it does provide a way of understanding conceptualization that is significantly different from those that assume processes of analytical abstraction or other rule-governed operations performed on elements of the kinds of symbol systems proposed in mainstream cognitive science. As St. Julien observes (chapter 10, this volume):

> Knowledge—insofar as that which enables competence can still be called knowledge—is found in the context, in structuring resources and discursive practices, in the habits that get us through the day. For the most part competence is more understandable as a matter of appropriate perception and habituated action than as formal reasoning over classical objects of knowledge. (p. 264)

Figure 7.11 illustrates how multiple triadic relationships can incorporate perception and habituated action in ways that can give rise to concepts as both generalized and situated semiotic practices. Two triads are presented. In both, the action of slicing 25 cents worth of cheese serves as an interpretant [i] that, through the mediation of the coins presented (either five nickels [r_1] or one quarter [r_2]), signifies a common monetary value [o]. "Twenty-five cents worth" thus becomes conceptually generalized as a value that can

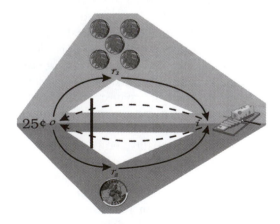

FIG. 7.11. Slicing two bits worth of cheese (a concept as a generalized and situated semiotic practice).

correspond not only to various coin combinations, but also to specific quantities of cheese or bread or other goods. Although this might be described as an abstract value, we should note that it has not become established in this illustration through the formal logical procedure of abstraction. Instead, it has been *conceived* as a general sign in a manner very much like that in which five nickels came to be *perceived* as the sign of an equivalent value.

At least in the case of such regularly encountered quantities, the value of the nickels will not be *calculated* by the "expert" cheese vendor, but simply *recognized*. Every time five nickels are encountered, they will differ in their physical arrangement. There might be a darkened dirty nickel, a Canadian nickel, or an old Indian head nickel, all variously showing heads or tails. The vendor is confronted with a different visual image every time. But this does not mean that, each time, the vendor must go through an algorithmic rule-governed procedure to ascertain the monetary value of the coins. In the case of five nickels, the expert does not even execute the rudimentary procedure of counting them; she simply *recognizes* them as 25 cents. Experts might recognize the value of five nickels more readily than that of five dimes or even four nickels. If so, this is because of the repeated and familiar practical relationship between five nickels and the frequently encountered monetary value of 25 cents. In that case, the *perception* of five nickels is no less abstract than the *conception* of 25 cents; the concept is not derived from the concrete objects through rule-governed processes of sensation, information processing, and calculation. Instead, in the manner described by St. Julien (chapter 10, this volume), the recognition of five nickels is itself arrived at through the unruly but reliably regular processes of (socially supported and constrained) perceptual pattern completion, and the pattern of five nickels, in particular, is more readily perceived because of its relation to an "abstract" quantity (25 cents) that may be semiosically more *solid* than the metal coins themselves, by virtue of the density of practical transactions and communications in which the value of that quantity is so well established. Quantities of cheese, coins, and monetary value are sustained in practical cognition through the habituated relationships among them, and among them and the terms of countless networks of other triads in which they are also involved.

We see here a conceptual generality of signs that coordinate *conception* with *perception* and action. Compare this with the view of Roschelle and Clancey (1992), who explained that the social-neural standpoint helps us see how

> . . . the emergence of new categories is a matter of re-using transient organizations of neural maps; structured cues from the physical and social world gradually can stabilize new relations of features and the world. Crucially, these maps coordinate perception and action—they do not *represent* how behavior or the world appears to an observer. (p. 12)

Again, they told us, "Representing is, in essence, coordinating perception with action; this coordination takes place in a dialectic between the social and neural processes" (p. 14). I believe that our examples of triadic signification do illustrate semiosic processes in which such coordination can take place. On the other hand, I think that these quotations from Roschelle and Clancey reveal an ambivalence in their use of "representation" that might now be clarified, in part, by differentiating between the senses of "representation" as *Vorstellung* or as *Darstellung* (helpfully discussed in Toulmin, 1972).

The kind of representation that is denied in the first quotation is more an example of *Vorstellung*. As Toulmin (1972) explained:

> By contrast [with *Darstellung*], the term *Vorstellung* suggests a "representation" as private or personal as a *Darstellung* is public. A *Vorstellung* "stands for", or symbolizes, something "in the mind" of an individual. The term carries the same burden as words like "idea" and "imagination": it is, in fact, the standard German translation for the Lockean term "idea", and runs into all the same difficulties. (p. 195)

Toulmin also explained that

> a *Darstellung* is a "representation", in the sense in which a stage-play serves as a theatrical representation, or in which an exhibition or recital provides a public presentation or representation of works of art or music. To *darstellen* a phenomenon is then to "demonstrate" or "display" it, in the sense of setting it forth, or exhibiting it, so as to show in an entirely public manner what it comprises, or how it operates . . . (p. 195)

Toulmin (1972) concluded that "the relationship between a *Darstellung* and the reality which it 'displays' or 'represents' is, accordingly, a relationship between two public entities" (p. 195). This conclusion is questionable in a couple of respects (at least as it pertains to our interest in representation, rather than his immediate purpose in explaining the established usage of the German word). First, we do not see the elements of representational signification as "entities" that can be identified existing in themselves; in general, we see the elements themselves produced and identifiably existing *as the terms* of their relationships with other elements. Toulmin's point that both elements are "public" is also an overstatement—understandable in the context of his criticism of the received framework of Kant, Locke, and Descartes. From our standpoint, however, we understand representational sign relations as including such things as the transient activation states and neural maps that Roschelle and Clancey (1992) described as occurring neurologically in individuals (pp. 11–12; cf. St. Julien, chapter 10, this volume). Although not "public," these also exist as terms of their relationships with other things and events in the world, including things and events outside the brain or psyche of any single individual. Our framework enables us to deny the very split between mind and world that is presumed in the Cartesian framework, and reflected in the Lockean notion of "private" representation that Toulmin is at such pains to rebut.

We should also note a possible apparent difference between *Darstellung* in the exhibition of a visual work of art and in the performance of a musical composition. Although it might be thought that the particular performance of a work of music "represents" the composition in the sense that any *token* represents a *type* (as when the sounds I vocally produce while speaking may be regarded as tokens representing their phonemic types, or the printed character *R* on this page is a token of the letter *R* in the Roman alphabet), this is clearly not the sense of *Darstellung* involved in the case of an exhibition of a painting or a sculpture. In both the visual and musical examples, however, *Darstellung* involves the work itself—the object represented—being actively engaged with in the world. If we recall that Toulmin used the works of art as an example in explaining the nature of representation in collectively developed and shared scientific concepts, it is easier to avoid the mistake of understanding this as a matter of (formal) types represented by (substantial) tokens. In both science and the arts, as well as in everyday practical cognition, this sense of *Darstellung* is not so much a matter of public versus private, but it is clearly something socially accomplished and not a matter of performing formal operations on some inward mental symbol system (as in *Vorstellungen*).

As Clancey and Roschelle (1991) explained in their discussion of an activity for learning physics concepts:

> Schema models are good for representing the ways of talking and seeing that the students bring to bear. . . . But schema models of interpretation require input concepts and relations . . . which are constructed in the activity itself. "Triggering a schema" is a perceptual process, but not a matter of matching given tokens. Perception involves coordinating current processes of talking, seeing, and moving with the processes that have been constructed previously. The result is always novel, though composed of past coordinations. To the extent that environment is regular, stable behaviors will develop. Representations are created and given meaning in the course of this perceptual process. (pp. 21–22)

As we have seen, Peirce's semiotic approach shows how such coordinations occur in triadic relationships, with perceived or conceived objects represented in the activity of interpretants through the mediation of the representamena. Considering the breadth of possible examples, we can see more clearly now why the kind of representation-as-coordination demonstrated by Clancey and Roschelle should not be restricted to the kinds of things that match their definition and examples of a representation as something that is recognized or claimed by somebody as a representation. The stability that they describe as a tendency of constrained novelty in the resulting coordinated behaviors (interpretants) is partly determined by the regularity of the object and its *Darstellung* in the triadic sign. This is what constitutes the sign as a representation of the object, and it does not depend on being claimed or otherwise acknowledged as such.

To account for the developmental aspect of representation noted by Clancey and Roschelle, it may be helpful at this point to add the last bits of Peircean arcana to be introduced in this chapter: the distinctions between immediate and dynamic objects, and immediate, dynamic, and final interpretants. As Short (1981) explained:

> The immediate object is the world, or some part of it, as the sign represents it to be, while the dynamic object is the world—or the relevant portion of it—that will actually determine the success or failure of any given interpretant of the sign. This success or failure will sometimes be manifest in the semeiotic process itself, namely, when there is opportunity to form more than one dynamic interpretant of the same sign. For then each interpretant implicitly adds to or corrects the preceding interpretant. (pp. 214–215)

In one of Short's examples of this process:

> Several physicians consulting can agree that a thermometer reading indicates that the patient has a fever, while disagreeing about what else this signifies. The immediate logical interpretant is that the patient has a fever; what their dynamic interpretants add to this will depend upon their collateral observations of the patient, of similar cases, and so on. The immediate object of the sign is fever; the dynamic object is the actual physical condition of the patient so far as that bears on the physicians' practical problem (for their goal is only practical, not theoretical). Sufficient collateral observations will produce dynamic interpretants close to the final logical interpretant, in which this dynamic object would be fully apprehended. (p. 216)

Finally, Short (1981) explained that "the final interpretant (toward which the dynamic interpretants of a sign tend) could, depending on the sign and the goal of interpretation, be either the feeling or the action or the thought which *would be* the ideally adequate interpretation" (p. 213) Thus, "the ultimate form of a logical interpretant is the testable form of that interpretant. The final logical interpretant is the logical interpretant that would survive all possible tests" (pp. 218–219).

We are now prepared to reconsider the nature of concepts as representational signs that coordinate between social and neurological levels. Let us recall the notorious Weight Watchers cottage cheese example:

In this case they [the dieters] were to fix a serving of cottage cheese, supposing that the amount allotted for the meal was three-quarters of the two-thirds cup the program allowed. The problem solver in this example began by muttering that he had taken a calculus course in college (an acknowledgment of the discrepancy between school math prescriptions for practice and his present circumstances).* Then after a pause he suddenly announced that he had "got it!" . . . He filled a measuring cup two-thirds full of cottage cheese, dumped it out on a cutting board, patted it into a circle, marked a cross on it, scooped away one quadrant, and served the rest. Thus, "take three-quarters of two-thirds of a cup of cottage cheese" was not just the problem statement but also the solution to the problem and the procedure for solving it. The setting was part of the calculating process and the solution was simply the problem statement, enacted with the setting. At no time did the Weight Watcher check his procedure against a paper and pencil algorithm, which would have produced $\frac{3}{4}$ cup $\times \frac{2}{3}$ cup $= \frac{1}{2}$ cup. Instead, the coincidence of problem, setting, and enactment was the means by which checking took place. (Lave, 1988, p. 165 [*footnote omitted])

Some questions were raised by critical discussants after Brown et al. (1989a) described this resolution as "inventive," and the dieter's solution path as "extremely expedient" and an example of situated cognition as used both by real practitioners and by "JPFs" ("Just Plain Folks"), as opposed to the noncontextualized procedures taught to students in school (p. 35). Instead of seeing this as an "inventive resolution" of the problem, Palincsar (1989) described it as "an act of desperation, born of ignorance." Asking "Where does this so-called resolution lead? Nothing has been learned that could be generalized," she noted her suspicion that "the underlying problem here is that, due to the decontextualized teaching of fractions, the Weight Watcher never internalized procedures for simple mathematical computations that could be used to solve a practical problem" (p. 7). Wineburg (1989) added the observation that this dieter "could not use a simple algorithm and a time-honored culinary tool—the fractionalized measuring cup" (p. 9).

Responding to the criticism, Brown, Collins, and Duguid (1989b) explained:

We do not doubt that it is useful to resort to algorithms in many cases, but we suggest that people will first try to deploy useful aspects of the task and their understanding of the context in order to limit and to share the representational and computational load. If this situated approach fails, they may, step by step, fall back on abstract algorithms. But we still need to understand the initial impulse to try a situated approach. And if this approach indeed succeeds, reflecting on and justifying that success is a productive learning experience. (p. 11)

The peculiar thing is that, for all the talk about whether or not algorithms should be used, or when and how, the only kind of thinking described by anyone in this exchange is algorithmic—whether "situated" or "abstract"—to the exclusion of nonalgorithmic responses that are possible on the basis of the more substantive and intuitive (rather than procedural and algorithmic) conceptual understanding that can be built up through engagement in triadic sign activity, involving the kinds of perceptual activity and habituated pattern-completion described by Clancey and Roschelle (1991) and by St. Julien (chapter 10, this volume).

Lave found it significant that the dieter did not use the paper-and-pencil algorithm that would have produced a solution in the form $\frac{3}{4} \times \frac{2}{3}$ cup $= \frac{1}{2}$ cup.[5] Notice, however, that "take three quarters of two thirds of a cup of cottage cheese" is also being used as an algorithm when it serves not only as the problem statement, "but also the solution to the problem and the procedure for solving it" (When the Weight Watcher "suddenly announced that he had 'got it,' " what he had in mind was a context-specific algorithm).

The paper-and-pencil algorithm would presumably involve canceling numerators and denominators, $\frac{3}{4} \times \frac{2}{3}$, to get the product, $\frac{1}{2}$. If the algorithm is executed properly, it will produce the correct answers; but I have actually seen first-year college undergraduates canceling numerators and denominators across unrelated problems! Advocates of rule-based theories and pedagogy would say that we need two sets of rules: one for knowing when to "apply" a given algorithm and the other for knowing how to apply it properly. Many critics have argued that the range of human abilities that can be accounted for in this way is quite narrow and exceptional (e.g., Dreyfus, Dreyfus, & Athanasiou, 1986; Winograd & Flores, 1987). When the task is one that can be accomplished in this way, we might still consider that it is worth sacrificing greater generalizability in the decontextualized rule-based approach for the sake of greater functional success and accessibility using more ad hoc, makeshift situation-specific algorithms. But comparisons on these instrumental functionalist grounds omit what I see as another distinct advantage of the situated approach, one that is more important, I believe, at least for the distinct educational purpose of the school curriculum.

I believe that situated approaches to problem solving should be appreciated not only in terms of their functional sufficiency, but more importantly (at least for educators and educational researchers) in terms of the substantial understanding that is required for the more inventive problem solving (and, perhaps more important, for the situationally responsive practical judgment in problem formulation), and that might not be required at all in getting correct results to predefined problems through rote application of procedural rules. I believe that education does properly aim for a more fundamental

---

[5]Notice that this should be $\frac{3}{4} \times \frac{2}{3}$ cup, not $\frac{3}{4}$ cup $\times \frac{2}{3}$ cup (as published). This is not meant to quibble, but to insist on the importance of such sign elements in developing an intuitive conceptual sense of the representation, rather than relying on either context-free or situation-specific algorithms without guidance from such conceptual comprehension.

conceptual understanding that might not be required for functional adequacy in solving this or that specific technical problem.

We have seen that although Brown, Collins, and Duguid (1989a, 1989b) criticized traditional notions of conceptuality, they were not dismissive of conceptualized learning; rather, they would propose a notion of conceptuality as something that perpetually develops from the kinds of situated cognitive activity exhibited by the Weight Watcher with his cottage cheese. Although I believe that they have validly distinguished such conceptualizing activity from the traditional rote learning and "application" of "concepts," I believe that they are still describing algorithmic procedures, which are now seen to include "microroutines" in which "parts of the cognitive task" are "off-loaded onto the environment" (1989a, p. 35) and people "deploy useful aspects of the task and their understanding of the context in order to limit and to share the representational and computational load" (1989b, p. 11). They contrast this situated approach with "the processing solely inside heads that many teaching practices implicitly endorse" (1989a, p. 35), as well as the "abstract algorithms" that it might be "useful to resort to" or "fall back on" when the situated approach is not successful (1989b, p. 11). The problem with these formulations is that they too narrowly restrict our view of cognition, in part through the dichotomization of purportedly nonalgorithmic activity situated in the environment versus abstract algorithmic activity "solely inside heads." This framework does not seem to provide a place for the role of such things as the pattern-completion and perceptual activity described by St. Julien (chapter 10, this volume) and by Clancey and Roschelle (1991).

I believe that a Peircean framework would more adequately account for how these processes participate with the other processes that operate together within cognitive activity. One glimpse of this possibility might be provided by considering a kind of conceptual understanding that mathematics instruction might aim for in the schools, and that is not a matter of algorithmic procedure (either abstract or situated), but that would also have been useful to the Weight Watcher who wants to eat just the right sized portion of cottage cheese.

In that case, the situated algorithm that was ultimately used has been described to us as an inventive and efficient way of getting the right answer, without any need for remembering the more abstract algorithms for formulating the problem as one that requires solving for x in x cup $= \frac{3}{4} \times \frac{2}{3}$ cup, and then performing the correct operations on the formula to find the correct answer. I want to argue, however, that without either recalling and executing those "abstract" calculations or inventing and executing situated calculations more concretely on the cottage cheese itself, a Weight Watcher with the conceptual understanding of mathematical relationships that we should be aiming for in school could have more efficiently and directly *recognized* $\frac{1}{2}$ cup of cottage cheese as the quantity desired.

When told to "take three fourths of two thirds of a cup," someone familiar enough with quantitative relationships will recognize "three fourths of two thirds" as a designation for the same value as "two thirds of three fourths" or simply "one half." If this were a matter of canceling numerators and denominators, then it would make no difference whether the quantity were represented as $\frac{3}{4}$ of $\frac{2}{3}$ or as $\frac{2}{3}$ of $\frac{3}{4}$. The latter is much more easily *recognized*, however, as another representation for the same quantity that is more often designated as $\frac{1}{2}$ (see Fig. 7.12). For someone who has developed a sufficiently "expert" familiarity with such quantitative relationships, there will be no need to remember that multiplication is a commutative operation (i.e., that $a \times b = b \times a$) and to "apply" a commutation procedure before deriving one form from the other. Instead of thinking about the forms of fractional expression, the person would be able to recognize the common value as directly as she could recognize the common value of five nickels and five other nickels, or one quarter, without first turning them so that they are all showing the same side (heads or tails), or "applying" some remembered rule about an Indian head nickel being equal to a Jefferson nickel, and then counting them and multiplying by 5 cents. In the cottage cheese example, there is no need to remember the commutativity of multiplication—or for canceling numerators and denominators, for that matter—because there is no need for multiplying any fractions. Instead, just as the cheese vendor can recognize five nickels as a value equal to the same amount of cheese as one quarter, so too could the Weight Watcher see "three fourths of two thirds" as calling for a half-cup of cottage cheese.

The kind of conceptual familiarity with fractional quantities and relationships that I am speaking of can be developed and habituated in the kind of triadically signifying practical activity illustrated in the cheese-selling example (Fig. 7.11). Far from being esoteric, rare, or academic, such familiarity

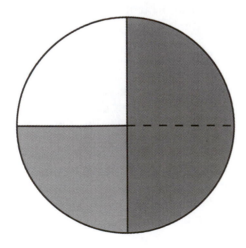

FIG. 7.12. One half as two thirds of three fourths.

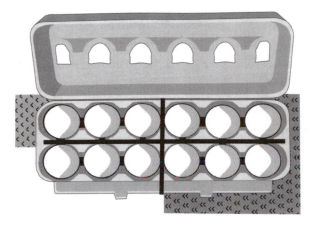

FIG. 7.13a. A half-dozen eggs (as two thirds of three fourths).

can be observed in the everyday activities of "Just Plain Folks" such as the adult workers in a milk processing plant reported and discussed in Scribner (1984, 1986), and the 5- to 16-year-old Brazilian candy sellers in Saxe (1990).

Like the coins and cheese slices in Fig. 7.11, physical objects participate in the active triadic sign activity in which more general signs or concepts are developed. In Scribner's study, for example, workers in a milk processing plant were deftly manipulating cases partially filled with cartons of milk to fill orders from their customers. For illustration purposes, Fig. 7.13a uses an egg carton showing one half as two thirds of three fourths in a palpable form that could participate in the formation of the more general conceptual relationships. Figure 7.13b presents a dozen eggs divided into thirds, with three quarters of two thirds again comprising half a dozen eggs.

FIG. 7.13b. A half-dozen eggs (as three fourths of two thirds).

Again, these illustrations might be easily confused with familiar classroom methods for teaching algorithmic processes. If we were contemplating using the eggs as manipulatives in teaching fractional arithmetic, the division of a dozen eggs into fourths and into thirds might be employed with equal effectiveness. But that is not the same thing as the kinds of situated learning and cognition observed by Scribner and by Saxe, which I would describe as being situated not only with respect to local and specific time and place but also with respect to their embeddedness within the dynamic structured networks of semantic and pragmatic relationships that make them consequential and significant within the practices and projects of people's real lives in the social world. In real life, we deal frequently with a "half-dozen" as a quantity of eggs or other familiar things, but there is probably less basis for intuitive familiarity with two thirds of a dozen.

On the other hand, a student whose life revolves around sharing six-packs (Fig. 7.14a) with two regular companions might be more likely to have formed a robust, intuitive conceptual familiarity with "half" as three fourths of two thirds (see Fig. 7.14b).

It is in our everyday lives that we are engaged in practical occasions for the situated development of more general conceptual understanding, but I believe that school instruction can make an important difference in the likelihood of

FIG. 7.14a. A six pack.

FIG. 7.14b. Half a six pack (as three fourths of two thirds).

gaining such conceptual development in everyday experience. Daily practical experience with six-packs, milk cartons, or Brazilian candies can be expected to produce robust intuitions of the quantitative relations that are most commonly encountered. But classroom practices in which conceptual understanding is itself featured as a practical objective could open up additional dimensions of more general mathematical relationships within which cognitive activity situated outside of the classroom can be more richly embedded and elaborated, so that the six-pack-swilling Weight Watcher is more likely to recognize half a cup as the desired quantity of cottage cheese.

Of course, most of us who are mathematically "Just Plain Folks," even with the kind of conceptual familiarity with mathematical relationships that I claim we should be aiming for in school instruction, would not see the value as "half a cup" in one single act of recognition. Most of us would see one-half only after recognizing the value as one that could be expressed equally as either $\frac{3}{4}$ of $\frac{2}{3}$ or as $\frac{2}{3}$ of $\frac{3}{4}$. Moreover, I am obviously taking advantage of the fortuitous convenience of the specific fractions that happen to be involved in this example. With these specific fractional amounts, JPFs with a conceptual grasp of the relationships could see the solution in just two steps of recognition (first, recognizing $\frac{3}{4}$ of $\frac{2}{3}$ as $\frac{2}{3}$ of $\frac{3}{4}$, and then recognizing $\frac{2}{3}$ of $\frac{3}{4}$ as $\frac{1}{2}$). This might, indeed, be regarded as a simple algorithm, or as a rule-governed procedure. Less convenient fractional quantities might require a procedure involving more than just two steps. Although conceptually grounded recognition does not totally obviate such procedures, the solution process cannot be accounted for simply as a rule-conforming process because the key steps in the process consist of nonalgorithmic recognition processes.

An appreciation of the situated character of real, practical cognition does not require us to dogmatically repudiate the use of algorithms or to concede that algorithmic procedures might provide a useful fallback that we can resort to if our preferred situated approach does not succeed. Few, if any, situated cognitive performances will be completely nonalgorithmic. What we need to understand, rather, is the orchestration of algorithmic and non-algorithmic processes within cognitive practices.

I have argued that the difference between situated cognition and abstract decontextualized formalisms is not that the latter are algorithmic whereas the former are not. Instead, I have argued that the formalistic algorithms are attempts to function adequately without the substantive conceptual under-standing that enables the ad hoc invention of the situated algorithms—and that this is a difference between rote learning and conceptual development. Considering what we have learned from Walkerdine about how she has seen the distinction between rote learning and conceptual development used in discourses and practices that systematically disparage the real intellectual achievements of female, minority, and working-class students, it is necessary for me to explain how I think my usage differs from what she has seen in those oppressive discourses. That explanation begins the final section of this chapter, which considers implications of the semiotic framework for issues of critical reflection and transcendence in cognition as a situated social process.

CRITICAL REFLECTION AND TRANSCENDENCE

Recalling Walkerdine's discussion of how a differentiation between rote learning and conceptual development has been used invidiously in the sup-pression of female, minority, and working-class students, it is incumbent on me now to reconsider the distinction that I have just been making, in light of her sobering observations.

The first point is that although I may be using the same terms, the distinction I am making is not the same as what she observed. "Conceptuality" in the discourse Walkerdine reported does in fact refer to the imagined abstract, analytical and formalistic context-independent "concepts" that are the farthest thing from the kind of richly embedded, substantive, social and physiological, situationally developed conceptual triadic signs that I have been discussing.

At the same time, I would not want to dodge Walkerdine's more fundamental point: The invidious distinction here is only one of the examples she used to make more general points about how our discursive practices—including those of educational researchers and theorists as well as practitioners, policymakers, and the general public—do not just represent reality but actually engender the realities that they presume to signify. Moreover, Walkerdine (1988, 1992) also demonstrated how our discursive practices are driven by dreams, desires, and fantasies that can be wildly unaccountable to any kind of an objective reality.

I am impressed by Walkerdine's demonstrations, and I am convinced that the phenomena she demonstrated are real (even if her discourse is itself fueled by her own desires and fantasies). For my part, I have no wish to deny the role of dreams, desires, and fantasies in the generation of my own discourse, nor would I want to lose sight of how these processes may compromise my quest for valid understanding. This assumes, as I do believe, that the differentiation between valid and invalid representations of cognition makes more sense than Walkerdine might recognize (cf. Agre, chapter 5, this volume, on how Walkerdine's Foucauldian stance differs from Lave's more Marxian approach, in which it is more meaningful to criticize a discourse as being ideological in the sense of expressing systematically false consciousness).

I want to argue, in fact, that one of the great virtues of the Peircean approach is the basis it reveals for understanding critical, reflective, and even transcendent practice as a potential that is intrinsic in the fundamental processes of semiosis. I believe that this is true of both the semiosic processes of cognition and of our processes of inquiry into cognition; and I believe that it is not only a valid point, but also an important one.

I would like to briefly discuss some of the importance of this point, before arguing more extensively for its validity. I begin by relating these concerns expressed by Petrie (1992).

> A lot more work needs to be done on "constructivist theories of learning" before we can be certain that they will be anything more than the latest educational fad, perverted beyond their meaning by superficial educationists (who did the same thing to Dewey, Piaget, Kohlberg, etc.)
>
> It is understandable if people of color are even more conservative than I am about the promise of "the new learning and teaching." We do not know whether these will ultimately be helpful in combatting the isms. Their contention is that just when folks of color figure out what they need to do to make it in the power structures, and they start teaching their children how to pass standardized tests and get into college, the white folks change the rules of the game and tell them they've got to do "whole language" or "constructivism," which may or may not get them into the power structure.
>
> The problem with that approach, to my way of thinking, is that it implicitly assumes that not only are there no absolute versions of knowledge (after all,

we all know that absolutist positions have been used to justify oppression for a long time), there are also no judgments of better or worse with regard to knowledge claims. That is, claims of a "better" conception of teaching and learning are NOTHING MORE than different political claims. So you end up saying that it's all just about political power anyway, and evidence and argument are irrelevant.

This leads me to what I have come to believe is another fundamental division in our intellectual lives—between those who start with a psychological approach and those who start with a sociological approach. To oversimplify only a little, psychologists talk about classroom teaching and learning; sociologists talk about organizational structures and power relations, which in their judgment completely overwhelm any individual teaching and learning that might go on. Indeed, they often reduce everything, including cognitive psychology, to yet another political ideology.

For their part, the psychologists tend to ignore the fact that very often, although perhaps not always, the social factors do constrain what we can do for individual children and do influence even the conception of how individuals teach and learn. The constructivist versions of teaching and learning, especially when they focus on the social construction of meaning, give us some hope of bridging the gap, but we are by no means there yet. . . . If we are to make real progress, we need to make the psychologists and sociologists talk to each other. (pp. 19–20)

Petrie's comments intersect with our discussion at a number of points. To begin with, his concerns about the potential uses and effects of "constructivism" are not unrelated to what Walkerdine witnessed in the English schools. The contrast that he drew between the sociologists and the psychologists may be reflected in a contrast between the socially and culturally oriented discourses of Lave and Walkerdine on the one hand, and the apparently more psychologically oriented discourses of Clancey and Roschelle and of Brown, Collins, and Duguid on the other hand—despite the fact that all of us argued the need for an approach that is at once both psychological and social, to the extent that we no longer see any psychological or social processes as such, but only human processes that can be analyzed (but only violently) in terms of their psychological or social aspects, moments, or elements.

I believe that what we see here is an overwhelming inertial or gravitational influence of the hegemonic discourse that is built on a system of dichotomies,[6] reflected in that between the psychological and social.

---

[6]See Whitson (1991b) for my interpretation of the Gramscian concept of hegemony. Briefly, I see the distinctive value of Gramsci's usage in its focus on the way disparate elements are structurally linked or "articulated" within a hegemonic system. Thus, the system finds a place for even the most oppositional elements and incorporates them within its own constitution. The most committed oppositional struggles can actually reinforce such hegemonic systems; to be truly counterhegemonic (and not just oppositional), it is necessary to dismantle and replace the ways that oppositions are articulated, and not just to support the disvalued or suppressed elements within those oppositions.

Consider Lave's (1992) compelling answer to the question: "Why bother pursuing a social, situated theory of learning?":

> In the broadest and baldest terms: 1) Theories of cognition, knowing, thinking, learning, etc., have traditionally taken the individual as the unit of analysis. 2) There are deep social inequalities in our world, in which socialization processes, including schooling, are deeply implicated. 3) Theories of the individual in the end are reduced to blaming the individual for the very social ills they suffer. 4) If such theories are incomplete and inadequately conceived in the first place, we have double reasons for reconsidering learning as part of social existence and as broadly as possible. (p. 1)

I would not disagree with Lave's argument here, which is carefully crafted to avoid being reduced either to a social or a psychological argument. Despite the explicit terms of her position, however, I am still concerned that the hegemonic discourse may be strong enough to translate her express arguments into readings that construe her discourse as a plea for situated cognition as an approach that is recommended for its attractiveness to those who share social or political commitments—as if approaches to the understanding of cognition and learning are matters of ideological "choice," to be chosen on the basis of "ideologies" viewed positivistically as arbitrary "value preferences" (as suggested in the concerns expressed earlier by Petrie).

This illustrates one of the reasons why I personally feel that it is important to argue for an approach that recognizes the socially situated nature of cognition and learning in a way that resists suggestions that the superior validity of such an approach is not contingent on such positivistically construed political agendas or ideologies. One virtue of the Peircean approach is that it reveals a basis, in the fundamental constitution of signs and sign activity, for a critical realism (both in cognition and the study of cognition) that is not reducible to the hegemonic discourse of positivistic subjectivism. What is at stake here, I believe, is nothing less than recognition of the basis for a critical potential that is inherent in the basis of all our semiosic practices and not merely contingent on "values," forces, or influences that are extrinsic to such practices.

It is the motivated triadicity of signs that both allows their ongoing, generative potential on the one hand and prevents them from getting lost into a completely indeterminate chain of arbitrary signifiers on the other. Derrida correctly noted that, unlike Husserl, Peirce did not see the sign as guaranteed by any foundational grounding in nonsignification—that is, by an originary "thing itself" (see, e.g., Derrida, 1967/1976, pp. 48–50). But in his concern to distinguish Peirce from Husserl in terms of how they understand the origins or the "genetic root-system" of signification, Derrida forgot that Peirce's sign is always a *triadic* affair, motivated not by a *genesis* in any continuously dominating originary signified, but by the ongoing tension between *genesis* and *telos*. There is no "transcendental signified" in Peirce, but there are transcendent possibilities inherent in the sign by virtue of the sign's *teleological* (rather than *genetic*) motivation. In my interpretation, it is the interests, concerns, or other teleological factors that determine a sign's orientation to the object, which motivate the production of an interpretant in responding to the representamen *as a sign of the absent object*, that is, an object that is not immediately present and does not govern this and subsequent interpretants as would a transcendental signified. The motivating orientation to the object is not lost, however, but remains implicit in the triadic signification of the object in relation to the interests, ends, purposes, concerns, and so forth that motivated its signification in the first place.

This does not presume a humanist position in which all is beholden to conscious or voluntary existentially self-determining purposes. To the contrary, it is Peirce whose definition of the sign avoided limiting semiosis to the scope of human agency. He did this, however, by invoking his notion of a scientific intelligence as anything (be it a process, system, agency, etc.) capable of modifying its production of interpretants on the basis of their success or failure as significations of the object to which the sign is oriented. This success is relative to the pragmatic and teleological motivation of the sign (it does not require re-presentation in the sense of somehow making the object fully present). A sign represents not only its object; it also represents itself to be sufficient to its office as a sign of that object, and any insufficiency can be reflectively responded to in modifications of the habits or practices in which the object is signified through the production of further interpretants.

This reflectively critical and potentially transcendent corrigibility is fundamental to Peirce's conception of semiosis, and stands in sharp contrast to the Saussurean conception, carried over into the poststructuralist semiotics of Derrida, Lacan, and others. Derrida's unbounded "play of signifiers" parallels the Lacanian chaining of signifiers that we saw in the semiotic processes described by Walkerdine. I do not doubt the serial representations described by Walkerdine, but I think that there is something missing from the Lacanian framework in which they have been described. Neglecting the triadic motivation of semiosis within ongoing human practices, this framework leaves the determination of the sign activity to be explained in terms of forces or processes located somewhere outside of the semiotic practices themselves. It is as if semiotic chaining were an instrument that could, without resistance, be pressed into the service of any governing social, political, or economic determination, so that social, political, and economic theories are required to explain how the trajectory of a particular series of dyadic significations has been determined from outside the chain itself.

The problem lies in an instrumentalist or functionalist view of signs, which the structuralist (and, by default, the poststructuralist) framework shares with some formulations of situated cognition. Recall, for example, how Brown,

Collins, and Duguid (1989a) invited us to consider conceptual knowledge as something similar to a set of tools:

> To explore the idea that concepts are both situated and progressively developed through activity, we should abandon any notion that they are abstract, self-contained entities. Instead it may be more useful to consider conceptual knowledge as, in some ways, similar to a set of tools.* Tools share several significant features with knowledge: They can only be fully understood through use, and using them entails both changing the user's view of the world and adopting the belief system of the culture in which they are used. (p. 33 [*footnote omitted])

Again, this is a salutary correction to the conceptions of cognition that these theorists are arguing against. We should note, however, how closely their conception of situated cognition parallels this description of *bricolage* by the structuralist Levi-Strauss (1962/1966):

> The "bricoleur" is adept at performing a large number of diverse tasks; but, unlike the engineer, . . . his universe of instruments is closed and the rules of his game are always to make do with "whatever is at hand," that is to say with a set of tools and materials which is always finite and is also heterogeneous because what it contains . . . is the contingent result of all the occasions there have been to renew or enrich the stock or to maintain it with the remains of previous constructions or destructions. (p. 17)

The parallel between bricolage and situated cognition theory is more than a superficial coincidence of language,[7] and the relationship between bricolage and Saussure's structuralist theory of signs is also more than coincidental.[8]

One consequence of the way "bricolage" has been defined in contradistinction to "science" or "engineering" is that the bricoleur is concerned only with an instrumental or functional adequacy in responding to technical problems with the set of tools and materials at hand in the immediate situation,

---

[7]See Turkle and Papert (1991) for an explicit use of "bricolage" in arguing for a situated "constructionist" approach to human cognition. Compare also Berry and Irvine (1986). Levi-Strauss' concept of bricolage is probably best known to cognitive psychologists through Gardner (1981). It is more familiar to folks in literary studies and philosophy through sources such as Derrida (1966/1978).

[8]Compare Levi-Strauss (1962/1966)

> It would be impossible to separate percepts from the concrete situations in which they appeared, while recourse to concepts would require that thought could, at least provisionally, put its projects (to use Husserl's expression) "in brackets." Now, there is an intermediary between images and concepts, namely signs. For signs can always be defined in the way introduced by Saussure in the case of the particular category of linguistic signs, that is, as a link between images and concepts. In the union thus brought about, images and concepts play the part of the signifying and signified respectively. (p. 18)

and stops short of any critical questioning of the general situation within which that situation is embedded. "It might be said that the engineer questions the universe, while the 'bricoleur' addresses himself to a collection of oddments left over from human endeavors, that is, only a subset of the culture" (Levi-Strauss, 1962/1966, p. 19).

Levi-Strauss was explicit in relating his distinction between bricoleurs and engineers or scientists back to the more fundamental Saussurean way of distinguishing between "concepts" and "signs."[9] I see these as examples of the kind of articulations in which oppressive hegemonic discourse is sustained. Unfortunately, I see potential articulations between "JPFs" and others as risking such assimilation to the hegemonic discourse. Levi-Strauss admitted that, in reality, the actual working conditions of scientists and engineers put them in a position much more like that of bricoleurs than is recognized in their idealized definitions; but he did not talk about occasions for his bricoleurs also to question the universe. In the same way (as we are reminded by Pea, 1990), we cannot presume that JPFs are only interested in functionally satisfying the demands of their immediate situations, or that they have no more than such functionalist expectations for their own schooling or the education of their children.

As Lave (1992) explained:

> We might not want to take the study of learning to be first and foremost the study of knowledge people are acquiring, though theories of learning have traditionally been based in epistemological analysis, in the philosophy of knowledge and knowing, hence on conceptions of the knowing, contemplating, (representing, problem solving . . .) person. In contrast, learning, viewed as socially situated activity, must be grounded in a social ontology that conceives of the person as an acting being, engaged in activity in the world. Learning is, in this purview, more basically a process of coming to *be*, of forging identities in activity in the world.
>
> In short, learners are never only that, but are becoming certain sorts of subjects with certain ways of participating in the world. (p. 3)

---

[9]Both the scientist and the "bricoleur" might therefore be said to be constantly on the look out for "messages." Those which the "bricoleur" collects are, however, ones which have to some extent been transmitted in advance—like the commercial codes which are summaries of the past experience of the trade and so allow any new situation to be met economically, provided that it belongs to the same class as some earlier one. The scientist, on the other hand, whether he is an engineer or a physicist, is always on the look out for *that other message* which might be wrested from an interlocutor [i.e., "nature" or "the universe"] in spite of his reticence in pronouncing on questions whose answers have not been rehearsed. Concepts thus appear like operators *opening up* the set [of intellectual and material resources] being worked with and signification [i.e., "signs," as opposed to "concepts"] like the operator of its *reorganization*, which neither extends nor renews it and limits itself to obtaining the group of its transformations. (Lévi-Strauss, 1962/1966, p. 20)

The fact that our own personal and social beings are formed within our semiosic activity precludes us from determining such activity exclusively according to the measure of prespecified instrumental or functional requirements of absolutely local situations, as if those situations were inhabited by beings whose identities and related needs, interests, and concerns were fully given in advance. This is one basic principle in the distinction between "technical" and "practical" activities and capabilities, which is taken up by Walkerdine and Lave in their ongoing efforts to help us understand "cognitive" activities within the social practices in which they are embedded.

Referring to the work of Bourdieu and others, Lave (1988) provided a needed warning against falling back on overly humanist theories of practice that neglect the processes and relationships that escape our consciousness and our control. I think Bourdieu (e.g., 1972/1977, 1980/1990) is right in his expectation that phenomenologically intentional activity takes place within the broader scope of processes and structures that we are generally unaware of, and over which we exercise no conscious control. However, the capability of triadic sign activity to modify itself on the basis of ongoing results also extends beyond the limits of our conscious subjectivity. This provides a basis for critical reflection in our cognitive activity that, although always situated, enables some transcendence of that very situation. In this and other ways, I believe that a Peircean semiotic framework has something to offer in our quest to understand human cognition as processes and achievements of situated social practices.

REFERENCES

The American Heritage Dictionary of the English Language (3rd ed.). (1992). Boston: Houghton Mifflin.

Bereiter, C. (1991). Implications of connectionism for thinking about rules. *Educational Researcher, 20*(3), 10–16.

Berry, J. W., & Irvine, S. H. (1986). Bricolage: Savages do it daily. In R. J. Sternberg & R. K. Wagner (Eds.), *Practical intelligence: Nature and origins of competence in the everyday world* (pp. 271–306). Cambridge, UK: Cambridge University Press.

Bourdieu, P. (1977). *Outline of a theory of practice* (R. Nice, Trans.). Cambridge, UK: Cambridge University Press. (Original work published 1972)

Bourdieu, P. (1990). *The logic of practice* (R. Nice, Trans.). Stanford, CA: Stanford University Press. (Original work published 1980)

Brown, J. S., Collins, A., & Duguid, P. (1989a). Situated cognition and the culture of learning. *Educational Researcher, 18*(1), 32–42.

Brown, J. S., Collins, A., & Duguid, P. (1989b). Debating the situation: A rejoinder to Palincsar and Wineburg. *Educational Researcher, 18*(4), 10–12, 62.

Clancey, W. J., & Roschelle, J. (1991, April). *Situated cognition: How representations are created and given meaning.* Paper presented at the meeting of the American Educational Research Association, Chicago.

Cussins, A. (1988). *The connectionist construction of concepts.* (SSL Research Report). Palo Alto, CA: Xerox Palo Alto Research Center.

Cussins, A. (1990). The connectionist construction of concepts. In M. A. Boden (Ed.), *The philosophy of artificial intelligence* (pp. 368–440). Oxford, UK: Oxford University Press.

Deledalle, G. (1992). Peirce's "sign": Its concept and its use. *Transaction of the Charles S. Peirce Society, 28*(2), 289–301.

Derrida, J. (1976). *Of grammatology* (G. Spivak, Trans. and preface). Baltimore: Johns Hopkins University Press. (Original work published 1967)

Derrida, J. (1978). Structure, sign and play in the discourse of the human sciences. In J. Derrida (Ed.), *Writing and difference* (A. Bass, Trans.) (pp. 278–293). Chicago: University of Chicago Press.

Dreyfus, H. L., Dreyfus, S. E., & with Athanasiou, T. (1986). *Mind over machine: The power of human intuition and expertise in the era of the computer.* New York: The Free Press.

Gardner, H. (1981). *The quest for mind: Piaget, Lévi-Strauss, and the structuralist movement* (2nd ed.). Chicago: University of Chicago Press. (Original work published 1972)

Gee, J. P. (1992). *The social mind: Language, ideology, and social practice.* Hadley, MA: Bergin & Garvey.

Greimas, A. J., & Cortés, J. (1982). *Semiotics and language: An analytical dictionary* (L. Crist, D. Patte, & others, Trans.). Bloomington: Indiana University Press. (Original work published 1979)

Hardwick, C. S. (Ed). (1977). *Semiotics and significs: The correspondence between Charles S. Peirce and Victoria Lady Welby.* Bloomington: Indiana University Press.

Heidegger, M. (1962). *Being and time* (J. Macquarrie & E. Robinson, Trans.). New York: Harper & Row. (Original work published 1927)

Henriques, J., Hollway, W., Urwin, C. V., & Walkerdine, V. (1984). *Changing the subject: Psychology, social regulation and subjectivity.* London: Methuen.

Holdcroft, D. (1991). *Saussure: Signs, system, and arbitrariness.* Cambridge, UK: Cambridge University Press.

Jenkins, J. J. (1974). Rember that old theory of memory? *Well, forget it! American Psychologist, 29*(11), 785–795.

Johnson, M. (1987). *The body in the mind: The bodily basis of meaning, imagination, and reason.* Chicago: The University of Chicago Press.

Lakoff, G. (1987). *Women, fire, and dangerous things: What categories reveal about the mind.* Chicago: University of Chicago Press.

Lave, J. (1988). *Cognition in practice.* Cambridge, UK: Cambridge University Press.

Lave, J. (1992, April). *Learning as participation in communities of practice.* Paper presented at the meeting of the American Educational Research Association, San Francisco.

Lave, J., & Wenger, E. (1991). *Situated learning: Legitimate peripheral participation.* Cambridge, UK: Cambridge University Press.

Levi-Strauss, C. (1966). *The savage mind* (G. Weidenfeld, Trans.). Chicago: University of Chicago Press. (Original work published 1962)

Merrell, F. (1992). *Sign, textuality, world.* Bloomington: Indiana University Press.

Palincsar, A. S. (1989). Debating the situation: A rejoinder to Palincsar and Wineburg. *Educational Researcher, 18*(4), 5–7.

Pea, R. D. (1990). Inspecting everyday mathematics: Reexamining culture-cognition relations [Review of *Cognition in practice: Mind, mathematics, and culture in everyday life* and *Culture and cognitive development: Studies in mathematical understanding*]. *Educational Researcher, 19*(4), 28–31.

Peirce, C. S. (1931–1935). *Collected papers of Charles Sanders Peirce* (Vols. 1–6, C. Hartshorne, & P. Weiss, Eds.). Cambridge, MA: Harvard University Press.

Petrie, H. (1992, March). The *Holmes Group Forum, 6*(3), 19-20 (e-mail correspondence to Kathleen Devaney, February 27, 1992).

Roschelle, J., & Clancey, W. J. (1992, May). *Learning as social and neural.* Revised version of a paper presented at the meeting of the American Educational Research Association, Chicago.

Saussure, F. de (1959). *Course in general linguistics* (C. Bally & A. Sechehaye, with A. Reidlinger, Eds.; W. Baskin, Trans.). New York: Philosophical Library. (Original work published 1916)

Saussure, F. de (1968). *Cours de linguistique générale [Course in general linguistics]* (Critical Edition by R. Engler, Ed.). New York: Philosophical Library. (Original work published 1916)

Saussure, F. de (1986). *Course in general linguistics* (C. Bally & A. Sechehaye, with A. Reidlinger, Eds.; R. Harris, Trans.). La Salle, IL: Open Court. (Original work published 1916)

Saxe, G. B. (1990). *Culture and cognitive development: Studies in mathematical understanding.* Hillsdale, NJ: Lawrence Erlbaum Associates.

Scribner, S. (1984). Studying working intelligence. In B. Rogoff & J. Lave (Eds.), *Everday cognition: Its development in social context* (pp. 9–40). Cambridge, MA: Harvard University Press.

Scribner, S. (1986). Thinking in action: Some characteristics of practical thought. In R. J. Sternberg & R. K. Wagner (Eds.), *Practical intelligence: Nature and origins of competence in the everyday world* (pp. 13–30). Cambridge, MA: Cambridge University Press.

Short, T. L. (1981). Semeiosis and intentionality. *Transactions of the C. S. Peirce Society, 17*(3), 197–223.

Toulmin, S. (1972). *Human understanding: The collective use and evolution of concepts.* Princeton, NJ: Princeton University Press.

Turkle, S., & Papert, S. (1991). Epistemological pluralism and the revaluation of the concrete. In I. Harel & S. Papert (Eds.), *Constructionism* (pp. 161–191). Norwood, NJ: Ablex.

Walden, R., & Walkerdine, V. (1983). *Girls and mathematics: From primary to secondary schooling.* London: Heineman.

Walkerdine, V. (1988). *The mastery of reason: Cognitive development and the production of rationality.* London: Routledge.

Walkerdine, V. (1990). *Schoolgirl fictions.* London: Verso.

Walkerdine, V. (1992, April). *Girls and schooling: Regulating gendered subjectivity in the curriculum.* Presentation at the College of Education, Louisiana State University, Baton Rouge.

Walkerdine, V., & The Girls and Mathematics Unit. (1989). *Counting girls out.* London: Virago.

Whitson, J. A. (1991a). *Constitution and curriculum: Hermeneutical semiotics of cases and controversies in education, law, and social science.* London: Falmer.

Whitson, J. A. (1991b). Post-structuralist pedagogy as counter-hegemonic praxis (Can we find the baby in the bathwater?). *Education and Society, 9*(1–2), 73–86

Wineburg, S. S. (1989). Remembrance of theories past. *Educational Researcher, 18*(4), 7–10.

Winograd, T., & Flores, F. (1987). *Understanding computers and cognition: A new foundation for design.* Reading, MA: Addison-Wesley.

Mathematizing and Symbolizing: The Emergence of Chains of Signification in One First-Grade Classroom

Paul Cobb
Vanderbilt University

Koeno Gravemeijer
Freudenthal Institute

Erna Yackel
Purdue University Calumet

Kay McClain
Vanderbilt University

Joy Whitenack
University of Missouri

The contention that knowing and doing mathematics is an inherently social and cultural activity has gained increasing acceptance in recent years. At least in the United States, this attempt to go beyond purely cognitive analyses reflects a growing disillusionment with mainstream psychology (Brown, Collins, & Duguid, 1989; Greeno, 1991; Schoenfeld, 1987). The theoretical basis for this position is inspired to a considerable extent by the work of Vygotsky and that of activity theorists such as Davydov, Leont'ev, and Galperin (Nunes, 1992). A second research tradition that also questions the adequacy of purely cognitive analyses of learning derives from symbolic interactionism (Blumer, 1969) and ethnomethodology (Mehan & Wood, 1975) as they have been developed for mathematics education (Bauersfeld, Krummheuer, & Voigt, 1988). In both these lines of research, social and cultural influences are not restricted to the process of learning, but are instead seen to extend to its products; increasingly sophisticated mathematical ways of knowing. Consequently, adherents to both positions reject the view that social interaction merely serves as a catalyst for otherwise autonomous cognitive development.

In their view, students' mathematical activity is social through and through and cannot be adequately understood unless it is placed in social and cultural context.

The primary difference between the two research traditions concerns the relative emphasis given to individual cognition and to collective communal practices. As a matter of course, researchers working in the sociocultural tradition initiated by Vygotsky give priority to social and cultural processes when accounting for an individual's mathematical activity (Kozulin, 1990; Wertsch, 1985). Thus, as Vygotsky (1979) himself put it, "the social dimension of consciousness is primary in time and in fact. The individual dimension of consciousness is derivative and secondary" (p. 30). From this perspective, the link between social and cultural processes and individual development is a direct one. Students' mathematical conceptions are said to be directly derived from or generated by interpersonal relations and their use of cultural tools (cf. Forman, 1996; Minick, 1987; van Oers, 1990). Analyses conducted in this tradition therefore leave little room for psychological approaches, such as constructivism, that focus on the individual.

The second of the two research traditions has elsewhere been called an emergent perspective (Cobb, Jaworski, & Presmeg, 1996). In this approach, individual thought and social and cultural processes are considered to be reflexively related, with neither attributed absolute priority over the other. Thus, if individual thought is social through and through, then social processes can be seen to be cognitive through and through. In this formulation, individual mathematical activity is seen to be necessarily socially and culturally situated. However, adherents to the emergent perspective treat the linkage between social and cultural processes and individual psychological processes as an indirect one (cf. Saxe & Bermudez, 1996; Voigt, 1994). Thus, they might talk of students' participation in particular cultural practices enabling and constraining their mathematical development, but not determining it. This approach therefore admits constructivist analyses of individual students' activity. However, it seeks to coordinate such analyses with analyses of the social and cultural processes in which the students participate and to which they contribute (cf. Balacheff, 1990a; De Corte, Greer, & Verschaffel, 1996; Hatano, 1993). The extent to which either a psychological or a social analysis is brought to the fore in any particular situation is a pragmatic issue that reflects the purposes at hand.

In summary, the sociocultural perspective treats mathematical learning as primarily a process of enculturation wherein students appropriate their intellectual inheritance; that is, the mathematical ways of knowing institutionalized by wider society. In contrast, the emergent perspective treats mathematical learning as both a process of active individual construction and a process of enculturation. The analysis presented in this chapter was conducted from this latter perspective and attempts to account for the developments that occurred in one U.S. first-grade classroom during mathematics instruction over a 3-month period. Our reasons for conducting the analysis were motivated by both theoretical and pragmatic concerns. Theoretically, we wanted to explore ways of accounting for students' mathematical development as it occurs in the social situation of the classroom. To this end, we describe the evolution of the mathematical practices established by the classroom community and consider the mathematical learning of individual children as they participated in and contributed to the development of these practices. In addition, we give particular attention to symbolizing as a central aspect of both these practices and individual children's activity. A notion that proved to be particularly useful in this regard was that of a chain of signification (Walkerdine, 1988; chapter 4, this volume). Pragmatically, the analysis constitutes a phase of an ongoing developmental research effort. The data were in fact collected during a year-long teaching experiment conducted in collaboration with the first-grade teacher. As a consequence, the conclusions arrived at in the course of the analysis feed back to inform our future work in classrooms. We take the specific implications of the analysis as a paradigm case to clarify the relation between the two general aspects of the research cycle, instructional development, and analyses of teaching experiments.

In the following pages, we first orient the reader by locating the analysis in the context of our prior research. To this end, we first outline the general framework used to interpret classroom events and discuss the instructional theory that guided the development of the instructional activities used in the teaching experiment. Next, we elaborate this framework as we document aspects of the classroom microculture and delineate both individual students' development and the evolution of classroom mathematical practices. In the final section of the chapter, we then step back to locate the analysis in a broader theoretical context by comparing and contrasting the approach taken with both sociocultural theory and theories of distributed cognition or distributed intelligence.

THEORETICAL ORIENTATION

Interpretive Framework

Against the background of our prior work, the analysis we present can be viewed as an elaboration of the interpretive framework outlined in Fig. 8.1. This framework originally grew out of our attempts to help a number of U.S. elementary school teachers radically revise their instructional practices. Consequently, although the framework is empirically grounded in this sense, the only claim we would make about it is that we have found it useful when attempting to support change at the classroom level. We therefore eschew the

Social Perspective	Psychological Perspective
Classroom social norms	Beliefs about own role, others' roles, and the general nature of mathematical activity in school
Sociomathematical norms	Mathematical beliefs and values
Classroom mathematical practices	Mathematical interpretations and activity

FIG. 8.1. An interpretive framework for analyzing the classroom microculture.

essentialist implication that the framework might somehow capture the structure of the classroom mathematical microculture independently of situation and purpose.

As a second caveat, it should be noted that the purview of the framework is restricted to what might be called the box of the classroom. Thus, explanations of classroom events developed in terms of the framework do not make reference to practices or institutions at the school or societal levels. This is not, of course, to deny the pervasive influence of both institutional arrangements at the school level and beyond, and of students' participation in a diverse range of out-of-school practices. However, we do contend that, for many purposes, it is sufficient to restrict the explanatory focus to social interactions and individual interactions located at the classroom level. For other purposes, it might well be essential to augment the framework, perhaps as shown in Fig. 8.2. Analyses in which we have found it necessary to go

Social Perspective	Psychological Perspective
General societal norms	Beliefs about what constitutes normal or natural development in mathematics
General school norms	Conception of the child in school— beliefs about own and others' role in school
Classroom social norms	Beliefs about own role, others' roles, and general nature of mathematics in school
Sociomathematical norms	Mathematical beliefs and values
Classroom mathematical practices	Mathematical conceptions

FIG. 8.2. Possible augmentation of the interpretive framework.

beyond the box of the classroom are reported by Yackel and Cobb (1993) and Yang and Cobb (1995).

In Fig. 8.1, the column heads Social Perspective and Psychological Perspective signify a focus on communal or collective classroom processes, and on individual students' activity as they participate in such processes. As we have noted, these individual and communal processes are considered to be reflexively related in an emergent approach. In the following paragraphs, we outline the framework by discussing social norms, then sociomathematical norms, and finally classroom mathematical practices.

Social Norms. In the course of our research, we, together with Terry Wood, have conducted a series of year-long classroom teaching experiments in collaboration with first-, second-, and third-grade teachers of 6-, 7-, and 8-year-old students. The social arrangements in these prior experiments typically involved small-group collaborative activity followed by whole-class discussions of students' interpretations and solutions. At the beginning of the first of these experiments conducted during the 1986 to 1987 school year, it soon became apparent that the teacher's expectation that students would verbalize how they had interpreted and attempted to solve tasks ran counter to their previous experiences of class discussions in school. The students had been in traditional classrooms in the previous school year and had typically been steered toward officially sanctioned solution methods during discussions. As a consequence, the students took it for granted that they were to infer what the teacher had in mind rather than to articulate their own understandings. The teacher with whom we collaborated coped with this conflict between her own and the students' expectations by initiating the renegotiation of classroom social norms. This process has been documented in some detail elsewhere (Cobb, Yackel, & Wood, 1989). For our current purposes, it suffices to note that the social norms for whole-class discussions that became explicit topics of conversation included explaining and justifying solutions, attempting to make sense of explanations given by others, indicating agreement and disagreement, and questioning alternatives in situations where a conflict in interpretations or solutions had become apparent. In many respects, an analysis of classroom social norms teases out what Erickson (1986) and Lampert (1990) called the classroom participation structure.

As indicated in Fig. 8.1, we take the teacher's and students' individual beliefs about their own role, others' roles, and the general nature of mathematical activity in the classroom to be the psychological correlates of classroom social norms. An analysis of social norms focuses on regularities in classroom social interactions that, from the observer's perspective, constitute the grammar of classroom life (cf. Voigt, 1985, 1996). Such an analysis treats these regularities as manifestations of consensual ways of knowing (Gergen, 1985). However, when the interactions are viewed from a psychological perspective that focuses on the teacher's and students' interpretations of their own and others' activity, it becomes apparent that there are differences in their individual beliefs. From this perspective, the most that can be said when interactions proceed smoothly is that the teacher's and students' beliefs fit in that each acts in accord with the other's expectations (Bauersfeld, 1988; von Glasersfeld, 1984). In psychological terms, renegotiations of social norms occurred in project classrooms when there was a lack of fit—when either the teacher's or a student's expectations were not fulfilled. In sociological terms, these renegotiations occurred when there was a perceived breach of a social norm (Much & Shweder, 1978). It was by capitalizing on such breaches that the teacher and, to an increasing extent, the students initiated the renegotiation of social norms and, in the process, influenced others' beliefs. These beliefs in turn found expression in their individual interpretations of situations that arose in the course of social interactions. This relationship between social norms and beliefs can be summarized by saying that individual interpretations that fit together constitute the social norms that both enable and constrain the individual interpretations that generate them. Such an account instantiates the reflexive relationship between the communal culture and individual experience of, and action in, the lived-in world (cf. Lave, 1988).

Sociomathematical Norms.   In considering the second aspect of the classroom microculture shown in Fig. 8.1, it can be noted that the classroom norms discussed thus far are not specific to mathematics, but instead apply to almost any subject matter area. For example, one would hope that students will challenge each other's thinking and justify their own interpretations in science and literature lessons as well as in mathematics lessons. As a consequence, it is also necessary to analyze normative aspects of whole-class discussions that are specific to students' mathematical activity (Voigt, 1995; Yackel & Cobb, 1996). Examples of such sociomathematical norms include what counts as a different solution, a sophisticated solution, an efficient solution, and an acceptable solution.

As part of the process of guiding the development of an inquiry mathematics microculture in their classrooms, the teachers with whom we have worked regularly asked the students if anyone had solved as task a different way and then explicitly rejected contributions that they did not consider mathematically different. It was while analyzing classroom interactions in these situations that sociomathematical norms first emerged as a focus of interest. The analysis indicated that, on the one hand, the students did not know what would constitute a mathematical difference until the teacher accepted some of their contributions, but not others. Consequently, in responding to the teacher's request for a different solution, the students were simultaneously learning what counts as a mathematical difference and helping to interactively constitute what counts as a mathematical difference in their classroom. On the other hand, the teachers in these classrooms were themselves attempting to develop an inquiry form of practice and had not, in their prior years of teaching, asked students to explain their thinking. Consequently, the experiential basis from which they attempted to anticipate students' contributions was extremely limited. They therefore had to respond to the students' contributions even though they had not consciously decided what constituted a mathematical difference. Thus, as was the case with general classroom norms, the negotiation of this (and of other) sociomathematical norms was not consciously planned by the teachers but instead emerged in the course of joint activity (Yackel & Cobb, 1996).

The analysis of this and other sociomathematical norms has pragmatic significance in that it clarifies the process by which teachers foster the development of intellectual autonomy in their classrooms. In this account, the conception of autonomy as a context-free characteristic of the individual is rejected. Instead, autonomy is defined with respect to students' participation in the practices of the classroom community. In particular, students who are intellectually autonomous in mathematics can draw on their own intellectual resources to make mathematical decisions and judgments as they participate in these practices. These students can be contrasted with those who are intellectually heteronomous and who rely on the pronouncements of an authority to know how to participate appropriately in the activities of the classroom community (Kamii, 1985; Piaget, 1973). As part of the process of supporting the growth of intellectual autonomy, the teacher guides the development of a community of validators by encouraging the devolution of responsibility (Brousseau, 1984). However, students can only take over these responsibilities to the extent that they have developed personal ways of judging that enable them to know-in-action both when it is appropriate to make a mathematical contribution and what constitutes an acceptable contribution. This requires, among other things, that students can judge what counts as a different solution, an insightful solution, an efficient solution, and an acceptable explanation. But these are the types of judgments that the teacher and students negotiate when establishing sociomathematical norms. We therefore contend that the students construct the specifically mathematical beliefs and values that enable them to act as increasingly autonomous members of a classroom mathematics community as they participate in the renegotiation of sociomathematical norms (Yackel & Cobb, 1996).

Classroom Mathematical Practices. The third aspect of the classroom microculture shown in Fig. 8.1 concerns the taken-as-shared mathematical practices established by the classroom community. This is the most underdeveloped part of the framework and one of our primary concerns when we present the analysis of the first-grade classroom. For the present, we follow

Balacheff's (1990b) suggestion that classroom mathematical practices evolve as the teacher and students discuss situations, problems, and solutions, and that they involve means of symbolizing, arguing, and validating. As an example, solution methods that involved counting by ones were established mathematical practices at the beginning of the school year in the second-grade classrooms in which we worked. Further, some of the students in these classes were able to develop solutions that involved the conceptual creation of units of 10 and of ones. However, when they did so, they were usually obliged to explain and justify their interpretations of number words and numerals. Later in the school year, solutions based on such interpretations were taken as self-evident by these classroom communities. The activity of interpreting number words and numerals in this way had been institutionalized as a classroom mathematical practice that was beyond justification. From the students' point of view, numbers were simply composed of tens and ones—it had become an established mathematical truth.

We take individual students' mathematical interpretations and activities to be the psychological correlates of classroom mathematical practices. In the case of the example, our analyses suggest that the students actively developed increasingly sophisticated numerical interpretations by curtailing and interiorizing their activity of counting by ones. However, these developments did not arise in vacua. They were not isolated, solo achievements, but instead occurred as the students participated in the classroom mathematical practices. Conversely, the evolution of those practices was made possible by and did not occur apart from the students' reorganization of their individual activities. It is for this reason that we consider individual students' mathematical learning and the development of classroom mathematical practices to be reflexively related. In this formulation, they are different sides of the same coin that reflect the observer's focus on the individual and on the collective respectively. Thus, as Whitson (chapter 7, this volume) puts it, there are only human processes that can be analyzed in terms of their psychological or social aspects, moments, or elements.

The reason for distinguishing between the psychological and social stances taken by the observer becomes apparent when we note that there are typically significant differences in individual students' mathematical interpretations even as they and the teacher participate in an established mathematical practice. In the case of the example, both classroom observations and individual interviews indicate that, despite the apparent unanimity, there were qualitative differences in individual students' numerical interpretations (Cobb, Wood, & Yackel, 1993). Thus, from the observer's perspective, the students' numerical interpretations were not necessarily shared, but instead fit, or were compatible, for the purposes at hand in that the students were able to communicate effectively without these differences becoming apparent. Each student assumed that his or her interpretation was shared by the others, and nothing occurred in the course of ongoing interactions that led the student to question this assumption (cf. Schutz, 1962).

The example of the shift from counting by one to creating units of ten and one is representative of our previous work in that it addresses only global changes in classroom mathematical practices. The challenge of accounting for mathematical development as it occurs in the social situation of the classroom requires that we identify changes in classroom mathematical practices at a more microscopic level. In doing so, it will be necessary to focus explicitly on the development of means of symbolizing as integral aspects of both classroom mathematical practices and individual children's activity. This issue is particularly critical in that ways of symbolizing play a central role in the domain-specific instructional theory that guided the development of the instructional activities used in the teaching experiment.

Instructional Development

The motivation for developing the interpretive framework we have described was primarily theoretical. Such work does have practical relevance in that analyses of classroom events or of individual students' mathematical activity typically lead to suggestions for educational improvement. However, it does not yield positive heuristics that can guide the development of instructional activities for students. In this regard, we have found it essential to draw on the theory of Realistic Mathematics Education (RME) developed at the Freudenthal Institute in the Netherlands.

It should be stressed that RME developed independently of the interpretive framework and of the encompassing emergent perspective. The compatibility between this theoretical perspective and RME is based in large part on similar characterizations of mathematics and mathematics learning. Both contend that mathematics is a creative human activity and that mathematical learning occurs as students develop effective ways to solve problems and cope with situations (Gravemeijer, 1994a; Streefland, 1991; Treffers, 1987). Further, both propose that mathematical development involves the bringing forth of a mathematical reality (Freudenthal, 1991). In sociological terms, this is a process of enculturation into a historically evolving interpretive stance (cf. Greeno, 1991; Saxe & Bermudez, 1996). In psychological terms, it involves the internalization and interiorization of activity via a process of reflective abstraction so that the results of activity can then be anticipated and activity itself becomes an entity that can be conceptually manipulated (Sfard, 1991; Thompson, 1996; von Glasersfeld, 1991).

One of the central tenets of RME is that the starting points of instructional sequences should be experientially real to students in the sense that they can immediately engage in personally meaningful mathematical activity (Gravemeijer, 1990; Streefland, 1991). In this regard, Thompson (1992) noted from the emergent perspective that "if students do not become engaged imaginistically in the ways that relate mathematical reasoning to principled experience, then we have little reason to believe that they will come to see their worlds outside of school as in any way mathematical" (p. 10). This tenet can also be seen to be consistent with the recommendations derived from investigations that have compared and contrasted mathematical activity in the classroom with that in out-of-school situations (Nunes, Schliemann, & Carraher, 1993; Saxe, 1991). As a point of clarification, it should be stressed that the term *experientially real* means only that the starting points should be experienced as real by the students, not that they should necessarily involve realistic situations. Thus, arithmetic tasks presented by using conventional notation might be experientially real for students for whom the whole numbers are mathematical objects. Further, we take it as self-evident that even when everyday scenarios are used as starting points, they necessarily differ from the situations as students might experience them out of school (Lave, 1993; Walkerdine, 1988). To account for students' learning, it is therefore essential to delineate the scenario as it is interactively constituted for pedagogical purposes in the classroom with the teacher's guidance.

A second tenet of RME is that in addition to taking account of students' current mathematical ways of knowing, the starting points should also be justifiable in terms of the potential endpoints of the learning sequence. This implies that students' initially informal mathematical activity should constitute a basis from which they can abstract and develop increasingly sophisticated mathematical interpretations as they participate in classroom mathematical practices. At the same time, the starting point situations should continue to function as paradigm cases that involve rich imagery and, thus, anchor students' increasingly abstract mathematical activity. This latter requirement is consistent with analyses that emphasize the important role that analogies (Clement & Brown, 1989), metaphors (Dörfler, 1991; Pimm, 1987; Presmeg, 1992; Sfard, 1994), intuitions (Fischbein, 1987, 1989), and generic organizers (Tall, 1989) play in mathematical activity.

In dealing with the starting points and potential endpoints, the first two tenets of RME hint at tension that is endemic to mathematics teaching. Thus, Ball (1993) observed that recent U.S. proposals for educational reform "are replete with notions of 'understanding' and 'community'—about building bridges between the experiences of the child and the knowledge of the expert" (p. 374). She then inquired, "*How* do I [as a mathematics teacher] create experiences for my students that connect with what they now know and care about but that also transcend the present? *How* do I value their interests and also connect them to ideas and traditions growing out of centuries of mathematical exploration and invention" (p. 375)?

RME's attempt to cope with this tension is embodied in a third tenet wherein it is argued that instructional sequences should involve activities in which students create and elaborate symbolic models of their informal mathematical activity. This modeling activity might involve making drawings, diagrams, or tables, or it could involve developing informal notations or using conventional mathematical notations. This third tenet is based on the psychological conjecture that, with the teacher's guidance, students' models of their informal mathematical activity can evolve into models for increasingly abstract mathematical reasoning (Gravemeijer, 1991). Dörfler (1989) made a similar proposal when he discussed the role of symbolic protocols of action in enabling reflection on and analysis of mathematical activity. Similarly, Kaput (in press) suggested that such records and notations might support the taking of activities or processes as entities that can be compared and can come to possess general properties. To the extent that this occurs, students' models would eventually provide what Kaput (1991) termed semantic guidance rather than syntactic guidance. In sociological terms, this third tenet implies a shift in classroom mathematical practices such that means of symbolizing initially developed to express informal mathematical activity take on a life of their own and are subsequently used to support more formal mathematical activity in a range of situations.

It can be noted that this third tenet of RME is consistent with Sfard's (1991) historical analysis of several mathematical concepts, including number and function. In line with the emergent approach, Sfard contended that the historical development of mathematics can be seen as a long sequence of reifications, each of which involves the transformation of operational or process conceptions into objectlike structural conceptions. However, she stressed that the development of ways of symbolizing has been integral to the reification process both historically and in students' conceptual development. Thus, although she is careful to clarify that the development and use of symbols is by itself insufficient for reification, she and Linchevski (1994) contended that mathematical symbols are manipulable in a way that words are not. In a similar vein, Bednarz, Dufour-Janvier, Poirier, and Bacon (1993) and van Oers (1996) both argued that, historically, the struggle for mathematical meaning can be seen in large part as a struggle for means of symbolizing.[1]

The third tenet suggests a possible point of contact with Vygotsky's sociohistorical theory of development. Semiotic mediation and the use of cultural tools such as mathematical symbols constitutes one of the two mechanisms that Vygotsky contended drives conceptual development, the other being interpersonal relations (Cole & Engestrom, 1993; Confrey, 1995; Vygotsky, 1934/1987). The primary difference between the emergent ap-

---

[1]We speak of symbolizing to stress that our focus is on the actual, concrete use of symbols for some purpose. In this regard, we follow Nemirovsky (1994) in distinguishing between symbol system and symbol use. A symbol system refers to the semantic and syntactic analysis of mathematical representations in terms rules. In contrast, "symbol-use [or symbolizing] is embedded in personal intentions, in specific histories, and in the qualities of a situation" (Nemirovsky, 1994).

proach and RME on the one hand and Vygotskian theory on the other concerns the underlying metaphor used to characterize learning in instructional situations. In Vygotskian theory, the central metaphor is that of the transmission of mathematical meaning from one generation to the next. Within this perspective, symbols are sometimes called carriers of meaning and are treated as primary vehicles of the enculturation process (van Oers, 1996). This metaphor does not, of course, imply a crude transmission view of communication. Instead, the fundamental claim is that students develop particular mathematical conceptions as they learn to use conventional symbols while engaging in particular sociocultural activities (Davydov, 1988). In this scheme, the teacher's role is frequently characterized as that of relating students' personal meanings to the cultural meanings inherent in the appropriate use of conventional symbols. The teacher's role might therefore be characterized as that of introducing conventional means of symbolizing and relating them to students' mathematical activity (cf. Forman, 1996; Tharp & Gallimore, 1988). An approach of this type can be characterized as top-down (Gravemeijer, in press), in that the teacher's role is framed as that of importing established cultural meanings into the classroom.

In contrast to the metaphor of transmission, the underlying metaphor in RME is that of the emergence of mathematical meaning in the classroom.[2] This metaphor is apparent in both the means of symbolizing developed in the classroom and in the characterization of the teacher's role. As is the case in Vygotskian approaches, RME acknowledges that the teacher is an institutionalized authority in the classroom. Further, the teacher might, on occasion, express this authority in action by introducing means of symbolizing as he or she redescribes students' contributions. However, as is apparent from the third tenet of RME, these means of symbolizing are not restricted to conventional mathematical symbols. In this approach, the instructional developer draws on both historical analyses and analyses of students' informal methods to invent means of symbolizing that students might see reason to use as they seek to achieve their mathematical goals (Gravemeijer, 1994a).

Instructional sequences therefore typically involve establishing nonstandard means of symbolizing that are designed both to fit with students' informal activity and to support their transition to more sophisticated forms of mathematical activity. These means are, in effect, offered to students as resources that they might use as they solve problems and communicate their thinking.

---

[2]It is important to differentiate the use of the emergence metaphor in the two aspects of the developmental research cycle—instructional development and classroom-based research. Developers working within RME use the metaphor as they engage in the first of these phases. In contrast, the previously discussed emergent perspective and associated interpretive framework refer to the second phase. Thus, although there is consistency between the two aspects, the events in any classroom can be analyzed in terms of emergence.

Crucially, students who engage in these ways of thinking are typically expected to explain their activity in terms of actions on mathematical objects.

This elaboration of the third tenet of RME clarifies that, in such an approach, ways of symbolizing are not construed as a means of bringing students into contact with established cultural meanings. Instead, they are considered to support the emergence of mathematical meaning in the classroom. To be sure, the teacher's and the instructional developer's understanding of the mathematical practices institutionalized by wider society provides a sense of directionality to this process of emergence. However, the basic metaphor is that of building up toward participation in these practices rather than bringing students into contact with cultural meanings. Within this scheme, the teacher's role is characterized as that of supporting the emergence of both individual and collective meanings. This entails guiding both the development of individual students' constructive activities and the evolution of classroom mathematical practices. Such an approach can legitimately be classified as bottom-up rather than top-down in that symbolic means are developed to support students' reconstruction of cultural meanings (Gravemeijer, 1994b).[3]

The contrast we have drawn between emergent and Vygotskian approaches should not mask our acceptance of Vygotsky's fundamental insight that semiotic mediation is crucially implicated in conceptual development (Vygotsky, 1981). As will become apparent, we also have considerable sympathy both with theories of distributed cognition (Dörfler, in press; Pea, 1987, 1993) and with van Oers' (1996) claim that the process of concept formation is synonymous with that of symbol formation. This gives rise to a significant theoretical challenge for us in that symbolizing frequently plays little, if any, role in emergent accounts of mathematical development (Kaput, 1991; Walkerdine, 1988). There are, of course, several notable exceptions to this generalization (e.g., Bednarz et al., 1993; Kaput, 1987; Mason, 1987; Nemirovsky, 1994; Pirie & Kieren, 1994; Sfard & Linchevski, 1994; Thompson, 1992). Nonetheless, semiotic mediation continues to be an underdeveloped theme. The issue is particularly pressing for us in light of the third tenet of RME. We, therefore, sought to elaborate the interpretive framework outlined in Fig. 8.1 when we analyzed events in the first-grade classroom.

THE FIRST-GRADE CLASSROOM

Ms. Smith's first-grade class was one of three first-grade classes at a private school in Nashville. The class consisted of 11 girls and 7 boys. The majority of the students were from middle to upper socioeconomic families. Most parents held professional occupations. There were no minority children in the classroom, although a small percentage attended the school. The students

---

[3]St. Julien's (chapter 10, this volume) example in which the reader is asked to distinguish eukaryotic and prokaryotic cells illustrates a bottom-up approach in science education.

in the class were representative of the school's general student population. Although not a Christian school, morals and values were part of the responsibility of schooling and children regularly participated in spiritual activities.

Ms. Smith was a highly motivated and very dedicated teacher in her fourth year of teaching, all at the first-grade level. She worked to create a learning environment that supported her students' learning and had developed very different teaching practices from most of the other teachers at the school. She voiced frustration with traditional mathematics textbooks and was attempting to reform her practice prior to our collaboration. She explained that her attempts to use a center approach had left her without the benefits of productive whole-class discussions. Although she highly valued students' ability to communicate, explain, and justify, Ms. Smith indicated that she had previously found it difficult to enact an instructional approach that both met her students' needs and enabled her to achieve her own pedagogical agenda. Nonetheless, her desire to change and her personal philosophy toward education were such that she constantly assessed both the instructional activities she used and her own practice. In addition, it soon became apparent that she had a relatively deep understanding of both first-graders' mathematical activity and the mathematical conceptions that constituted her instructional goals. She was therefore, in many respects, an atypical teacher.

THE DATA

During the school year, we developed four instructional sequences in collaboration with Ms. Smith. Video-recorded individual interviews were conducted with all the children in September, December, January, and May, and a total of 106 mathematics lessons were recorded using two cameras. During whole-class discussions, one camera focused primarily on Ms. Smith or on children who came to the whiteboard to explain their thinking. The second camera focused on the students as they engaged in discussions while sitting on the floor facing the whiteboard. Additional documentation consists of copies of all the children's written work and three sets of daily field notes that summarize classroom events.

The data selected for the analysis reported in this chapter comprise the January and May interviews and 54 lessons video-recorded during the second semester of the school year. During this part of the school year, approximately half the classroom time involved whole-class discussions in which the teacher posed tasks, frequently by using an overhead projector. The remaining time was devoted to either individual or small-group work, followed by whole-class discussions of students' interpretations, solutions, and ways of symbolizing. When they worked individually, the children were encouraged to solicit assistance from each other and to share their thinking.

The approach used to analyze a large, longitudinal data set of this type draws on Glaser and Strauss' (1967) constant comparison method and is discussed in some detail by Cobb and Whitenack (in press).

In presenting the analysis, we first document aspects of the classroom microculture by describing the social norms and sociomathematical norms established in Ms. Smith's classroom. We then briefly summarize the children's mathematical development during the first semester and, against this background, focus on the evolution of classroom mathematical practices during the second semester.

ASPECTS OF THE CLASSROOM MICROCULTURE

Classroom Social Norms

The classroom social norms were documented by analyzing video-recordings and transcripts of five whole-class discussions conducted on October 7, October 20, December 8, January 10, and April 13. The classroom participation structure was found to be remarkably consistent across these lessons. The field notes of three observers who made daily observations indicate that the five selected lessons are representative of the larger data corpus.

Normative aspects of whole-class discussions that were stable across the school year included:

1. The students were expected to explain and justify their reasoning. For the most part, they raised their hands to indicate that they wanted to make a contribution and waited for Ms. Smith to call on them. Further, although they were directed to speak to the entire class, they sometimes spoke to Ms. Smith, but in a voice loud enough for all to hear. When they gave explanations, they frequently began by speaking in the first person (e.g., "I thought about . . .", "I knew . . ."), thereby implying personal agency. Some completed their explanations in this voice, whereas others continued in more generic second-person terms (e.g., "if you had . . .", "then you take . . .").

2. On those occasions where a child's contribution was judged to be invalid in some way by the classroom community, Ms. Smith frequently intervened to clarify that this child had acted appropriately by attempting to explain his or her thinking. Further, Ms. Smith emphasized that such situations did not warrant embarrassment.

3. The children were expected to listen to and attempt to understand others' explanations. When children gave explanations, Ms. Smith directed them to speak loudly enough for all to hear. On occasion, she asked the listening students to raise their hands if they solved a task the same way or if an explanation made sense to them. From time to time, she sanctioned

students who did not appear to be participating as active listeners, typically by mentioning them by name.

4. Ms. Smith frequently commented on or redescribed children's contributions, sometimes noting their reasoning on the whiteboard or overhead projector as she did so. The children for their part were expected to reject redescriptions that did not, in their view, give an adequate account of their reasoning. Thus, although Ms. Smith expressed her institutionalized authority in action when she redescribed the children's solutions, the children were the authorities about their mathematical thinking.

As the following representative episode from January 10 illustrates, the social norms documented thus far frequently gave rise to a sequence of teacher–student–teacher–student turn-taking. In the episode, Ms. Smith referred to a picture of a cookie jar projected on the whiteboard as she posed a task corresponding to 8 + 9:

> There were eight cookies in the cookie jar [writes 8 in the jar] and then we put, we did that . . . we had eight cookies in the cookie jar and then we did this [writes +9 in a box she has drawn to the right of the jar.]

The episode begins as Jordan explains his answer of 17:

Jordan: See, I . . .
Teacher: (Interrupts) Say it louder because Jan says they're having trouble hearing you over there.
Jordan: See, I started with the 9 and then added the 8.
Teacher: You started with the 9 and then you added 8? Did you, did you count up to 8, is that what you did?
Jordan: By fours.
Teacher: OK. Thank you. Jordan said he did it by counting. . . . Did someone else figure it out a different way? Bob.
Bob: I knew if you took one, if you had 9 and then . . . plus 8 and then you took one away from the 8 and put it with the 9 and you would have 7 left and that would make 17.
Teacher: [Writes as Bob speaks]

$$9 + 8 = \underline{\quad}$$
$$\bigwedge$$
$$1 \quad 7$$

$$9 + 1 = 10$$
$$10 + 7 = 17$$

Karen:

Did you understand what Bob said? Did that make sense? [Students raise their hands.] Did someone do it a different way? Karen?

I knew that if 8 plus 8 was 16 and you have one more it would be 17.

Ms. Smith redescribed and notated this solution and that of the next child, who explained, "I thought about 9 plus 9 being 18, and if I had 8 plus 9 then that would be 17." This pattern of turn-taking was repeated as four more children explained different thinking strategy solutions.

Teacher:

One thing that y'all did . . . we have a whole bunch of different ways to figure out 8 plus 9. And what that says, that makes me think that you were listening while your friends were talking so you would know if your way was a different way or not or if your way was a way that someone else had already done it. It was important that you were listening to what your friends were saying.

Episodes frequently concluded with summary statements of this type in which Ms. Smith attempted to clarify her expectations for the students.

It is readily apparent that Ms. Smith regulated the turn-taking in this exchange. The primary occasion when the sequence of student explanation followed by teacher comment or redescription broke down was when students questioned explanations that they either did not understand or considered invalid. In making such interjections, students contributed to the establishment of two further classroom social norms:

5. Students were expected to indicate nonunderstanding and, if possible, to ask the explainer clarifying questions.

6. Students were expected to indicate when they considered solutions invalid, and to explain why they did not accept the solution.

In the following episode, which also occurred on January 10, Ms. Smith used the cookie jar graphic to pose a task corresponding to 14 − 6. One child, Joseph, said that he had used a physical device called the arithmetic rack to solve the task. He explained that he had made two collections of seven beads, taken six away from one of these collections, and knew immediately that eight beads were left.

Teacher:

Raise your hand if you understand what Joseph said. Raise your hand if that makes sense to you. [Several students do not raise their hands.] OK, if that doesn't make sense to you, what could you ask Joseph to help you understand it?

Donald: I don't understand how you started out with the 14 . . .

Joseph: No, I did 7 and 7 equals 14, and I broke the 7 up into 6 and 1 and I had, I added the 1 to the 7 then it would be 8.

Jan: I don't understand how you broke the 6 and 1 down.

Joseph: You know 7 plus 1 will make, I mean 6 plus 1 would make 7.

Jan: Yeah, but what about the 8?

Joseph: Oh, the 8, um I had, I had about 7. [T places an arithmetic rack on the overhead projector and makes two collections of 7 beads.] See that 7 right there next to the other 7? [T separates one of the collections of 7 into 6 and 1.] I had that one right there and the 7 to make 8.

Jan: Oh.

Teacher: Joseph, you've done a really nice job explaining that. I think it might help some people if they could see what you're saying. [T moves beads on the arithmetic rack as Joseph explains his solution.]

Jan: I get it. . . . That's a good way.

Teacher: Thank you for your question, Jan. Donald, did you have a different way?

Donald: Yeah.

Teacher: Give your attention to Donald.

The focus on understanding as realized in activity was such that the children typically challenged solutions with which they disagreed by saying that they did not understand, and then explained why they considered the solution to be invalid. The two overriding values that appear to characterize the microculture established in Ms. Smith's classroom were those of active participation and of attempting to understand. At the end of the whole-class discussion on January 10, Ms. Smith articulated these values as follows:

> Thanks very much for thinking about cookies with me. And, but most of all, thanks for listening to one another and trying to figure out if you had a different way and listening to what your friends said to see if that made sense. Several of you were asking questions when someone's explanation didn't make sense to you and that's really important because we really want to understand each other.

Sociomathematical Norms

It will be recalled that classroom social norms are not specific to mathematics, but can apply to any subject matter area. In contrast, sociomathematical norms are specific to mathematical activity. We continue our documentation of the classroom microculture by discussing what counted as an acceptable explanation, a different solution, and an insightful and efficient solution in Ms. Smith's classroom. These sociomathematical norms were identified by analyzing the same five whole-class discussions considered when documenting the classroom social norms. As was the case with social norms, the sociomathematical norms proved to be consistent across these lessons.

In the most general terms, acceptable explanations involved the description of actions on what were, for the children, mathematical objects. For example, in the first of the two episodes presented when discussing social norms, Bob explained, "I knew if you *took* 1, if you *had* 9 and then . . . plus 8 and then you *took* 1 away from the 8 and *put* it with the 9 and you would *have* 7 left and that would make 17" (italics added).

In explicating his reasoning, Bob used the metaphor of acting in physical reality (cf. Cobb, 1989; Williams, 1992). Bloor (1976) contended that this physical metaphor constitutes the ultimate scheme with which we think. More recently, Sfard (1994) elaborated the entailments of this metaphor for mathematics education. She noted that it involves a shift away from the view of mathematical activity as information processing and toward an interpretation of it as bringing forth and acting in a virtual mathematical reality. This latter interpretation is at least partially consistent with Bereiter's (chapter 11, this volume) discussion of a world of immaterial knowledge objects. We, for our part, have argued that the individual and collective experience of acting in a mathematical reality is a crucial aspect of meaningful mathematical activity (Cobb, Wood, Yackel, & McNeal, 1992). Explanations such as that given by Bob can be contrasted with those that involve following procedural instructions. In the latter case, an explanation specifies a procedure for manipulating conventional mathematical symbols that do not necessarily refer to anything beyond themselves.[4]

The sociomathematical norm of what constituted an acceptable explanation was extremely stable and well-established. We did not find a single instance in the five lessons where a child's explanation was challenged on the grounds that the types of mathematical reasons given were unacceptable. This does not, of course, imply that the children had to explicitly invoke the metaphor of physical reality when they made a contribution. For example, the child who gave an explanation immediately after Karen in the first episode said, "I thought about 9 plus 9 being 18, and if I had 8 plus 9 then

---

[4]Walkerdine (chapter 4, this volume) follows Lacan (1977) in arguing that semiotic chains are carried along the metaphoric axis, and this no longer exists in school mathematics discourse. As we noted elsewhere, Walkerdine's focus is on the traditional school mathematics microculture rather than discourse within an inquiry mathematics microculture (Cobb & Bauersfeld, 1995). This latter discourse, it should be noted, is compatible with mathematicians' views of their activity: "Mathematicians know that they are studying an objective reality. To an outsider, they seem to be engaged in an esoteric communication with themselves and a small clique of friends" (Davis & Hersh, 1981, pp. 43–44).

that would be 17." Against the background of the basis for communication established by the classroom community, Ms. Smith and the other children seemed to take it for granted that this child was speaking about relationships between quantities as mathematical objects when she said, "9 plus 9 being 18," and "8 plus 9 . . . would be 17." Crucially, children who gave explanations of this type were expected to elaborate on them by speaking in terms of the physical metaphor or by actually manipulating a physical device such as the arithmetic rack if other children indicated that they did not understand.

Ms. Smith made reference to a second sociomathematical norm, that of what counted as a different mathematical solution, at the end of both the first episode and the entire whole class discussion.

> [Y]ou were listening while your friends were talking so you would know if your way was a different way or not or if your way was a way that someone else had already done it.
> [T]hanks for listening to one another and trying to figure out if you had a different way.

As Ms. Smith noted, the children were usually able to judge for themselves what constituted a mathematical difference by January of the school year. This made possible a devolution of responsibility that enabled her to take a less directly evaluative role. Although it was not stated explicitly, two criteria appear to have been involved when solutions were judged as different in additive situations such as those exemplified in the sample episode. One concerned differences in quantitative interpretations (e.g., a task interpreted as $6 + \_\_\_ = 14$ rather than $14 - 6 = \_\_\_$) and the other involved differences in computational processes wherein numerical quantities were decomposed and recomposed in different ways.[5]

The sample episodes are also helpful in clarifying the sociomathematical norm of what counted as a sophisticated and insightful solution. It is apparent from the first episode that Ms. Smith responded differentially to the children's contributions. In particular, she inferred that Jordan, the first child to respond, had counted and merely commented, "Jordan said he did it by counting." In contrast, the remaining seven children who made contributions in the first episode explained thinking strategy solutions. In each case, Ms. Smith redescribed the child's explanation, noting his or her reasoning as she did so. This differential treatment of the children's contributions served to indicate that Ms. Smith particularly valued what she and the students called grouping solutions.[6] The fact that, by January, most of the students typically

---

[5]These two criteria correspond to the distinction that Thompson (1994) made between quantitative reasoning and evaluating an unspecified number.

[6]As grouping solutions involve the constitution and recognition of patterns, Ms. Smith's emphases are consistent with the connectionist approach outlined by St. Julien (chapter 10, this volume) and the implications of the Peircean model of sign activity as developed by Whitson (chapter 7, this volume).

offered thinking strategy solutions indicates that this specifically mathematical value was generally taken as shared in Ms. Smith's classroom. In our view, the establishment of this sociomathematical norm was a critical aspect of her effectiveness as a reform teacher (McClain, 1995).

Analysis of the sampled whole-class discussions conducted on October 7 and October 20 indicates that this norm was already established just a few weeks after the beginning of the school year. For example, in the first of these two lessons, Ms. Smith posed tasks designed to support the students' development of spatial patterns. She and the children had previously developed the scenario of a pumpkin seller who packed his pumpkins in crates of ten. Ms. Smith used a ten frame to represent a crate and, in one task, made the following configuration on the overhead projector:

She showed the configuration to the students for one or two seconds and then asked, "What did you see?" They almost all raised their hands and Ms. Smith called on Donald, who explained that he related this task to a previous one that involved a row of four and three pumpkins.

Donald:	Four plus 3 makes 7, so one up of 7 is 8.
Teacher:	O.K., Donald . . . Raise your hand if you thought of it kind of like Donald thought about it. [Several students raise their hands.]
Teacher:	Casey, did you see something else?
Casey:	I saw 8.
Teacher:	You also saw 8.
Casey:	I saw 4 plus 4.
Teacher:	You saw it as 4 plus 4.

In contrast to these grouping solutions, the next child to make a contribution, Jordan, explained that he had counted. Although the overhead projector was still turned off, he went to the screen and pointed to locations as he counted '1, 2, . . . , 8.' His pointing actions made the following arrangement:

$$1 \quad 3 \quad 5 \quad 7$$
$$2 \quad 4 \quad 6 \quad 8$$

Teacher:	O.K., let's just look at it together [turns on the overhead projector] and think about what people are seeing.

In this last exchange, Ms. Smith accepted Jordan's counting solution without comment. Thus, as in the January episodes, she treated counting and grouping solutions differentially. It should be noted that she did not always respond to counting solutions in this unenthusiastic manner. Conversations with her outside the classroom revealed that, in her view, Jordan was capable of producing more sophisticated solutions. We, as classroom observers, agreed with this judgment.

The differential treatment of the two types of solutions continued as Ms. Smith summarized the students' contributions, but without referring to Jordan's solution. She explained that "some people said that they just saw 4 plus 4 right away [notates the solution]," and that "other people said that they thought about it and what they had just seen before, 4 plus 3 [notates the solution]." Jan then raised her hand.

Teacher:	Jan, did you think about it a different way?
Jan:	[Goes to the screen]. I saw 6 and I saw 2 more and that makes 7.
Teacher:	O.K.
Jan:	I mean 8.
Teacher:	O.K., Jan said that she saw 6 [briefly covers 2 counters with her hand] and then she saw 2 more. And 6 and 2 would be 8 [notates the solution].

The next child to give an explanation walked to the screen and pointed to the display:

Darren:	Like um . . . 2 plus 2 plus 2 . . . I mean like 2 plus 2 plus 2 plus 2.
Teacher:	O.K., that's another way you could also see it. 2 plus 2 plus 2 plus 2 equals 8 [notates the solution].
Jordan:	That's how I did it.
Teacher:	And that's what Jordan had said too. He saw it as four groups of 2 together.

Consistent with her responses to Donald's and Casey's explanations, Ms. Smith explicitly legitimized Jan's and David's grouping solutions. In the course of the exchange, Jordan appeared to reconceptualize his prior counting solution when he heard David's explanation, thereby making the transition from counting by ones to grouping, at least in this specific situation.

In our view, the manner in which Ms. Smith indicated that grouping solutions were particularly valued enabled her students to become aware of developmentally more sophisticated ways of thinking (cf. Voigt, 1995). Their problem-solving efforts therefore had a sense of directionality. At the same time, Ms. Smith took care to ensure that her students did not merely imitate grouping solutions. Thus, she continued to accept counting solutions and actively solicited them from children who, she judged, were not yet capable of developing grouping solutions. Our classroom observations indicate that these children were legitimate members of the classroom community who continued to actively participate. In addition, the requirement that explanations carry the significance of acting on mathematical objects served to delegitimize contributions that did not have quantitative significance. Children were therefore typically ineffective on the rare occasion when they did attempt to blindly imitate a sophisticated grouping solution.

In summary, we have illustrated three sociomathematical norms that were relatively stable throughout the school year (McClain, 1995). These concern what counted as an acceptable explanation, a different solution, and an insightful or sophisticated solution. In our view, the students developed specifically mathematical values that made possible a devolution of responsibility in the classroom as they participated in the establishment of these sociomathematical norms. We now take both these norms and the social norms as background and provide an orientation for the analysis of the classroom mathematical practices by outlining the instructional sequences developed during the first semester and the children's mathematical growth during the second semester.

SYNOPSIS OF THE FIRST SEMESTER

Collectively, the children's mathematical capabilities at the end of the first semester were unusual when compared with those of children who have experienced traditional first-grade instruction. As these collective capabilities constitute the basis from which classroom mathematical practices evolved during the second semester, it is important to document them.

The children's mathematical growth during the first semester occurred as they participated in the enactment of two instructional sequences, Patterns and Partitioning and the Arithmetic Rack. The development of the first of these sequences was motivated by a preliminary analysis of the individual interviews conducted in September. These interviews indicated that 6 of the 18 students had considerable difficulty in using their fingers as substitutes for other items.[7] For example, the tasks presented included elementary story problems such as:

---

[7]It is important to stress that we view interviews as social events in which the interviewer and child negotiate their obligations and expectations. The interviews proved to be powerful predictors of the children's activity in the classroom, indicating that the two situations as realized in interaction were commensurable (cf. Lave & Wenger, 1991). The statement that, say, a child had difficulty in using his or her fingers as substitutes for other items is a shorthand for the more elaborate statement that, in the course of his or her participation in the interview, the child acted in ways that justify making this inference about his or her socially situated capabilities. A more detailed discussion of the role of interviews in teaching experiments can be found in Cobb (1995).

"Can you pretend that you have 3 apples?" Child nods. "Can you pretend that I have 2 apples?" Child nods. "How many apples do we have together? You have 3 and I have 2." For these 6 children, the possibility of putting up fingers as perceptual substitutes for the apples did not seem to arise even when they were prompted. As a consequence, they were not able to make a quantitative interpretation of the situation described in the task statement. Drawing on the work of Neuman (1987), we developed the Patterns and Partitioning sequence that had as its goals the development of flexible finger patterns, imagined spatial patterns, and the conceptual partitioning of collections of up to 10 items. A detailed account of this sequence as it was realized in the classroom can be found in Whitenack (1995). The sample episode given to document sociomathematical norms in which Ms. Smith presented a ten frame containing 8 items illustrates one of the spatial pattern tasks. The sequence involved 19 lessons from September 22 until October 22.

The Arithmetic Rack sequence began immediately after the Patterns and Partitioning sequence was completed, and involved 25 lessons that ended on January 10. Its intent was to support students' development of increasingly sophisticated quantitative interpretations of additive situations and of thinking or derived fact strategies. The rack is a physical device that consists of two rods on each of which are five red beads and five white beads (Gravemeijer, 1994b; Treffers, 1990). To use the arithmetic rack, the student moves beads from right to left either by counting individual beads or by moving several beads at a time. For instance, a student might show seven (beads) by moving three beads on the top rod and three on the bottom rod, and then move an additional bead.

The rack was designed to fit with thinking strategy solutions that have been documented in the research literature (Carpenter, 1980; Cobb, 1983; Steinberg, 1985). One of the goals of the Patterning and Partitioning sequence was in fact to make it possible for the students to create patterns that signified the results of curtailed counting activity when they acted with the rack. In particular, our intent was that the children would be able to interpret a collection of, say, five red and two white beads on one rod as juxtaposed numerical composites of five and two. They might then not have to count all the beads, but might instead either know immediately that there were seven beads (cf. Whitson, chapter 7, this volume) or just count the white beads, "6, 7." Classroom observations indicate that all but one of the children moved beyond counting by ones when they acted with the rack relatively early in the instructional sequence.

The potential fit with students' thinking strategy solutions can be clarified by considering a specific case. Suppose, for example, that a student has made a collection of nine beads by moving five beads on the top rod and four beads on the bottom rod, and has formulated the intention of finding how many more are needed to make 16. To complete the solution, the student might move five beads on the top rod and two on the bottom rod (see Fig. 8.3a.) Alternatively, the student might first move one additional bead on the bottom rod and three on the top rod and three on the bottom rod (see Fig. 8.3b.) From the observer's point of view, a going-through-ten strategy is implicit in the student's activity in the first example, and a doubles strategy is implicit in the second example. The instructional challenge is then to guide the emergence of such aspects of children's activity as explicit topics of conversation in the classroom.

Whitenack (1995) documented both the instructional sequence as it was realized in the classroom and the manner in which Ms. Smith addressed this challenge. Her analysis reveals that the arithmetic rack was initially consti- tuted in the classroom as a model of a scenario involving a double-decker bus. Later, it functioned increasingly as a model for arithmetical reasoning in classroom discourse. This was exemplified in the classroom episode from January 10 in which Joseph explained to Donald and Jan how he had solved a task corresponding to 14 − 6. In that instance, Joseph had actually acted with a rack, but explained without referring to the rack, "I did 7 and 7 equals 14, and I broke the 7 up into 6 and 1 and I had, I added the 1 to the 7 then it would be 8." The two episodes from January 10 in which Ms. Smith developed the cookie jar scenario illustrate one of several situations in which tasks were posed toward the end of the Arithmetic Rack sequence. At this point in the sequence, the children were free to choose whether they wanted to use an arithmetic rack. Most were able to produce grouping, thinking strategy solutions without using a rack.

A comparison of the individual interviews conducted in September and January indicates that all 18 children had made significant progress as they

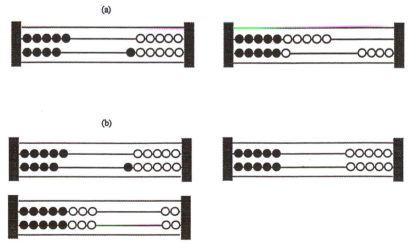

FIG. 8.3. Strategies for showing 16 using the arithmetic rack: (a) going-through-ten, and (b) referencing doubles.

participated in the enactment of the Patterns and Partitioning and Arithmetic Rack sequences. During the September interviews, the children typically attempted to count to solve a wide range of tasks, the methods ranging from counting all on fingers to counting on or counting down subvocally. As has been noted, six of the students were unable to use their fingers as perceptual substitutes during the September interview. Further, only two children spontaneously used thinking strategies, and each did so on only one occasion.

In the January interviews, the only tasks presented that involved sums and minuends to 20 were addition and subtraction number sentences. Ten children spontaneously used thinking strategies to solve all the sentences posed to them, and another three did so for at least half of the sentences presented. The remaining five children were all in the initial group of six who had difficulty in using their fingers as perceptual substitutes in September. These children solved smaller sentences with sums and minuends of 10 or less by using finger patterns, thinking strategies, or, occasionally, by counting. However, only one of these children used a thinking strategy to solve any of the larger number sentences. Two attempted to create finger patterns beyond 10 with limited success by imagining additional fingers, and two counted on and counted down by ones. It should, however, be noted that these five children produced a wider range of thinking strategy solutions in classroom discussions than they did in the interviews. In the former setting, their activity was supported by attempts to understand others' explanations, by acting with the rack, and by symbolizing their reasoning.

The January interviews corroborate that grouping solutions involving either thinking strategies or finger patterns had been institutionalized in the classroom during the first semester. It is also apparent from the January interviews that the capabilities the children developed reflect the history of their participation in particular classroom mathematical practices (cf. Whitenack, 1995). The influence of the children's activity with a physical device, the arithmetic rack, is clearly evident. This observation is consistent with contemporary accounts of distributed cognition (Dörfler, in press; Pea, 1993) and with Vygotsky's (1981) contention that intellectual development is mediated by the use of tools. This issue of the influence of tool use also comes to the fore in the second semester, and it is there that we discuss it in some detail.

STUDENTS' MATHEMATICAL DEVELOPMENT DURING THE SECOND SEMESTER

As was the case with the first semester, the students' mathematical growth during the second semester was atypical when compared with that of first graders who have experienced traditional instruction. However, in contrast to the first semester, we had several concerns in our role as mathematics educators who had some responsibility for the children's learning. We first summarize the children's activity in the January and May interviews and then clarify these concerns.

Our overall intent during the second semester was to support the children's development of increasingly sophisticated quantitative interpretations and their development of estimation and mental computation strategies for solving a wide range of additive tasks involving numbers to 100. Two of the task sets posed in both the January and May interviews involved number sentences and story problems. The number sentences were: 16 + 9, 28 + 13, 37 + 24, 39 + 53, 42 − 18, 53 − 26, and 74 − 37. Specific tasks were posed to individual children at the discretion of the interviewer. Two parallel sets of story problems were constructed. Children were randomly asked to complete one set in the January interview and the second set in the May interview. The text of one set of problems was:

> There are 43 pages in Jill's book. She has read 24 pages. How many pages does she have to read?
>
> It's Susie's father's birthday. There are 42 candles on his birthday cake. He blows out some of them. 17 are still burning. How many did he blow out?
>
> There are 52 children in the library. There are only 26 chairs in the library. How many more chairs are needed?
>
> Joe and Bob each grab a handful of M&M candies out of a jar. Joe gets 53 and Bob gets 28. How many does Joe need to put back so that he and Bob have the same number of candies?

Each problem was accompanied by a graphic that the interviewer referred to while reading the story to the child. The interviewer was free to vary the wording as he or she attempted to communicate with the child. For example, in the case of the last task, the interviewer might point to a picture of two boys and explain that Joe and Bob were friends before asking if it was fair that Joe had 53 candies and Bob had 28. The child might then be asked, "How many does Joe need to put back so it is fair?"

It is important to note that in terms of the standard classifications of problem types (e.g., Carpenter & Moser, 1982), all the story problems presented are considered to be relatively challenging. Further, the numbers specified in the problem statements were selected so that the children could not merely partition them into a tens part and a ones part and solve each as a separate task.

As one child moved from the school shortly before the end of the school year, only 17 children are included in the analysis. In the January interviews, seven children developed grouping solutions to solve at least the first two addition number sentences presented, 16 + 9 and 28 + 13. Several of these solutions appeared to be elaborations of the thinking strategy solutions the children had developed during the first semester. The range of solutions for 28 + 13 was:

$$28 + 2 = 30; \ 30 + 10 = 40; \ 40 + 1 = 41 \tag{2}$$
$$28 + 10 = 38; \ 38 + 3 = 41 \tag{2}$$
$$28 + 3 = 31; \ 31 + 10 = 41 \tag{1}$$
$$20 + 13 = 33; \ 33 + 8 = 41 \tag{1}$$
$$20 + 10 = 30; \ 30 + (8 + 2) = 40; \ 40 + 1 = 41 \tag{1}$$

A further four children attempted unsuccessfully to solve these two addition sentences by developing grouping solutions. These sentences were not posed to the remaining six children in light of their performance on the smaller number sentences with sums and minuends to 20.

Significantly, none of the 18 children were able to solve any of the subtraction sentences presented by developing grouping solutions. It is also noteworthy that only one child developed solutions that involved partitioning both addends (e.g., 28 + 13 solved as 20 + 10 = 30; 30 + (8 + 2) = 40; 40 + 1 = 41). The preponderance of solutions in which the children incremented in numerical composites or groups beyond one addend clearly indicates the influence of the classroom mathematical practices in which they participated during the first semester. This general orientation was also evident in the May interviews. There, 10 of the 17 children solved all the addition and subtraction sentences presented by either incrementing or decrementing. The range of solutions for 42 − 18 was:

$$42 - 2 = 40; \ 40 - 10 = 30; \ 30 - 6 = 24 \tag{3}$$
$$42 - 10 = 32; \ 32 - 2 = 30; \ 30 - 6 = 24 \tag{2}$$
$$42 - 10 = 32; \ 32 - 2 = 30; \ 30 - 1 = 29; \ 29 - 5 = 24 \tag{1}$$
$$42 - 10 = 32; \ 32 - 3 = 29; \ 29 - 5 = 24 \tag{1}$$
$$42 - 10 = 32; \ 32 - 4 = 28; \ 28 - 4 = 24 \tag{1}$$
$$42 - 2 = 40; \ 40 - 6 = 34; \ 34 - 10 = 24 \tag{1}$$
$$42 - 2 = 40; \ 40 - 10 = 30; \ 30 - 2 = 28; \ 28 - 4 = 24 \tag{1}$$

As can be seen, there was considerable uniformity in the children's solutions. All but one of these children either subtracted 10 and the remaining 8 in some manner, or 2 to leave 40, then 10 and 6.

Two of the other seven children developed partitioning solutions to the addition sentences but decremented to solve the subtraction sentences. Another child also partitioned to solve addition sentences, but then attempted to solve the subtraction sentences by taking smallest from largest (e.g., 42 − 18 = 36 because 4 − 1 = 3 and 8 − 2 = 6). The remaining four children were all in the group of six who, in the September interviews, had difficulty in using their fingers as perceptual substitutes. One said that she could not solve the first sentence presented, $16 + 9$. The other three each solved several addition sentences by developing a variety of different types of solutions. For example, two counted successfully to solve $28 + 13$ while keeping track on their fingers and explained that they had added 10 and then 3. In addition, two spontaneously used a type of notation that was developed in the classroom during the second semester, the empty number line. Further, these three children were all able to solve subtraction sentences such as $32 - 7$ either by counting down or by developing grouping solutions.

In summary, the comparison of the children's solutions to number sentences presented in January and May indicates that all but one made considerable progress.[8] A similar pattern emerges when we consider the students' solutions to the story problems. In the January interviews, the first story problem was posed to 11 of the children who had developed relatively sophisticated solutions to prior tasks. Only four of these children were able to initiate a solution attempt. In each case, the child appeared to partition numbers (e.g., in the first story problem, 43 interpreted as 40 and 3, and 24 as 20 and 4). However, in the social setting of the interview, they were not able to coordinate units of ten and of one, and instead focused solely on the tens part, reasoning either $20 + 20 = 40$ or $40 - 20 = 20$. Their quantitative interpretations of the tasks therefore appeared to be appropriate, but they were yet to develop strategies for evaluating the unspecified number.

In the May interviews, at least one story problem was posed to all 17 children, and the complete set of four problems was presented to nine children. Ten of the children successfully solved all the story problems presented to them. These children's solutions to one of the following two story problems from the parallel problem sets were:

There are 52 children in the library. There are only 26 chairs in the library. How many more chairs are needed?

or

Joe and Bob each grab a handful of M&M candies. Joe got 52 and Bob got 26. How many more candies does Bob need to have as many as Joe?

$26 + 10 = 36; 36 + 10 = 46; 46 + 4 = 50; 50 + 2 = 52; 26$ (3)
$26 + 10 = 36; 36 + 10 = 46; 46 + 5 = 51; 51 + 1 = 52; 26$ (1)
$26 + 4 = 30; 30 + 2 = 32; 32 + 10 = 42; 42 + 10 = 52; 26$ (1)

---

[8]Even the child who said she could not solve $16 + 9$ had made some progress. In January, she relied exclusively on finger patterns and was unable to solve tasks in which the sum or minuend was more than 10. In May, she counted on or counted down to solve sentences such as $9 + 5$ and $11 - 4$. Further, she now successfully solved smaller sentences such as $6 - 2$ by reasoning, "Take away the 6 and the 5." Here, one can see, in naissant form, a possible origin of more sophisticated decrementing solutions.

$26 + 4 = 30; \ 30 + 2 = 32; \ 32 + 20 = 52; \ 26$ (1)
$26 + 4 = 30; \ 30 + 10 = 40; \ 40 + 10 = 50; \ 50 + 2 = 52; \ 26$ (1)
$26 + 4 = 30; \ 30 + 10 = 40; \ 40 + 12 = 52; \ 26$ (1)
$52 - 4 = 48; \ 48 - 2 = 46; \ 46 - 10 = 36; \ 36 - 10 = 26$ (1)
$30 + 26 = 56; \ 29 + 26 = 55; \ 28 + 26 = 54; \ 27 + 26 = 53;$ (1)
$26 + 26 = 52; \ 26$

Four of these 10 children actually wrote number sentences as they solved the task, whereas the other six solved the task entirely mentally. As can be seen, there was considerable uniformity in the first eight solutions.

Of the remaining seven children, two attempted to develop similar solutions but sometimes had difficulty in keeping track as they incremented or decremented. A third child attempted unsuccessfully to produce partitioning solutions to all four tasks presented. Another three children attempted to symbolize their reasoning by using empty number line notations. However, in the case of two of these children, their notating activity appeared to be imitative and to have limited numerical significance for them.[9] Finally, one child attempted to produce a partitioning solution to the only task presented to her and, like several children in the January interview, reasoned $20 + 20 = 40$.

In summary, the children generally made significant progress during the second semester in their quantitative interpretations of additive tasks and in the strategies they developed to solve these tasks. By traditional standards, their performance was reasonably impressive. However, three aspects of their activity gave rise to concern. First, we have noted that there was a significant uniformity in the children's solutions to both the number sentences and story problems presented in the May interviews. Differences were, for the most part, limited to the specific sequence of increments or decrements they made. Second, and relatedly, most of the children who produced grouping solutions repeatedly incremented or decremented by steps of 10. For example, solutions such as the following were not uncommon for the number sentence $39 + 53$: $39 + 10 = 49, 49 + 10 = 59, 59 + 10 = 69, 69 + 10 = 79, 79 + 10 = 89, 89 + 3 = 92$. This suggests that specific numerical interpretations and particular ways of calculating may well have been institutionalized in the classroom. Third, several children solved all tasks in certain task sets by using just one type of strategy. Thus, although these children's activity appeared to have numerical significance for them, they seemed to enact routine computational processes. The children's lack of flexibility can be contrasted with the January interviews, where they

---

[9]As imitative activity of this type was rare in the classroom, these responses may have reflected those children's construal of the interview as a situation in which they were expected to produce solutions.

typically used several different thinking strategies to solve the small number sentences. These latter solutions can be classified as insightful in that they were based on specific numerical patterns that the children established when interpreting the tasks (cf. Whitson, chapter 7, this volume). This orientation of capitalizing on task-specific numerical relationships was not as evident in the May interviews.

It should be clear that the concerns we have expressed were contrary to both our own and the teacher's intentions for the children's mathematical development. The analysis of the classroom mathematical practices established during the second semester therefore has practical significance in that it can feed back to inform the revision of the instructional sequences.

MATHEMATICAL PRACTICES ESTABLISHED BY THE CLASSROOM COMMUNITY

Two instructional sequences were developed during the second semester; the Candy Shop and the Empty Number Line. Classroom observations and a preliminary analysis of video recordings indicate that the children's activity during the Candy Shop sequence was generally consistent with our expectations. This was not, however, the case for the Empty Number Line sequence as it was realized in this classroom. Concomitantly, there appeared to be a qualitative difference in the nature of classroom discourse between the two sequences. The classroom mathematical practices established during both sequences are therefore of interest.

The Candy Shop Sequence

The instructional intent of the Candy Shop sequence was to support the students' initial coordination of units of ten and one. The sequence involved 12 lessons conducted between February 2 and February 24. Initial instructional activities involving numbers to 100 were introduced in January, prior to the beginning of the sequence. There, Ms. Smith had gradually increased the size of the numbers as she posed tasks in scenarios similar to those used at the end of the Arithmetic Rack sequence. In addition, she made bags of 100 unifix cubes available for the children to use. Consistent with our expectations, most of the children counted collections of single cubes when they solved these tasks. We speculated that, in repeatedly counting in this fashion, the children might develop at least a gross quantitative understanding of numbers to 100.

Ms. Smith first introduced the Candy Shop sequence on February 2 by developing a narrative with the children about a candy shop owned by a character called Mrs. Wright. Ms. Smith was an excellent storyteller and was able to involve her students in events in the candy shop as the narrative unfolded in subsequent lessons. As a consequence, the scenario appeared to be experientially real for all the children, and many in fact came to believe that Mrs. Wright was a real person.

The first issue Ms. Smith raised with the children concerned counting and organizing the candies. Ms. Smith explained that Mrs. Wright kept different types of candies in big jars, and that she counted them out one by one for customers. However, this often took her a long time, and there was sometimes a long line of customers waiting to be served. The children were asked to suggest what Mrs. Wright might do. They made a wide range of suggestions that included hiring someone to help her in the shop and putting the candies into bags. Ms. Smith acknowledged that Mrs. Wright could have followed any of their proposals, but that the solution she chose was to pack her candies into rolls. The next issue addressed was that of how many candies to put in a roll given that Mrs. Wright wanted to fill her customers' orders quickly. Once the children had made several suggestions (e.g., 5, 10, 20), Ms. Smith clarified that there were several possibilities and explained that Mrs. Wright decided to put 10 candies in each roll. Thus, in the course of this ongoing conversation, the notion of packing candies into rolls of 10 was developed as a convention in the candy shop.[10]

In the next instructional activity, the children were given bags of unifix cubes and asked to act as packers who were helping Mrs. Wright in her shop. Before they began, however, they were asked to estimate how many rolls they thought they would make. This question seemed to orient the children to monitor their activity of creating composites of 10. In several subsequent activities, the children continued to estimate and then empirically check the number of rolls that could be created in a variety of different situations. Ms. Smith then drew on the children's activity of packing candies and making bars of 10 unifix cubes when she introduced a second type of instructional activity. In this activity, the children were shown a pictured collection of rolls and individual candies on the overhead projector and asked to figure out how many candies there were in all. Solutions in which the children first specified the number of candies in the rolls and then added on the number of loose candies quickly became established as a routine

---

[10]It is important to stress that the instructional intent for establishing this convention was not to introduce rolls and individual candies as an external representation of the base-ten numeration system. Thus, the children were neither expected to somehow discover salient mathematical properties of the rolls and candies, nor to connect them in some unexplained way to preestablished cultural meanings. Instead, in line with RME, the scenario of the shop was developed as a starting-point situation in which the children might group objects into collections of 10. Later in the sequence, Ms. Smith supported the children's reorganization of their initial packing and unpacking activity by guiding the development of symbolic models of that activity.

practice of the classroom community. For example, on February 8, Ms. Smith showed the children a picture of two rolls and three individual candies. Anna explained her answer of 23 as follows: "Ten plus 10 makes . . . um . . . 20, and if you add 3 more it would be 23." Another child, Sarah, subsequently gave a similar explanation to a task involving three rolls and two pieces.

Sarah: (Goes to the screen.) I know that 10 plus 10 makes 20, and I added one more to make 30 (points to the rolls), and I added two more (points to the loose pieces) and they were . . . 32.

Teacher: Thank you Sarah. Sarah saw the three rolls (points to the rolls) and she knew it would be 10 plus 10, plus 10 more pieces in those rolls to make 30, and then 32 (points to the loose pieces).

In contrast to Ms. Smith, neither Anna nor Sarah referred to the rolls or candies, but instead reported their calculational processes directly. In the broader context of our observations, this suggests that the numerical interpretations they made of the pictures were self-evident and beyond comment. The task as they understood it appeared to be that of adding up the numerical amounts signified by the pictured rolls and candies.

This routine mathematical practice evolved as the teacher and students discussed the next task presented:

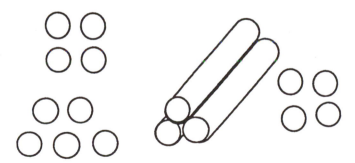

Casey, the first child to make a contribution, gave an explanation that was difficult for Ms. Smith and the other children to follow in which he seemed to indicate that he had mentally grouped 10 of the loose candies together.

Teacher: How did you figure it out, Casey?

Casey: Well, I knew there was 13 pieces not counting the rolls, all those pieces that are loose,

Teacher: OK.

Casey: and then those three rolls make 30 and if you go up and I
                got past 10, and I got to 13, so I got past 30, and then I
                knew if you added 10 and 3, and I used up two of those, I
                mean three of those (points toward the screen from his po-
                sition sitting on the floor). You have 30, and you add the
                10, you used up the 10 on the 30 and then you had 3 left
                and that made 43.

Ms. Smith then asked Casey to repeat his thinking, presumably in an
attempt to understand his thinking. On this occasion, Casey clarified that
the 10 he had previously mentioned was a composite of two fives.

Teacher: OK, come [to the screen] and point to the 30 you're talking
                about. Pay close attention, I heard somebody say they didn't
                really understand.
Casey: (Goes to the screen) Here's the 30.
Teacher: OK, he pointed to these three rolls, that's 30 pieces.
Casey: And then I have 5 and 5 (points to a group of five candies,
                and to groups of four and one candies), and that used up
                the 30 because it made 10 and I got 40, and then I have 3
                left and then I have 40, and then it's 43.

At this juncture, Ms. Smith began to redescribe Casey's solution, possibly
to check her interpretation with him.

Teacher: Casey, you said this was 30 (writes 30 beneath the rolls).
                Then you have 5 here (circles a group of five candies).
Casey: Yes.
Teacher: Then you had (circles a group of four candies).
Casey: Four, and then that one over there made 5. (T circles the
                candy he points to.) So that's 10. I used up that 30 right
                there, I used up that 30 with 10, you see 30 is a whole entire
                10 almost, it's not really a whole entire 10—after 39 comes
                40 and that used up the 10.

Here, in speaking of 30 as being almost an entire 10, Casey appeared to
be saying that the number sequence in the 30s (i.e., 31, 32, . . . , 39) almost
made 10, and that an additional increment to 40 would complete the 10—the
group of 10 loose candies would be used up.

Teacher: So there's the 30 that he used (points). Now does everybody
                see the 10 that he used? He had 5 there, and then you saw
                he had 4 and 1 more made another 5. So did you add the
                5 and 5 to make 10?

Casey:	Yes.
Teacher:	So then you had 30 plus 10 and that got you up to 40.
Casey:	Yes.
Teacher:	And then you still had these 3 more (circles the group of three candies) made 43.
Casey:	Yes.

In the course of this exchange, Casey and Ms. Smith together interactively constituted an explanation. Casey initially appeared to refer to the number sequence when he explained his thinking. However, Ms. Smith interpreted his contributions exclusively in terms of making groups, and he accepted this redescription. It is via implicit negotiations such as this in which meanings subtly shift and slide that classroom mathematical practices often emerge.

The account of Casey's solution as making groups became taken as shared by the classroom community as the exchange continued.

Jan:	I don't understand about the four and the one.
Teacher:	It's like this Jan. Pretend like this one is right there instead of right there (draws a candy next to the group of four and crosses out the candy she had previously circled). Then what would you have (points to the groups of five and four)?
Jan:	Ten.
Teacher:	Is that what you were thinking about Casey?
Casey:	Yes.
Teacher:	Pretending that this one . . .
Jan:	Oh, I know what it is.
Casey:	If you have 5, 5, is 10; 30, use up the 30, then you get 40, then you use this 3, 43.

In giving this final explanation, Casey appeared to assume that the process of establishing the groups was self-evident. The only thing that remained to be explained was the calculational process.

This approach of grouping the individual candies quickly became a routine mathematical practice. The next task that Ms. Smith posed was:

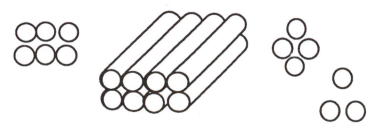

Anna was the first child to give an explanation.

Anna: I know that 4 plus 4 is 8, and if there was 8 rolls there would be 80 pieces . . . and if you added 6 more it would be 86, and . . .

Teacher: Those 6 over there (points to a collection of six candies).

Anna: Yes.

Teacher: OK, so you've used those and those to get 86 (writes 80 + 6 = 86). OK, then what did you do?

Anna: And then I added 4 more to make . . . and it made 90.

Teacher: (Writes 86 + 4 = 90.) OK.

Anna: I think it would be 93.

Teacher: OK, how did you know you needed 3 more after you got 86 and 4 you said was 90?

Anna: And then I added 3 more to the 90, it would be 93.

Teacher: So then 3 added, those last 3 (writes 90 + 3 = 93). She said that made 93.

In the course of this exchange, the task as it was interactively constituted by Anna and Ms. Smith appeared to be that of grouping the loose candies in ways that facilitated a computational process. Ms. Smith summarized this realization of the task as follows:

Teacher: Anna, could we say this? You thought about how many pieces were in the rolls first, and that was 80. And then you did a group at a time, you added the group of 6 first, and then you added the group of 4 to get 90, and then you added the group of 3 and that made 93.

Anna: Yes.

When Ms. Smith subsequently called on other students to explain their thinking, she indicated that solutions that involved grouping were particularly valued.

Teacher: Is there another way you could group to figure out 93?

Bob: (Walks to the screen.) I think it's 93 because I took this 6 (points) and I broke it up and I took 1 away and I put it with the 4 (points) to make 5 and 5, to make 10, and I knew that was 80, so it would be 90, and then 93.

As she redescribed Bob's solution, Ms. Smith wrote the arithmetical sentences:

$$\begin{matrix} 4 & 6 \\ & \diagdown\diagup \end{matrix}$$
$$80 + 10 = 90$$
$$90 + 3 = 93$$

In addition, she asked the class, "Does Ms. Wright have enough [candies] to make another roll?" In doing so, she both suggested an interpretation of Bob's explanation in terms of situation-specific imagery and indicated that his creation of a group of 10 was of particular significance.

The emergence of this mathematical practice was consistent with our instructional intent in that the act of conceptually creating numerical composites of 10[11] became an explicit topic of conversation. It is important to note that most of the children could participate in this practice even though they gave solutions that instantiated a range of qualitatively distinct interpretations. Anna and Sarah, for example, were two of the children who had difficulty in using their fingers as perceptual substitutes at the outset of the teaching experiment. The process by which this practice emerged appeared to be bottom-up rather than top-down, in that it grew out of the children's activity with Ms. Smith's guidance. The possibility that the children might make contributions that fit with her pedagogical agenda was reasonably high, given their prior experiences during the first semester. In particular, Casey's and Bob's activity of creating a composite of 10 appears to elaborate a practice established during the Arithmetic Rack sequence, the going-through-10 strategy. They, in effect, created a composite of 10 when they added the loose candies in order to go through a decade (i.e., 40 in Casey's case and 90 in Bob's case). Given their prior activity with the arithmetic rack, it also appears to be more than coincidence that they both established 10 as a composite of two groups of five.

It should be clear from our discussion of the sample episodes that a bottom-up process of emergence involves active negotiation. The appropriate metaphor for it might therefore be that of guided reconstruction rather than invention or a natural unfolding. We saw that in the exchange with Casey, Ms. Smith redescribed his solution in terms of making groups. There is every indication both in the episodes we presented and in subsequent lessons that Casey reconceptualized his own prior activity as he participated in this exchange. It was, we believe, because Casey could make this reconceptualization that he accepted Ms. Smith's interpretation.[12] This active individual construction in interaction was critical in our view and indicates why, for our purposes, it is inadequate to say merely that Casey appropriated Ms. Smith's interpretation of his solution. For example, we can imagine an alternative scenario in which a child gives a similar explanation but rejects Ms. Smith's redescription of it because he or she cannot reconceptualize the initial solution

---

[11]A distinction is made in the analysis between 10 as a numerical composite and 10 as a composite unit. Ten as a numerical composite refers to a collection of 10 units of one that are yet to be taken as a single entity or unit. In contrast, the 10 units of one are integrated into a single unit in the case of 10 as a composite unit (Steffe, Cobb, & von Glasersfeld, 1988).

[12]As we noted when discussing the classroom social norms, the children did, on occasion, reject Ms. Smith's redescriptions when the redescriptions were inconsistent with their interpretations of their mathematical activity. The children were, in effect, the authorities about their own mathematical activity.

in the way that Casey did. An account of the difference between these two scenarios makes reference to the children's situated interpretive activity.

The practice of evaluating collections of rolls and candies by creating composites of 10 became increasingly routine in subsequent lessons. In addition, it constituted the basis from which a further classroom mathematical practice developed. This new practice emerged when the children were asked to generate different partitionings of a given collection of candies. To introduce the instructional activity, Ms. Smith explained that Mrs. Wright was interrupted when she was counting out candies and putting them into rolls. In an exchange that occurred on February 25, the last lesson of the Candy Shop sequence, Ms. Smith posed a task of this type by inquiring:

> Teacher: What if Mrs. Wright had 43 pieces of candy, and she is working on packing them into rolls. What are different ways that she might have 43 pieces of candy, how many rolls and how many pieces might she have? Sarah, what's one way she might find it?

The discussion proceeded smoothly in that the children, as a group, generated the various possibilities with little apparent difficulty. Their contributions were:

> Sarah: Four rolls and three pieces.
> Ellen: 43 pieces.
> Kendra: She might have two rolls and 23 pieces.
> Darren: She could have three rolls, 12 pieces, I mean 13 pieces.
> Linda: One roll and 33 pieces.

The teacher, for her part, recorded each of their suggestions on a whiteboard as follows:

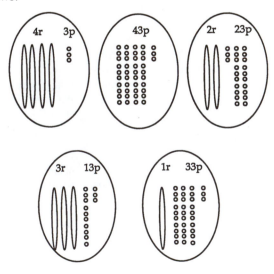

The analysis of this and other observations indicates that most of the children could flexibly create composites of 10 as they participated in this type of instructional activity. The activity of conceptually creating and decomposing composites of 10 therefore appeared to have emerged as a classroom mathematical practice in this setting, where the children could rely on situation-specific imagery. In contrast to the previous instructional activity in which the children evaluated pictured collections of candies, Ms. Smith now drew pictures to record the results of their conceptual activity.

As the episode continued, one of the children, Karen, indicated that she had something she wanted to say and went to the whiteboard at the front of the classroom.

Karen: Well see, we've done all the ways. We had 43 pieces . . .

Teacher: OK.

Karen: And, see, we had 43 pieces (points to 43p) and right here we have none rolls, and right here we have 1 roll (points to 1r 33p).

Teacher: OK, I'm going to number these, there's one way . . . no rolls (writes "0" next to 43p).

Karen: And there's one roll, there's two rolls, then there's three, and there's four.

Teacher: (Numbers the corresponding pictures 1, 2, 3, 4.)

In making this contribution, Karen initiated a shift in the discourse from generating possible ways the candies might be packed to operating on the results of that generative activity. Most of the other children also took the need to produce an ordering as self-evident, and a second child proposed an alternative scheme for numbering the pictures. A further shift then occurred in the discourse as the children explicitly negotiated different ways of ordering and labeling the configurations.

A central aspect of Ms. Smith's role in this episode was to redescribe the children's contributions by drawing pictures and labeling the number of rolls and candies in each (e.g., 4r 3p, 43p). The children might have reasoned with the pictures[13] when they generated alternative ways in which the candies could be packed. For example, some children might have imagined breaking one or more rolls in a given configuration into 10 individual candies. Alternatively, they might have imagined integrating one or more collections of 10 candies into a roll. It is important to stress, however, that Ms. Smith did not simply make these transformations apparent to the children when she drew the pictures. Instead, the children's generative activity reflected the

---

[13]Our rationale for saying that the children reasoned with the pictures rather than that they used the pictures as intellectual resources to support their reasoning is discussed in the last section of this chapter.

intellectual capabilities they had developed as they participated in prior classroom mathematical practices. For the sake of example, suppose that Darren, the child who suggested three rolls and 13 pieces, had mentally transformed a collection of 10 candies in the previous configuration (2r 23p) into a roll. To do so, he would, at a minimum, have had to interpret the pictured collection of 23 pieces as comprising two numerical composites of 10. In addition, he would have had to interpret the pictured rolls as composites of 10 candies rather than as single, indivisible entities. Darren may, of course, have made a far more sophisticated numerical interpretation when he contributed to the discussion. This does not, however, invalidate the point of our illustration, namely that reasoning with the pictures involves significant intellectual capabilities.

In this account, we have noted that the pictures might well have played a central role in some of the children's reasoning. Thus, in line with current theories of distributed cognition, we observe that the presence of the pictures might have profoundly influenced the nature of the children's mathematical activity. At the same time, we have also stressed the children's constructive activities. They could reason with the pictures in this way because the pictured rolls and collections of candies signified numerical composites of 10 for them. In other words, the children's experience of these composites as being there on the whiteboard waiting to be manipulated reflected the intellectual capabilities they had actively constructed as they participated in and contributed to the evolution of classroom mathematical practices. Consequently, in the point of view we are advancing, the view of learning as a process of active construction is considered to be compatible with the notion that intelligence is distributed.

Reflections on the Candy Shop Sequence

In our analysis of the Candy Shop sequence, we have characterized the process by which classroom mathematical practices emerge as one of negotiation. The evolution of mathematical practices when this instructional sequence was realized in the classroom can be divided into three phases. In the first, the children used unifix cubes to simulate the activity of packing candies. The children's performance in the January interviews suggests that both this activity and its results had a range of qualitatively distinct meanings for them. However, there is reason to believe that the bars of 10 unifix cubes came to signify at least numerical composites of 10 for most of the children. In the second phase of the sequence, the practice of evaluating pictured collections of rolls and candies by creating composites of 10 emerged. We noted that this practice appeared to be an elaboration of practices established during the Arithmetic Rack sequence. In addition, this practice appeared to evolve from the children's simulated packing activity. Previously, the children had physically created entities that carried the significance of numerical composites of 10 by packing. In the second phase of the sequence, the children interpreted pictured rolls as signifying numerical composites, indicating that the results of the packing activity were now taken as a given. Thus, an aspect of the children's activity that was, for some, implicit in the first phase became explicit during the transition to the second phase. A similar phenomenon occurred during the transition to the third phase, in which the children generated alternative partitionings. Consider, for example, Bob's solution during the second phase of the sequence in which he evaluated a pictured collection of 8 rolls and 13 candies by creating an additional composite of 10, reasoning "80, so it would be 90, and then 93." Here, Bob in effect created 9 composites of 10 and 3 as an alternative partitioning of 93. In the third phase, the generation of these implicit alternatives became an explicit focus of activity. Further, whereas in the second phase, the children created composites of 10 by mentally grouping pictured candies, in the third phase, Ms. Smith drew pictures to express the results of their conceptual activity. The transition from the second to the third phase can therefore be seen to involve a shift in the way that the children reasoned with pictured collections.

With regard to the instructional theory that guided the development of the Candy Shop sequence, the pictured collections initially functioned as models of the results of packing activity. They subsequently functioned as models for arithmetical reasoning when the children generated alternative partitionings. Our account of the evolution of mathematical practices therefore documents the process by which a model of became a model for in the course of ongoing classroom interactions. This same process can also be seen to instantiate what Walkerdine (1988), following Lacan (1977), might term the emergence of a chain of signification (cf. Whitson, chapter 7, this volume). In particular, Ms. Smith and her students interactively constituted the following chain of signification[14]:

signified$_1$ —	signifier$_1$ —	signifier$_2$ —	signifier$_3$
candies	unifix cubes	pictured collections	verbal enumerations recorded as 3r 13p etc.

Together with Walkerdine (1988), we consider that a sign comprises a signified/signifier pair. It is important to stress that at each link in a chain of signification, the preceding sign combination becomes the signified of the succeeding sign combination. This can be illustrated as follows:

---

[14]This analysis gives an overview across the entire sequence. A separate analysis can, of course, be conducted for individual episodes. In the exchanges involving Casey and Bob, the chain of signification includes calculational terms and number sentences.

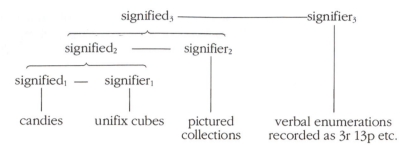

As Walkerdine (1988) observed, succeeding signifiers may initially be established as substitutes for preceding terms, with the assumption that the sense of those terms is preserved through links along the chain. However, terms that originated in relation to certain concerns and interests are in fact displaced by the terms of succeeding signs as these are taken over by other practices motivated by different concerns and interests. In this process, a sign combination such as candies/unifix cubes is said to slide under the succeeding signifiers—in our case, picture collections and verbal enumerations.

Walkerdine's (1988) sociolinguistic perspective is of interest in that it emphasizes that the original sign combination is not merely concealed behind succeeding signifiers. Instead, the meaning of the sign combination evolves as a chain of signification is constituted. In the case of the Candy Shop sequence, this evolution of meaning corresponds to a process of mathematization wherein what was previously said or done in activity subsequently becomes objectified as a focus of activity and topic of conversation. Initially, the meaning of the candies/unifix cubes combination was constituted within the story about Mrs. Wright's candy shop. They were items that needed to be packed to make it possible to serve customers efficiently. Here, the concerns and interests were those of a simulated commercial buying and selling practice. By the end of the sequence, the concerns and interests were primarily mathematical and involved structuring a collection of candies in different ways. Here, rolls now instantiated numerical composites of 10 and individual candies instantiated abstract units of one. The practice of packing candies by making bars of 10 unifix cubes had been displaced by that of conceptually creating and decomposing image-supported composites of 10.

In this chain of signification, the interactive constitution of the link between $sign_1$ (candies/unifix cubes) and $signifier_2$ (pictured collections) corresponds to the establishment of the pictured collections as a model of the results of the packing activity. The constitution of the link between $sign_2$ and $signifier_3$ (verbal enumerations) corresponds to the establishment of the pictured collections as a model for arithmetical reasoning. This relationship between Walkerdine's work and the theory of RME is potentially significant in that RME emerged from attempts to develop instructional sequences whereas Walkerdine offered a way to analyze what might be going on in classrooms. These two perspectives therefore deal with the two interrelated phases of developmental or transformational research—instructional development and classroom-based research. The coordination of these two perspectives might make it possible to address these two phases of the research and development process in a unified way. However, to effect such a coordination, we supplement Walkerdine's approach in two ways.

First, Walkerdine's (1988) focus was on the discourse of traditional school mathematics. She observed that possible referents in this discourse are restricted to material entities and concluded that the purpose of doing mathematics in school is to produce formal statements that do not signify anything beyond themselves. As a consequence, her analysis did not address the creation and manipulation of experientially real mathematical objects, a key feature of meaningful mathematical activity for us. Given our focus on the discourse of inquiry mathematics, we build on her sociolinguistic approach by considering the taken-as-shared mathematical reality that the classroom community creates as it constitutes a chain of signification. In the case of the Candy Shop sequence, for example, we suggested that the activity of generating alternative partitionings by creating and decomposing numerical composites of 10 emerged as a classroom mathematical practice. We therefore infer that Ms. Smith and her students took initial steps in constituting a taken-as-shared mathematical reality in which numbers can be composed of units of 10 and one as the need arises. In this view, the emergence of a chain of signification and of a taken-as-shared mathematical reality are therefore seen to be reflexively related.

The elaboration we have made to Walkerdine's (1988) approach is consistent with our attempt to account for mathematical learning by coordinating psychological and sociological analyses. As we illustrated during the discussion of the Candy Shop sequence, individual students' contributions to the constitution of a mathematical reality can be analyzed in psychological terms. Such an account would necessarily treat students' activity as being socially situated and would analyze their reorganization of that activity as they participate in the evolution of classroom mathematical practices. Given that signification is inherent to these practices, an account of this type would also address Walkerdine's important observation that languaging and symbolizing typically play little if any role in constructivist accounts of mathematical development.

The second elaboration we would make to Walkerdine's approach has been suggested by Whitson (chapter 7, this volume). As he observes, an analysis conducted in terms of the chaining of signifiers does not consider the interests, concerns, and purposes that motivate signification in the first place. We have attempted to address this issue by documenting the social norms and sociomathematical norms, and by describing the instructional activities as they were interactively constituted in the classroom. For example, in the second of the two episodes we presented, Ms. Smith's motivation for drawing pictures was to record the students' contributions as they fulfilled their obligation of proposing different partitionings. More generally, it was as Ms. Smith and the students fulfilled their obligations while discussing their mathematical activity that they interactively constituted chains of signification.

In summary, we have related the analysis of the classroom mathematical practices that emerged in the course of the Candy Shop sequence to both the theory of RME and to Walkerdine's (1988) sociolinguistic perspective. In doing so, we discussed the possibility of developing an account of the evolution of classroom mathematical practices that is compatible with the domain-specific instructional theory that guided the development of the instructional sequences. We suggested that to realize this possibility, it is necessary to supplement the notion of a chain of signification by attending to the interests and purposes that motivated signification, and by specifying the taken-as-shared mathematical reality that emerges as a chain of signification is constituted. We continue to explore this possibility by considering the mathematical practices that emerged when the second instructional sequence, the Empty Number Line, was realized in the classroom.

The Empty Number Line Sequence

The instructional intent of the Empty Number Line sequence was to support students' continued construction of increasingly sophisticated concepts of 10, and their development of flexible mental computation strategies. The intent can be further clarified by noting a distinction between two general types of computational strategies made in the research literature (cf. Beishuizen, 1993). In one type, the child partitions numbers separately into a tens part and a ones part and adds or subtracts them separately (e.g., 39 + 53 is found by reasoning 30 + 50 = 80, 9 + 3 = 12, 80 + 12 = 92). In the second type of strategy, the child increments or decrements directly from one number (e.g., 39 + 53 found by reasoning 39 + 50 = 89, 89 + 3 = 92). These two types of strategies appear to reflect two different ways of interpreting two-digit numerals and number words that Cobb and Wheatley (1988) called collection-based and counting-based interpretations, respectively, and that Fuson (1990) called collected multiunits and sequence multiunits. The Empty Number Line sequence was specifically designed to support the development of counting-based rather than collection-based conceptions and strategies. The metaphor implicit in these conceptions is that of counting activity that can be curtailed or chunked. In contrast, the Candy Shop sequence was designed to support the development of collection-based numerical interpretations in which the implicit metaphor is that of collections of items that can be partitioned and recomposed.

The Empty Number Line sequence as it was realized in the first-grade classroom involved 46 lessons conducted between February 17 and May 12.

For the purposes of this analysis, it is sufficient to document the classroom mathematical practices established during the first 2 months of the sequence. The initial instructional activities in the sequence as it was originally outlined by its developers involved the use of a bead string composed of 100 beads (Treffers, 1991). The beads were of two colors and were arranged in groups of 10. In line with the tenets of RME, the developers recommended that the Empty Number Line should emerge as a model of students' activity with the structured bead string. We decided to modify the sequence by omitting these instructional activities because the bead string did not itself serve as a means by which children might explicitly model their prior problem-solving activity.[15] Instead, we speculated that the classroom mathematical practices established during the Arithmetic Rack and Candy Shop sequences might constitute an adequate starting point for the Empty Number Line sequence.

The primary means of symbolizing developed during the instructional sequence was that of an empty number line on which the children recorded their arithmetical reasoning. Gravemeijer (1994b) gave the following examples of strategies for solving 65 − 38 that have been notated in this way:

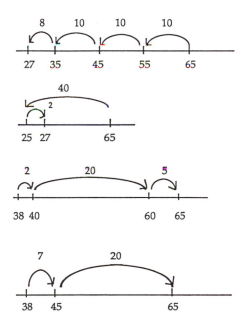

---

[15]More specifically, in the instructional sequence as envisioned by its developers, the bead string is introduced directly and does not emerge as a model of informal mathematical activity in a situation that is experientally real for students. As a consequence, it is necessary to treat the bead string as a thing in itself and to teach children desired ways of interpreting and acting with it. This seemed somewhat artificial as a starting point of the instructional sequence.

The conjecture underlying the development of the instructional sequence was that the empty number line would initially emerge as a model of children's informal arithmetical reasoning, but that it would subsequently become a model for increasingly abstract yet personally meaningful arithmetical activity.

Ms. Smith first introduced the empty number line notation to symbolize the children's reasoning during a whole-class mental computation activity, called Target on February 17. The children had engaged in this instructional activity on several previous occasions and were familiar with it. To pose tasks, Ms. Smith drew a vertical line on the whiteboard and marked two numbers on it. For example, she posed the first task on February 18 by drawing:

Referring to the scenario of the Candy Shop, she then asked the children to pretend that they have six pieces of candy, explained that a customer wants 13 pieces of candy, and asked them to figure out how many additional pieces they need. Three children offered solutions to this first task:

Anita: Seven—I thought if we were at 6 and we wanted to get up to 13, we would need 7.

We note in passing that Anita's talk of "wanting to get up to" is consistent with the use of a vertical line to pose tasks. The line was in fact oriented vertically to support this taken-as-shared metaphor of a quantity increasing or decreasing (cf. Lakoff & Johnson, 1980).

Casey: Six plus 6 is 12, and 7 and 7 is 14, so 6 plus 7 is 13 because it has to be in between.

Donald: Six plus 6 is 12, so 6 plus 7 is 13 because we need one more.

Ms. Smith verbally redescribed both Anita's and Casey's solutions, and wrote number sentences to record Casey's reasoning. In contrast, she recorded Donald's solution by notating on the vertical line as follows:

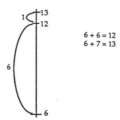

Ms. Smith differentiated between the children's solutions in this way because Donald's solution was the only one that appeared to involve counting-based reasoning. It fit with this way of notating whereas those that involved collection-based reasoning did not. Our prior observations of the Target activity had in fact indicated that a number of children would offer counting-based solutions, thereby making it possible for Ms. Smith to initiate the development of this way of notating by capitalizing on their contributions.

Ms. Smith continued to differentiate in this way between solutions that reflected counting-based reasoning and those that appeared to involve collection-based reasoning in both the remainder of this lesson and in the subsequent lessons. Classroom observations and a review of the video recordings indicate that all but one of the children were soon able to participate by offering efficient noncounting solutions. Further, by the fifth session involving Target on February 23, the children usually described their solutions in ways that made it possible for Ms. Smith to notate their thinking on the vertical line. It is important to stress that Ms. Smith at no point required that the children's explanations fit this way of notating. Instead, the shift in the children's solutions appeared to reflect the changing role that the vertical line and Ms. Smith's notating played in their activity.

Initially, Ms. Smith simply recorded the children's explanations. However, some of the children soon appeared to solve tasks by reasoning with the line. In particular, these children seemed to imagine numerical quantities that could be symbolized by jumps on the line, thereby anticipating ways of symbolizing that had previously occurred only after they explained their thinking. These children could, however, only reason with the line because Ms. Smith's symbolic acts of marking jumps had numerical significance for them. The children's ability to make these numerical interpretations in turn reflected their participation in prior classroom mathematical practices, particularly those established during the Arithmetic Rack sequence.

It should be noted that the children's reasoning with the line might have involved a concomitant change in the Target activity as it was interactively constituted in the classroom. Initially, the taken-as-shared goal appeared to be to evaluate an unspecified number. However, for some of the children, the instructional activity might have become to specify numerical jumps on the vertical line, and then add them. This shift in the nature of the instructional activity via a process of implicit negotiation together with the changing role of the vertical line in the children's activity explain why almost all of the children were able to develop relatively sophisticated grouping solutions.

Solutions that involved going-through-decade had become routine by the fifth session involving target on February 23. Jordan, for example, solved a task corresponding to 18 + ___ = 25 as follows:

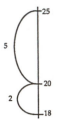

Jordan: It's 7. If you add 2 more it's 20, so 5 more is 25.

Teacher: Who thought about it like Jordan did?

(Approximately half the class raise their hands.)

Teacher: Who thought about it a different way?

Donald: I knew that 8 and 2 is 10, and 18 is like it except it has an extra 10, and 20 has an extra 10 than 10, and 5 more 25.

Teacher: (Redescribes Donald's explanation by referring to the symbolic record created when notating Jordan's solution.)

The predominance of these types of solutions appeared to be a direct consequence of the practices established during the Arithmetic Rack sequence. These ways of solving tasks by reasoning with the vertical line in fact appeared to constitute a new classroom mathematical practice.

The children's written responses to a subsequent instructional activity conducted on March 3 allow us to assess the extent to which they solved target tasks by imagining jumps on the vertical line. In this instructional activity, the children worked individually to complete target tasks that were presented on activity sheets. The statement of each task involved a vertical line with the initial and target numbers marked. At the outset, Ms. Smith asked the children to make a record of their thinking so that others could understand how they solved the tasks. In making this request, she stressed that the only criterion for ways of recording was that they be comprehensible to others. For the first task, which corresponded to 9 + ___ = 15, all 17 children gave six as their answer. One child wrote that she had used one of the available arithmetic racks, eight wrote number sentences or used elements of other notations developed during the Arithmetic Rack sequence, seven both wrote sentences and marked jumps on the vertical line, and one only marked jumps on the line. This pattern of responses provides an additional indication that the classroom mathematical practices that emerged during the Target activity were adaptations of those established during the Arithmetic Rack sequence. This inference corroborated by the observation that although the reasoning of the 16 students who recorded their thinking was diverse, in 15 cases it involved the numerical relationships 10 + 5 = 15 or 15 − 5 = 10. In the ensuing whole-class discussion, Ms. Smith reproduced some of the children's written records on the whiteboard and initiated a conversation in which ways of notating became an explicit focus of attention.

In summary, the vertical line that Ms. Smith drew appeared to be interactively constituted as a number line during the Target activity, in that the jumps appeared to have numerical significance for the children. To be sure, there were qualitative differences in the children's interpretations. For example, it is possible that some of the children might have interpreted the jumps as a sequence of hops from the starting number to the target number. For these children, the jumps would signify simple unitary quantities (e.g., 7 and 3 more is 10, and 3 more is 13). For other children, the jumps might have signified incremental increases (or decreases) in the starting number (e.g., 7 increased by 3 is 10, so 7 increased by 6 is 13). For the remainder of the analysis, we speak of the children reasoning with the empty number line with the understanding that their activity with the line had a range of qualitatively distinct numerical meanings.

At this point in the teaching experiment, the instructional challenge as we saw it was to support the children's development of reasoning with the empty number line to 100. To this end, we capitalized on the children's familiarity with the candy shop scenario by developing a trading game that the children played in pairs. In introducing the game, Ms. Smith explained that the candy in Mrs. Wright's shop cost 1¢ per piece. When playing the game, one child in each pair acted as the sales clerk in the shop and the other as the customer. At the beginning of the game, the customer had a bag containing plastic 1-cent, 5-cent, and 10-cent coins. The sales clerk had 100 candies (i.e., 100 unifix cubes arranged in bars of 10) and a cash register (i.e., a sheet of paper divided into columns headed 1¢, 5¢, and 10¢). To play the game, the children threw two dice to determine how many candies the customer would buy. The customer then paid the sales clerk, who put the coins in the cash register and gave the customer the appropriate number of candies. The children continued until the supply of candies had been exhausted. The number of each coin denomination provided was such that the customer quickly ran out of pennies, and the sales clerk had to give change.

This was in fact the third version of a trading game that we piloted during the teaching experiment. We had judged the two previous versions inadequate because some of the implicit suppositions and assumptions of the game that were self-evident to us proved to be counterintuitive to the children. In contrast, Ms. Smith was able to introduce this third version with little difficulty by initiating a discussion of out-of-school commercial transactions. The children played the game on three occasions with great enthusiasm, and their engagement in it appeared to be self-sustaining. Our instructional intent was simply that they would experience the gradual decrease in the initial supply of 100 candies and the increase in the amount of money in the cash register. Ms. Smith did in fact direct the children to check how many candies were left in the shop and how much money was in the cash register after each transaction. Some pairs ignored this directive, whereas others made written records in nonstandard notations on their own initiative.

Ms. Smith drew on the buying-and-selling scenario simulated in the trading game when she introduced a subsequent whole-class instructional activity on March 8 called Incrementing and Decrementing. In the incrementing version, she explained that there was no money in Mrs. Wright's cash register at the beginning of the day and then repeatedly described and, with a child, acted out transactions in which a sequence of customers bought candies. For each transaction, she asked the children to calculate the amount of money that was now in the cash register. As they did so, she recorded the cumulative total by constructing a vertical number line. For example, she drew the number line shown below to record the money in the cash register for sales of six candies, one roll, one roll, one roll, one roll, two candies, and one roll.

```
            58
   +10  
            48
   +2   
            46
   +10  
            36
   +10  
            26
   +10  
            16
   +10  
            6
   +6   
            0
```

We expected that the children would count by ones once tasks involved quantities beyond the range of those dealt with in the Arithmetic Rack sequence. We had in fact suggested to Ms. Smith that she repeatedly specify transactions involving one roll so that the children could abstract regularities from the successive results of counting (e.g., 16, 26, 36, 46). They might then curtail counting activity and begin to increment by 10. However, contrary to our expectations, the children's solutions were collection-based rather than counting-based and involved partitioning. For example, for the last three transactions recorded on the number line, the children explained:

Sarah: It's 46. Thirty and 10 more makes 40, and 6 more is 46.
Terri: Forty-eight—6 plus 2 is 8, so 46 plus 2 is 48.

Joseph: Fifty-eight—I know 5 tens are 50, and I add the 8 with it—58.

Another child subsequently formulated this partitioning strategy as a general method for adding 10.

These novel partitioning solutions appear to reflect the children's prior participation in the classroom mathematical practices established during the Candy Shop sequence almost a month earlier. In the last phase of that sequence, the activity of generating alternative partitionings of a collection of candies by creating and decomposing composites of 10 was an established practice. In this incrementing activity posed in the candy shop scenario, the interpretation of numbers as collection-based entities that could be partitioned into a tens part and a ones part appeared to be self-evident to the children. Further, almost all the children were able to participate in this practice, indicating that these numerical interpretations were taken as shared.

Anna was the first child to give a nonpartitioning explanation. There was, by this time, a total of 78 cents in the cash register and an additional 3 cents were placed in it.

Anna: Um, 81.
Teacher: Anna thinks now she would have 81 cents. How did you figure that out?
Anna: If you had 78 and you added 3, and you added 2 more that would make 80, and if you added 1 more, that would make 81.

Teacher: (Writes 78 + 2 = 80, 80 + 1 = 81 and draws as she redescribes Anna's explanation.)
Ellen: That's the way I thought about it.
Teacher: Is that the way you thought about it? Thank you.
Sarah: It's a good way.
Teacher: You think that's simple for you, it makes sense to you?

This going-through-a-decade solution appeared to reflect Anna's prior participation in the mathematical practices established during the Target activity. Anna's interpretation of the task might have been supported by Ms. Smith's drawing of a jump of three beyond 78 on the number line when she posed the task. It is important to note that a partitioning interpretation of this task would give rise to an additional complication that does not arise with, say, a task corresponding to 68 + 10. In the case of 68 + 10, the children might have recognized almost immediately that the result was 78 on the basis of imagery developed while participating in the Candy Shop sequence (cf. Whitson, chapter 7, this volume). For 78 + 3, however, they might recognize this as 70 and 11, but would then have to consciously calculate the result. In contrast, they might have recognized almost immediately that 78 was 2 less than 80, so an additional 1 would be 81. This experience of recognizing the result as 81 might in fact have motivated Sarah's comment that, "It's a good way." Significantly, Anna, Ellen, and Sarah were three of the children who had difficulty in using their fingers as perceptual substitutes at the beginning of the school year. It can also be observed that, by this point in the school year, the children took the initiative in indicating the mathematical interpretations and solutions they particularly valued.

In the remainder of this lesson, and in the next one in which the Incrementing and Decrementing activity was conducted (March 15), children continued to offer partitioning solutions that were grounded in imagery of the candy shop situation. For example, Terri gave the following explanation for a decrementing task in which there were 80 candies in the shop and a customer bought 4.

> Terri: I know that 10 plus, I mean 6 plus 4 is 10, so if you took away 4 from 80, you should have 76 'cause 6 plus 4 is 10 and 80 is 8 10s, and I messed up. Ten take away 4 is 6, so take away 4 should be 76.

However, going-through-a-decade solutions became increasingly common. For example, Joseph explained his answer of 66 to a decrementing task corresponding to 76 − 10 as follows:

> Joseph: I took away the 6.
> Teacher: You took away the 6 (writes 76 − 6).
> Joseph: I mean 5 because 5 and 5 is 10.
> Teacher: OK.
> Joseph: Because 6 and 4 would be 10. And then, so I took away the 6, and then I took away the 5 and that left me with 4.

Ms. Smith then asked Joseph how much was left when he took away six, and he clarified:

> Joseph: That left me with 70. And then I took away the other 5, the other 4, no, actually it's 66.

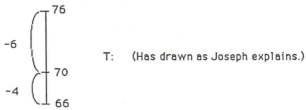

T: (Has drawn as Joseph explains.)

Another child then explained her solution to the next task posed, 66 − 10, as follows.

Anita: It's sort of like Joseph's way for the other one. I took the 6 and then I took away 4 more to get me down to 56.

The extent to which the children related their collection-based solutions to counting-based solutions that involved going-through-a-decade is open to question. These solutions might in fact have been alternative, unrelated approaches for the children that were based on differing numerical interpretations. The children's development of the collection-based methods can be traced to the mathematical practices established in the final phase of the Candy Shop sequence. In those practices pictured collections of rolls and candies served as models for arithmetical reasoning. Now, in the absence of such pictures, many of the children engaged in semantically grounded arithmetical reasoning in which conventional verbal and written symbols signified conceptual actions on taken-as-shared arithmetical objects. In terms of Greeno's (1991) environmental metaphor, these children could be said to be acting in an emerging arithmetical environment in which they simply recognized numerical relationships.

These unanticipated collection-based interpretations did not fit with our instructional intent of supporting the students' construction of increasingly sophisticated counting-based concepts and mental computation strategies. In retrospect, the children's going-through-a-decade solutions were also problematic from the point of view of our instructional agenda. This can be clarified by considering the development of these solutions from the going-through-ten solutions established during the Arithmetic Rack sequence. It will be recalled that, during the Target Activity, these latter solutions were symbolized by drawing number lines. The empty number line was subsequently extended to 100 during the Incrementing and Decrementing activity and served as a record of simulated transactions in the candy shop. However, the classroom mathematical practices associated with these transactions had been established during the Candy Shop sequence and were collection-based rather than counting-based. As a consequence, they did not provide a semantic grounding for the going-through-a-decade solutions that were symbolized on the number line. The empty number line had, in effect, emerged as a model of the transactions in the Candy Shop per se, rather than of the children's activity in that situation. As a consequence, the practice of going-through-a-decade appeared to be a calculational generalization of the going-through-ten strategy, rather than as a mathematization grounded in counting-based imagery for quantities to 100.

It should be stressed that this analysis is retrospective. At this point in the teaching experiment, we actually thought that the going-through-a-decade practice was grounded in the children's prior activity of playing the trading game and that the number line had been interactively constituted as a model of their activity in that situation. It was, in fact, to support this semantic grounding that Ms. Smith acted out transactions with a child when she posed incrementing and decrementing tasks. Our inferences concerning the quality of the children's activities initially appeared to be confirmed by the facility with which the children, working in pairs, created number lines to tell stories about what happened in the candy shop. However, events in the classroom a few days later on March 30 led us to revise our view.

In this pivotal lesson, Ms. Smith posed addition and subtraction tasks by drawing a horizontal empty number line, and by describing transactions in the candy shop, but without acting them out. One of the tasks posed corresponded to 90 − 8 (i.e., Mrs. Wright has 90 pieces of candy and she sells 8 of them). Terri and Jan justified the answer of 82 by giving a collection-based and a counting-based explanation, respectively. At this point, Donald attempted to justify his answer of 83.

> Donald: OK, if you have 90 pieces of candy and it couldn't be 82 'cause the 90, if you're counting it and taking away one, well it would just be the 98, it, you would be counting something extra. So you would take away 2; the 98 and the 99.

Donald appeared to misspeak when he said 98 and 99 instead of 88 and 89. At first glance, it might seem that he had arrived at his answer of 83 by counting backwards starting from 90 rather than 89. However, his comments in the remainder of the episode indicated that his interpretation of the task was relatively sophisticated. Collectively, these comments suggest that, for him, the ninth decade when counting comprised 80, 81, 82, . . . , 89. The 90 to which he referred appeared to be of special significance in that it signified an additional item beyond this decade. By this reasoning, the solution to 90 − 8 involved taking away the 90 and then 7 from the decade 80, 81, . . . , 89. The result for Donald was then 83 rather than 82.

As the exchange continued, Ms. Smith questioned Donald in an attempt to understand his thinking.

> Teacher: We're at 90, we have 90 pieces. You said if you took away one of those pieces you would have . . . (draws).

> Donald: 89. If you took away another one you would have 88. You've got 3 pieces [taken] away.

Teacher:	Now wait a second. You took away, Donald, you said you took away 1 piece, and that left you with 89. Is that what you said?
Donald:	(Nods.)
Teacher:	Then you took away one more piece, and that left you with 88. Is that right? (Draws.)

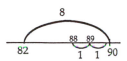

Donald:	Right.
Teacher:	So how many pieces have you taken away so far?
Donald:	Three.
Teacher:	OK, show me where are the three pieces you took away.
Donald:	The 90, 98, I mean the 90, the 89 and the 88 (points to the drawing).

For Donald, three rather than two candies had to be taken away to leave 88 because there was an additional candy beyond the ninth decade, the 90. Following this line of reasoning, 90 take away 2 would be 89 because it was necessary to take away the 90 and then one from the ninth decade.

In the subsequent discussion, several students voiced objections to Donald's claim that 83 candies would be left. Most of these contributions specified calculation processes but did not explicate underlying numerical interpretations. For example, Mark argued:

Mark:	Donald, if you minus 7 that would be, minus 8 from 90 would be 82 but if you minus 7 that would be 83, but we're not taking away 7, we're taking away 8 instead of 7.

To this, Donald responded:

Donald:	But I still think it's 83 'cause you're counting the 90 which you have to 'cause if you have 90 pieces and if you didn't count the 90, you'd just have 89 [pieces].

Presumably, from Donald's point of view, Mark and the other objectors were failing to take away the 90 beyond the ninth decade and were acting as though there were only 89 candies (i.e., 80, 81, . . . , 89).

At this juncture, Joseph offered an argument that eventually made it possible for numerical interpretations to become an explicit topic of conversation.

Joseph: Pretend this is 90 (holds up all 10 fingers).

Teacher: OK, pretend this is 90 (holds up her fingers). 10, 20, 30, 40, 50, 60, 70, 80, 90 (closes and opens her fingers with each counting act to simulate counting numerical composites of 10).

Joseph: If you take away one, do you see Donald (closes one finger), 1, 2, 3, . . . 8 (closes a further 7 fingers). 82. 'Cause see, watch. 1, 2, 3, . . . 8 (again closes 8 fingers). Eight. (Holds up his 2 extended fingers) Two more.

Joseph then repeated his argument at Ms. Smith's direction. She redescribed his activity with reference to the empty number line, and, in summary, said:

Teacher: OK (holds up all 10 fingers) he took away these 8 (closes 8 fingers) so he still has these 80 (points to the number line) and then these 2 left (holds up her 2 extended fingers).

However, this explanation did not resolve the situation. Kendra countered, "But that would leave the 80 and 81." Thus, Donald was not alone in making an unanticipated interpretation of the number line. Bob then volunteered:

Bob: I don't think it's 83 or 82. I think it's 81.

Joseph: No. This would make 10, 90 (holds up 10 fingers). 1, 2, 3, . . . 8 (closes 8 fingers).

Bob: But you've gotta count the 80, too.

Donald promptly elaborated Bob's claim, but to justify his answer of 83.

Donald: But wait a minute. These are 2 (points to Joseph's 2 extended fingers). Took away 8 and got 2, count the 80, you have 83.

As we have noted, for Donald, the ninth decade comprised 80, 81, 82, . . . , 89. Joseph's two remaining fingers signified 81 and 82, but the 80 from this decade had not been taken away. Consequently, in his interpretation, there were three additional candies, those signified by 80, 81, and 82. Bob and Kendra also seemed to assume that the ninth decade comprised 80, 81, 82, . . . , 89. However, they appeared to reason that taking away eight as indicated by Joseph folding down eight fingers would leave the candies signified by 80 and 81, and so there would be 81 candies left.

The children's contributions indicate that they were attempting to fulfill their obligation of attempting to understand each other's explanations. Further, these explanations appeared to carry the significance of acting on experientially real mathematical objects at least for the speaker. The difficulty was that Ms. Smith and the children interpreted the empty number line in a variety of different yet personally meaningful ways. They were, in fact, unable to establish an adequate basis for communication during the remaining 10 minutes of the lesson. This was the case even though Ms. Smith redescribed several of the children's explanations in considerable detail by referring to the empty number line she had drawn.

We previously noted that the empty number line as a way of symbolizing was first developed to record transactions in the candy shop per se, rather than to model counting-based practices involving quantities of up to 100. As a consequence, the children had to create a semantic grounding for the empty number line individually and privately by interpreting it in terms of counting activity. In looking through the notation to counting activity, they were in effect imagining an activity that could have given rise to this way of symbolizing. However, in their attempts to understand, they reconceptualized counting in a variety of different ways that now made it impossible for them to communicate effectively.

This analysis indicates that, contrary to our intentions, the empty number line was constituted in the classroom by means of a top-down rather than a bottom-up process. On the following day, March 31, Ms. Smith attempted to guide the development of a taken-as-shared semantic grounding for the empty number line. To this end, she placed bars of 10 unifix cubes end to end on a ledge at the bottom of the whiteboard. As she did so, she asked the children to pretend that each bar was a roll of candies. She then drew an empty number line directly above the unifix cubes and marked 0 on it directly above the beginning of the first bar. On the basis of our classroom observations, we inferred that the cubes could carry the significance of abstract units of one for the children, and that the bars of 10 could instantiate composite units of 10 for them. Thus, as a consequence of the children's participation in prior classroom mathematical practices, these were not the same unifix cubes or candies that were introduced at the beginning of the Candy Shop sequence. Our intent was that the children would refer to and, if necessary, count the cubes to explain their thinking with the empty number line. We conjectured that this might facilitate communication, and that the children might reorganize their reasoning with the empty number line. We also speculated that the arrangement of bars of 10 of different colors might make it possible for the children to curtail their going-through-a-decade reasoning. For example, they might come to recognize that, say, 38 plus 10 was 48 because two cubes of the next bar would remain uncounted if they were to count 10 on from 38. The sequence of unifix cubes can in fact be viewed as a substitute for the bead string that we omitted from the instructional sequence as it was originally outlined by its developers.

The first instructional activity that Ms. Smith and the children engaged in on March 31 was Incrementing and Decrementing. In redescribing the children's solutions, Ms. Smith partitioned the train of unifix cubes at the appropriate points and drew jumps on the empty number line directly above the blocks of cubes. For example, she symbolized a going-through-a-decade solution to a task corresponding to 56 − 10 as follows:

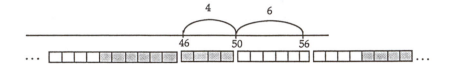

Further, she on occasion asked the children which pieces of candy (unifix cubes) would be needed to get from, say, 34 to 40. In contrast to the previous lesson (March 30), there were no instances where the children appeared to talk past each other for any length of time. Further, several of the children did appear to modify their interpretations of the number line. For example, Donald explained his answer of 18 to a task corresponding to 20 − 2 by saying, "you take away the 20 and the 19 leaves 18."

Despite these encouraging observations, we judged that neither this lesson nor those that succeeded it were entirely successful. Our primary concern was that the classroom discourse was, for the most part, concerned with computational processes rather than underlying numerical interpretations and focused on the specific jumps that students made on the number line to arrive at an answer. This might well have reflected the way in which the empty number line to 100 had originally been constituted by means of a calculational generalization of the going-through-ten strategy. Thus, although the children reorganized their reasoning with the empty number line, they continued to view it as a means of symbolizing mental computations. For example, four lessons later on April 19, Ms. Smith posed a task corresponding to 64 − 29 in the scenario of the candy shop. In giving her explanation, Karen simply specified a sequence of jumps that Ms. Smith recorded on an empty number line—take away 4 to leave 60, take away 10 to leave 50, take away 10 to leave 40, take away 5 to leave 35.

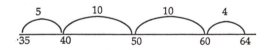

Explanations of this type were quite typical. Further, although such explanations did themselves become topics of conversation, the issues addressed concerned aspects of the computational process rather than its semantic grounding (e.g., why Karen first took away 4, or how she knew that she had taken away 29).

In the course of these discussions, two general types of computational strategies became institutionalized. In the first, illustrated by Karen's solution, the child adds or subtracts to complete a decade (e.g., $64 - 4 = 60$), then adds or subtracts tens (e.g., $60 - 10 = 50$, $50 - 10 = 40$, and finally adds or subtracts the remaining amount (e.g., $40 - 5 = 35$). The second type of solution is exemplified below for the same task, $64 - 29$.

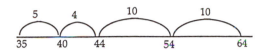

In this case, the child first adds or subtracts tens and then adds or subtracts the remaining amount, often by going through a decade (e.g., $44 - 4 = 40$, $40 - 5 = 35$). These two computational strategies comprised the mathematical practice of reasoning with the number line as it was interactively constituted in this classroom.

Several children did on occasion offer solutions that involved jumps greater than 10 (e.g., $64 - 29$ solved by reasoning $64 - 20 = 44$, $44 - 4 = 40$, $40 - 5 = 35$). However, others objected that it was difficult for them to follow such solutions and that solutions involving jumps of 10 were easier to understand. The objection in these instances was not that such solutions were invalid, but that some of the children did not immediately know the result of adding, say, 30 to 49. It was a consequence of these objections that the solutions were implicitly delegitimized.

The final significant development in the Empty Number Line sequence occurred when Ms. Smith began to record students' reasoning with the empty number line by writing number sentences. For example, shortly after Karen had explained how she had solved $64 - 29$, Bob attempted to clarify how he knew that she had taken away 29.

Bob: You see, I knew that she already took away the 4 (points to the empty number line) so now she's down to 60. (T writes $64 - 4 = 60$.) And then she took away 2 tens and that got her down to 40 (T writes $60 - 10 = 50$, $50 - 10 = 40$.) And then I knew if she took away 5 that would get her down to 9 (of the 29 she was taking away.)

In the ensuing discussion, Bob clarified that 2 tens, 4, and 5 made 29. The important point for our purposes is the way in which Ms. Smith notated Bob's description of Karen's solution. Drawing number lines and writing sentences subsequently became two of the primary ways in which the children symbolized their activity when they worked individually.

The analysis we have presented of the mathematical practices established during the empty number line sequence allows us to clarify the concerns we expressed when analyzing the children's May interviews. We noted that there was considerable uniformity in the children's solutions to tasks presented during the interviews and that most children repeatedly incremented or decremented by 10. The limited flexibility of their activity in the interviews appears to reflect their participation in the classroom mathematical practices established during the final phases of the instructional sequence. We have seen that these practices emerged via a process of calculational generalization rather than semantically grounded mathematization and that the focus of discussions was on aspects of computational processes rather than underlying numerical interpretations.

Lest we mislead the reader, it is also important to stress that the children's participation in the practices that involved reasoning with the empty number line appeared to have numerical significance for them. This was documented most clearly on April 25 and 26 when one of the researchers asked children on-camera how they were solving tasks during individual work. The tasks were addition and subtraction story problems. An unmarked empty number line was provided beneath each task statement and most of the children did attempt to solve the tasks by reasoning with the number line. However, in no case did their activity appear to be blindly imitative. Instead, the children attempted to semantically ground their activity. As a consequence, there were significant differences in the ways they acted with the line that reflected the qualitatively distinct meanings they had developed for it while participating in prior classroom mathematical practices. For example, Sarah drew the following number line when she solved a task corresponding to 62 − 34:

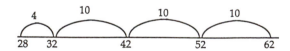

However, before doing so, she counted out 62 unifix cubes arranged as 6 bars of 10 and 2 individual cubes. She then slightly separated 34 cubes arranged as 3 bars of 10 and 4 cubes from the remainder of the collection before she began to draw.

Sarah: Take away 10 (removes a bar of 10 and draws the jump from 62 to 52) 52. Take away 10 (removes another bar of 10 and draws the jump from 52 to 42) 42. And then you take away one more [10] (removes a third bar of 10 and draws the jump from 42 to 32) 32. Take away 4 more (removes four cubes and counts the remaining cubes) 28.

Clearly, Sarah could have solved this task by simply using the unifix cubes. However, in drawing the number line, she reorganized her activity, in effect monitoring and analyzing what she was doing as she took away the 34 cubes. In the process, she created a semantic grounding for her activity with the number line in that a bar of 10 signified a composite unit of 10 for her.

A second child, Ellen, drew the following number line when she solved a task corresponding to 31 + 24.

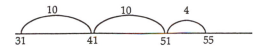

She first marked 31 on the number line and then counted-on 10 from 31 on her fingers before drawing the jump from 31 to 41. She again counted-on 10 before drawing the jump from 41 to 51, but then immediately drew the jump from 51 to 55. Based on the analysis of Ellen's May interview and of other observations of her classroom activity, we infer that in the absence of situation-specific imagery, she actually had to count by ones to create numerical composites of 10 (cf. Steffe, Cobb, & von Glasersfeld, 1988). Had she not reasoned with the empty number line, she might have attempted to count-on 24 from 31, but would have been unable to keep track. In reasoning with the number line, she reorganized her counting activity and created a protocol of action that could facilitate her reflection on what she had done.

As has been noted, Sarah and Ellen were two of the children who could not use fingers as perceptual substitutes at the beginning of the school year. It was encouraging from our point of view that they had developed personally meaningful ways to reason with the number line. The explanations that two further children, Kendra and Leigh, gave to the researcher illustrate the range of the children's reasoning. Kendra solved a task corresponding to 34 + 27 by drawing:

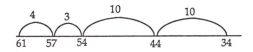

Kendra: I added 10.
Researcher: And that put you at what?
Kendra: 44. And I added 10 more and that made 54.
Researcher: Why did you add 3? You could have added 10 more.
Kendra: Well, I added it 'cause . . . well, this is 27.
Researcher: So you were trying to make 27?
Kendra: It would be 30 [if I added another 10].
Researcher: Oh, it would be too many? So you were keeping track in your mind?

The jumps that Kendra drew appeared to signify composite units of 10, and the record she created of her ongoing activity enabled her to monitor and keep track of what she was doing. This was also the case for Leigh's solution to the same task.

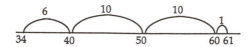

Leigh: I started at 34 and 6 more to get to 40. I added 10 more to get to 50. And I added 16 so far 'cause 10 and 6 is 16.
Researcher: And you're kind of keeping track in your mind?
Leigh: And then 10 more would be 26. And I saw that I only needed one more and that became 61.

Here, Leigh's activity with the empty number line appeared to carry the significance of a double increment. A jump of 10 seemed to increase both the quantity she was adding (e.g., 10 and 6 is 16) and the quantity she began with (e.g., 10 more to get to 50). She solved a range of tasks by double incrementing in the May interview without drawing a number line or writing sentences.

In the account we have given of the Empty Number Line sequence as it was realized in Ms. Smith's classroom, it is clear that the children's participation in practices that involved the use of the line profoundly influenced their reasoning as documented in the May interviews. We have also attempted to document that, within the microculture established in this classroom, the children had to develop ways of acting with the empty number line that had numerical significance for them in order to be effective. Their view of the jumps they drew as signifying composite units reflected intellectual capabilities that they had developed as they contributed to the evolution of the classroom mathematical practices.

Reflections on the Empty Number Line Sequence

We noted when discussing the Candy Shop sequence that the model of/model for transition described in the theory of RME can be seen to instantiate the emergence of a chain of signification. The signifying relationships that we speculated might emerge during the Empty Number Line sequence were:

| signified₁ | — | signifier₁ | — | signifier₂ |

signified$_1$ — signifier$_1$ — signifier$_2$

| | | |
mathematical pratices   empty   number
established during the   number line   sentences
Arithmetic Rack and
Candy Shop sequence

In particular, we hoped that the empty number line would initially serve as a model *of* forms of reasoning developed during the Arithmetic Rack and Candy Shop sequences. We conjectured that their activity with the number line would subsequently take on a life of its own and would function as a model *for* increasingly abstract yet personally meaningful mathematical reasoning that could be symbolized by writing number sentences.

The signifying relationships that actually were constituted by the classroom community were:

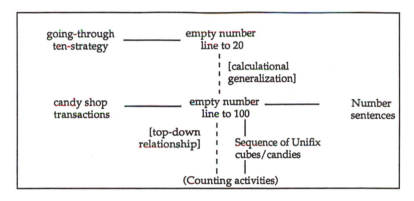

We noted that the empty number line to 100 was first developed to symbolize transactions in the candy shop, and that it supported the calculational generalization of the going-through-ten strategy. However, because the empty number line symbolized transactions in the candy shop rather than the children's arithmetical activity in that scenario, it did not serve as a model *of* their initially informal activity. Difficulties first became apparent when we attempted to support the emergence of the empty number line as a model *for* arithmetical reasoning. The children's contributions to a whole-class discussion on March 30 indicated that they reasoned with the empty number line in a variety of idiosyncratic although personally meaningful ways that made it difficult for them to communicate effectively. Crucially, it appeared that the process of constituting the empty number line was actually top-down rather than bottom-up, in that the children had to look through the notation and imagine an activity that could have given rise to this way of symbolizing. In Nemirovsky's (1994) terms, this involved coordinating two realms of experience, those of counting and of number lines. Significantly, these two realms can be seen to instantiate the sociocultural distinction between personal meaning (counting) and cultural meaning (the number line) (cf. Lektorsky, 1984; Leont'ev, 1981; van Oers, 1996). Thus, the emergence of the empty number line as it occurred in this classroom was consistent with a sociocultural perspective wherein the teacher's role is characterized as that of mediating between children's personal meanings and their cultural inheritance.

We introduced the sequence of unifix cubes/candies once we became aware of these difficulties. The bars of 10 cubes appeared to carry the significance of numerical composites of 10 for the children, and the individual cubes appeared to signify abstract units of one. Our intention was that the empty number line might be reconstituted as a model of the children's reasoning with these materials. Subsequent observations in which we documented the children's activity as they worked individually indicated that we had some success in this regard. The chain of signification that finally emerged was therefore:

$$\begin{array}{ccccc}
\text{signified}_1 & - & \text{signifier}_1 & - & \text{signifier}_2 \\
| & & | & & | \\
\text{(sequence of} & & \text{empty} & & \text{number} \\
\text{unifix cubes/candies} & & \text{number line} & & \text{sentences} \\
\text{composite units of 10} & & & & \\
\text{and abstract units of 1)} & & & &
\end{array}$$

It should, however, also be noted that the classroom discourse dealt almost exclusively with computational processes. Possibly as a consequence of its initial emergence via a process of calculational generalization, reasoning with the empty number line was constituted as a computational activity.

Thus far, this discussion of the Empty Number Line sequence has been conducted in sociological rather than psychological terms. We previously observed that an analysis that focuses only on the emergence of chains of signification has little to say about the creation and mental manipulation of experientially real mathematical objects. In this regard, we contend that it is entirely legitimate to bring individual children's constructive activities to the fore against the background of their participation in classroom mathematical practices. Such an analysis might document individual children's reorganizations of their activity and attempt to account for these reorganizations by using notions such as internalization, interiorization, and reflective abstraction. In our analysis, we have taken these constructive processes as background and have, for the most part, focused on the mathematical practices in which children participated as they reorganized their activity.

We conclude this discussion of the Empty Number Line sequence on a pragmatic note by observing that the analysis has immediate implications for our ongoing work in the classroom. It reveals that, initially, the empty number line did not emerge as a model of the children's informal mathematical activity. The primary reason for this shortcoming was that the mathematical practices established during the Candy Shop sequence were collection-based, whereas the empty number line was designed to fit with and to support the development of linear, counting-based reasoning.[16] It therefore

---

[16]It should be acknowledged that the bead string proposed by the developers of the Empty Number Line sequence was designed to avoid this conflict between collection-based classroom practices and counting-based reasoning. The informal measuring activities that we plan to

seems essential to radically modify the first part of the intended instructional sequence. In particular, new instructional activities are needed to support the construction of counting-based composites of 10 that are grounded in situation-specific imagery. To this end, we developed instructional activities that involved informal linear measuring and planned to use them in a classroom teaching experiment in collaboration with Ms. Smith during the 1995 through 1996 school year.[17]

DISCUSSION

We turn now to locate the analysis of the Candy Shop and Empty Number Line sequences in a broader theoretical context. To this end, we first clarify the relationship between mathematical learning and the social situation of development that is implicit in our analysis. We then consider the relation between the two general phases of developmental research, instructional development

---

develop will involve acting with a measurement stick that is structured in a similar way to the bead string. Our intent is to support the emergence of the measurement stick as a model of students' activity in experientially real situations.

[17]From this brief summary of our future plans, the reader might be misled into assuming that we will merely follow a traditional formative-evaluation approach of implementing a ready-made instructional sequence, and then evaluating its effectiveness. It is therefore important to clarify that the cyclic process of thought experiment and teaching experiment central to developmental research occurs at a variety of levels (cf. Gravemeijer, 1994b). At the most basic level, this cyclic process concerns the design and tryout of individual instructional activities on a day-to-day basis. At this microlevel, the researcher envisions both an instructional activity as it might be realized in the classroom, and the students' learning as they participate in it. The instructional activity is then enacted in the classroom, and an analysis of what happens is used to guide the design of the next instructional activity to be enacted in the same classroom. We touched on the design process at this microlevel during the discussion of the two instructional sequences when we mentioned both the children's unanticipated interpretations and the challenges we encountered during the teaching experiment.

At a second level, the cyclic process concerns an entire instructional sequence. The thought experiment at this level involves a local instructional theory that underlies a possible sequence of instructional activities. In the case of the Candy Shop and Empty Number Line sequences, for example, the local theory centered on conjectured model of/model for transitions. The teaching experiment at this level consists of trying out the entire sequence, in the course of which it is modified and refined on a daily basis as described. In addition, the revision of the entire sequence can also be guided by a retrospective analysis conducted once the experiment is completed. The analyses we have presented of the two instructional sequences as they were realized in Ms. Smith's classroom exemplify this process.

At a third level, the cyclic process is more distanced from classroom practice. The goal is to develop a domain-specific instructional theory by generalizing from various local instructional theories. The general tenets of RME instantiate a theory of this type. The empirical grounding of these tenets is provided by the cyclic alternation at the two lower levels. The issues considered in the final discussion section of this chapter also represent an attempt to step back from the specifics of the two instructional sequences.

and classroom-based research, that emerges from the analysis. Finally, we compare and contrast the approach we have taken with both sociocultural theory and theories of distributed cognition or distributed intelligence.

Learning in Social Context

One of our initial goals when analyzing the two instructional sequences was to elaborate the interpretative framework shown in Fig. 8.1. This goal was motivated by our broader concern to explore ways of accounting for mathematical learning as it occurs in social context. To this end, we first delineated aspects of the classroom microculture by documenting the classroom social norms and sociomathematical norms. Against this background, we then analyzed the mathematical practices that emerged as the instructional sequences were realized in the classroom. Within the encompassing classroom microculture, these classroom mathematical practices can be seen to constitute the local social situation of the children's development. Consequently, in specifying sequences of such practices, we have documented the evolving situations in which the children participated and learned.

This approach to learning in social context is generally consistent with the position developed by Lemke (chapter 3, this volume). In Lemke's view, we always perceive, act, and learn by participating in the self-organization of systems which are larger than our own organism. He calls these larger systems ecosocial systems because their ecology is semiotic; it is an ecology of meaning making, of taking one thing as a sign for another. In the case of our analysis, the ecosocial system is the community of practice constituted by Ms. Smith and her students in the classroom. As Lemke observes, such systems are self-organizing, developmental systems in which each stage sets up the conditions necessary for the occurrence of the next stage. With regard to our analysis, the classroom mathematical practices identified at a particular point in the school year can be seen to constitute the conditions for the emergence of the subsequent practices. For example, the practices developed during the Arithmetic Rack and Candy Shop sequences set up conditions for the emergence of the going-through-a-decade strategy as a calculational generalization, but did not set up the conditions for the emergence of the empty number line as a semantically grounded mathematization.

In the view that both we and Lemke are advancing, learning can be characterized as "an aspect of self organization, not just of the human organism as a biological system, but of the ecosocial system in which that organism functions as a human being" (p. 42). For Lemke, this implies that individuals "are constructs and products of the activity of the larger self-organizing system, the community and its semiotic ecology" (p. 47). Similarly, we have suggested that the children's participation in the semiotic ecology of the classroom community enabled and constrained their mathematical learning. However, we would also want to add that the larger self-organizing system, the community of practice in the classroom, can be viewed as the construct and product of Ms. Smith's and the children's attempts to coordinate their individual activities. In this formulation, the relationship between individual students' mathematical activity and the semiotic ecology that constitutes the social situation of their development is reflexive (cf. Cobb et al., 1993). This interpretive stance therefore offers an alternative to strong social or discursive perspectives wherein it is assumed that cognitive processes are produced by social or discursive practices (Lave & Wenger, 1991; Walkerdine, chapter 4, this volume). As has been suggested elsewhere (Cobb, 1994), the issue for us is not that of choosing which of these two characterizations gets the relation between the psychological and social or discursive realms right. We again follow Whitson (chapter 7, this volume) in suggesting that what are seen are human processes that can be analyzed in either psychological or social terms, depending on the purposes at hand. In our case, the purposes derive from classroom-based developmental research and, in this setting, we contend that a focus on individual students' constructive activities and the social situation of their development can be productive.

Instructional Development and Developmental Research

The analysis of the mathematical practices established by the classroom community offers an account of the Candy Shop and Empty Number Line sequences as they were enacted in the classroom. In arguing that these sequences as they were realized in interaction with the local situation of the children's development, the analysis draws together the two general aspects of developmental or transformational research—instructional development and classroom-based research. We elaborated this linkage in the course of the analysis by relating the model of/model for distinction that guided the instructional development process to Walkerdine's (1988) notion of a chain of signification.

The model of/model for distinction is, in effect, a conjecture about the semiotic ecology that might be constituted when an instructional sequence is enacted in the classroom, and about individual children's development as they participate in the evolution of this ecology. During the analysis of both instructional sequences, we illustrated that the model of/model for distinction can be interpreted as a conjectured chain of signification. In addition, we clarified that the semiotic ecology actually established by the classroom community can be described as the emergence of a chain of signification. It was by drawing on this single set of interrelated constructs that we were able to coordinate the two aspects of the developmental research process. This in turn made it possible for us to capitalize on both the positive heuristics for instructional development proposed by the theory of RME and on an established interpretive framework within which to analyze what transpired in the classroom when instructional sequences are realized in interaction.

It is important to stress that Walkerdine's (1988) notion of a chain of signification offers an account of the process by which signifiers can take on a life of their own, freed from the domination of signifieds that might have initially provided a realistic grounding for the mathematical signs established by the classroom community. As a consequence, this notion is particularly well suited to our purposes as mathematics educators. During our reflections on the Candy Shop sequence, we clarified that a sign comprises a signified/signifier pair. In the course of the discussion, we also noted that a chain of signification is constituted as a sign slides under a succeeding signifier. In the case of the Candy Shop sequence, the chain of signification established by Ms. Smith and her students was:

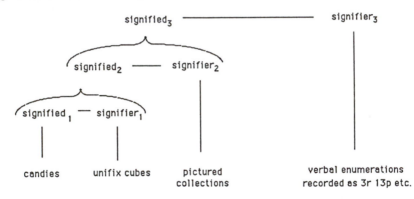

We also observed that, during the Empty Number Line sequence, the children gave collection-based solutions to Incrementing and Decrementing tasks (e.g., 36 + 10 solved as "30 and 10 more makes 40, and 6 more is 46"). As these solutions reflected the children's prior participation in the mathematical practices established during the Candy Shop sequence, it is reasonable to add a further link to the previous chain:

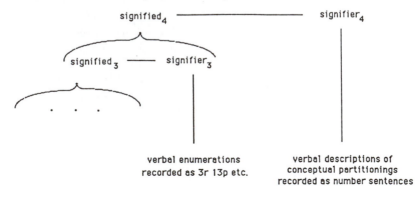

It is important to stress that in Walkerdine's (1988) account, the meaning of the original sign combination (i.e., candies/unifix cubes) is not merely masked by succeeding signifiers as a chain of signification is constituted. Instead, its meaning evolves as signs, that originated in relation to certain concerns and interests, slide under subsequent signifiers. The preceding diagram can be reorganized to bring this aspect of the chain of signification to the fore.

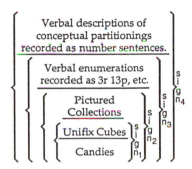

This, in sociolinguistic terms, is an account of the process of mathematization.

As Whitson (chapter 7, this volume) observes, an analysis of this type does not address the interests, concerns, and purposes that motivate signification. In this regard, it is important to stress that the chain of signification shown was constituted as the children participated in and contributed to the evolution of the classroom mathematical practices. The taken-as-shared motivation for signification can therefore be specified by delineating the concerns and interests of these practices. For example, the meaning of the candies/unifix cubes combination ($sign_1$) was constituted within the scenario about Mrs. Wright's shop, in which the concerns and interests were those of a simulated commercial buying and selling practice. In contrast, the concerns and interests that motivated the constitution of the final link in the chain, $sign_4$, were primarily computational.

It is also important to note that an account given solely in sociolinguistic terms is potentially behaviorist in that to act rationally or to know means no more and no less than to act in accord with the norms and standards of the community. However, Lemke (chapter 3, this volume) argues that:

> because practices are not just performances, not just behaviors, not just material processes or operations, but meaningful actions, actions which have relations of meaning to one another in terms of some cultural system, one must learn not just what and how to perform, but also what the performance means, in order to function and be accepted as a full member of a CoP [Community of Practice]. One must know the meaning in order to appropriately deploy the practice, to know when and in what context to perform how. Or one must know because knowing is a condition of membership. (p. 43)

In our terms, this development of meaning involves the creation and manipulation of experientially real mathematical objects. We attempted to take account of this during the analysis of the two instructional sequences by considering the taken-as-shared mathematical reality that emerged as the classroom community constituted chains of signification. For example, we argued that the children's reasoning with the empty number line had numerical significance for them even though its motivation appeared to be computational. More generally, in discussing the development of arithmetical meanings, we were in effect considering how the meaning of the original sign combination in a chain evolved as the chain was constituted.

We have suggested that an attention to meaning and to the emergence of a taken-as-shared mathematical reality admits a psychological analysis. The focus of this perspective is on individual students' internalization and interiorization of mathematical activity via reflective abstraction as they participate in classroom mathematical practices. Clearly, given that signification is central to these practices, it is also integral to the process of reflective abstraction. In this regard, a parallel can be observed between the process of constituting a chain of signification and the conceptual activity of the students who contribute to this process. In particular, we have seen that as a chain of signification emerges, signifiers come to take on a life of their own, freed from the domination of signifieds that might have initially provided a realistic grounding for signs. Similarly, Steffe et al.'s (1983, 1988) detailed psychological analyses of individual children's mathematical development documented a series of conceptual reorganizations whereby children's activity was gradually freed from the tyranny of perception. These reorganizations, which are seen as instances of reflective abstraction, have been characterized more generally by Thompson (1992) in terms of three qualitatively distinct types of individual imagery. It seems reasonable to suggest that Steffe et al. and Thompson on the one hand, and Walkerdine (1988) on the other, are giving alternative psychological and sociolinguistic accounts of similar developments. Analyses that explicitly coordinate these two theoretical perspectives might therefore further clarify the relation between signification and conceptual reorganization. The analysis we have presented in this chapter represents one attempt to move in this direction.

Emergent and Sociocultural Perspectives

In the introductory section of this chapter, we drew several contrasts between sociocultural and emergent approaches in mathematics education. The most fundamental of these concerned the underlying metaphors used to characterize learning in instructional situations. We suggested that the central metaphor in sociocultural approaches is that of the transmission of mathematical meaning from one generation to the next, and that in emergent approaches it is that of the individual and collective emergence of mathematical meaning in the classroom. It is important to stress that our focus in the introductory discussion was on the entailments of these two metaphors for instructional development and the teacher's role. Our focus now shifts to the second aspect of the developmental research cycle, that of interpreting what occurs as instructional sequences are realized in interaction in the classroom.

It is apparent from our discussion of chains of signification that we fully accept Vygotsky's fundamental insight that semiotic mediation is crucially involved in students' conceptual development. The issue at hand is that of accounting for or explaining the nature of this involvement. This issue is significant because it is often assumed that a sociocultural stance must necessarily be adopted if the central role of semiotic mediation is to be addressed. The analysis we have presented constitutes an alternative that admits the psychological view of learning as active individual construction, but sees it as inextricably bound up with processes of signification.

In sociocultural accounts of semiotic mediation, social and cultural processes are given precedence over individual psychological processes. For example, in one line of explanation associated most directly with Vygotsky, cultural tools such as conventional mathematical symbols are said to be internalized and to become psychological tools for thinking (Davydov & Radzikhovskii, 1985; Rogoff, 1990). In a second line of explanation associated with Leont'ev (1978), individuals are said to appropriate cultural tools to their own activity. Both formulations distinguish between sociohistorically developed cultural meanings embodied in the appropriate use of the tool and students' personal meanings. Further, both give accounts of learning that reflect the transfer metaphor. In each case, learning is characterized as the process by which students inherit the cultural meanings that constitute their intellectual bequest from prior generations.

In concert with sociocultural approaches, the alternative explanation that we have given emphasizes the central role of signification. However, learning is viewed as a process of active individual construction, as well as a process of enculturation. Further, ways of symbolizing are treated as emergent phenomena interactively constituted by the classroom community. Students are seen to reorganize their mathematical ways of knowing as they participate in the classroom mathematical practices that necessarily involve signification as integral aspects. It is our contention that an interpretive approach of this type is better suited to the purposes of developmental research in that it provides greater precision than sociocultural approaches. For example, a sociocultural analysis of the Empty Number Line sequence might account for the children's learning in terms of their appropriation or internalization of a particular way of symbolizing. Such an analysis does not specify the evolving social situation of the children's development—the instructional sequence as it was realized in interaction in this particular classroom. In addition, it has difficulty in accounting for qualitative differences in individual children's mathematical interpretations, except to the extent that they can be tied to the children's participation in different out-of-school communities of practice (cf. Crawford, 1996; Newman, Griffin, & Cole, 1989). Both these issues were, however, addressed in the analysis of the Empty Number Line sequence we presented and have implications for the revision of the instructional sequences and for the follow-up teaching experiment we plan to conduct.

In this discussion, we have been careful to tie our preference for an emergent analysis to the purposes of developmental research. We would therefore acknowledge that a sociocultural approach might well be preferable for other purposes. With regard to the relationship between the two interpretive stances, an emergent analysis might be said to recast appropriation processes by specifying how they are realized in interaction by the members of a specific community (cf. Cobb, Jaworski, & Presmeg, 1996). What, at the global level of the reproduction of the culture, is viewed as a process of transmission becomes, at the local level, a process of emergence in which students' constructive activities and the practices in which they participate are considered to be reflexively related.

Distributed Intelligence

In acknowledging Vygotsky's central insight concerning semiotic mediation, the approach we are advancing holds several points in common with theories of distributed intelligence. This latter perspective has evolved from mainstream American psychology and draws heavily on Vygotsky's (1981) treatment of cultural tools. The central tenet of this viewpoint is that intelligence is distributed "across minds, persons, and the symbolic and physical environments, both natural and artificial" (Pea, 1993, p. 47). In Dörfler's (in press) formulation, this implies that thinking

> is no longer located exclusively within the human subject. The whole system made up of the subject and the available cognitive tools and aids realizes the thinking process. . . . Mathematical thinking for instance not only *uses* those cognitive tools as a separate means but they form a constitutive and systematic part of the thinking process. The cognitive models and symbol systems, the sign systems, are not merely means for expressing a qualitatively distinct and purely mental thinking process. The latter realizes itself and consists in the usage and development of the various cognitive technologies.

This contention that cognitive technologies are integral to intellectual development is consistent with our analysis of the children's learning in the first-grade classroom. As Pea (1993) and Dörfler (in press) noted, tools are not merely amplifiers of human capabilities, but they lead to the reorganization and restructuring of activity. This phenomenon was documented repeatedly during both the Candy Shop and Empty Number Line sequences. In the Candy Shop sequence, for example, the children's development of collection-based interpretations of 10 occurred as they acted with unifix cubes and reasoned with the pictured collections. Similarly, in the second sequence, the children developed the ways of thinking documented in the May interviews as they participated in classroom mathematical practices that involved reasoning with the empty number line. Interventions made by a researcher on April 25 and 26 to document individual children's activity in the classroom illustrated various ways in which the children reorganized their activity as they reasoned with the number line. More generally, the distributed view of intelligence is partially consistent with the theory of RME that guided the instructional development process. In particular, the model of/model for distinction reflects the assumption that the development of ways of symbolizing involves the reorganization of thought.

It is important to note that the distributed view of intelligence attempts to transcend the traditional dualism between activity and the world. The account we have given of developments in the first-grade classroom is also nondualist. We have emphasized that the children participated in and contributed to the development of the classroom mathematics practices. By virtue of this participation, they were necessarily acting in a taken-as-shared world of signification that, in Lemke's (chapter 3, this volume) terms, constituted the semiotic ecology of the classroom community. Further, we have suggested that the relationship between individual children's activity and the classroom mathematical practices is reflexive. The children's activity and the world in which they acted can therefore be viewed as mutually constitutive. As Whitson (chapter 7, this volume) observes, an approach of this type that begins with activity in a world of signification and meaning simply bypasses a number of traditional philosophical issues including the classical problem of reference.

Thus far, we have emphasized several points of convergence between the distributed view of intelligence and the analysis of the first-grade classroom. We now turn to consider two issues that differentiate these approaches. The first concerns the tool metaphor and the second concerns the characterization of the individual in distributed accounts of intelligence. In each case, the differences we discuss instantiate the contrast between the sociocultural and emergent perspectives.

The significance that Vygotsky (1981) attributed to cultural tools can be traced to Marx's (1890) definition of man as a tool-making animal. Vygotsky apparently drew on Engel's (1925) elaboration of this view to argue that human history is the history of artifacts that makes possible the mastery of nature. In developing the tool metaphor, Vygotsky focused on the technologylike aspects of culture that support the control of the environment (e.g., language, counting systems, and writing) and ignored a variety of other aspects (e.g., systems of law, moral thinking, art, and religion) (van der Veer & Valsiner, 1991). As Dewey (1909/1977) observed, this instrumental orientation separates the means of thought from the ends of thought (cf. Prawat, 1995). Dewey illustrated this point by contrasting two alternative ways of thinking about the role of scaffolding in the construction of a building. In one, it is viewed as an external piece of equipment, and in the other, it is considered to be integral to the activity of building. "Only in the former case can the scaffolding be considered a *mere* tool. In the latter case, the external scaffolding is *not* the instrumentality; the actual tool is the action of erecting the building, and this action involves the scaffolding as a constituent part of itself" (Dewey, 1977, p. 362; cited in Prawat, 1995). Dewey's contention was that the characterization of the scaffolding as an external tool necessarily treats it as a means of constructing predetermined types of buildings. As a consequence, the characterization does not account for either the development of ways of building that involve the use of scaffolding, or for the concomitant evolution of the ends, the types of buildings that could be constructed. Whitson (chapter 7, this volume) makes a similar point when he notes that this view of thought is concerned only with an instrumental or functional adequacy in responding to technical problems with the set of tools and materials at hand in the immediate situation, and stops short of any critical questioning of the general situation within which that situation is embedded. However, the critical questioning of underlying assumptions is precisely what is involved in the restructuring of activity. An internal tension therefore seems to arise in distributed views of intelligence, in that explanations cast in terms of the metaphor of an external tool do not account for a phenomenon of central interest—the process of reorganizing activity.

We can clarify the point that Dewey and Whitson made by noting that when we talk of a tool, we necessarily do so as observers of already-developed forms of activity. In effect, we distance ourselves from the activity and treat it as a given entity that can be dissected into ends and means. This, it should be stressed, is a perfectly adequate way of talking for many purposes. For example, we could describe the interpretive framework presented earlier in this chapter as a tool and note that we used it to analyze the first-grade classroom. Here, the framework is treated as something preconstructed and objectified that can be picked up and used for a given purpose: that of analyzing individual and collective activity during mathematics instruction. However, this way of talking does not address the processes of learning and reorganization inherent in the development of the framework. It is, of course, precisely the process of coming to know that is of direct relevance to our purposes as mathematics educators.

This same argument holds when we consider the development of ways of symbolizing and notating. For example, we could simply talk of the first-graders using the empty number line as a problem-solving tool. However, this characterization does not account for the evolution of the children's activity such that they eventually became able to reason with the empty number line. In general, distributed accounts of intelligence provide compelling demonstrations that tool use can result in changes in forms of activity. For example, in one common illustration, it is argued that the use of the computer makes possible a shift to conceptual planning and problem solving because computational processes can be offloaded to the computer. Illustrations of this type indicate a possible reorganization by, in effect, comparing before and after snapshots. However, they do not specify the process of transition from one snapshot to the other in which the ends evolve along with the means. For our purposes, it is important to move beyond global explanations framed in terms of the tool metaphor and analyze the process of reorganization in which the ends and means are seen to be interdependent.

In the alternative that Dewey (1977) proposed to the tool metaphor, artifacts are considered to be constituent parts of purposeful human activities. This general orientation was taken when analyzing the first-grade classroom. It was, in fact, to locate artifacts in activity that we spoke of the children reasoning with, say, the empty number line, rather than of them using the empty number line as a problem-solving tool. A frequently cited illustration given by Bateson (1973) further clarifies what is involved in treating the artifact as integral to activity. "Suppose I am a blind man, and I use a stick. I go tap, tap, tap. Where do I start? Is my mental system bounded at the hand of the stick? Is it bounded by my skin? Does it start halfway up the stick? Does it start at the tip of the stick" (p. 459)? For Bateson, the person acting and the artifact acted with are inseparable. Significantly, in making this point, Bateson approached activity from the inside rather than from the observer's perspective. He asked us to pretend to be a blind person and to imagine the nature of his or her experience when using the stick. This actor's perspective can be contrasted with the observer's perspective inherent in sociocultural and distributed intelligence approaches wherein artifacts are typically treated as external, culturally given tools that function as carriers of meaning from one generation to the next. From the actor's perspective, the ends and means are seen to be inseparable. In the case of Bateson's illustration, for example, the tool is the act of tapping with the stick, not the stick, per se. It is therefore self-evident from this point of view that acting with an artifact can involve the restructuring of activity for the straightforward reason that to act with an artifact is to engage in a different form of activity. The approach exemplified by the analysis we have presented might therefore be thought of as distributed intelligence with a phenomenological twist.

The second point of contrast between distributed intelligence and the approach we took when analyzing the first-grade classroom concerns the characterization of the individual. As we have seen, in distributed accounts of intelligence, cognition is said to be stretched over the individual, the social context, and tools. This entire functional system is considered to be the only legitimate unit of analysis, and would in fact appear to constitute the mind (Pea, 1993). Formulated in this way, distributed intelligence challenges several central tenets of mainstream American psychology. For example, it rejects the traditional separation between internal representations in the head and external representations in the world. Nonetheless, distributed intelligence still carries vestiges of its development from mainstream psychology even as it reacts against it. This is particularly apparent in the debate between Pea (1993) and Salomon (1993) on the legitimacy of the individual as a unit of analysis.

Salomon (1993) contended that, in distributed accounts of intelligence, "the individual has been dismissed from theoretical consideration, possibly as an antithesis to the excessive emphasis on the individual by traditional psychology and educational approaches. But as a result the theory is truncated and conceptually unsatisfactory" (p. 111). Salomon subsequently argued that some competencies are not distributed but are instead solo achievements, and that the individual is the appropriate unit of analysis in such cases. Pea (1993), for his part, countered that many tools and social networks are invisible, and that intelligence is distributed even in the case of apparently solo intelligence and purely mental thinking processes. Despite these differences in perspective, Pea and Salomon appear to agree on at least one point. The individual of whom they both speak is the disembodied creator of internal representations who inhabits the discourse of mainstream psychology. It is this theoretical individual who features in Pea's claim that intelligence is distributed across the individual, tools, and social context. In developing his viewpoint, Pea, in effect, attempted to equip this mainstream character with cultural tools and place it in social context. However, in doing so, he implicitly accepted the traditional characterization of the individual and preserved it as a component of tool–person systems even as he explicitly rejected it. As a consequence, he found it difficult to give Salomon a compelling reason why this theoretical individual should not be taken as a unit of analysis. In our view, this second tension in distributed accounts of intelligence can be traced to the assumption that mainstream psychology offers the only possible conception of the individual. For Pea and for Salomon, one either accepts the mainstream characterization or one rejects the very notion of the individual as a legitimate unit of analysis.

The alternative approach that we have proposed is based on a different conception of the individual in which physical devices, notations, and symbol systems are viewed as constituent parts of human activities. In the case of Bateson's (1973) example of the blind person, what Pea (1993) might have called the person–stick system is, when viewed from the actor's perspective, simply an instance of a person negotiating his or her environment.

Similarly, a child reasoning with the empty number line might, from the perspective of distributed cognition, constitute a child–tool system. However, in our analysis, this was interpreted as an instance of the child engaging in mathematical activity of which the empty number line is a constituent part. In general, the children in this analysis are not the putative creatures of traditional psychology. Instead, their cognition is seen to be embodied, or to be located in activity (Johnson, 1987; Piaget, 1970; Winograd & Flores, 1986). Further, rather than representing a world, they are portrayed as enacting a taken-as-shared world of signification (Varela, Thompson, & Rosch, 1991). Consequently, whereas distributed accounts of intelligence dismiss the individual from theoretical consideration, the approach we have taken places the actively cognizing individual in a central role. With this shift in the characterization of the individual, the entire dispute between Pea and Salomon dissipates, in that activity can be analyzed in psychological or social terms as the need arises.

CONCLUSION

A primary reason for conducting the analysis of the first-grade classroom was to explore ways of accounting for learning as it occurs in the social context of the classroom. This was a pressing issue, in that we did not have adequate ways of understanding what might be going on in the classrooms where we conduct developmental research. In our view, it seems essential to go beyond traditional, individualistic accounts of learning, but without uncritically accepting Vygotskian alternatives that were developed for other purposes. To this end, we have outlined a perspective that preserves Vygotsky's key insights, although leaving room for the conception of children as active constructors of their ways of knowing. This approach gives particular attention to signification by focusing on the ways of symbolizing, notating, and acting with physical materials established by a classroom community, and on students' mathematical development as they participate in such processes. We also illustrated that this approach draws together the two general phases of the developmental research cycle, instructional development and classroom-based research. This latter aspect of the approach leads us to hope that analyses conducted along these lines might contribute to current reform efforts in mathematics education.

ACKNOWLEDGMENT

The analysis reported in this chapter was supported by the National Science Foundation under grant No. RED-9353587. The opinions expressed do not necessarily reflect the views of the Foundation.

REFERENCES

Balacheff, N. (1990a). Future perspectives for research in the psychology of mathematics education. In P. Nesher & J. Kilpatrick (Eds.), *Mathematics and cognition* (pp. 135–148). Cambridge, MA: Cambridge University Press.

Balacheff, N. (1990b). Towards a problematique for research on mathematics teaching. *Journal for Research in Mathematics Education, 21*, 258–272.

Ball, D. L. (1993). With an eye on the mathematical horizon: Dilemmas of teaching elementary school mathematics. *Elementary School Journal, 93*, 373–397.

Bateson, G. (1973). *Steps to an ecology of mind.* London: Paladin.

Bauersfeld, H. (1988). Interaction, construction, and knowledge: Alternative perspectives for mathematics education. In T. Cooney & D. Grouws (Eds.), *Effective mathematics teaching* (pp. 27–46). Reston, VA, and Hillsdale, NJ: National Council of Teachers of Mathematics and Lawrence Erlbaum Associates.

Bauersfeld, H., Krummheuer, G., & Voigt, J. (1988). Interactional theory of learning and teaching mathematics and related microethnographical studies. In H.-G. Steiner & A. Vermandel (Eds.), *Foundations and methodology of the discipline of mathematics education* (pp. 174–188). Antwerp, Belgium: Proceedings of the TME Conference.

Bednarz, N., Dufour-Janvier, B., Poirier, L., & Bacon, L. (1993). Socioconstructivist viewpoint on the use of symbolism in mathematics education. *Alberta Journal of Educational Research, 39*, 41–58.

Beishuizen, M. (1993). Mental strategies and materials or models for addition and subtraction up to 100 in Dutch second grades. *Journal for Research in Mathematics Education, 24*, 294–323.

Bloor, D. (1976). *Knowledge and social imagery.* London: Routledge & Kegan Paul.

Blumer, H. (1969). *Symbolic interactionism: Perspectives and method.* Englewood Cliffs, NJ: Prentice-Hall.

Brousseau, G. (1984). The crucial role of the didactical contract in the analysis and construction of situations in teaching and learning mathematics. In H.-G. Steiner (Ed.), *Theory of mathematics education* (pp. 110–119). Occasional paper 54. Bielefeld, Germany: Institut für Didaktik der Mathematik.

Brown, J. S., Collins, A., & Duguid, P. (1989). Situated cognition and the culture of learning. *Educational Researcher, 18*(1), 32–42.

Carpenter, T. P. (1980). Heuristic strategies used to solve addition and subtraction problems. In R. Karplus (Ed.), *Proceedings of the Fourth International Conference for the Psychology of Mathematics Education* (pp. 317–321). Berkeley: University of California.

Carpenter, T. P., & Moser, J. M. (1982). The development of addition and subtraction problem solving skills. In T. P. Carpenter, J. M. Moser, & T. A. Romberg (Eds.), *Addition and subtraction: A cognitive perspective* (pp. 9–24). Hillsdale, NJ: Lawrence Erlbaum Associates.

Clement, J., & Brown, D. E. (1989). Overcoming misconceptions via analogical reasoning: Abstract transfer versus explanatory model construction. *Instructional Science, 18*, 327–361.

Cobb, P. (1983). *Children's strategies for finding sums and differences.* Unpublished doctoral dissertation, University of Georgia, Atlanta.

Cobb, P. (1989). Experiential, cognitive, and anthropological perspectives in mathematics education. *For the Learning of Mathematics, 9*(2), 32–42.

Cobb, P. (1994). Where is the mind? Constructivist and sociocultural perspectives on mathematical development. *Educational Researcher, 23*(7), 13–20.

Cobb, P. (1995). Mathematical learning and small group interaction: Four case studies. In P. Cobb & H. Bauersfeld (Eds.), *Emergence of mathematical meaning: Interaction in classroom cultures* (pp. 25–129). Hillsdale, NJ: Lawrence Erlbaum Associates.

Cobb, P., & Bauersfeld, H. (1995). Introduction: The coordination of psychological and socio-logical perspectives in mathematics education. In P. Cobb & H. Bauersfeld (Eds.), *Emergence of mathematical meaning: Interaction in classroom cultures* (pp. 1–16). Hillsdale, NJ: Lawrence Erlbaum Associates.

Cobb, P., Jaworski, B., & Presmeg, N. (1996). Emergent and sociocultural views of mathematical activity. In L. P. Steffe, P. Nesher, P. Cobb, G. Goldin, & B. Greer (Eds.), *Theories of mathematical learning*. Mahwah, NJ: Lawrence Erlbaum Associates.

Cobb, P., & Wheatley, G. (1988). Children's initial understandings of ten. *Focus on Learning Problems in Mathematics, 10*(3), 1–28.

Cobb, P., & Whitenack, J. W. (in press). A method for conducting longitudinal analyses of classroom videorecordings and transcripts. *Educational Studies in Mathematics.*

Cobb, P., Wood, T., & Yackel, E. (1993). Discourse, mathematical thinking, and classroom practice. In N. Minick, E. Forman, & A. Stone (Eds.), *Education and mind: Institutional, social, and developmental processes* (pp. 91–119). New York: Oxford University Press.

Cobb, P., Wood, T., Yackel, E., & McNeal, G. (1992). Characteristics of classroom mathematics traditions: An interactional analysis. *American Educational Research Journal, 29,* 573–602.

Cobb, P., Yackel, E., & Wood, T. (1989). Young children's emotional acts while doing mathe-matical problem solving. In D. B. McLeod & V. M. Adams (Eds.), *Affect and mathematical problem solving: A new perspective* (pp. 117–148). New York: Springer-Verlag.

Cole, M., & Engeström, Y. (1993). A cultural-historical approach to distributed cognition. In G. Salomon (Ed.), *Distributed cognitions* (pp. 1–46). New York: Cambridge University Press.

Confrey, J. (1995). How compatible are radical constructivism, sociocultural approaches, and social constructivism? In L. P. Steffe & J. Gale (Eds.), *Constructivism in education* (pp. 185–225). Hillsdale, NJ: Lawrence Erlbaum Associates.

Crawford, K. (1996). Cultural processes and learning: Expectations, actions, and outcomes. In L. Steffe, P. Nesher, P. Cobb, G. Goldin, & B. Greer (Eds.), *Theories of mathematical learning*. Mahwah, NJ: Lawrence Erlbaum Associates.

Davis, P. J., & Hersh, R. (1981). *The mathematical experience.* Boston: Houghton Mifflin.

Davydov, V. V. (1988). Problems of developmental teaching (part II). *Soviet Education, 30*(9), 3–83.

Davydov, V. V., & Radzikhovskii, L. A. (1985). Vygotsky's theory and the activity-oriented approach in psychology. In J. V. Wertsch (Ed.), *Culture, communication, and cognition: Vygotskian perspectives* (pp. 35–65). New York: Cambridge University Press.

De Corte, E., Greer, B., & Verschaffel, L. (1996). Mathematics learning and teaching. In D. Berliner & R. Calfee (Eds.), *Handbook of educational psychology.* New York: Macmillan.

Dewey, J. (1977). In J. A. Boydston (Ed.), *John Dewey, The middle works, 1899–1924* (Vol. 2, pp. 362–363). Carbondale: Southern Illinois University Press.

Dörfler, W. (1989). Protocols of actions as a cognitive tool for knowledge construction. In *Proceedings of the Thirteenth Conference of the International Group for the Psychology of Mathematics Education* (pp. 212–219). Paris: PME.

Dörfler, W. (1991). Meaning: Image schemata and prototypes. In F. Furinghetti (Ed.), *Proceedings of the fifteenth conference of the International Group for the Psychology of Mathematics Education* (Vol. 1, pp. 17–32). Genoa, Italy: Università di Genova, Dipartimento di Matematica.

Dörfler, W. (in press). Computer use and views of the mind. In C. Keitel & K. Ruthven (Eds.), *Learning from computers: Mathematics education and technology.* New York: Springer-Verlag.

Engel, F. (1925). *Dialektik der Natur* [Dialectics of nature]. Berlin: Dietz Verlag.

Erickson, F. (1986). Qualitative methods in research on teaching. In M. C. Wittrock (Ed.), *The handbook of research on teaching* (3rd ed., pp. 119–161). New York: Macmillan.

Fischbein, E. (1987). *Intuition in science and mathematics.* Dordrecht, The Netherlands: Reidel.

Fischbein, E. (1989). Tacit models and mathematical reasoning. *For the Learning of Mathematics,* 9(2), 9–14.

Forman, E. (1996). Forms of participation in classroom practice: Implications for learning mathematics. In L. Steffe, P. Nesher, P. Cobb, G. Goldin, & B. Greer (Eds.), *Theories of mathematical learning.* Mahwah, NJ: Lawrence Erlbaum Associates.

Freudenthal, H. (1991). *Revisiting mathematics education.* Dordrecht, The Netherlands: Kluwer Academic Publishers.

Fuson, K. C. (1990). Issues in place-value and multidigit addition and subtraction learning. *Journal for Research in Mathematics Education, 21,* 273–280.

Gergen, K. J. (1985). The social constructionist movement in modern psychology. *American Psychologist, 40,* 266–275.

Glaser, B. G., & Strauss, A. L. (1967). *The discovery of grounded theory: Strategies for qualitative research.* New York: Aldine.

Gravemeijer, K. (1990). Context problems and realistic mathematics instruction. In K. Gravemeijer, M. van den Heuvel, & L. Streefland (Eds.), *Contexts, free productions, tests, and geometry in realistic mathematics education* (pp. 10–32). Utrecht, The Netherlands: OW & OC Research Group.

Gravemeijer, K. P. E. (1991). An instruction-theoretic reflection on the use of manipulatives. In L. Streefland (Ed.), *Realistic mathematics education in primary school* (pp. 57–76). Utrecht, The Netherlands: CD-ß Press.

Gravemeijer, K. P. E. (1994a). *Developing realistic mathematics education.* Utrecht, The Netherlands: CD-ß Press.

Gravemeijer, K. (1994b). Educational development and developmental research. *Journal for Research in Mathematics Education, 25*(5), 443–471.

Gravemeijer, K. (in press). Mediating between concrete and abstract. In T. Nunes & P. Bryant (Eds.), *How do children learn mathematics?* Mahwah, NJ: Lawrence Erlbaum Associates.

Greeno, J. G. (1991). Number sense as situated knowing in a conceptual domain. *Journal for Research in Mathematics Education, 22,* 170–218.

Hatano, G. (1993). Time to merge Vygotskian and constructivist conceptions of knowledge acquisition. In E. A. Forman, N. Minick, & C. A. Stone (Eds.), *Contexts for learning: Sociocultural dynamics in children's development* (pp. 153–166). New York: Oxford University Press.

Johnson, M. (1987). *The body in the mind: The bodily basis of reason and imagination.* Chicago: University of Chicago Press.

Kamii, C. K. (1985). *Young children reinvent arithmetic.* New York: Teachers College Press.

Kaput, J. J. (1987). Towards a theory of symbol use in mathematics. In C. Janvier (Ed.), *Problems of representation in the teaching and learning of mathematics* (pp. 159–195). Hillsdale, NJ: Lawrence Erlbaum Associates.

Kaput, J. J. (1991). Notations and representations as mediators of constructive processes. In E. von Glasersfeld (Ed.), *Constructivism in mathematics education* (pp. 53–74). Dordrecht, The Netherlands: Kluwer.

Kaput, J. J. (in press). Overcoming physicality and the eternal present: Cybernetic manipulatives. In R. Sutherland & J. Mason (Eds.), *Visualization and technology in mathematics education.* New York: Springer-Verlag.

Kozulin, A. (1990). *Vygotsky's psychology. A biography of ideas.* Brighton, UK: Harvester Wheatsheaf.

Lacan, J. (1977). *Ecrits: A selection.* London: Tavistock.

Lakoff, G., & Johnson, M. (1980). *Metaphors we live by.* Chicago: University of Chicago Press.

Lampert, M. (1990). When the problem is not the question and the solution is not the answer: Mathematical knowing and teaching. *American Educational Research Journal, 27*(1), 29–63.

Lave, J. (1988). *Cognition in practice: Mind, mathematics and culture in everyday life.* New York: Cambridge University Press.

Lave, J. (1993). Word problems: A microcosm of theories of learning. In P. Light & G. Butterworth (Eds.), *Context and cognition: Ways of learning and knowing* (pp. 74–92). Hillsdale, NJ: Lawrence Erlbaum Associates.

Lave, J., & Wenger, E. (1991). *Situated learning: Legitimate peripheral participation.* New York: Cambridge University Press.

Lektorsky, V. A. (1984). *Subject object cognition.* Moscow: Progress Publishers.

Leont'ev, A. N. (1978). *Activity, consciousness, and personality.* Englewood Cliffs, NJ: Prentice-Hall.

Leont'ev, A. N. (1981). The problem of activity in psychology. In J. V. Wertsch (Ed.), *The concept of activity in Soviet psychology* (pp. 37–71). Armonk, NY: Sharpe.

Marx, K. (1890). *Das Kapital.* Berlin: Dietz Verlag.

Mason, J. (1987). What do symbols represent? In C. Janvier (Ed.), *Problems of representation in the learning and teaching of mathematics* (pp. 73–82). Hillsdale, NJ: Lawrence Erlbaum Associates.

McClain, K. J. (1995). *The teacher's proactive role in supporting students' mathematical growth.* Unpublished doctoral dissertation, Vanderbilt University, Nashville, TN.

Mehan, H., & Wood, H. (1975). *The reality of ethnomethodology.* New York: Wiley.

Minick, N. (1987). The development of Vygotsky's thought: An introduction. In R. W. Rieber & A. S. Carton (Eds.), *The collected works of Vygotsky, L. S.: Problems of general psychology* (Vol. 1, pp. 17–38). New York: Plenum.

Much, N. C., & Shweder, R. A. (1978). Speaking of rules: The analysis of culture in breach. *New Directions for Child Development, 2,* 19–39.

Nemirovsky, R. (1994). On ways of symbolizing: The case of Laura and the velocity sign. *Journal of Mathematical Behavior, 13*(4), 389–422.

Neuman, D. (1987). *The origin of arithmetic skills: A phenomenographic approach* (Göteborg Studies in Educational Sciences, 62). Göteborg, Sweden: Acta Universitatis Göthoburgensis.

Newman, D., Griffin, P., & Cole, M. (1989). *The construction zone: Working for cognitive change in school.* New York: Cambridge University Press.

Nunes, T. (1992). Ethnomathematics and everyday cognition. In D. A. Grouws (Ed.), *Handbook of research on mathematics teaching and learning* (pp. 557–574). New York: Macmillan.

Nunes, T., Schliemann, A. D., & Carraher, D. W. (1993). *Street mathematics and school mathematics.* New York: Cambridge University Press.

Pea, R. D. (1987). Cognitive technologies for mathematics education. In A. H. Schoenfeld (Ed.), *Cognitive science and mathematics education* (pp. 89–122). Hillsdale, NJ: Lawrence Erlbaum Associates.

Pea, R. D. (1993). Practices of distributed intelligence and designs for education. In G. Salomon (Ed.), *Distributed cognitions* (pp. 47–87). New York: Cambridge University Press.

Piaget, J. (1970). *Genetic epistemology.* New York: Columbia University Press.

Piaget, J. (1973). *To understand is to invent.* New York: Grossman.

Pimm, D. (1987). *Speaking mathematically: Communication in mathematics classrooms.* London: Routledge & Kegan Paul.

Pirie, S., & Kieren, T. (1994). Growth in mathematical understanding: How can we characterise it and how can we represent it? *Educational Studies in Mathematics, 26,* 61–86.

Presmeg, N. C. (1992). Prototypes, metaphors, metonymies and imaginative reality in high school mathematics. *Educational Studies in Mathematics, 23,* 595–610.

Prawat, R. S. (1995). Misreading Dewey: Reform, projects, and the language game. *Educational Researcher, 24*(7), 13–22.

Rogoff, B. (1990). *Apprenticeship in thinking: Cognitive development in social context.* Oxford, UK: Oxford University Press.

Salomon, G. (1993). No distribution without individuals' cognition: A dynamic interactional view. In G. Salomon (Ed.), *Distributed cognitions* (pp. 111–138). New York: Cambridge University Press.

Saxe, G. B. (1991). *Culture and cognitive development: Studies in mathematical understanding.* Hillsdale, NJ: Lawrence Erlbaum Associates.

Saxe, G. B., & Bermudez, T. (1996). Emergent mathematical environments in children's games. In L. P. Steffe, P. Nesher, P. Cobb, G. Goldin, & B. Greer (Eds.), *Theories of mathematical learning.* Mahwah, NJ: Lawrence Erlbaum Associates.

Schoenfeld, A. H. (1987). What's all the fuss about metacognition? In A. H. Schoenfeld (Ed.), *Cognitive science and mathematics education* (pp. 189–216). Hillsdale, NJ: Lawrence Erlbaum Associates.

Schutz, A. (1962). *The problem of social reality.* The Hague, The Netherlands: Martinus Nijhoff.

Sfard, A. (1991). On the dual nature of mathematical conceptions: Reflections on processes and objects as different sides of the same coin. *Educational Studies in Mathematics, 22,* 1–36.

Sfard, A. (1994, September). *The development of the concept of concept development: From God's eye view to what can be seen with mind's eye.* Paper presented at the Symposium on Trends and Perspectives in Mathematics Education, Klagenfurt, Austria.

Sfard, A., & Linchevski, L. (1994). The gains and the pitfalls of reification—The case of algebra. *Educational Studies in Mathematics, 26,* 87–124.

Steffe, L. P., Cobb, P., & von Glasersfeld, E. (1988). *Construction of arithmetical meanings and strategies.* New York: Springer-Verlag.

Steffe, L. P., von Glasersfeld, E., Richards, J., & Cobb, P. (1983). *Children's counting types: Philosophy, theory, and applications.* New York: Praeger.

Steinberg, R. M. (1985). Instruction on derived fact strategies in addition and subtraction. *Journal for Research in Mathematics Education, 16,* 337–355.

Streefland, L. (1991). *Fractions in realistic mathematics education. A paradigm of developmental research.* Dordrecht, The Netherlands: Kluwer.

Tall, D. (1989). Concept images, generic organizers, computers, and curriculum change. *For the Learning of Mathematics, 9*(3), 37–42.

Tharp, R. G., & Gallimore, R. (1988). *Rousing minds to life.* New York: Cambridge University Press.

Thompson, P. W. (1992). Notations, principles, and constraints: Contributions to the effective use of concrete manipulatives in elementary mathematics. *Journal for Research in Mathematics Education, 23,* 123–147.

Thompson, P. W. (1994). Images of rate and operational understanding of the Fundamental Theorem of Calculus. *Educational Studies in Mathematics, 26,* 229–274.

Thompson, P. W. (1996). Imagery and the development of mathematical reasoning. In L. Steffe, P. Nesler, G. Goldin, & B. Greer (Eds.), *Theories of mathematical learning.* Mahwah, NJ: Lawrence Erlbaum Associates.

Treffers, A. (1987). *Three dimensions: A model of goal and theory description in mathematics instruction—The Wiskobas Project.* Dordrecht, The Netherlands: Reidel.

Treffers, A. (1990). Rekentot twintig met het rekenrek [Addition and subtraction up to twenty with the arithmetic rack]. *Willem Bartjens, 10*(1), 35–45.

Treffers, A. (1991). Didactical background of a mathematics program for primary education. In L. Streefland (Ed.), *Realistic mathematics education in primary school* (pp. 21–57). Utrecht, The Netherlands: CD-ß Press.

van der Veer, R., & Valsiner, J. (1991). *Understanding Vygotsky: A quest for synthesis.* Cambridge, MA: Blackwell.

van Oers, B. (1990). The development of mathematical thinking in school: A comparison of the action-psychological and the information-processing approach. *International Journal of Educational Research, 14,* 51–66.

van Oers, B. (1996). Learning mathematics as meaningful activity. In L. Steffe, P. Nesher, P. Cobb, G. Goldin, & B. Greer (Eds.), *Theories of mathematical learning.* Mahwah, NJ: Lawrence Erlbaum Associates.

Varela, F. J., Thompson, E., & Rosch, E. (1991). *The embodied mind: Cognitive science and human experience*. Cambridge, MA: MIT Press.

Voigt, J. (1985). Patterns and routines in classroom interaction. *Recherches en Didactique des Mathematiques, 6*, 69–118.

Voigt, J. (1994). Negotiation of mathematical meaning and learning mathematics. *Educational Studies in Mathematics, 26*(2–3), 273–298.

Voigt, J. (1995). Thematic patterns of interaction and sociomathematical norms. In P. Cobb & H. Bauersfeld (Eds.), *Emergence of mathematical meaning: Interaction in classroom cultures* (pp. 163–202). Hillsdale, NJ: Lawrence Erlbaum Associates.

Voigt, J. (1996). Negotiation of mathematical meaning in classroom processes. In L. P. Steffe, P. Nesher, P. Cobb, G. Goldin, & B. Greer (Eds.), *Theories of mathematical learning*. Mahwah, NJ: Lawrence Erlbaum Associates.

von Glasersfeld, E. (1984). An introduction to radical constructivism. In P. Watzlawick (Ed.), *The invented reality* (pp. 17–40). New York: Norton.

von Glasersfeld, E. (1991). Abstraction, re-presentation, and reflection: An interpretation of experience and Piaget's approach. In L. P. Steffe (Ed.), *Epistemological foundations of mathematical experience* (pp. 45–67). New York: Springer-Verlag.

Vygotsky, L. S. (1979). Consciousness as a problem in the psychology of behavior. *Soviet Psychology, 17*(4), 3–35.

Vygotsky, L. S. (1981). The genesis of higher mental functions. In J. V. Wertsch (Ed.), *The concept of activity in Soviet psychology* (pp. 144–188). Armonk, NY: M. E. Sharpe.

Vygotsky, L. S. (1987). Thinking and speech. In R. W. Rieber & A. S. Carton (Eds.), *The collected works of Vygotsky, L. S.: Problems of general psychology* (Vol. 1, pp. 39–288). New York: Plenum. (Original work published 1934)

Walkerdine, V. (1988). *The mastery of reason*. London: Routledge.

Wertsch, J. V. (1985). *Vygotsky and the social formation of mind*. Cambridge, MA: Harvard University Press.

Whitenack, J. W. (1995). *Modeling, mathematizing, and mathematical learning as it is situated in the classroom microculture*. Unpublished doctoral dissertation, Vanderbilt University, Nashville, TN.

Williams, S. (1992, August). *Kerygma and being-for-the-other: A continental view of classroom discourse*. Paper presented at the International Congress on Mathematical Education, Québec City, Canada.

Winograd, T., & Flores, F. (1986). *Understanding computers and cognition: A new foundation for design*. Norwood, NJ: Ablex.

Yackel, E., & Cobb, P. (1993, April). *Classroom microcultures reform in mathematics education*. Paper presented at the annual meeting of the American Educational Research Association, Atlanta, GA.

Yackel, E., & Cobb, P. (1996). Sociomath norms, argumentation, and autonomy in mathematics. *Journal for Research in Mathematics Education, 27*, 458–477.

Yang, M. T.-L., & Cobb, P. (1995). A cross-cultural investigation into the development of place value concepts in Taiwan and the United States. *Educational Studies in Mathematics, 28*, 1–33.

CHAPTER NINE

Thinking, Learning, and Reading:
The Situated Sociocultural Mind

James Paul Gee
Clark University

This chapter is ultimately about reading, but it will take a while to get there. I first look at how children acquire the concepts associated with words. This suggests a view of mind, meaning, and learning that stresses the situated and sociocultural nature of all of them and contains important implications for educational theory and practice. Then I turn to the nature of reading, both in terms of textual types (genres) and content, arguing that the model of concept acquisition sketched earlier is also a model of reading. Finally, I briefly discuss the implications of this model in the context of debates over the death of the literary canon and proposals for critical or resistant reading. I do this because I want to suggest how talk about the mind, far from precluding political discussion, invites it.

Before I begin in earnest, I want to say something about the theoretical underpinnings of the approach I take here, so that readers can situate it within the large body of literature relevant to the sociocultural nature of thinking and language. The claim that thinking and meaning are *situated* (i.e., that they are dove-tailed to particular purposes and social contexts) is now a popular one and stems from work in a variety of disparate areas, where the meaning of the word *situated* itself takes on somewhat differently situated meanings. The approach I take in this chapter is an attempt to render the notion of situated cognition (and situated word meaning) accessible and usable for readers from a variety of backgrounds while taking a particular perspective on it. I have sought an approach that captures something at the heart of many different accounts of situated cognition in a variety of disciplines. Although I have certainly been influenced by standard work on situated and distributed cognition (e.g., Brown, Collins, & Duguid, 1989; Lave, 1988; Lave & Wenger, 1991; Rogoff, 1990), the theoretical underpinnings of my account also reside in a variety of other areas.

I was originally inspired by connectionist theories of how the mind works in cognitive science. Connectionism is a family of viewpoints in cognitive science that claims that the human mind is not so much a calculator and rule follower on the order of a digital computer (as traditional cognitive accounts hold), but a flexible and adaptable pattern recognizer (P. M. Churchland, 1989; P. S. Churchland, 1986; P. S. Churchland & Sejnowski, 1992; A. Clark, 1989, 1993). There is not space here for a technical account of connectionism and its relationship to socially situated theories of meaning (but see Gee, 1992a, for an accessible account). However, the idea that we humans are primarily adept at recognizing, using, and transforming patterns (that, in a sense, all thinking works a lot like seeing and recognizing) is argued in work that goes beyond, and sometimes disagrees with the technical details of, connectionism (e.g., Hofstadter, 1995; Margolis, 1987, 1993; Nolan, 1994).

Not only is thinking a good deal like seeing (i.e., built around fluidly changing perspectives, patterns, and images built up in context), but it intimately involves acting and probing in and on the world. This aspect of thought is nicely captured in Schon's (1983, 1987) well-known work on reflective practitioners. Schon stressed how experts (whether architects, teachers, musicians, etc.) build up their arsenal of concepts through reflection not just on, but in practice. Their concepts are intimately tied to practical situations and courses of action and are fluidly adapted and changed in actual practice. Their concepts do not sit formed once and for all in their heads in grand isolation from the vicissitudes of practice and judgment.

Another inspiration for my approach in this chapter is activist accounts of the development and use of concepts, work quite compatible with both connectionism and with Schon's ideas, but stemming from cognitive psychologists. Psychologists like Barsalou (1987, 1991, 1992) have argued that we do not just passively retrieve prefabricated concepts out of our heads as the need for them is triggered by our experiences. Rather, we actively put together the features that will compose a customized version of the concept to fulfill the thinking and communicating needs we face and the goals we form. In some cases, this constructive process is strikingly apparent, as when I ask you what might unite things like my small child, my pet cat, my valuable painting, and my treasured photo album, and you place these disparate things under a concept like "things I would save first if my house was on fire." But even with common words like *coffee, light, democracy,* and so forth, the argument is that in context, these common labels name a fairly concrete pattern that we have actively put together to fit our needs and purposes in context (e.g., liquid-in-a-cup vs. grains-in-a-tin).

Just such an activist account of concept formation (and word meaning) has also come from a quite different source, namely Kress' work (e.g., Kress, in press) in social semiotics. Kress traced the early development of signs (words and pictures, e.g., a child using four circles to represent a car) and argues that children pick features (here, circles) that are apt in a given context and for a specific purpose to serve as a representation (here, for car). Children exemplify clearly a process that Kress (and I) argues occurs in the cognitive and social practices of adults as well:

> Signs are motivated conjunctions of meaning and form, in which the meanings of the sign-maker lead him or her to the apt, plausible, motivated expression of meaning in the most apt form. This process rests on the *interest* of the maker of the sign, which leads her or him to focus on particular aspects of the object to be represented as being, at this moment, criterial. (p. 5)

Kress' account of the child who picks circles to stand for wheels and wheels to represent a whole car indicates clearly the close ties between the view of thinking and meaning I have taken here and the copious research on analogies and analogical thinking. Work on analogical thinking has argued that what looks like a general concept or schema is often composed of and/or originally developed out of a specific set of analogies. For example, in research typical of this domain, Gick and Holyoak (1983; see also Holyoak & Thagard, 1995) gave subjects specific analogies. For example, they compared a doctor fighting a tumor by directing relatively weak x-rays at it from a variety of different directions (so as to concentrate the rays on the tumor without concentrating them too heavily on any other tissue) to a firefighter extinguishing an oil-well fire by using multiple small hoses, or to a general attacking a central fortress by sending small numbers of troops along a variety of different roads leading to the fortress, each of which could accommodate only small numbers without setting off alarms. The subjects, through exposure to multiple such analogies, eventually formed and used a more general convergence schema (much like a general-seeming concept). The formation of such a schema requires exposure to multiple concrete examples and is always tied more or less to such concrete exemplars, although in the expert, the schema becomes increasingly accessible and is triggered by and adapted to novel problems (i.e., the schema allows new concrete examples/patterns of the schema to be constructed, transformed, and adapted—new situated meanings to arise).

The study of the use of analogies and the growth of schemas raises an issue that I address directly in this chapter: if concepts and word meanings are situated (i.e., they are, in actual use, fairly concrete patterns customized to context) then what gives them their feeling of generality? To answer this question, I have turned away from typical schema theory in psychology (which I find too tied to private minds and too little tied to social practices).

Instead, I have used research on cultural models, stemming from psychological anthropologists who study discourse in social and cultural contexts (D'Andrade & Strauss, 1992; Holland & Quinn, 1987). Cultural models allow us to relate people's everyday folk theories (i.e., the shared stories that they use to explain their experiences) to more formal theories in academic disciples. Such relationships are sometimes quite overt: for example, I later discuss research (Harkness, Super, & Keefer, 1992) on middle-class parents who explain any new and disruptive behavior on the part of their toddlers as a stage that the child is going through in his or her growth toward independence (a highly valued goal for this group). Other parents see such behavior as the already too-independent behaviors of unsocialized children who need to be disciplined toward cooperativeness (Philipsen, 1975, 1990). The first cultural model of children's development, of course, is strikingly close to academic views of child development in child psychology. Of course, the folk theory and the academic one have engaged in a great deal of collusion (through shared class interests and self-help guide books).

Finally, my account is directly inspired by sociological and historical studies of scientists at work (Latour, 1987; Lynch, 1985; Pickering, 1992). Such studies show that working scientists do not just apply general theories and deduce neat and logical conclusions from them. Rather, they coordinate themselves (in body and mind) with instruments, tools, symbolic and linguistic expressions, other people, objects being studied, and places like laboratories so as to chain all these together into a coherent pattern or configuration that works. Here we see patterns not in the mind, but actual material configurations of objects, tools, people, and activities in the world. The scientist's mind, too, I argue, is peopled with such coordinations and connections, or with the materials to actively construct them and put them into action. The pattern "strongly focused and directed light fit for purposes X, Y, and Z" that serves as a contextually specific meaning of *light* (namely, in regard to lasers) is, itself, in actuality, but one element that the scientist uses to coordinate and get coordinated in real-world configurations of thinking, doing, and acting.

My account, then, is my version of a way to combine work on connectionism, concept formation, reflective practice, cultural models, and the sociology of science with an account of how children acquire the meanings of words (where we start next) and a sociocultural approach to language and literacy. The final goal, however, is to say something that is applicable to the practices and values of education in regard to multicultural classrooms and a multicultural world.

CHILDREN ACQUIRING CONCEPTS

The nature of words, especially written words, gives us a misleading, because overly general and asocial, view of both *meaning* and *mind*. A brief look, however, at how children go about acquiring the concepts associated with words can serve as an antidote to this view of meaning and mind, and can suggest a better one. Consider, then, the case of a little girl learning the word *shoe*. At first, she used the word only for the shoes in her mother's closet. Eventually, however, she overextended (E. Clark, 1993) the meaning of the word (beyond what adults would use it for) and used it, not only in situations where shoes were involved, but also while handling her teddy bear's shoeless feet, passing a doll's arm to an adult to be refitted on the doll, putting a sock on a doll, and when looking at a picture of a brown beetle (Griffiths, 1986). At this point, the little girl associated the word with a variety of different contexts, each of which contained one or more salient features that could trigger the use of the word. The picture of the beetle is associated with the word *shoe* presumably in virtue of features like shiny and hard and oval shaped; the doll's arm merits the word *shoe* in virtue of features like fit-able to the body and associated with a limb of the body, and so forth.

But this little girl must come eventually to realize that the features associated with a word are not just a list to be applied as they arise serially. Rather, they are correlated in certain ways, and these correlations are important for applying the word (A. Clark, 1993). For example, in the case of shoes, features like hard, shiny, formal, solid color, and with thin laces tend to go together, picking out a certain set of shoes (formal shoes), and features like soft, colored trim, thick laces, and others tend to go together, picking out a different set of shoes (e.g., athletic shoes). There are other feature correlations that pick out other sorts of shoes. And there are feature correlations like having a shape contoured to a human foot, covering a significant amount of the foot, flexible enough to fit on the foot, but relatively rigid that hang together in such a way that they pick out a very large class of the whole set of shoes, although even these are not a necessary and sufficient set of conditions for shoes in general. There are still borderline cases, like moccasins (not really hard enough) and sandals (do not really cover enough). When the child reaches this point, she is finding patterns and subpatterns in the contexts in which the word *shoe* is used (Barsalou, 1992).

But the child cannot stop with patterns. For adults, the concepts associated with words involve more than knowledge of feature correlations and patterns. They also involve a (sometimes rather rough and ready) explanation of the correlations or patterns (Anglin, 1977; Keil, 1979, 1989): Why do these things hang together this way? That is, the correlated features (patterns) are required to make sense within some kind of cause–effect model or theory of the domain (here, feet and footwear). These explanations, models, or theories, however, are very often tacit, largely unconscious, or, at least, not easily articulated in any very full fashion, and they are often incomplete in some ways. This does not mean that they are not also often very deep and rich in their own way.

In the case of our example, the correlated features hang together because of things to do with the fact that humans wear clothes (and shoes in particular) for protection, but that they are also items of fashion (style), and that different sorts of clothes are better or poorly suited for different tasks and activities, and that all these things vary with one's social or cultural group or subgroup. The child eventually comes to form a theory (really, we should say the child comes to share with his or her community a more or less tacit theory) of the shoe domain, a theory in which higher-order concepts like protection, style, and activities play a role. This theory makes sense of the patterns the child has found, and, in turn, may well lead the child to discern yet deeper or more complicated patterns. Because such theories are rooted in the practices of the sociocultural groups to which the learner belongs, I refer to them as *cultural models* (Gee, 1992a; Holland & Quinn, 1987). Bits and pieces of a cultural model are in people's heads, although much of it resides in the practices and settings of cultural groups and, thus, need not take up residence inside heads.

In my rendition of the child acquiring the meaning of a new word, I have taken the view, which is becoming progressively more common in work in cognitive science and the philosophy of mind, that the human mind is, at root, a pattern recognizer (Bechtel & Abrahamsen, 1990; A. Clark, 1993; Margolis, 1987, 1993; Rumelhart, McClelland, & the PDP Group, 1986). To acquire a concept, learners must have both numerous examples (experience) and must uncover the patterns and subpatterns in those examples that are the ones explicated by their socioculturally situated theories (Nolan, 1994). Because the world is infinitely full of potentially meaningful patterns and subpatterns in any domain, something must guide the learner in selecting the patterns and subpatterns to focus on. This something resides in the cultural models of the learner's sociocultural groups and the practices and settings in which they are rooted. Because the mind is a pattern recognizer and there are infinite ways to pattern features of the world, of necessity, although perhaps ironically, the mind is social (really, cultural) in the sense that sociocultural practices and settings guide the patterns in terms of which the learner thinks, acts, talks, values, and interacts (Gee, 1992a). This need not, however, mitigate each learner's own agency—because each individual belongs to multiple sociocultural groups, the cultural models and patterns associated with each group can influence the others in unique ways, depending on the different mix for different individuals (Kress, 1985). And, of course, each individual is biologically and, in particular, neurally quite different from every other one (and the patterns are stored in networks of neurons. See Crick, 1994).

CONCEPT ACQUISITION AS THREE DIALOGUES

The process of concept development is dynamic, interactive, and socioculturally situated. One way to look at the process is in terms of three dialogues. The child carries out a dialogue with the world in which he engages in actions; that is, probes the world and reflects while acting (reflection-in-action) and after acting (reflection-on-action) on the ways in which the world talks back (Schon, 1987). The child's actions and reflections are directed by and, in turn, help to revise his cultural models. The interaction of the child's action-reflection and his cultural models constitute the child's dialogue with the sociocultural world.

The child's actions and reflections (guided as they are by his cultural models) are also directed by and, in turn, help to revise the patterns he is uncovering through the mind and brain as a feature extractor and pattern recognizer. The child, through his action and reflection, becomes a self-teacher, training his own mental networks of associations (patterns). The interaction of the child's action and reflection (guided by cultural models) and the patterns he is uncovering constitutes dialogue with his own mind as a pattern recognizer. Figure 9.1 diagrams this interactive picture.

What we see here is a system made up of the world, the mind, and society, a system in which the boundaries between these three are not airtight and clearly separable. We can take various routes through the system: Actions can change patterns that, in turn, change cultural models; cultural models can modify patterns that, in turn, cause us to act in certain ways, ways that may change patterns and, in turn, cultural models.

This picture sets us up to ask a very specific and important question: When the child acts and reflects, probes the world and gets a result, on what basis does the child determine the significance—and the acceptability—of the result? The very form of this question makes it clear that the child must evaluate the answer coming back from the world, must determine whether he or she likes it or not, whether it is good or not. Otherwise, why use the answer in reflection and subsequent dialogues with his or her own mind and with the social and cultural worlds? If the child likes it, then he or she will use it to revise the patterns he or she is finding and the theories he or she is developing. The child can only determine what he or she likes, what is a good result, in terms of an appreciative system—a set of goals and values (D'Andrade & Strauss, 1992; Schon, 1987). Such a system is always part and parcel of any cultural model, and many cultural models share a range of values with others so that we can talk about various master

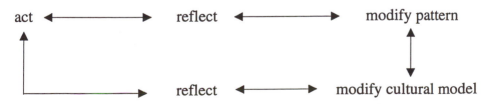

FIG. 9.1. The dynamic and interactive nature of the mind at work in forming concepts.

goals and values in a social group or culture. The child revises patterns and theories based on the values and goals encapsulated in the appreciative systems connected to cultural models.

Thus, we need to make the role of values and evaluation explicit. We get, finally, a picture like that in Fig. 9.2.

Although it is not germane to this chapter, I suggest that any pedagogy that does not speak, and speak directly, to each element in the diagram in Fig. 9.2 is not going to lead to authentic participation in, or even an authentic feeling for, the domain the learner is being inducted into.

THE MISLEADING NATURE OF WORDS AND CONCEPTS

The term *concept* is deeply misleading; it hides what is really important in learning, I believe. The model in Fig. 9.2 is meant to try to bring out these important, but sometimes hidden, features. Words fool us because they look very general and make us think that what is in the mind is itself very general, but it is not.

A word like *coffee*, for instance, appears to be a general term, standing for a general, decontextualized concept in the mind. But this is not, it turns out, true. The word *coffee* is, rather, associated with a number of more

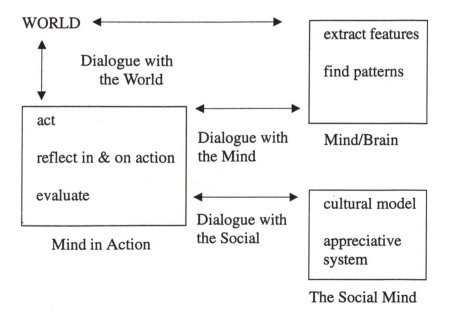

FIG. 9.2. The mind–world–society system and the role of values and appreciations.

specific patterns of experience tied to particular sorts of contexts (Barsalou, 1987, 1991, 1992; A. Clark, 1993). These patterns represent midlevel generalizations, not too specific and not too general, not totally contextualized, not totally decontextualized. The word *coffee* is associated with midlevel contextualized patterns like the following: coffee as a liquid that is found in various containers (e.g., coffee cups); coffee as beans found in various sorts of containers like bags; coffee as ground up grains found in things like tins and bags; coffee as berries growing on a bush; coffee as a flavor of various foods, like ice cream and candy; and so forth. It is with these midlevel patterns—not a general, generic coffee simpliciter—that we operate in and on the world.

Although such midlevel patterns or representations are not referred to much in our everyday theories of the mind, nor in many formal theories in psychology and education, they are deeply important because they are the level at which the mind learns and works. But because they have been ignored until recently they do not even have an agreed-on label as of yet. I call them (*midlevel*) *situated meanings* (just *situated meanings* for short). Situated meanings are, I argue, crucial to learning—without them, learning is either too general or too specific and useless for any critical or deep purposes. Of course, in schooling, many learners are crippled because they either have some induction into a cultural model (theory) without any real feeling for the situated meanings connected to it (this is too general), or they have some feeling for the situated meanings and ability to work with and recognize them in situ, but do not really have much feeling for the larger cultural model that connects and explicates them (this is too specific). We return to this matter soon.

Having argued that the meanings of words are not general concepts, we might very well now ask why, if situated meanings drive learning and practicing on the world, we have the feeling that the word coffee is associated with something more general, something that unites and rises above these midlevel patterns? Part of the answer is simply the fact that the single word exists, and we are misled by this fact to think that a single, general meaning exists. But another part of the answer is that the cultural model associated with *coffee* gives us this feeling of generality. This explanatory theory tells us that coffee grows, is picked, and is then prepared as beans or grain to make into a drink, as well as into flavorings for other foods; it tells us, as well, the when, where, who, and how about coffee from the perspective of our sociocultural groups (and their view of other groups).

It is important to realize that to know a situated meaning is not merely being able to say certain words, for example, "a cup of coffee," but to be able to recognize a pattern (e.g., a cup of coffee) in a variety of settings and variations—this is what makes situated meanings both contextualized and somewhat general. To see this point in another domain, one more important for education, consider the notion of light in physics. First of all, our everyday cultural model for light is not the same as the model (theory) of light in physics—that model is the specialized theory of electromagnetic radiation. It is more overt and articulated than most cultural models.

In physics, light is associated with a variety of situated meanings—for example, as a bundle of waves of different wavelengths, as particles (photons) with various special (e.g., quantum-like) properties, as a beam that can be directed in various ways and for various purposes (e.g. lasers), as colors that can mix in various fashions, and more. If one wants to start practicing with light so as to learn physics, one has to get experiences that lead to the acquisition of a few situated meanings (midlevel, contextualized patterns in one's pattern recognizer that can guide action). Otherwise, one really cannot understand what the theory of light has to explain, at least not in any way that could efficaciously guide pattern recognition and action and reflection.

But I must admit now that I myself do not understand (in any embodied way) these various physically situated meanings well enough to really have a deep understanding, despite the fact that I have read and can recite lots of the cultural model (theory) behind light in physics. To really teach me, you would have to ensure that I got experiences that allowed my mind/brain to really recognize patterns at the level of situated meanings. And what does it mean to recognize these? Situated meanings are correlations of various features, they are patterns that associate various features with each other, for example, light-as-a-particle-that-behaves-in-terms-of-various-sorts-of-contrived-(experimental)-observations-in-certain-characteristic-quantum-like-ways. To recognize such things is to be able to re-cognize (reconstruct in terms of one's pattern recognizing capabilities) and to act on and with these various features and their associations in a range of contexts. One's body and mind has to be able to be situated with—coordinated by and with—these correlated features in the world. Otherwise, you have my sort of understanding.

As it is, I cannot really understand what it means to say that light is a wave, even less that it is composed of various waves of different wavelengths, although I can say it. I just have not had the action-and-reflection experiences that would have made this pattern, this correlation of features, meaningful and recognizable in a way useful for practice, and, thus, for building on in the further development of patterns and theories. Thus, too, I cannot, in any deep way, be said to understand the theory of light in physics (although I could pass some tests on it, perhaps) because that theory is what makes (partial) sense of the various patterns connected to the word *light*.

Situated meanings are, then, a product of the bottom-up action and reflection with which the learner engages the world, and the top-down guidance of the cultural models the learner is developing or being apprenticed to. Without both these levels, the learner either ends up with something too general (a cultural model poorly connected to contextualized, midlevel patterns) or with something too specific and contextualized, something that functions too much like a proper name (the word just applies here, I do not really know why).

One final example may make the matter clear: The way we recognize a friend's face is a good example of a situated meaning. The pattern that makes us recognize our friend in various health conditions and across various ages, even when we have not seen her for some time, is not too specific (it is capable of dealing with a good deal of variation across contexts so we can recognize our friend after she has lost a lot of weight), but it is not too general (it is tied to that person's particularity so that we do not confuse her with look alikes). I cannot recognize light-as-bundle-waves-of-different-frequencies when I am exposed to experiences (in print or in action) where it plays a role in the way I can recognize a familiar face. Situated meanings are both general and specific, they are generalized across variations and contexts, but they are nonetheless tied to sorts of contexts; thus, they are neither totally contextualized nor decontextualized. They are very useful tools, indeed. It is unfortunate that they have played so little role, until recently, in theories of learning and pedagogy. They suggest that a certain sort of familiarity—the sort that I have with faces I can recognize—ought to be a key goal of any pedagogy for deep understanding.

CULTURAL MODELS

I have stressed thus far the importance of the embodied and enacted form of understanding represented by situated meanings, as against the idea that words and concepts are general. I want now to turn to the importance of values (evaluation) and cultural models. So far, we have talked about children acquiring the meanings of new words. But the processes we have uncovered apply to all learning, at whatever age. Thus, I turn now to adults.

A recent study of middle-class parents in Cambridge, Massachusetts, in the United States, talking about their young children (Harkness, Super, & Keefer, 1992) throws a good deal of light onto the operation of cultural models and their connection to values and evaluation. Two notions were highly salient in the talk of these parents: One was the notion of stages of development through which children pass; the other was the notion of the child's growing desire for independence as the central theme giving point and direction to these stages. For example, consider how one mother talked about her son David:

> . . . he's very definitely been in a stage, for the last 3 or 4 months, of wanting to help, everything I do, he wants to help. . . . And now, I would say in the last month, the intensity of wanting to do everything himself is . . . we're really into that stage. . . . I suppose they're all together . . . ya, I suppose they're

two parts of the same thing. Independence, reaching out for independence. Anything he wants to do for himself, which is just about everything, that I move in and do for him, will result in a real tantrum. (pp. 165–166)

David's mother later gave, as an example of his wanting to do things for himself, an episode where she had opened the car door for him when he was having a hard time getting out of the car: "He was very upset, so we had to go back and . . . close the door" (p. 166). She also attributed David's recent dislike of being dressed or diapered to his growing sense of independence: ". . . he's getting to the point where it's insulting, and he doesn't want to be put on his back to have his diaper changed" (p. 166).

However, in the same interview, David's mother also mentioned another behavior pattern. To get David to sleep, she strapped him into his car seat and pretended to be taking him for a drive. He almost immediately fell asleep, and then she returned home, leaving him in the car with a blanket to take a nap: "But he goes to sleep so peacefully, without any struggle, usually" (p. 167). Although this latter pattern is a repeated daily routine, nonetheless David's mother does not talk about this behavior as part of a stage. Rather, she said, the behavior "just sort of evolved" (p. 167). This is somewhat remarkable. Being strapped into a car seat and taken for a ride that inevitably ends in a nap might be seen as inconsistent with David's need for independence—just as having his diaper changed is—and thus equally cause for being insulted (p. 167).

Ironically, another pair of parents in the same study used their daughter's active resistance to being put in a car seat as an example of "this whole stage of development" and "the sort of independence thing she's into now," but in the same interview said, "the thing that's interesting is that she allows you to clean her up, after changing her, a lot more easily than she used to. She used to hate to be cleaned up. She would twist and squirm" (p. 168). So, here, too, parents appeared to be inconsistent. They took the child's desire not to be manipulated into a car seat as a sign of a growing desire for independence, but are not overly bothered by the fact that this desire does not seem to carry over to the similar event of having her diaper changed. And, oddly, this little girl exemplifies just the reverse pattern from David (who resented having his diaper changed, but willingly got strapped into the car seat, even to take a nap).

Many parents—and many others in our culture—consider stages to be real things that are inside their children. Further, they interpret these stages as signposts on the way to becoming an independent (and a rather de-socialized) person. But, it appears, parents label behaviors as part of a stage only when these behaviors represent new behaviors of a sort that could be seen as negative or difficult, and that require, from the parents, new sorts of responses. Behaviors that are not problematic in the parent–child relationship—for example, David yielding to naps in his car seat or the little girl yielding peacefully to being diapered—are not labeled as stages. Furthermore, the parents interpret these potentially negative behaviors that get labeled as stages in terms of a socioculturally valued notion of independence, a notion that other sociocultural groups may well view as socially disruptive or as antisocial (e.g., see Philipsen, 1975, 1990).

These parents' notions of stages and independence are part of a partially conscious and partially unconscious cultural model attached to these words. The cultural model need not be fully in any parent or child's head, consciously or unconsciously, because it is available in the culture in which these parents live—through the media, through written materials, and through interaction with others in the society. It exists in the ways in which these parents coordinate and are coordinated by the resources (i.e., other adults and children, expressions, books, media, etc.) through which they perform their social practices. The cultural model explains the child's behavior in a culturally appropriate manner and offers direction for the parents' responses to the behavior. Theories like this one help people to organize the flow of daily events and behavior—the patterns they can recognize as situated meanings—into a larger meaningful framework.

In this example, we see a cultural model well connected to situated meanings (e.g., child demanding to do things for himself) that are selected and interpreted in terms of the values embedded in the cultural model. I now turn to the unfortunate consequences of having cultural models (theories) that are not tied to mastery of the situated meanings they connect and explicate. In this case, one gets colonized by values that do not actually apply in one's practice in and on the world (which is always at the level of situated meanings). Consider, then, in this regard, a common U.S. cultural model of success or getting ahead, as discussed by D'Andrade (1984), a cultural model that is deeply embedded in some parts of U.S. society:

> It seems to be the case that Americans think that if one has ability, and if, because of competition or one's own strong drive, one works hard at achieving high goals, one will reach an outstanding level of accomplishment. And when one reaches this level one will be recognized as a success, which brings prestige and self-satisfaction. (p. 95)

So pervasive is this cultural model in U.S. culture that D'Andrade (1984) went on to say: "Perhaps what is surprising is that anyone can resist the directive force of such a system—that there are incorrigibles" (p. 98). However, people from different social groups within U.S. society relate to this cultural model in quite different ways. Strauss (1992, see also 1988, 1990), in a study of working-class men in Rhode Island (United States) talking about their lives and work, found that they accepted this cultural model of success. For example, one working man said, "I believe if you put an effort into *anything*, you can get ahead. . . . If I want to succeed, I'll succeed. It has to be, come from within here. Nobody else is going to make you succeed but yourself . . . And, if anybody disagrees with that, there's something wrong with them" (p. 202).

However, most of the men Strauss studied did not, in fact, act on the success model in terms of their career choices or in terms of how they carried out their daily lives. Unlike many white-collar professionals, these men did not choose to change jobs or regularly seek promotions. They did not regularly sacrifice their time with their families and their families' interests for their own career advancement or self-development. These men recognized the successs model as a set of values and, in fact, came to judge themselves by this model, concluding that they had not really been successful and lowering their self-esteem.

The reason these men did not actually act on this model was due to the influence of another cultural model, a model that did effect their actual behaviors. This was the cultural model of being a breadwinner. Unlike the individualism expressed in the success model, these workers, when they talked about their actual lives, assumed that the interests of the family came ahead of the interests of any individual in it, including themselves. For example, one worker said:

> [The worker is discussing the workers' fight against the company's proposal mandating Sunday work] But when that changed and it was negotiated through a contract that you would work, so you had to change or keep losing that eight hours pay. With three children, I couldn't afford it. So I had to go with the flow and work the Sundays. (p. 207)

This is in sharp contrast to the white-collar professionals studied in Bellah, Madsen, Sullivan, Swidler, and Tipton (1985), professionals who carried their individualism so far as to be unsure whether they had any substantive responsibility to their families, if their families' interests stood in the way of their developing themselves as individuals. These Rhode Island workers accepted the breadwinner model not just as a set of values with which to judge themselves and others. They saw the values connected with the model not as a matter of choice, but rather as inescapable facts of life (e.g., "had to change," "had to go with the flow"). Thus, these values were much more effective in shaping their routine daily behaviors. In fact, this very distinction—between mere values and hard reality (the facts)—is itself a particularly pervasive cultural model within Western society.

In contrast to these working-class men, many white-collar professionals work in environments where daily behaviors conform to the success model more than daily behaviors on the factory floor conform to this model. For these professionals, then, their daily observations and social practices have given them the ability to recognize and act on situated meanings that reinforce the cultural model for success. They practice the model, identify with it, and become experts as part and parcel of one integrated social process. For them, in contrast to the working-class men Strauss (1992) studied, the success model, not the breadwinner model, is seen as an inescapable fact of life, and, thus, for them, this model determines not just their self-esteem, but many of their actual behaviors.

The working-class men Strauss studied are, in a sense, colonized by the success model. They have allegiance to its values but have not come to recognize and enact the situated meanings it is, in fact, about. They use it, a model that actually fits the observations and behaviors of other groups in the society, to judge themselves and lower their self-esteem. But, as we have seen, because they then fail to identify themselves as actors within that model, they cannot codevelop the very expertise that would allow and motivate them to practice it. In turn, they leave such expertise to the white-collar professionals, some of whom made the worker work on Sunday against his own interests and wishes. On the other hand, many of these white-collar professionals fail to see that their very expertise in terms of the success model is connected to their failure to be substantive actors in their families or larger social and communal networks.

My knowledge of the physics of light is more akin to the workers' relationship to the cultural model of success. I can recite bits and pieces of it and I have allegiance to its values, in large part, but I cannot enact it in word, deed, or perception because I am not familiar with—able to re-cognize and act on and with—its situated meanings. I am, then, for better or worse, colonized by it, as I am, of course, by a good deal of the rest of my education.

LITERACY

The model of meaning acquisition that I have diagrammed in Fig. 9.2 is (perhaps somewhat surprisingly) also a model of reading. And it is a model of reading at two levels: the level of text types and the level of content. Consider the level of types of texts, first. At this level, the notion of a genre—as typified social action (Miller, 1984) and not just textual form—functions like a word (e.g., the words *shoe* or *light*) in our previous discussion. Like words, genres have a spurious generality. But there is really no such thing in general as a report, an explanation, an argument, an essay, a novel, a narrative, a business letter, a scientific article, and so forth. Rather, these are like the words *shoe* or *light*. They are each instantiated in situated meanings (most of which have no labels of their own). For example, in certain academic fields, things like "an essay review," "a theoretical piece," "a typical research-based journal article," or "an overview of the literature" ("a review article") are situated meanings. These are tied together, are made understandable, not in terms of some generic genre label like *article* or *essay*, but in terms of a cultural model of the production of work in the academic fields whose situated instances these are. What generality we feel genre labels like *report*, *essay*, or *novel* have is, like our earlier discussion of words, a matter of having a word (e.g., *novel*, report) and our cultural model of novels or reports, the (partial) theory (rooted in practice and social institutions) that correlates and explicates the situated instances and their connections (some of which may only be historical).

Although I cannot devote space here to the issue in any depth, I might point out that the model in Fig. 9.2 bears, in some respects, on current debates over the notion of genre as the basis of pedagogical approaches to writing and other aspects of the curriculum (Kress, 1985; Martin, 1985, 1991; Swales, 1990). Although I support much of this work, I do believe that thinking there is such a thing as a prototypical report, essay, explanation, or novel is a mistake; even more is it a mistake to think that exposure to such a thing is the basis for learning genres. The basis for learning genres, like the basis for learning any meanings, is in getting (lots of) experiences, guided by cultural models, that allow learners to become familiar with—to recognize and be able to act on and with—situated meanings (situated instances of genres). The cultural models (connected to practices and institutions, to communities that share certain interests, goals, and values) and the situated meanings are the heart of the matter. General genre terms are just words.

I want now to turn to the issue of the application of the model in Fig. 9.2, not to types of texts, but to the content of what we read. I spend a bit more time on this issue. First, let us consider the role of cultural models (and their concomitant values) in reading for content. Intriguingly, cultural models attached to the sorts of situated meanings one expects to find in certain texts are sometimes so strong that the reader does not have to actually see the text! Consider, in this respect, a typical reading test, like the reading portion of the SAT (the Scholastic Aptitude Test required for admittance to many U.S. colleges). I reprint (from Owen, 1985, pp. 134–135) several questions from an SAT test (which has been released because it is no longer in use). The questions are about a reading passage that I do not reprint. You might try, nonetheless, to answer them:

1. The main idea of the passage is that
   (A) a constricted view of [this novel] is natural and acceptable
   (B) a novel should not depict a vanished society
   (C) a good novel is an intellectual rather than an emotional experience
   (D) many readers have seen only the comedy [in this novel]
   (E) [this novel] should be read with sensitivity and an open mind

2. The author's attitude toward someone who "enjoys [this novel] and then re-
   marks 'but of course it has no relevance today' " (lines 21–22) can best be
   described as one of
   (A) amusement
   (B) astonishment
   (C) disapproval
   (D) resignation
   (E) ambivalence

3. The author [of this passage] implies that a work of art is properly judged on
   the basis of its
   (A) universality of human experience truthfully recorded
   (B) popularity and critical acclaim in its own age
   (C) openness to varied interpretations, including seemingly contradictory ones
   (D) avoidance of political and social issues of minor importance
   (E) continued popularity through different eras and with different societies

I first saw these questions in Owen's book *None of the Above: Behind
the Myth of Scholastic Aptitude* (1985). Owen claimed that he, and many
others, could answer such questions correctly without looking at the reading
passage associated with the questions. The answers seemed obvious to me
as well. So I decided to test Owen's claim (Gee, 1992b). I gave the questions
reprinted here, as well as other SAT reading questions, without their accom-
panying reading passages to undergraduates in the honors program at the
university at which I then worked. These students were primarily recruited
into the honors program by their SAT scores, so they are very good at the
test. I gave these questions to three honors classes, nearly 100 students
overall. About 80% of these students answered all of the reprinted questions
correctly. In fact, virtually no student missed the answer to Question 3 (which
is *A*). I might add, however, that when I gave these same questions to my
regular undergraduate classes, a great many more of the students answered
them incorrectly.

So how did my honors students manage this? Consider, in this regard,
Question 3. The correct answer is *A*. Now, avant garde literary critics certainly
do not believe that a work of art is properly judged on the basis of its
universality of human experience truthfully recorded. In fact, they believe
something much closer to answer *C*: that a work of art is properly judged on
the basis of its openness to varied interpretations, including seemingly
contradictory ones. And my honors students did not, in actual fact, believe that
a work of art is properly judged on the basis of its universality of human
experience truthfully recorded, either. They were, in fact, prone to believe
something much closer to answer *E*: that a work of art is properly judged on
the basis of continued popularity through different eras and with different
societies.

So, why did my honors students answer *A* to Question 3? They did so because they immediately recognized, in this question and the others, a certain set of values connected to a particular cultural model. They recognized a value like *truth and beauty transcend cultures*, so they knew that the answer to Question 3 was *A*. They recognized a value like *truth and beauty transcend time*, so they knew that the answer to Question 2 was *C*. And they recognized a value like *truth and beauty are open (and only open) to people who are appropriately sensitive and open-minded* (i.e., people who are not ideological), thus they knew that the answer to Question 1 was *E*.

But, you will insist, how could my honors students know that the passage the Educational Testing Service printed in front of these questions did not, in fact, contravene these values? They knew this because they knew perfectly well that the prestigious institutions in our society that they have passed through and from which they have garnered distinction claim to hold these values. They knew perfectly well that the Educational Testing Service, which designs the SAT, would never print a passage that contravened them.

The sorts of values that constitute the correct answers to the SAT questions—that is, that truth and beauty transcend cultures and time, and that they are open to appropriately sensitive and open-minded people—represent what Kernan called the romantic-traditional view of literature in his book, *The Death of Literature* (1992). Kernan argued that this view of literature, as well as the category of literature itself—so much a construction of this view—is on its deathbed. However, every honors student knows very well that although the romantic-traditional view may well be dead on our streets and within our avant garde, it is, at least for the time being, alive and well at the gates of status and power in our society. It is, for instance, alive and well at the Educational Testing Service.

The sociologist Bauman, in his book *Intimations of Postmodernity* (1992), also argued that the sorts of values underlying the answers to these SAT questions are dead or dying in the postmodern world. He argued that as the world became modern and conditions became global, the first response—the response of the old classical colonial and industrial capitalism—was to attempt to claim universality and correctness for Anglo-Western culture and its values. The first response was to colonize the rest of the world, to attempt to homogenize other cultures in the image of the Western middle class. But the new postindustrial and postcolonial capitalism has found virtue in diversity. Bauman put the matter as follows:

> Contrary to the anguished forebodings of the "mass culture" critics of the 1950s, the market proved to be the arch-enemy of uniformity. The market thrives on variety; so does consumer freedom and with it the security of the system. The market has nothing to gain from those things the rigid and re-

pressive social system of "classical" capitalism promoted: strict and universal *rules*, unambiguous criteria of *truth, morality and beauty*, indivisible *authority of judgement*. But if the market does not need those things, neither does the system. The powers-that-be lost, so to speak, all interest in universally binding standards. . . . (p. 52)

So here we see people (namely, honors students) reading texts they have not seen (i.e., correctly answering questions about their content) solely on the basis of their mastery of a cultural model (really a set of related cultural models) and their allegiance to its values (at least, in action at test time), its modes of evaluation, and its appreciative system. This model organizes and explicates the sorts of situated meanings that these students expect to find in texts, at least the sorts of texts they will be tested on as gates to future power in their society. But, of course, they have mastered this cultural model so well precisely because they have also mastered recognizing the situated meanings that the cultural model stands behind (and we momentarily see some of these). That is why the SAT reading test works: It selects the readers who have had the right sorts of experiences to recognize the right sorts of situated meanings, the sorts the cultural model selects and explicates.

Having discussed the role of cultural models in reading, let us turn to the role of situated meanings, the analogues of coffee-as-a-liquid-in-certain-types-of-characteristic-containers. Here we consider a study by Hemphill (1992) of the Harvard Graduate School of Education, who investigated how high school students from different socioeconomic backgrounds read various canonical works of literature. We just look at two cases, a girl named Maria and a girl named Mary (these are, of course, pseudonyms) The two girls were discussing the poem "Acquainted with the Night" by Robert Frost.

Maria responded (orally) as follows to individual lines from the poem (I have removed speech hesitations and repairs from the transcript):

I have passed by the watchman on his beat.
I think he's trying to say that though he [has] like seen the sadder situations. And the watchman meaning I would think a cop was on his daily routine. The watchman still couldn't stop the situation that was happening. Which was probably something bad. Or you know dishonest. But he still was able to see what was going on.

And dropped my eyes unwillingly to explain.
Oh well this line's making me think that well the watchman caught him. And he was ashamed of what he was doing. And he didn't want to explain his reasons for his own actions to the watchman. Cause he was so ashamed.

Mary responded in an essay she wrote as follows (I cite only parts of the essay):

Figuratively, Frost is describing his life. "Acquainted with the night" meaning having been depressed. "If I have looked down the saddest city lane" can be interpreted that he's had some really tough times.

In the third stanza, he says "I have stood still . . ." Maybe he has stopped during his walk of life and heard people with different paths or lives calling him but he later finds they were not calling him after all.

There is a slight undertone of death in the last two or three lines. The clock symbolizing the time he has left. The clock telling him that he can't die yet however much he may want to.

. . . the reader, if he looks closely can see past the words on the paper and into Robert Frost's soul.

What we see here are the sorts of situated meanings that compose one's overall interpretation or response to a text. For example, Maria uses (recognizes) situated meanings like "Something bad is happening and an authority figure can't stop it" and "An authority figure catches one doing something bad and one is ashamed." Mary is using (recognizing) situated meanings like "People's lives are like paths or walks through landscapes" or "Time passing as shown by things like clocks is associated with aging and death." These students recognize different situated meanings (midlevel patterns of meaning in the texts) and these different situated meanings are connected to different cultural models of the sorts of content they are reading within the type of (situated) text they take themselves to be reading.

Maria appears to operate within a cultural model that finds significance in relating the text to narrative schemes that come from the reader's everyday life and experiences. In her world, if people are out late at night and avoiding contact with police, they are in all likelihood in trouble. This cultural model also seems to stress social contacts and relationships between people. The reader reads from her own experience to the words and back again to her social experience. I have elsewhere pointed out that this way of reading is rather typical of many groups when they are not operating with allegiance to school-based essayist literacy (Gee, 1990/1996).

Mary appears to operate within a cultural model that finds significance in treating concrete details and actions as symbols for more universal emotions and themes. The reader, by looking closely (close reading), can "see past the words on the paper and into Robert Frost's soul," but that soul is a concrete universal, described in such convincing peculiarity that it none-theless comes to resonate with universal meaning for all our souls. This cultural model of reading texts of this (situated) type, of course, was quite explicitly delineated by people like T. S. Eliot and William Carlos Williams, among other canonical (Anglo) modernists (Dijkstra, 1978; Perkins, 1976). Needless to say, Hemphill (1992) found that students like Maria fared less well than students like Mary in English classes. And that is, of course, because canonical modernism is a cultural model that is still held in high regard in high school English and literature classrooms and in many colleges, until students get to their theory classes.

It is now standard procedure, in work on critical literacy and cultural studies, to reverse traditional values and condemn Mary's sort of response (as tied to an elitist canon) and praise Maria's (as culturally authentic). However, in a world driven by ethnic hatred and violence, where people are mutilated and killed simply for not being like us, I would argue, rather, that we are in need of both cultural models. The one because it sees human commonality in concrete particularity; the other because it ensures that this commonality will not become detached from the world of social relationships and lived experience. However, having both will not be all that easy. And that, at last, leads to my conclusion.

CONCLUSION

Learning to read situated texts of certain types is like learning the meanings of words. It is a matter of having lots of experiences that allow one to become familiar with patterns and subpatterns, that is, with what I have called situated meanings (both of text types like a-New England-modernist-imagistic-poem and their situated contents) guided by cultural models that explicate and evaluate these situated meanings, and are, in turn, ultimately formed by and out of them.

The literary canon represented the values, models, and situated meanings of the powerful in Western culture (in several different senses of the word *power*). That is why being inducted into these values, models, and situated meanings was so good, for better or worse, for forming one's subjectivity in line with the values and interests of the powerful. But that is also why such induction was also good for deep resistance to this subjectivity, because through such induction some people managed to become familiar with and re-cognize the faces of power in Western society. Witness, in this regard, how many minorities and working-class people used mastery of the canon as a way to found their own resisting subjectivity.

Massive social, cultural, economic, political, academic, and technological changes have all but led to the death of the canon and its associated cultural models and situated meanings (Faigley, 1992; Giddens, 1990; Harvey, 1989; Kernan, 1992; Poster, 1990; Smith, 1988). And I do not want either to praise or to help bury the canon, but to point to some of the implications of its impending death. We have seen that words are tied to situated meanings explicated by cultural models. These cultural models exist only through the active work of what I call Discourses, with a capital *D* (Gee, 1990/1996, 1992a). Discourses are sociohistorical coordinations of people, objects (props), ways of talking, acting, interacting, thinking, valuing, and (sometimes) writing and reading that allow for the display and recognition of socially significant identities, like being a (certain sort of) African American, boardroom executive, feminist, lawyer, street-gang member, theoretical physicist, 18th-century midwife, 19th-century modernist, Soviet or Russian, schoolchild, teacher, and so on through innumerable possibilities. If you destroy a Discourse (and they do die), you also destroy its cultural models, situated meanings, and its concomitant identities.

So, too, for reading. The canon was a prop of a long-running Discourse in Western history. I suggested earlier that we need cultural models of situated textual meanings like both Maria's and Mary's. Maria's alone is too specific—one needs to read beyond one's experience, however much one most certainly needs to read from within it as well. Mary's alone is too general, too much in danger of representing one group's experience as if it is universal, natural, and uniquely valuable. And that, of course, is one of the many reasons the canon is being attacked.

But with the death of the canon, what will replace Mary's sort of cultural model of reading situated texts and content? We cannot simply offer up new reading formations, call them critical or resistant or whatever, and leave it at that. It is not that simple. We would have to replace the long sociohistorical work that went into the formation of the Discourse that upheld the canon. We would have to create a new Discourse, and Discourses are not born in a day. They are the products of groups and struggle and history; they are formations of new commonalties, new forms of common wealth, with all the attendant dangers of othering that that can imply. Without new cultural models of situated texts and content to replace the canonical Discourse, Maria will have no way to read, to interpret, beyond herself and her own culture and lifeworld—and part of the point of the attack on the canon is—or ought to have been—that no one's culture, neither Maria's nor Mary's, is natural and adequate on its own to the task of perceiving, acting in, and transforming the world, especially a multicultural world.

There are, of course, bits and pieces emerging that may be signposts to new social practices, new cultural models, new situated text types and meanings. For example, much of the work drawing on Bakhtin (e.g., 1986), and more recent Russian theorists like Lotman (e.g., 1988), using notions like the internal heterogeneity of texts, intertextuality, dialogicality, and multivocality, as well as much work in semiotics more generally (e.g., that stemming from Halliday; e.g., 1978), certainly holds out great promise, especially if it can transcend the use of radical ideas merely to renew the subjectivities of traditional academic Discourses, a practice all too common in our universities. The ferment circling around new interactive technologies—such as students mutually annotating and contributing to a progressively displaced (perhaps, even canonical) primary text in a hypertext technology—also holds out great promise for new social practices and new multicultural and multivocal communities sharing a common wealth. But here, again, it is too early to tell if these new technologies will be captured by the social gravity of old forms of hierarchy and power.

In the sense in which the Discourse that upheld the canon used the word reading, we cannot read again, on its death, without jointly imagining and putting into practice a new Discourse that is situated between the specifics of each of our group memberships and the old, dying universals of the canonical Discourse. Such a task is barely begun, perhaps barely imaginable at times in a world where things fall apart and the center cannot hold. But it is, nonetheless, what I take our task to be.

REFERENCES

Anglin, J. M. (1977). *Word, object, and conceptual development.* New York: Norton.

Bakhtin, M. (1986). *Speech genres and other late essays* (V. W. McGee, Ed.; C. Emerson & M. Holquist, Eds.). Austin: University of Texas Press.

Barsalou, L. W. (1987). The instability of graded structure in concepts. In U. Neisser (Ed.), *Concepts and conceptual development: Ecological and intellectual factors in categorization* (pp. 101–140). New York: Cambridge University Press.

Barsalou, L. W. (1991). Deriving categories to achieve goals. In G. H. Bower (Ed.), *The psychology of learning and motivation: Advances in research and theory* (Vol. 27, pp. 1–64). New York: Academic Press.

Barsalou, L. W. (1992). *Cognitive psychology: An overview for cognitive scientists.* Hillsdale, NJ: Lawrence Erlbaum Associates.

Bauman, Z. (1992). *Intimations of postmodernity.* London: Routledge.

Bechtel, W., & Abrahamsen, A. (1990). *Connectionism and the mind: An introduction to parallel processing in networks.* Oxford, UK: Basil Blackwell.

Bellah, R. N., Madsen, R., Sullivan. W. M., Swidler, A., & Tipton, S. M. (1985). *Habits of the heart: Individualism and commitment in American life.* Berkeley: University of California Press.

Brown, J. S., Collins, A., & Duguid, P. (1989). Situated cognition and the culture of learning. *Educational Researcher, 18,* 32–42.

Churchland, P. M. (1989). *A neurocomputational perspective: The nature of mind and the structure of science.* Cambridge, MA: MIT Press.

Churchland, P. S. (1986). *Neurophilosophy: Toward a unified science of the mind/brain.* Cambridge, MA: MIT Press.

Churchland, P. S., & Sejnowski, T. J. (1992). *The computational brain.* Cambridge, MA: Bradford/MIT Press.

Clark, A. (1989). *Microcognition: Philosophy, cognitive science, and parallel distributed processing.* Cambridge, MA: MIT Press.

Clark, A. (1993). *Associative engines: Connectionism, concepts, and representational change.* Cambridge, UK: Cambridge University Press.

Clark, E. V. (1993). *The lexicon in acquisition.* Cambridge, UK: Cambridge University Press.

Crick, F. (1994). *The astonishing hypothesis: The scientific search for the soul.* New York: Scribner's.

D'Andrade, R. (1984). Cultural meaning systems. In R. A. Shweder & R. A. LeVine (Eds.), *Culture theory: Essays on mind, self, and emotion* (pp. 88–119). Cambridge, UK: Cambridge University Press.

D'Andrade, R., & Strauss, C. (Eds.). (1992). *Human motives and cultural models.* Cambridge, UK: Cambridge University Press.

Dijkstra, B. (Ed.). (1978). *A recognizable image: William Carlos Williams on art and artists.* New York: New Directions.

Faigley, L. (1992). *Fragments of rationality: Postmodernity and the subject of composition.* Pittsburgh, PA: University of Pittsburgh Press.

Gee, J. P. (1996). *Social linguistics and literacies: Ideologies in discourses* (2nd ed.). London: Taylor & Francis. (Original work published 1990)

Gee, J. P. (1992a). *The social mind: Language, ideology, and social practice.* New York: Bergin & Garvey.

Gee, J. P. (1992b). Reading? *Journal of Urban and Cultural Studies, 2,* 65–77.

Gick, M. L., & Holyoak, K. J. (1983). Schema induction and analogical transfer. *Cognitive Psychology, 15,* 1–38.

Giddens, A. (1990). *The consequences of modernity.* Stanford, CA: Stanford University Press.

Griffiths, P. (1986). Early vocabulary. In P. Fletcher & M. Garman (Eds.), *Language acquisition: Second edition* (pp. 279–306). Cambridge, UK: Cambridge University Press.

Halliday, M. A. K. (1978). *Language as social semiotic: The social interpretation of language and meaning.* London: Edward Arnold.

Harkness, S., Super, C. M., & Keefer, C. H. (1992). Learning to be an American parent: How cultural models gain directive force. In R. D'Andrade & C. Strauss (Eds.), *Human motive and cultural models* (pp. 163–178). Cambridge, UK: Cambridge University Press.

Harvey, D. (1989). *The condition of postmodernity.* Oxford, UK: Basil Blackwell.

Hemphill, L. (1992, September). *Codeswitching and literary response.* Conference on literacy and identity, Carlisle Education Center, Sponsored by the Literacies Institute, Newton, MA.

Hofstadter, D., & the Fluid Analogies Research Group. (1995). *Fluid concepts and creative analogies: Computer models of the fundamental mechanisms of thought.* New York: Basic Books.

Holland, D., & Quinn, N. (Eds.). (1987). *Cultural models in language and thought.* Cambridge, UK: Cambridge University Press.

Holyoak, K. J., & Thagard, P. (1995). *Mental leaps: Analogical in creative thought.* Cambridge, MA: MIT Press.

Keil, F. (1979). *Semantic and conceptual development.* Cambridge, MA: Harvard University Press.

Keil, F. (1989). *Concepts, kinds, and cognitive development.* Cambridge, MA: MIT Press.

Kernan, A. (1992). *The death of literature.* New Haven, CT: Yale University Press.

Kress, G. (1985). *Linguistic processes in sociocultural practice.* Oxford, UK: Oxford University Press.

Kress, G. (in press). Writing and learning to write. In D. Olson & N. Torrance (Eds.), *The handbook of human development in education: New models of learning, teaching, and schooling.* Oxford, UK: Blackwell.

Latour, B. (1987). *Science in action.* Cambridge, MA: Harvard University Press.

Lave, J. (1988). *Cognition in practice.* Cambridge, UK: Cambridge University Press.

Lave, J., & Wenger, E. (1991). *Situated learning: Legitimate peripheral participation.* Cambridge, UK: Cambridge University Press.

Lotman, Y. M. (1988). Text within a text. *Soviet Psychology, 26,* 32–51.

Lynch, M. (1985). *Art and artifact in laboratory science: A study of shop work and shop talk in a research laboratory.* London: Routledge & Kegan Paul.

Margolis, H. (1987). *Patterns, thinking, and cognition: A theory of judgment.* Chicago: University of Chicago Press.

Margolis, H. (1993). *Paradigms and barriers: How habits of mind govern scientific beliefs.* Chicago: University of Chicago Press.

Martin, J. R. (1985). *Factual writing: Exploring and challenging social reality.* Geelong, Victoria, Australia: Deakin University Press.

Miller, C. R. (1984). Genre as social action. *Quarterly Journal of Speech, 70*, 151–167.

Nolan, R. (1994). *Cognitive practices: Human language and human knowledge.* Oxford, UK: Blackwell.

Owen, D. (1985). *None of the above: Behind the myth of scholastic aptitude.* Boston: Houghton Mifflin.

Perkins, D. (1976). *A history of modern poetry: From the 1890s to the high modernist mode.* Cambridge, MA: Harvard University Press.

Philipsen, G. (1975). Speaking "like a man" in Teamsterville: Culture patterns of role enactment in an urban neighborhood. *Quarterly Journal of Speech, 61*, 26–39.

Philipsen, G. (1990). Reflections on speaking "like a man" in Teamsterville. In D. Carbaugh (Ed.), *Cultural communication* (pp. 21–25). Hillsdale, NJ: Lawrence Erlbaum Associates.

Pickering, A. (Ed.). (1992). *Science as practice and culture.* Chicago: University of Chicago Press.

Poster, M. (1990). *The mode of information: Poststructuralism and social context.* Chicago: University of Chicago Press.

Rogoff, B. (1990). *Apprenticeship in thinking: Cognitive development in social context.* New York: Oxford University Press.

Rumelhart, D. E., McClelland, J. L., & the PDP Research Group (1986). *Parallel distributed processing: Explorations in the microstructure of cognition: Vol. 1. Foundations.* Cambridge, MA: MIT Press.

Schon, D. A. (1983). *The reflective practitioner.* New York: Basic Books.

Schon, D. A. (1987). *Educating the reflective practitioner.* San Francisco: Jossey-Bass.

Smith, B. H. (1988). *Contingencies of value: Alternative perspectives for critical theory.* Cambridge, MA: Harvard University Press.

Strauss, C. (1988). *Culture, discourse, and cognition: Forms of belief in some Rhode Island working men's talk about success.* Unpublished doctoral dissertation, Harvard University, Cambridge, MA.

Strauss, C. (1990). Who gets ahead? Cognitive responses to heteroglossia in American political culture. *American Ethnologist, 17*, 312–328.

Strauss, C. (1992). What makes Tony run? Schemes as motives reconsidered. In R. D'Andrade & C. Strauss (Eds.), *Human motives and cultural models* (pp. 197–224). Cambridge, UK: Cambridge University Press.

Swales, J. M. (1990). *Genre analysis: English in academic and research settings.* Cambridge, UK: Cambridge University Press.

CHAPTER TEN

Explaining Learning:
The Research Trajectory of
Situated Cognition and the
Implications of Connectionism

John St. Julien
University of Illinois, Urbana–Champaign

Situated cognition is characterized by a concern for competence and an insistence that competence cannot be ignored (e.g., Lave, 1985). Competence, understood as the ability to act on the basis of understanding, has been a fundamental goal of education. But it is a painful fact of educational life that knowledge gained in school too often does not transfer to the ability to act competently in more "worldly" settings. Situated cognition resolves this dilemma by offering a new explanatory structure within which to explain competence.

From the viewpoint of situated cognition, competent action is not grounded in individual accumulations of knowledge but is, instead, generated in the web of social relations and human artifacts that define the context of our action. This focus shifts our explanations of the competence we observe from knowledge held by an individual to the social context of the activity we are examining. This shift brings a strangely welcome resolution to the transfer problem by making transfer an unreasonable expectation—the sort of knowledge we once supposed failed to transfer is simply not the basis of the competence for which we hoped. This reframing allows us to explore new, and potentially more productive, ways of understanding human competence.

The relief that such a resolution brings should not lead educators to miss the probability that this analysis, like the one it displaces, may bring new blind spots with unfortunate consequences for our students' developing abilities. The very concern for competence that motivates situated cognition compels us to ask: How are we to explain instances in which it appears that transfer does occur and that students have learned something in school that applies to a worldly problem? Certainly this occurs much less often than we have been fond of telling ourselves. But just as surely, it does occur. I argue that situated cognition can be seen as the key to understanding knowledge, but that this will still leave education missing an understanding of learning that will allow us to understand both the failure and the success of transfer. I discuss my hope that by turning connectionism's insights into perception and category formation, we can glean the beginnings of such a learning theory. Taken in tandem, these two ways of recasting education's traditional assumptions concerning knowledge and learning may provide us with the binocular vision that will allow us to see the problems of instructional design in useful relief. The results of one attempt to bring this position into practice are used illustratively.

THE RESEARCH TRAJECTORY
OF SITUATED COGNITION

I forgo the temptation to define situated cognition in favor of presenting a story of its engagement with a broad problem area that has shaped its research trajectory.

It should be noted that the narrative I relate is an intentional one (as narratives tend to be). That is, I tell it in the hope that it will usefully organize educational understandings of the potential of these fields. It is certainly not the only story that could be told. Its virtue, insofar as it has any, must lie in its educational utility.

Classical theories of knowledge and learning, which form a background to this story, are familiar enough that I only sketch them here. The classical approach holds that the world is made up of objects and the relations between them. We say that someone knows something when one holds in the mind isomorphic copies of these objects and their relations. Learning is the process of bringing, somehow, these objects-in-the-world into the mind. Reasoning is understood as the manipulation of these objects in the mind according to deductive rules.

Researchers concerned with competence and the problem of transfer were (and are) faced with this cultural preunderstanding. Knowledge is understood as consisting of objects detached from the world and located in the mind. Knowledge that is objective in this sense should be available for use in any situation. This classical preunderstanding gives us the problem of transfer as one in which objective knowledge is not used when appropriate. Education has traditionally discussed this as an application problem.[1]

---

[1]Most crucially in U.S. educational discourse, it has been Bloom's (1952) taxonomy that has organized this problem as application. Although critiques are legion and persuasive, it remains the basis of practices (official lesson plans, state curricula) that organize teaching.

The availability of knowledge is assumed. The classical set of assumptions lead one to conclude that transfer or application problems are generated when knowledge is too closely identified with the particular situation in which it is gained. Thus, the usual analysis of the problem with knowledge learned in school is that it was overly embedded in schooling and, in this sense, insufficiently abstract. This understanding led to solutions that attempted to make the knowledge more and more objective and less and less identified with any particular context of acquisition or use.[2] Thus, solutions written within the classical tradition rely on strengthening the opposition between objective knowledge and the particular situation. But more efficient techniques for making knowledge independent of context, for instance decomposing complex skills into their presumed elements and systematically teaching these elemental skills, had the disheartening effect of making them harder to recall and less likely to be used in any circumstance.[3]

Researchers began to notice, or at least treat more seriously, the other side of the transfer problem: the relative efficacy of knowledge gained in the context of use.

The first movement onto the path of situated cognition is taken when the researcher, usually in profound frustration with a lack of consistent research findings concerning knowledge use,[4] decides to take a close look at what happens outside of schools that leads to the relative success of knowledge gained in those settings.

But the researcher starts with the problem already stated by tradition. In this instance, one starts with a difference to be explained: the difference between the knowledge acquired in school and the knowledge acquired in the context of application for subsequent competence. This sets up context, schooling, and knowledge as the elements to somehow be brought into productive contact with the competence that is to be explained. This line of research also proves frustrating initially. It proves difficult to locate the sort of knowledge that the research tradition connected with schooling expects to locate (e.g., Lave & Wenger, 1991; Walkerdine, 1988). Formal, mathematical reasoning, for instance, appears vanishingly rare, even in situations such as grocery shopping, which would seem to call for constant calculation.

It is at this point that knowledge and the traditions that undergird formal schooling's assumptions concerning knowledge come into question. The question becomes, "If there is no recognizable knowledge out there, then what produces competence?" The response entails bringing different tradi-

---

[2]For example, foundationally: Bloom (1952).

[3]This is not a new research finding, see: Bartlett (1932/1977). That we persist in designing curricula around an abstract concept of knowledge is an index of our cultural commitment to the concept.

[4]See: Rogoff (1984) and Rogoff and Morelli (1989) for retrospective overviews that reflect this position.

tions into play—among them anthropology, activity theory, cognitive science, phenomenology, ethnomethodology, poststructuralism, semiotics, and linguistics—in an attempt to find another way of understanding the relationships involved. Based on both the inconsistency of research results and the traditions that are brought into play, work in this developing tradition pays more and more attention to the small-grained particulars of everyday social activity. But it does this in a particular way—it does not pay more attention to the individual and to individual psychology, which had been the mainstay of traditional research into the problematic.[5] The resulting fine-grained analysis of social interaction, done while holding individuality in abeyance, reveals a landscape quite different from the traditional picture. Knowledge—insofar as that which enables competence can still be called knowledge—is found in the context, in structuring resources and discursive practices, in the habits that get us through the day. For the most part, competence is more understandable as a matter of appropriate perception and habituated action than as formal reasoning over classical objects of knowledge.

In a curious way, situated cognition has restated the importance of a theory of knowledge. Some things remain the same: Knowledge remains the foundation of competence; knowledge continues to transcend the bounds of the personal. Knowledge can still be considered to reside in objects. But things change as well: Knowledge is firmly material; it is distributed outside the head; knowledge is decidedly social and always situationally contingent.

This trajectory has led in the direction of an ever smaller grained and more particular analysis of the social patterns in which competence seems to be invested. It questions dichotomy, particularly the dichotomy of the individual and the world, on a basis that emphasizes the material and the social rather than the psychological. Situated cognition has greatly broadened the multidisciplinary basis for understanding knowledge in a way that profoundly alters its meaning. The project of bringing context, knowledge, and schooling into productive contact with competence has yielded to a reframing in which context and knowledge are brought together in the situation and the competence a person exhibits is a complex, socially constructed result of a cognition that spans the formerly separate categories.

The classical problem facing researchers concerned with competence has been transformed. Not solved, but changed in a way that allows productive research to proceed; situated cognition is a very real step forward. However, each new structure of explanation sets up its own blind spots and it behooves us, as educators, to ask what blind spot this theoretical framework might suggest. Situated cognition helps explain the problem of unsuccessful transfer, a problem that was inexplicable when viewed against the background

---

[5]For succinct expositions of ths viewpoint from situated perspectives, see Lave and Wenger (1991) and Walkerdine (1984).

of a classical understanding. But situated cognition, taken seriously, makes a problem of the opposite condition. How is successful transfer explained? Knowledge acquired in one context should simply not exist in another situation where the appropriate social, material, and linguistic supports are lacking. And yet, we all know that this does happen. The 3-year-old in the chaotic confusion of an airline terminal for the first time recognizes and is comforted by the familiar ballness of the newly purchased red ball, where all else is strange. It may not seem strange that this is so, steeped as we all are in the traditional understanding, but situated cognition makes it strange.

Situated cognition challenges, at a very fundamental level, the mythos of the rational, sovereign individual. But some way of understanding the person as a semiautonomous thinker is still necessary if we are to explain instances in which acting persons are the locus of successful transfer across situations.

If we are at all sympathetic with the concern for competence that motivates situated cognition, a concern for this issue arises. As long as those working from various situated positions have difficulty accounting for successful transfer, a path remains open for those who would abandon the advances of situated cognition and continue to infer that, in comparison with the rational, objective, generalizable knowledge that has always been the most valued form of thinking and rationality, situated perspectives are unable to account for the most valuable sorts of knowledge.

TRADITION AND SITUATED COGNITION'S CHALLENGE

It is worth pausing in our journey to notice that although situated cognition is usually positioned as a startlingly new perspective, it has some very clear antecedents in our intellectual history. To simply list a few names: McCulloch in perceptual psychology, Bartlett in psychology, Mead and Bendedict in anthropology, G. H. Mead in sociology, and Dewey in both education and philosophy have all questioned the easy dichotomy of human and world. And yet the tradition in which we are embedded does not reflect these insights.

I want to ask: Why not? If situated approaches to cognition have been implicit in the most sophisticated approaches to the problems of learning (including socialization and perception as forms of learning), then why have practices not been adopted that reflect these insights? Crucially for educators, why has education not been noticeably affected by these insights into our basic task of encouraging learning?

I suspect that a major reason is that taking such a viewpoint on learning implies deep differences from the culturally canonical position on individuality and thought. It is hard to imagine a more difficult and counterintuitive position than one that asks people to see that the very experience of their self and their thought is historically specific, culturally interpreted, and potentially problematic. Thorough-going situated perspectives go further and make the claim that not only is our self-conception problematic, it is wrong— or at least profoundly misleading. Previous impulses in the direction represented by situated cognition have failed to overcome this barrier that is strategically situated in our very perception of ourselves. Insights emerging from the various isolated disciplines were simply swamped by the larger framework that supported the canonical position. Perception became an isolated professional field, anthropology was marginalized, and perspectives in psychology and education were ignored or their meaning was transformed in their implementation. The history of Dewey's insertion into the discourses of both philosophy and education is instructive in this regard.[6]

We need to ask ourselves, "What is to prevent the same things from happening to situated cognition?" A hopeful answer would be that the movement in this direction is more broadly based than in the past and is not entirely captured within discrete disciplinary frameworks. Recent intellectual history holds out the example of cognitive science whose major strength lies in the fact that researchers from a number of different disciplinary frameworks came to the conclusion that the mental really did matter, and developed a transdisciplinary field in concert.[7]

Situated approaches can be read to claim that the broad coalition that constitutes cognitive science is not yet broad enough: The individual is too narrow a construction to contain all the regularities that we want to explain. Situated approaches locate these regularities in the social and socially conditioned phenomenal world and the individual's link to that world. It argues for a fine-grained analysis of this connection.

I would like to introduce the possibility that even this is not yet broad enough to serve the purposes of educators (see also Lemke, chapter 3, this volume). Situated cognition broadens the attempt to understand cognition in the direction of the social and in the direction of particular experiences of the social. Such a move is surely necessary. And yet some part of the reasoning process still does take place within the head. If we agree that *cognition* is rightly seen as including a broader, external, and socially constructed sense of this term, the term *thinking* may be reserved for those processes that do take place in the head—however intertwined they must be with the social. The fine-grained analysis that situated cognition takes in its analysis of the interaction between world and self has led to a productive questioning of that dichotomy. Paralleling this move, it seems reasonable to assume that a similar fine-grained analysis of the actual, material processes that constitute the relation between the mind and the brain will be similarly

---

[6]As it is with much of Dewey's work, it seems more fruitful to go to Dewey when discussing misinterpretations and misappropriations than to his commentators. See Dewey (1949, 1965).

[7]The central citation, and the one that arguably defined the field (although it is now seriously outdated in its particulars) is Gardner (1985).

fruitful and will lead to a similarly informative blurring of the difference that our dichotomous, cultural preunderstanding gives us.

Given its canonical character, the traditional explanation needs no research-based findings to support the naturalness of its understanding of thought. But situated cognition and related alternate perspectives such as phenomenology and triadic semiosis (Whitson, chapter 7, this volume) that postulate other patterns of explanation need a firm basis for claiming that thought (in-the-head thought) is actually something other than our tradition gives us to posit a credible alternative to the traditional understanding of cognition.

What is needed is a conception of the person thinking (in-the-head thought) that is at once compatible with situated cognition's insights and that offers a principled way to understand how successful transfer might occur across practices and situations. The person needs to be understood as neither discontinuous nor unproblematically integrated with the situation in which they find themselves acting. A biologically constrained understanding of learning and thinking that spans the distance from the material processes underlying individual learning to the social organization of available knowledge needs to be sought in order to provide this credible basis.

CONNECTIONISM

Connectionism can be seen as a perspective that blurs the distinction between the mind and the brain in ways that parallel situated cognition's blurring of the distinction between the self and the world. By taking the brain itself seriously as a metaphor of mind, connectionism discards logocentric views embedded in mechanical, computer, and deductive metaphors of human thought. Connectionist points of view have introduced questions from a perceptual and biological perspective that parallel those that situated cognition introduces from the other, social, side of the divide that the Cartesian individual creates in our cultural self-understanding. Connectionists insist that the type of objects of knowledge on which the classical tradition is founded are physiologically impossible. Knowing is necessarily conditioned on experience in this alternate account; the relationship between the world and the self is one of interdependence built over time.[8] This perspective also repositions context effects as constitutive rather than as unfortunate sorts of error to which humans are prone. Pattern completion based on a particular history rather than logical deduction is the basic primitive operation in this conception of how the mind works. Connectionist understandings of perception and category formation begin to fill in the missing material proc-

---

[8]Rumelhart, Smolensky, McClelland, and Hinton (1986).

esses that must support terms like *internalization, appropriation*, and *learning*.[9]

The link between the situational plasticity of perception and the context dependence of learning has been noted, if not emphasized, by those in both the situated cognition and the connectionist camps. Gladwin (1985), for instance, remarking on studies of calculation in nonschool settings, said, "In most cases the calculation takes place in what looks like a recognition process, where the solution is recognized even as the problem is identified" (p. 207). Connectionists Rumelhart et al. (1986), discussing their view that external symbols are the key to formal reasoning, remarked, "Roughly speaking, the view is this: We are good at 'perceiving' answers to our problems" (p. 45). Clancey and Roschelle, in a paper presented at the 1991 AERA convention, arrived at a similar position concerning the value of a perceptual approach to learning.

This is just the sort of position concerning in-the-head thought that situated cognition needs in order to counter the naturalized claims of the classical tradition that real, valuable thought is objective, abstract, and logical. Such a culturally prescribed position remains attractive even to those who understand that it is fundamentally illusory and allows them to continue to advocate a model of knowledge that results in asking students to simulate a computer (Bereiter, chapter 11, this volume).

An alternate vision of cognition built on a perceptual or connectionist basis suggests that knowledge objects are acquired in the same manner as is, say, a chair or any material object: through socially mediated experience. Abstract knowledge objects are presumed to be built in the same way and to face the same context-bound constraints. The trick is to make sure that the history of its acquisition shapes a representation in which the knowledge object and its use is recalled in appropriate situations. Even in so abstract a domain as mathematics, situated perspectives add real explanatory power (Cobb, chapter 8, this volume; see also St. Julien, 1994a). One example of how this shaping can occur in a way that does without the lists of objective features and facts that our traditional model of knowledge makes necessary and that makes the resulting representation more available in its eventual context of use is contained in the supplement at the end of this chapter. Its experience-based format stands in contrast to the usual lists of features

---

[9]Bereiter, in his 1991 *Educational Researcher* article "Implications of Connectionism for Thinking About Rules," begins to reflect on the educational implications of a connectionist approach to learning. The debate on the nature of learning has been vigorous but largely centered on opposing developmental and cognitive brands of psychology, whereas the contrast suggested here is between competing cognitive perspectives. See Fodor's (1980) chapter "On the Impossibility of Acquiring 'More Powerful' Structures" for a contrasting position that influentially concludes that learning as we usually think of it is impossible based on the Chomskian idea that learning is nothing more than the elaboration of innate axioms.

(presence of nucleus, double cell membranes, etc.) that form the basis of traditional instruction. New technology makes this perceptual style of learning more readily accessible to the student and enables the researcher or teacher to include time and activity constraints that print-based materials make difficult or impossible (St. Julien, 1994b).

Connectionist research argues that objective, abstract thought is difficult for real, material reasons and that where it is achieved, it is built on the basis of a quite different set of processes than the deductively logical manipulation of objects that the classical tradition gives us.[10] Reciprocally, connectionist perspectives need the social perspective as well. Connectionists are currently hobbled by the difficulty of locating the source of the regularities that do appear. A deep understanding of perceptual processes precludes connectionists from taking objects that appear during perception as natural—indeed, explicating the process through which such differences are noted is the primary appeal of these approaches. It is largely the everyday practices of human interaction that differentiate these objects from the Jamesian background of blooming, buzzing confusion. These formative practices are delineated in the more fully articulated social perspectives.

THE PRACTICAL INSPIRATION

But my conviction that these two ways of bridging the gap introduced by the sovereign individual are compatible and educationally useful is not simply a product of analysis. The perspectives discussed here might lead one to suspect this conviction emerges out of problems encountered in practice. In this instance, the catalyst was an attempt to design instructional materials with which to teach the prokaryote–eukaryote distinction in biology education. What is salient in this context is the way in which neither socially situated practice nor connectionist perception were sufficient by themselves to give the kind of purchase on the problem that was possible with both.

What we desired to do was to make accessible to students the categories of experience that ordered the world of our experts. We wanted them to be able to simply perceive a cell as prokaryote or eukaryote before attempting an analysis of features.

The traditional way of teaching taxonomic distinctions (and not only taxonomic distinctions) is to present the student with a list of essential features to memorize. The purpose of memorizing this list is to give the students the essential facts that they can apply to classifying objects according to the presence of these critical features. This way of understanding learning is problematic because it assumes that we can learn the features of an object

---

[10]See, for example: Cussins (1990) for an especially closely reasoned exposition of this position.

before the object can be recognized. In practice, although students are able to memorize the list, they are not thereby able to recognize the object.

The claim made here is that we have things backwards. People who are competent in a field, people we usually think of as experts or simply as competent, are the producers of such facts. Facts, rules, and features are first used by experts among experts. They are helpful in discussing marginal cases, cases where the usual fluid, unremarkable competence has broken down. Facts, rules, and features provide the socially agreed on framework within which the fully competent can support each other when working on a difficult problem. They are not the atomistic elements on which competence is built and they cannot serve this function (Dreyfus & Dreyfus, 1987); that would be putting the cart before the horse. Competence is the basis for the production of facts, not the building blocks of competence. But we in education—and in the culture as a whole—have believed that competence in a field was built on classical knowledge, on facts and rules and essential features. But this is quite simply wrong. Taxonomic features are not the building blocks of competence; they are a discursive product of such competence.[11]

The student had to see the objects their teachers saw before there would be any hope that their teachers' discussion of the features of these objects could be anything but opaque and mystifying. Students needed to be able to recognize objects as being prokaryote on the basis of a systematic perceptual difference from objects labeled eukaryote in order for the discussion of the presence or absence of nuclei to make sense in the lab.[12]

Connectionist theorizing suggests ways to understand an experience-based, nonanalytic process of category formation, but is of no help in determining how to select and order experiences so that of all the differences potentially available in the field of perception, the ones corresponding to the eukaryote–prokaryote distinction would stand out. Indeed, perceptual categorization alone simply has nothing to say about what is perceived. It does suggest that categorization proceeds along different lines than our tradition gives us. Connectionist categorization is most similar to Wittgenstein's (1958) understanding of categorization.[13] Unlike classical, feature-defined categories, connectionist categories have no firm boundaries. And unlike Roschian

---

[11]For an excellent discussion of the discursive production of competence in school settings, see Gee (1992).

[12]I have resolutely avoided overtly opening questions of meaning and philosophical intentionality in this chapter. Here, however, the subject seems hard to avoid. I do not want to imply that the list of features that students learn about cells is meaningless. It is very meaningful—a large proportion of these students will gain entry to medical school on the basis of their facility in memorizing such lists. I do want to say that such lists do not and cannot subserve the sort of competence on which this chapter focuses.

[13]Compare, for instance, Wittgenstein's (1958) discussion of language games in the first 50 pages of Philosophical Investigations and McClelland and Rumelhart's (1986) discussion of memory in "A Distributed Model of Human Learning and Memory" in Parallel Distributed Processing, Volume 2.

categories, they are not organized around central instances.[14] Rather, the history of the person interacting with the world, experience, is the basis of category formation.

Situated cognition and the tradition from which such work descends effectively describe the choice-narrowing, situated structures that act to support cognition in the social field but offer no help in filling out their assumption that experience is the basis for such ordering. Combining connectionist insight into the process of learning categories with situated cognition's fine-grained analysis of how knowledge is structured into the world of phenomena begins to allow progress toward a pedagogy that bridges the gap between knowledge (in-the-world sort of knowledge) and learning (in-the-head sort of learning). Bridging that gap is necessary to design ways of teaching students new categories of perception in a way that is a useful approximation of the community's understanding of the domain.

In our pilot study, when one task was to recognize a picture of a particular cell as either prokaryotic or eukaryotic, students who had been prepared using the alternate condition did much better than those using the traditional textbook treatment. We were quite surprised at the degree of confidence that resulted.[15]

That we are fairly successful at this, using a single set of only five examples of each category, leads me to the pedagogically hopeful conclusion that constraining the design of instruction both socially and perceptually can be a powerful tool for designing instructional practices. Students can begin to learn the categories that order the world of expertise prior to actually entering that community of practice. The uncomfortable opposition constructed within the educational community between the utility of apprenticeship models for competence and the liberative values of an enlightenment view of schooling is, on this account, unnecessary.[16] Schools may serve both masters.[17]

---

[14]Rosch in her later work emphasized "prototype effects" rather than prototypes. This difference intends to restrict her claims to the observed data (such as reaction time) and to avoid a commitment idea that prototypes isomorphically structure representation. See Lakoff's (1987) *Women, Fire, and Dangerous Things*, especially pp. 39–46, for a clear summary of Rosch's late position. The evidence leading to the abandonment of the strong position is here read as a strong argument in favor of the on-the-fly sort of categorization formation that is implied by connectionism. The implications of such a position are profound: There is no stable representation in memory. On this account, these folk psychological terms are reflections of social rather than psychological organization.

[15]See: St. Julien (1994b). For instance, analysis of categorization tasks using micrographs considered particularly difficult revealed that the difference between the treatments was significant at the .001 level.

[16]See, for example: the debate centering around disciplinary cultures and apprenticeship initiated by Palincsar's (1989) and Wineburg's (1989) challenges to Brown, Collins, and Duguid (1989a) and their response (1989b).

[17]Although the point made here is fairly limited to saying that serving both masters is possible, a strong argument can be made that this dual focus is necessary to attain the goals of either group. See Whitson (1988).

In lieu of an extended discussion of the findings of our study, a description of the instrument, and a recounting of the design process that would attempt to validate the truth of my claims about the study's meaning,[18] a supplement follows this chapter that will allow you to participate in an activity similar to the one with which we faced our students. I hope that this socially organized instance of perceptual learning will be a more likely ground for learning—that is, that you will come to share my perceptions—than would be the case for a discursive recounting of facts about such a study.

It is my hope that out of the confluence of the perspectives of connectionism and situated cognition, a material theory of learning can be formulated to displace the descriptive theorizing that currently characterizes knowledge acquisition. A solid theory of the material constitution of learning, spanning the range from structured external symbols that are materially present in the world to a connectionist approach to the learning of these socially organized categories, should prove invaluable to our hopes of building a pedagogy that enhances our students' competence. It is this hope that finally, I submit, motivates us all.

SUPPLEMENT

One implication of this chapter is that people learn most easily when engaged in activity of a special sort. I have claimed that this activity is one of perceptual learning (or category formation) that is mediated by socially organized practices that situate knowledge in the world.

An implication of this in its turn is that a chapter such as this about something as strange as the organizing mediation of social practices in perceptual category formation is bound to be difficult, opaque, and mystifying. What is wanted is an activity that will make use of the sort of learning that I claim is easier.

Hence, this interactive appendix that is designed to allow for the sort of experience that leads to categorical learning. I hope that you will demonstrate to yourself that you can do something that the traditional ways of thinking about learning cannot explain.

Instructions

Figure 10.1 contains three rows of cells. The cells on the left are eukaryotic cells, the ones in the middle are unknown, and the ones on the right are prokaryotic. Your task is to decide with which group, prokaryote or eu-

---

[18]For a more complete description of the project, see St. Julien (1994b); for another perspective, see: Wandersee (1992) "The Graphic Representation of Biological Knowledge."

Eukaryotic Cells

Prokaryotic Cells

Unknown Cells

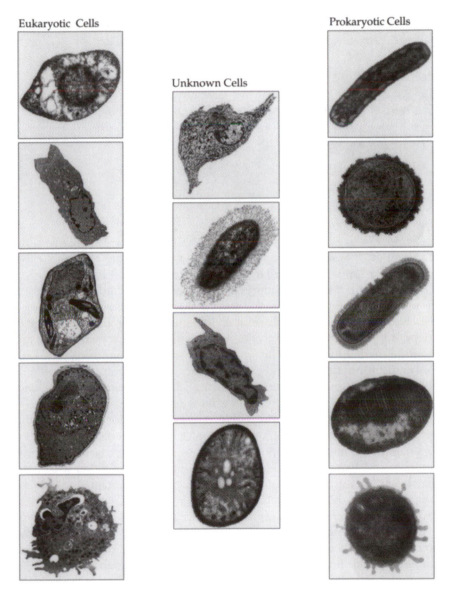

FIG. 10.1.

karyote, the images in the center belong. The distinction that biologists have in mind has to do with complexity.

Work on it for a few minutes, note your choices, and I will let you know how microbiologists would complete the task and then discuss the practices that were used to guide category formation in this instance.

Discussion

First, here is the way that biologists perform this division:

Unknown #1: Eukaryote

Unknown #2: Prokaryote

Unknown #3: Eukaryote

Unknown #4: Prokaryote

Consider your probable performance on this task. A large majority of the people in most groups I have worked with agree with the biologists either three or four times—with the largest number agreeing all four times.

Success at this task is very impressive and very poorly understood. People are able to generate categorical distinctions quite accurately with an extremely meager experiential base in a domain in which almost none have any prior knowledge. Almost everyone is surprised at their own success and understand what they did as just guessing. I want to claim that you should not be surprised, that this kind of task is something you and all people do well; that the process of pattern recognition that underlies this competence is the most basic of all human intellectual talents.

Understanding that pattern recognition is what we do well implies that the sorts of deductive logics and essentialist feature recognition that are dominant in our cultural tradition and embodied in our textbooks are things we do poorly. Practices based on our dominant cultural tradition will, therefore, be poor sites for learning, precisely because they embody poor assumptions concerning the basis of learning.

But if this presentation is surprisingly successful, what about it leads you to make the distinction competently? I want to claim that there are two interdependent things going on that make this possible: pattern perception and situated practice—and that these two are mutually constraining.

Pattern perception belongs to the world of biology, physiologically based psychology, and neurology, whereas situated practices belong to the emphatically social worlds of culture, Foucaultian analysis, semiosis, and activity theory. We are used to thinking of the biological and the social as perhaps naturally and certainly analytically separate.

I think we are wrong.

Pattern Recognition

The idea of pattern recognition discussed here is one that is informed by connectionist perspectives. Connectionism is an offshoot of cognitive psychology that takes the constraints imposed by the material organization of the brain seriously when speculating on mental activity. Connectionist claims about mental activity imply a radically different way of understanding mental entities in general—a number of which are suggestively congruent with the observations of situated cognition. The one I want to focus on here is the claim that pattern recognition is the basic mental process and, as such, it is the ground for all that we call learning. Consider the example of the prokaryotes and the eukaryotes. Using a single page designed to amplify pattern recognition, most people are able to do very well in making an unfamiliar technical distinction in biological taxonomy.

Participants have so little to go on that most of our usual explanations do not seem reasonable here. They do not know the rules of the domain and so could not have deduced their conclusions. I deliberately did not give anyone the essential features that we usually think are necessary to learn recognition didactically. And few have any relevant domain-specific knowledge.

It is tempting to simply conclude, by process of elimination, that what is left is pattern recognition and that therefore pattern recognition must be what explains this. That, however, is not enough. Pattern recognition can be regarded as a basis for a theoretical framework of learning. What it does not and cannot do is be the basis of a theoretical framework for knowledge. If we as educators are to design instruction in which knowledge already known in various communities is learned by our students, we need both.

Pattern recognition can begin to tell us how we come to recognize objects in the world. But there are infinite ways to divide up our experience. There is nothing natural about the categories of eukaryotic and prokaryotic.

Pattern recognition cannot tell us which objects are to be formed. For that, we need situated cognition or something very like it. It would be a mistake to assume that all that went on when you worked the examples was simply pattern recognition.

Situated Practice

The page containing the images that you just classified trades on a whole set of already given social practices, practices that are no more natural than the eukaryote–prokaryote distinction itself. These work because we are familiar with them, but that very familiarity tends to make them invisible in our everyday lives.

For instance, look at how unity is represented. Grouping things together that we intend to represent as a category is an old and well-understood practice. Most folks looking at that page would be tempted to conclude that there are 3 things represented there, not 14.

Or look at how difference is structured: The two categories are on opposite sides of the page. We expect that they will not be simply different from each other, but also opposed in some crucial way.

The unnamed category is in the center, a position that denotes its ambiguity in relation to both of the named categories. The differing number of images helps set this center row off as different from the other two.

Then, of course, I told you what was going on—language is a practice as well. With it, I alerted you to the domain in which the division was being made and to its broad taxonomic purpose.

Then, I hinted that complexity was at stake. That gave you a particular, relational difference as a dimension along which to order the two groups.

In a slightly different vein, the academic role of most readers of this text (and the writer) attests to the fact that at some point, we got pretty good at taking tests. You are bound to suspect that I was unlikely to make all four unknowns members of one category. That leaves 3 and 1 and 2 and 2 as possible patterns. Two and 2 is the most likely. If you feel sure about a couple of the images, you can use patterns such as these to fill in most likely guesses for the ones that are still uncertain.

It is important to notice that all this is not cheating. It is an attempt to build knowledge into the world so that the learner would recognize a particular pattern in the material given. The activity of sorting in this way— without rules, prototypes, or essential features—is crucial to forming a category perceptually. The practices discussed previously constrain the activity of choosing which image goes with which column by trading on knowledge already embedded in the problem presentation. Opposition, unity, ambiguity, linguistic ordering, and cultural knowledge of testing regularities all constrain the possible pattern—out of the plenitude of possible patterns— that the learner will settle on. It is highly unlikely that a student, given a page of unordered, uncommented-on images, would discover anything resembling the taxonomic distinction this activity attempts to teach. Such a student would have only pattern perception to rely on, and pattern perception alone is not enough. But practices that do not acknowledge the constraints of perception, like our traditional ones that center around lists of features, are also unlikely to result in category formation. Any categories formed during the traditional presentation of this distinction are the result of fortuitous factors peripheral to the design of the learning experience.

This argues that socially structured categories of perception are the ground for recognizing objects in the world as objects. Such objects, in their turn, are tools that are used in later pattern perception. Columns-as-unities is an object that our individual histories, with the deployment of such columns by others, has given a particular meaning: unity. In the example under discussion, this practice was deployed—consciously by the designer/teacher and unconsciously by most readers/students—to build the categories *eukaryote* and *prokaryote*. In turn, these categories, deployed as objects that structure experience, can be called on to make other patterns available. For instance, once a class accurately perceives cells as either prokaryotic or eukaryotic, it would be a relatively simple matter to label one pattern of difference, present in eukaryotes and absent in prokaryotes, a nucleus.

Constrained by both connectionist ideas about category learning and existing practices that situate knowledge, an approach such as this enables the teacher to design a learning experience that begins to make available the categories through which the community of biologists structure their world.

ACKNOWLEDGMENTS

The microscopy research discussed in this chapter was supported by NSF-LASER grant (1991) HDR 01: "Exploring Microstructures: Introducing Biology Students to the Images, Tools, and Applications of High-Tech Microscopy." Other members of the research team, without whom this chapter would not have been possible, were, from Life Sciences: Drs. Becky Demler, Cindy Henk, Sharon Mathews, and Marion Socolofsky, from Education: Drs. Catherine Cummins and Jim Wandersee.

This chapter benifited extensively from the criticism and support of the educational community at LSU and subsequently, the students in the Social Cognition course at UIUC. Appropriately, perhaps, it is to the challange of this community of practice as much as to any individual within it that I owe thanks.

REFERENCES

Bartlett, F. C. (1977). *Remembering—A study in experimental social psychology*. Cambridge, UK: Cambridge University Press. (Original work published 1932)

Bereiter, C. (1991). Implications of connectionism for thinking about rules. *Educational Researcher, 20*, 10–16.

Bloom, B. S. (Ed.). (1952). *Taxonomy of educational objectives: The classification of educational goals, handbook 1: The cognitive domain*. New York: McKay.

Brown, J. S., Collins, A., & Duguid, P. (1989a). Situated cognition and the culture of learning. *Educational Researcher, 18*(1), 32–42.

Brown, J. S., Collins, A., & Duguid, P. (1989b). Debating the situation. *Educational Researcher, 18*(4), 10–12, 62.

Clancey, W. J., & Roschelle, J. (1991, April). *Situated cognition: How representations are created and given meaning*. Paper presented at AERA conference, Chicago.

Cussins, A. (1990). The connectionist construction of concepts. In M. A. Boden (Ed.), *The philosophy of artificial intelligence* (pp. 368–440). Oxford, UK: Oxford University Press.

Dewey, J. (1949). Appendix: Letter to a friend. In J. Dewey & A. F. Bently (Eds.), *Knowing and the known* (pp. 313–329). Boston: Beacon.

Dewey, J. (1965). Preface. In J. Dewey, *The influence of Darwin on philosophy* (pp. iii–vi). Bloomington: Indiana University Press.

Dreyfus, H. L., & Dreyfus, S. E. (1987). From Socrates to expert systems: The limits of calculative rationality. In P. Rabinow & W. M. Sullivan (Eds.), *Interpretive social science: A second look* (pp. 327–350). Berkeley: University of California Press.

Fodor, J. (1980). Chapter 6: On the impossibility of acquiring "More Powerful" structures. In M. Piatelli-Palmarini (Ed.), *Language and learning, the debate between Jean Piaget and Noam Chomsky* (pp. 142–162). Cambridge, MA: Harvard University Press.

Gardner, H. (1985). *The mind's new science.* New York: Basic Books.

Gee, J. P. (1992). *The social mind: Langauge, ideology and social practice.* New York: Bergin & Garvey.

Gladwin, H. (1985, Fall). In conclusion: Abstraction versus 'how it is'. *Anthropology and Education Quarterly, 16,* 207–213.

Lakoff, G. (1987). *Women, fire, and dangerous things: What categories reveal about the mind.* Chicago: Chicago University Press.

Lave, J. (1985, Fall). Introduction: Situationally specific practice. *Anthropology and Education Quarterly, 16,* 207–213.

Lave, J., & Wenger, E. (1991). *Situated learning: Legitimate peripheral participation.* Cambridge, UK: Cambridge University Press.

McClelland, J. L., & Rumelhart, D. E. (1986). A distributed model of human learning and memory. In J. L. McClelland, D. E. Rumelhart, & the PDP Research Group (Eds.), *Parallel distributed processing. Vol. 2: Psychological and biological models* (pp. 170–215). Cambridge, MA: MIT Press.

Palincsar, A. S. (1989). Less charted waters. *Educational Researcher, 18*(4), 5–7.

Rogoff, B. (1984). Introduction: Thinking and learning in social context. In B. Rogoff & J. Lave (Eds.), *Everyday cognition: Its development in social context* (pp. 1–8). Cambridge, MA: Harvard University Press.

Rogoff, B., & Morelli, G. (1989). Perspectives on children's development from cultural psychology. *American Psychologist, 44,* 134–141.

Rumelhart, D. E., Smolensky, J. L., McClelland, J. L., & Hinton, G. E. (1986). Schemata and sequential thought processes in PDP models. In J. L. McClelland, D. E. Rumelhart, & the PDP Research Group (Eds.), *Parallel distributed processing. Vol. 2: Psychological and biological models* (pp. 7–57). Cambridge, MA: MIT Press.

St. Julien, J. (1994a, April). *Social constructivism: Vygotskian activity and connectionist representation.* Paper presented at the American Educational Research Association conference, New Orleans.

St. Julien, J. (1994b/1995). Cognition and learning: The implications of a situated connectionist perspective for theory and practice in education. (Doctoral dissertation, Louisiana State University, 1994). *Dissertation Abstracts International, 55/11,* 3404A.

Walkerdine, V. (1984). Developmental psychology and the child-centered pedagogy: The insertion of Piaget into early education. In J. Henriques, W. Holloway, C. Unwin, C. Venn, & V. Walkerdine (Eds.), *Changing the subject* (pp. 153–202). London: Methuen.

Walkerdine, V. (1988). *The mastery of reason: Cognitive development and the production of rationality.* London: Routledge.

Wandersee, J. (1992, June). *The graphic representation of biological knowledge: Integrating words and images.* Paper presented at the NATO Conference on the Structure and Acquisition of Biological Knowledge, Glasgow, Scotland.

Whitson, J. A. (1988). The politics of "non-political" curriculum: Heteroglossia and the discourse of "choice" and "effectiveness". In W. F. Pinar (Ed.), *Contemporary curriculum discourses* (pp. 279–330). Scottsdale, AZ: Gorsuch Scarisbrick.

Wineburg, S. S. (1989). Remembrance of theories past. *Educational Researcher, 18*(4), 7–10.

Wittgenstein, L. (1958). *Philosophical investigations* (G. E. M. Anscombe & R. Rhees, Eds.). Oxford, UK: Blackwell.

CHAPTER ELEVEN

Situated Cognition and How to Overcome It

Carl Bereiter
The Ontario Institute for Studies in Education

The first half-century of American psychology is often represented nowadays as a dark age of rat-running and rote verbal-learning experiments, which ended only when it was overwhelmed by the rise of the new cognitive psychology that started in the 1950s (cf. Gardner, 1985). But throughout that early period, there was a strain of mainstream experimental psychology that dealt with what we would now call situated learning. It was rat psychology, to be sure, but it was a psychology of situated rat behavior. The central tenet was that animals do not simply learn responses, they learn their environments. Run rats in a maze under typical tightly controlled conditions, and they learn a fixed route to the goal. Change things a little and they are lost. But let them run around on their own and they quickly learn the whole maze, so that they can get from wherever you drop them to wherever they want to go by an efficient route. Tolman (1949) was responsible for the seminal experiments and also for the proposal that place learning, as he called it, is mainly perceptual and not behavioral. It was Woodworth (1958), however, for some time the dean of U.S. experimental psychologists, who made the most forceful effort to shift the mainstream of experimental psychology toward a consideration of organisms interacting with their environments. "If behavior consists in an active dealing with the environment" (p. 300), he said, "and if it depends very largely on learning, it must depend on what we can properly call 'learning the environment.' " He then went on to elaborate:

If we said, "learning about the environment," we should imply the sort of information that can be picked in conversation and reading. What we mean is a direct acquaintance with persons, places, and things—the kind of learning that occurs when we see a person, hear him talk, watch him act, and participate with him in social activity. . . . (Woodworth, 1958, p. 300)

I would like to credit Woodworth with having arrived at the basic idea of situated cognition by the unlikely route of animal experimental psychology. Despite his eminence, his 1958 book seems to have been largely ignored. Interesting observations, but they do not lead anywhere theoretically—that was the opinion expressed by professors of mine at the time. Woodworth was a couple of decades too early. His ideas would find a ready reception now.

Woodworth and his environment-learning rats are of more than historical interest, however. Contemporary ideas about situated cognition, having come to us from anthropology, are heavily loaded with human cultural concerns. They are connected with Vygotsky and his belief in the social origins of cognitive structures. As several of the chapters in this volume indicate, situated cognition has also gotten itself connected with feminism and educational radicalism. We tend to forget that animal cognition is situated, as well.

In order to consider such an idea as overcoming situated cognition, it is important to appreciate that, no matter how deeply enmeshed in culture human cognition may have become, its situatedness has a biological basis. Rat cognition is situated in a world of mazelike tunnels formed by the framing of building walls and floors. Learning such environments is what rat learning is geared to. Rat intelligence involves leveraging off the structural properties of such environments for purposes of escape, gaining entry, food gathering, and so on. Of course, rat cognition is situated in a world that also contains other rats—but it is a stretch to say that it originates on a social plane. Our brain, like the rat's, evolved as an adaptation to our environment. The environment, of course, changes, and many of the most striking changes have been brought about through our own doing. But those changes have occurred too recently to have had much effect on our own evolution, which for most of its period took place in a world little affected by our presence.

OUTGROWING ANIMAL COGNITION

Thus, we do not come by situated cognition through a cultural or learning process. Our brains evolved to deal with situations in which we find ourselves. We have, however, managed to transcend our animal heritage in certain ways, and in this chapter I argue for the value of viewing these as ways of overcoming the situatedness of cognition. Like other adventures in overcoming nature, overcoming the situatedness of cognition has risks as well as benefits and is, in a fundamental sense, illusory. But identifying the risks and benefits and separating illusion from reality is part of the program I am advocating here.

The most obvious way in which we humans transcend our animal heritage is through transforming physical environments and creating new social structures and practices along with them. The second way is through acquiring expertise, which enables us to function in a novel environment much as if we had evolved within it (Bereiter & Scardamalia, 1993).

Environmental transformation and expertise are to be found in every society, but there is a third way of transcending biological givens that is much less common and that represents a far more radical departure from the kinds of cognitive adaptations we share with other species. This is the kind of departure most dramatically exemplified by science. It amounts to creating a world of immaterial knowledge objects and acquiring expertise in working with them. Although these knowledge objects may refer to spatially and temporally located situations, they are not bound to those situations. Thus, this third way represents a stronger sense in which humans may be said to overcome the situatedness of cognition. The third way, furthermore, greatly extends the other two. A modern city is a physical environment within which human beings have developed many new forms of practice and expertise, but this environment could not exist were it not for centuries of development of abstract knowledge now put to use in the construction of tall buildings, electrical power grids, heating and air-conditioning systems, and the countless other technological underpinnings of a modern city.

These three kinds of advances beyond animal cognition map nicely on to Popper's (1972) metaphoric schema of three worlds—World 1 being the material world of inanimate and animate things (including human beings), World 2 the subjective world of individual mental life, and World 3 the world of immaterial knowledge objects. Lacking other handy labels, I use Popper's terms without implying a necessary commitment to other aspects of Popper's epistemology.

Situated cognition researchers have contributed substantially to our understanding of the relations between Worlds 1 and 2, arguing that these are much more directly and intimately connected than previous cognitive theories had supposed. But they have not done the same for World 3. Instead of according knowledge existential status in its own right, as epistemologists have traditionally done, they have tried to account for it in terms of the practices of particular groups, such as scientists or mathematicians; concrete embodiments of knowledge, such as books and instruments; and, occasionally, as content in individual minds—as mental models, for instance (Greeno, 1994).

Although these are important aspects of knowledge, they seem to me to miss the core. That core is represented in the metaphor of World 3—a world, wholly created by the human intellect, that enables us, for better or worse, to escape the situational embeddedness of cognition. Without that core, formal education becomes meaningless (as, indeed, some advocates of situated cognition seem to believe it is). Again, for better or worse, formal education is our individual escape route from the confines of situated cognition.

CAN THERE BE NONSITUATED COGNITION?

Greeno, a leading exponent of situated cognition, expressed dissatisfaction with the term. It seems to refer to a type of cognition and, thus, to imply that there also exists a type of cognition that is not situated (Greeno, 1994). Situativity theorists (to use Greeno's suggested replacement term) deny this: All cognition is situated and could not be any other way. If we accept this premise, then the title of this chapter, "Situated Cognition and How to Overcome It," is an oxymoron.

But, in fact, there is nonsituated cognition, and situativity theorists have devoted a lot of effort to criticizing it. The catch is that nonsituated cognition is not found in nature (at least not in nature as it is known to earthlings); it is found only in machines. Most of artificial intelligence has been constructed according to a model radically at variance with the kind suggested by situativity theory. In situated cognition, people (or other agents) carry on activity in the world, adapted to the constraints and affordances of the environment. Cognition is the individual or collective process by which people negotiate these constraints and affordances, according to their individual or collective purposes. Machine intelligence of the classic AI variety is not like that. Cognition is an entirely internal process of symbol manipulation (Vera & Simon, 1993). Interaction with the outside world is done by means of transducers that translate inputs from sensors into symbols that the machine can manipulate or that translate symbols into actions. Thus, a robot controlled by AI of this kind will contain a plan—for getting from Point A to Point B, let us say—that controls how data from its visual sensors are translated into symbols that its program can then convert into instructions to its servomechanisms so that the plan is executed through physical movement. The robot may also contain a program for revising the plan in case of mishap. One very important line of argument in favor of situated cognition comes from roboticists, who find that this kind of robot cognition does not work very well (Beer, 1991). It is too slow and crude and prone to catastrophic failure. But these kinds of criticisms acknowledge that there is such a thing as nonsituated cognition, making the case that it is not a very good kind of cognition for getting around in the world.

The existence of nonsituated cognition, albeit artificially created, is, I believe, profoundly important for understanding human cognition and its situatedness. For one thing, it allows us to talk about advantages and disadvantages of situated cognition, which would make no sense if there were nothing to compare situated cognition to. It also affords the possibility of identifying degrees of situatedness. With such possibilities in view, it is no longer absurd to talk about overcoming situated cognition. The questions are: Why would anyone want to, and how could it be done?

ADVANTAGES AND DISADVANTAGES
OF SITUATED COGNITION

If we take rule-based AI[1] as exemplifying nonsituated cognition, then looking at what it does well and poorly (compared to human beings) may offer us insights into the advantages and disadvantages of situated cognition. Using rule-based programs, computers are much better than we are at carrying out long chains of reasoning and at exhaustively searching memory (Anderson, 1985). Thus, they excel at chess. The best programs, which can beat all but a few human experts, succeed by reasoning farther ahead and along more paths than their human opponents (Charness, 1991). We are abysmally bad at searching memory in a listwise fashion. Try naming the 50 United States—or some other familiar set of about that size, if the states are not familiar enough. Almost everyone misses one or two and has a terrible time finding the missing ones, whereas computers have no trouble with this sort of task.

What we do remarkably well in comparison to rule-based AI is recognize patterns—for instance, recognizing a face from the past, even though it has aged 20 years since last we saw it. Computers, by contrast, have trouble identifying letters of the alphabet under the normal variations of handwriting and typography, a task many preschool children can handle easily. Another relative strength of human cognition is associative retrieval—for instance, reading a research report and being reminded of a related finding from a decade past, on a slightly different topic. This is a chancy business for us, but rule-based AI cannot do it at all unless the stored items have been appropriately indexed beforehand (Schank, Collins, & Hunter, 1986). Pattern recognition and associative retrieval seem to be the means by which we grasp analogies and metaphors, and this gives us a great imaginative edge over the literal-minded machine (Margolis, 1987).

---

[1]The qualifier *rule-based* is necessary because there has lately emerged a different kind of AI, connectionism (Rumelhart, 1989), which functions much more like situated cognition. Throughout this chapter, however, when I refer to AI, I always mean the rule-based kind, whether the qualifier is attached or not.

The relative strengths of computer and human cognition directly reflect differences between nonsituated and situated cognition. Rule-based AI works very well when all the necessary information can be explicitly represented and indexed, as is the case with a game of chess or a gazeteer. The rule-based system can then go to work on its stored information and produce a result appropriate to the part of the real situation of which it contains a representation; for example, it can compute a move appropriate to a real chess game. When all the necessary information is coded into rules or propositions, formal logic comes to the fore as a powerful tool for arriving at decisions, and logical operations are what computers excel at. The trouble is that the great bulk of real-world situations cannot be represented in this way. Chess games can, but as simple a game as tag cannot. This is because chess has a set of rules that allow all the possible moves to be computed, whereas the possibilities inherent in a dozen kids running around on a playground are, for practical purposes, limitless. Representations are necessarily abstractions. Abstractions based on Newton's laws work for physical situations involving a small number of inanimate objects, but when objects have minds of their own and can twist and dodge the way agile children can, such abstract representations become relatively useless. It is not that Newton's laws cease to hold, of course; it is just that the variables are too numerous and are impractical to measure and compute.

A tag-playing robot would need a different kind of mind from the one that rule-based AI would give it. Instead of a mind that works on internal representations of the playground and the participants, it would need a mind more directly attuned to the physical and social environment, responding quickly to opportunities for tagging, switching from one pursuit to another the instant that a more promising target presented itself. In short, it would need situated cognition.

At this point, my account sounds like much of what appears in the situated cognition literature. The situated actions of just plain folks come off as flexible, adaptive, and elegant—in a word, intelligent—whereas action based on formal procedures and principles comes off as brittle, plodding, insensitive to nuance—in a word, stupid. It is time, therefore, to look at the other side. Although nonsituated cognition may not be very good for guiding a robot in a game of tag, it has proved capable of guiding a space vehicle to Mars. Surely there is a lesson for us in that.

THE PROBLEM OF TRANSFER

The main weakness of situated cognition is, it seems, precisely its situatedness. In traditional language, the limitations of situatedness are referred to as problems of transfer. What we learn in one situation, we often fail to apply in another. Situativity theory helps us to understand why this is so. The progress of situated learning consists of increasingly fine attunement to the constraints and affordances of the particular situation. Thus, as learning proceeds, it tends to become less and less generalizable to other situations. In your first job as a store clerk, you will begin by learning many things that are applicable to store clerking in general—how to address customers, ring up sales, bag purchases, watch for shoplifters, and so on. But as the weeks go on, your skills will become more and more specific to the particular store and its merchandise, clientele, management, physical layout, staff, and so on.

Advanced stages of situated learning may, in fact, begin to yield negative transfer, as habits are acquired that will need to be overcome in a new situation. There is a deeper problem of transfer, however. Elsewhere, I have tried to show that what mainly fails to transfer is learned intelligent behavior (Bereiter, 1995). The course of situated learning typically has the aspect of a progression from being inept and prone to stupid mistakes to being competent and smart. Although important parts of what is learned in one situation may transfer to a new one, the part that does not transfer is likely to include the being smart. Again, this makes sense in light of situativity theory, for being smart just means becoming so nicely attuned to specific constraints and affordances of a situation that you can effortlessly cope with whatever problems arise.[2] In a new situation, you are liable to have to start over being stupid.

If, categorically, learned intelligent behavior is not transferrable from old situations to new, this has grave implications for education, if not for humankind in general, what with the accelerating pace of change. But there we have an irony worth pondering. The accelerating pace of change is increasingly driven by technological innovations, virtually every one of which is an instance of transfer of intelligent behavior from one situation to another. I do not want to make space travel out to be the highest achievement of human intelligence, but it is surely our most colossal example of transfer of learning. No amount of situated cognition or legitimate peripheral participation would get people to the moon and back.[3] It took something more to produce that kind of transfer, and we must try to pin down what that is. Failing in that, we may face a future in which a small number of people have caught on to some secret of transferrable learning, and thus are able to keep creating and adapting to new situations, while the rest of us find it increasingly difficult to cope.

---

[2]This is how Dreyfus and Dreyfus (1986) characterized expertise—a characterization that we criticize as failing to distinguish experts from experienced nonexperts (Bereiter & Scardamalia, 1993).

[3]This is not to deny that situated learning played a part. Astronauts did, after all, do part of their training near Sudbury, Ontario, where years of mineral extraction had produced a terrain closely approximating what was expected to be found on the moon.

Greeno, Smith, and Moore (1993) offered a situated account of transfer, attributing it to constraints or affordances that are common across situations. This account differs from older, nonsituated accounts in that constraints and affordances are not characteristics of either the environment or of the person, considered separately, but of the relationship between person and environment. Thus, transfer is a matter of the same kind of relationship coming into play in different situations. I think that is a valuable conceptual advance on this timeworn problem, but I also believe that it raises issues that can only be dealt with by introducing ideas of nonsituated cognition.

To constitute an interesting case of transfer, the constraints and affordances of two situations must appear different on the surface. In one of the classic transfer problems, people learn a clever way of beaming x-rays at a tumor and then are given the opportunity to apply this knowledge to figuring out a clever way for Crusaders to attack a castle. Without prompting, people seldom exhibit transfer; but if told that the solution to the first problem should suggest a solution to the second, more people will make the connection. Thus, transfer in such cases is anything but automatic. People have to be looking for a relationship. And what kind of relationship is it? The word that comes to mind is *abstract*. It is a relationship based on formal, structural, or logical correspondences. In the tumor and castle example, the abstract idea is focus—things following converging paths to produce maximum effect where they meet.[4] To discover such abstract relationships, however, one has to carry out something quite different from ordinary situated action. One has to create symbolic representations of situations and carry out operations on those symbols. In other words, one has to act more like a computer and less like a creature of nature.

LEARNING BEYOND WHAT THE SITUATION CALLS FOR

Flora and Dora are both A students in Algebra I. The next year, they take Algebra II. Flora again aces the course, whereas Dora finds herself at a loss and just manages to scrape by with the C minus awarded to students who try hard but do not get it. Here we have an apparent case of the same learning transferring for one person but not for another. Few mathematics educators would buy that interpretation, however. They would conjecture that Flora and Dora learned quite different things in Algebra I. What Flora learned evidently provided a good basis for Algebra II, whereas what Dora learned did not. So it is not that something failed to transfer for Dora, it is that she failed to learn what was transferrable. How are we to account for these different learnings, and how do they relate to situated cognition?

---

[4]Thus, converging x-rays destroy the tumor but have less effect on the surrounding tissue; converging tunnels enable large numbers of troops to reach the castle simultaneously.

In the last 20 years, there has been quite a bit of research on the Floras and Doras of the world. Even without the research, it is easy to divine that Flora probably understood the mathematics presented in Algebra I and that Dora did not, getting by instead on rote procedures. What the research has done is give us an idea of what Flora did differently from Dora in order to produce this result. Stepping down from algebra to arithmetic, a nice example of this research comes from Resnick and Neches (1984). They examined a practice common in elementary arithmetic, in which children carry out operations with concrete objects that mirror such symbolic operations as borrowing and carrying (or regrouping, as it is now called). Most children, although they were able to carry out both the concrete and the symbolic operations, failed to make a connection between them. Some children did make the connection, however. On interviewing the children, it was found that the children who made the connection reported that they were trying to make a connection.

That may not sound very surprising, but consider it from the standpoint of situated cognition. Clearly, the situation was designed to afford experimenting with the relationships between concrete and symbolic quantitative operations. But any situation affords innumerable opportunities for inquiry. Why we would exploit one and not another—or any at all, for that matter—depends partly on our own goals and partly on, to put it broadly, what the situation calls for. Generically, the situation in which the children in Resnick and Neches' study found themselves was that of schoolwork (Doyle, 1983). A schoolwork situation is rather like that in a garment factory. Although a number of workers may be present in the same room, each one is independently engaged in carrying out a task specified by the supervisor or teacher. What the situation calls for is defined by the task constraints. The tasks are usually defined in such a way as not to put undue strain on the capacities of those performing them. There usually are time constraints, however, and so there is motivation to find ways of satisfying task requirements that economize on time. Another characteristic shared by schoolwork and garment work is a very limited time horizon. Although the teacher or supervisor may have long-range objectives, the students or workers are not expected to look beyond the immediate day's task. (School projects are an exception, as their name implies.)

Given these characteristics of schoolwork, it then becomes remarkable that some children would take it on themselves to try to discover a logical connection between the concrete and symbolic components of the task they were assigned to carry out. The task assignment did not require it. The task components were easily enough executed that it was unlikely that an impasse would drive them to deeper analysis. And the time horizon, suggesting that it would all be over soon, offered no reason to think ahead to the possible relevance of the current task to future situations.

Returning to Flora and Dora, their first-year algebra class probably provided opportunities—through textbook explanations and worked examples, class discussions, and problems—to develop a basic understanding of algebraic functions. But what the situation actually called for was just solving lots of linear equations. By learning a few procedures and applying them carefully, an assiduous student could solve the equations without any need for conceptual understanding. That, we may surmise, is what Dora did. It worked well through Algebra I. But then she got to Algebra II and encountered an explosion of different types of equations and complications in procedures for solving them. Try as she might, she made frequent errors. Having no sense of how algebra related to arithmetic, she never checked her answers with trial values. (Perhaps arithmetic did not make much sense to her, either, and therefore provided no basis on which to build an understanding of algebra.) Consequently, her errors went uncorrected and the marks on her schoolwork plummeted.

Flora, we surmise, did acquire an understanding of algebra in the course of her first year. But on the basis of related research, we may further surmise that this did not just happen. Despite the fact that the situation did not actually call for it, Flora must have expended effort in trying to understand what algebra was about and how it connected with what she already knew. This is what Scardamalia and I have elsewhere defined as intentional learning (Bereiter & Scardamalia, 1989). Intentional learning is primarily a matter of goals rather than strategies. Examining the goal-related statements of people studying computer programming, Ng and Bereiter (1991) were able to identify three levels of goals. The first and most common are task completion goals. In the Flora and Dora case, these would be goals associated with correctly completing assigned algebra problems. At the next level are instructional goals. These are goals related to what the teacher or textbook is trying to teach. They can vary greatly in how explicitly and saliently they are put before the student. In a typical algebra textbook, they would be discernible from section headings and the like, but they could easily be ignored in the pursuit of task completion goals. Finally, and rather rare, are knowledge-building goals, which pertain to the learner's personal agenda for constructing knowledge. Among other things, the three kinds of goals differ greatly in their time horizons. In a conventional algebra class, the time horizon for task completion goals is usually the next day. The time horizon for instructional goals is likely to be the next examination, or, at most, the end of the course. The time horizon for knowledge-building goals, by contrast, may extend indefinitely far into the future, and may also extend into the past, encompassing a history of past learning that is consciously built on in the present.

To succeed in Algebra II, the student must at least have achieved some of the instructional goals implicit in Algebra I. Merely achieving task completion goals, even doing very well at them, would not suffice. To be on track for becoming a mathematician, it is probably also necessary to be pursuing knowledge-building goals—goals that extend beyond the instructional goals of the immediate course and that involve, in effect, reconstructing mathematical knowledge in one's own way and following out its implications (cf. Popper & Eccles, 1977, p. 461).

These three levels of goals differ in their level of abstractness. Correspondingly, we may say that they differ in their degree of situatedness. Action in pursuit of task completion goals is highly situated, being directly linked to manifest constraints of the situation. The pursuit of instructional goals is less so. And when we get to pursuing knowledge-building goals, we are talking about action that is only weakly connected with the immediate situation, that consists largely of mental work on symbolic objects, some of which are abstracted from the current situation but others of which originate quite outside it.

Situativity theorists might concede that something like this continuum of abstraction exists, but they would argue that the more abstract kind of mathematical activity is just as situated as the more concrete. This is where the relational character of situativity becomes important. Although Flora and Dora may be in the same physical environment, they are in different situations. The affordances and constraints are different, reflecting their differing motives and capacities. But even though one may be plodding through a workbook assignment while the other is reflecting on the nature of mathematical functions, each is engaged in a cultural practice that is adapted to situational constraints and affordances.

I do not want to argue the contrary. With a concept as elastic as situatedness, it would be impossible to exclude any activity from it categorically. What I do want to argue for, nevertheless, is the value of thinking of situatedness as varying along a continuum. Both ends of the continuum are limits that might be approached but could never be reached. At the extreme situated end would be organisms so fully and rigidly adapted to one particular environment that they could never survive in any other. The organisms that live in the steaming pool at the base of Old Faithful come to mind as possible candidates for this end of the continuum, but no doubt even they have some range. To mark the other end of the continuum—to make the other end of the contiuum even imaginable—we must invoke rule-based artificial intelligence. With such a continuum in mind, we can grant that Flora and Dora, along with all animal organisms, demonstrate situated cognition, but at the same time we can make something of the idea that in their mathematical behavior, Flora is farther toward the nonsituated end than Dora. In the next sections, I try to show what can be made of this idea.

LEARNING TO SIMULATE A COMPUTER

The pioneers of artificial intelligence did not suppose that they were creating something to stand at the opposite pole from natural cognition. On the contrary, they thought, and many still maintain, that the computational systems they created were reasonable simulations of human intelligence. These systems were, after all, based on what common sense and 2,000 years of philosophy told us is the nature of human intelligence—that it consists of the ability to reason and figure things out on the basis of information coming from the outer world. AI systems did that, and did it with kinds of tasks that challenge human reasoning abilities: playing chess and other intellectual games, solving logical and mathematical puzzles, diagnosing illnesses. Moreover, fine-grain comparisons between machine and human behavior indicated that machines tended to carry out their tasks in humanlike ways, encountering humanlike difficulties, and even following time courses similar to those of human reasoners (e.g., Anderson, 1983; Newell & Simon, 1972).

How could it have come about, as situativity theorists suggest, that these AI pioneers were all barking up the wrong tree, designing something radically at variance with what natural cognition is really like? To answer that question, we had better open it up and ask as well how common sense and 2,000 years' worth of philosophers could have made the same mistake. The answer, I think, lies in introspection.

We are conscious of only a small part of our cognitive activity. In routine activities, such as driving a car or reading a newspaper, we process vast amounts of information, but we tend to be conscious of it only when some mental effort is involved—when a problem arises or when something comes up that makes us think. Thus, when philosophers or just plain folks reflect on the nature of cognition, their introspective database consists of these rather exceptional events. This is like doing an ethnography of a people based solely on observing riots and demonstrations.

During these exceptional cognitive events, we find ourselves formulating problems and hypotheses, recalling rules and facts, and engaging in spurts of if–then reasoning. The great fallacy of traditional theory of mind has been to assume that the rest of cognition consists of these same sorts of things, carried out unconsciously (Dreyfus, 1988). A more realistic and productive view, which situatitivy theorists have helped advance, is that these symbolic processes are themselves exceptional and by no means representative of the great bulk of cognitive activity. Situativity theorists have helped us to appreciate the great unconscious part of cognition.[5] My purpose here is to

---

[5]Although Freud is justly credited with winning a place for the unconscious in psychology, he held to the classic view that unconscious structures and processes are similar to conscious ones. It is the content of the unconscious that Freud treated as distinct, as well as the processes by which certain content is rendered unconscious.

look again at the exceptional conscious part, to reflect on what it is for and how it relates to unconscious situated cognition.

The following is no doubt an overstatement, but it will serve to launch the discussion: The mental processes that we are conscious of are processes that do not come naturally (which probably has much to do with why they are conscious). They are acquired processes, culturally mediated, that enable the brain to act as if it were a different kind of device from what it had evolved to be. The device we simulate in our conscious thinking is a logic machine—a machine that finally, in the current century, people have been able actually to build. Thus, according to this conjecture, the computer does not simulate human cognition. Instead, human cognition is able to simulate the computer—although, until this century, the computer existed only as an idealization of a certain form of intelligence and not as a physical reality.

According to Kitto (1954), the ancient Greeks believed they had discovered logical reasoning, and they treated it as a sort of information technology to be exploited and disseminated. According to Piaget (Inhelder & Piaget, 1958), contemporary adolescents often have the same notion when they first become able to carry out formal logical operations. They think they can now figure out everything. Such enthusiasms are consistent with a cognitive achievement that, at least subjectively, brings new powers. They are also, however, a signal to us to be on guard against overextended claims.

Young children and tribal peoples unfamiliar with the syllogism have often been regarded as lacking in reason, and much of modern research in anthropological and developmental psychology has gone into demonstrating that this is not the case. Logicality, it turns out, is to be found in all peoples and at very young ages, provided one looks for it in situations where the people have had a chance to develop some knowledge and competence (Donaldson, 1978; Scribner, 1979). So what is it, then, that the Greeks thought they had discovered and that adolescents keep rediscovering? Piaget and Inhelder (1958) seemed to have had it basically right. It is one thing to think logically about concrete reality; it is something else to think logically about propositions (which may or may not refer to concrete reality).

In a famous study that was originally taken to demonstrate the lack of logical reasoning in uneducated people, Luria (1976) presented Russian peasants with syllogistic reasoning problems such as, "In the Far North, where there is snow, all bears are white. Novaya Zemlya is in the Far North. What color are bears there?" Luria found that the peasants tended to waffle on such problems, protesting that they were really not all that familiar with conditions in Novaya Zemlya and advising Luria to go check with someone who had been there. By contrast, collective farm workers who had had some education promptly responded that the bears in Novaya Zemlya are white.

Without speculating too deeply about thought processes, we can say with confidence that the more educated workers did not actually know that the bears in Novaya Zemlya were white. What they knew, rather, was that the two given propositions implied that the bears in Novaya Zemlya are white. Either proposition could be false or there could be no such place as Novaya Zemlya or there might be no bears there at all. These may have been some of the considerations that bothered the peasants, for they are legitimate concerns when it comes to thinking about the real physical world—Popper's World 1. But in the kind of language game that we call logical reasoning, none of these considerations count. Certain propositions are taken as given, and at issue are propositions that follow from them. This is action carried out in World 3, which is a world that was probably unknown to the illiterate peasants.

By itself, World 3 is just a world of language games carried out by what might as well be arbitrary rules. The great power of World 3, the thing that makes it exciting to people when they discover it, is that when one works with premises that are true with respect to World 1, then valid conclusions from these premises turn out also to be true with respect to World 1. Conversely, if valid conclusions turn out not to be true with respect to World 1, this is a signal that something is wrong with the premises. Disciplined movement back and forth between World 1 and World 3 gives us the hypothetico-deductive method and opens up vast possibilities for theory development, problem solving, and design.

Such heady talk is, of course, the basis of positivism, and it is subject to all the criticism that has been leveled against that overly optimistic philosophy. It furthermore overlooks the large and vital role of informal, unarticulated, impressionistic, and embedded knowledge (Bereiter & Scardamalia, 1993). This is not the place for a critique of pure reason, however. The point I am trying to make is that a significant and empowering change takes place when one catches on to treating ideas as objects of inquiry. Once we get good at it, it seems perfectly natural and we tend to forget that there was ever a time when we did not do so. But it is always effortful, open to serious error. It is not how we function most of the time, and it may well be that a large part of the human population never functions that way.

In human development, several theorists have characterized cognitive development along similar lines. Donaldson (1978), after documenting the logicality of young children's behavior, proposed that during subsequent cognitive development, this logicality becomes less situation-dependent— thus, in some sense, less situated. Karmiloff-Smith (1992) proposed a theory even more closely aligned with the present argument. She portrayed cognition as going through a series of representational redescriptions, such that knowledge that was originally implicit in skills finally comes to be rendered sufficiently explicit that it can be applied in different domains and in the service of goals different from those that gave rise to it.

SCHOOLING AND KNOWLEDGE WORK

Although situated cognition researchers have taken a lively interest in learn-ing, both in and out of school, they have not come up with anything that could be called a new educational vision. Instead, situativity theorists have tended to endorse various innovations of a social constructivist cast, inter-preting them within their own frameworks. As has been pointed out (Wine-burg, 1989) and acknowledged (Brown, Collins, & Duguid, 1989), however, the educational ideas coming from situativity theorists have not advanced notably beyond those of Dewey. The main difficulty, I would suggest, is that situativity theory has not been able to provide a cogent idea of the point of schooling. This difficulty, in turn, derives from a serious confusion between product and process.

If the work of a community of practice is manufacturing paint, for instance, there is no difficulty in separating the process from the product. One may view the manufacturing of paint as situated activity without also having to regard the paint as situated. The paint will be used in all kinds of remote and unknown situations. The fact that the paint may also be used by the people who make it—to paint their shop walls, for instance—still introduces no confusion. But when the product of an activity is knowledge, and the knowledge is mainly of use to the people who produce it, confusion can be well nigh total.

The source of the confusion is that knowledge production, like any kind of human activity, takes place in some physical and social situation, and accordingly situated knowledge also develops. This is knowledge constituted in the practice of the community and intimately involved with the affordances and constraints of the situation. But this is not the same as the knowledge that is the product of the situated activity, any more than the situated knowl-edge of the workers in the paint factory is the same as the paint they produce.

Some knowledge-production situations are less confusing than others, however, so let us consider one of those first. A forensic chemistry laboratory produces knowledge of a particular kind. Through analysis of materials obtained at a crime scene, knowledge is produced that contributes to creating an account of what went on at the scene. In this case, it is not difficult to distinguish between the knowledge embedded in the practice of the chemists and the knowledge that they deliver to the detectives. The two kinds of knowledge relate to entirely different situations. The distinction becomes trickier if the chemists are doing basic research. In this case, the knowledge they produce relates to their own practice as well as to others'. But with a little effort, the distinction can be maintained. It is not so much different from the paint-makers being users of the paint they produce. If, however, chemical research is being carried out by students in a school laboratory, then the distinction becomes even less obvious. This is because the students are likely to be the only users of the knowledge they produce. Nevertheless, I believe that the school situation, like the other situations in which knowledge is created, can best be understood by striving to distinguish knowledge implicit in the process from knowledge that is the product of the process.

No such distinction is normally made in education, even with the popularization of constructivist ideas. The results of knowledge construction are thought of as entirely internal—internal to the minds of individual students under most construals, or internal to the distributed cognition of the classroom community under construals influenced by sociocultural theories (Cobb, 1994). Accordingly, constructivism becomes more or less synonymous with learning by discovery, and it competes—not always successfully—with direct instruction (Harris & Graham, 1994).

But students can produce knowledge objects—theories (or theorylike conjectures, at any rate), interpretations, historical accounts, problem statements, defenses based on evidence, and so on. These may be embodied in reports or presentations, but not necessarily. When students use a networked computer database as a discourse medium, they can produce quite substantial knowledge objects without the need for any more tangible product than the electronic record of the discourse itself (Bereiter, Scardamalia, Cassells, & Hewitt, in press; Scardamalia, Bereiter, & Lamon, 1994).

The observable goings-on in this activity that we call collaborative knowledge building fall easily within the spectrum of what others might call constructivist learning, cognitive apprenticeship, inquiry learning, or talking science. The distinctiveness is conceptual; it is a matter of how teachers and students conceive of what they are doing and the effect this has on efforts to do it better. One thing that must be recognized about the many exciting experiments in educational uplift that are going on (it is true of all the ones I have knowledge of, and so I confidently generalize to the rest) is that reality falls well short both of the ideal and of the exemplary episodes reported in the literature. Hence, in pedagogy as in science, improvability is of the essence. The following are ways in which a knowledge-building conceptualization of schooling offers advantages over other approaches that regard both knowledge construction and the knowledge produced as situated:

1. The focus of classroom activity shifts from improving students' minds to improving their theories or other knowledge objects. This is a clearer objective and one that students and teachers alike can more readily track.

2. A developmental continuum may be recognized that runs from unconscious learning in early childhood (Montessori, 1967) to self-aware, intentional learning (Bereiter & Scardamalia, 1989) and then to inquiry that is focused on the external world and finally to inquiry that is focused on World 3 objects as they relate both to the external world and to one's own purposes

(Scardamalia, Bereiter, & Lamon, 1994). Helping students advance along this continuum then becomes a meaningful educational objective.

3. Production of knowledge objects inevitably involves building on or otherwise dealing with existing knowledge objects (hence Newton's avowal that he stood upon the shoulders of giants). Consequently, familiarity with culturally significant World 3 objects—the goal of cultural literacy (Hirsch, 1987)—comes about naturally rather than through a didactic regimen.

4. The problem of inert knowledge (Whitehead, 1929) is effectively circumvented. Progressive education sought to avoid inert knowledge by having learning come about naturally through the social life of the community. But the social life of school communities does not naturally give rise to much learning of an abstract or theoretical nature. The most immediate and obvious use of knowledge objects is in creating new ones—in creating new understanding either of particular phenomena or of a class of phenomena. Students experience the power of concepts in science and other disciplines by using them to help solve problems in their own knowledge-building efforts.

5. Knowledge building is not in competition with instruction. In real life, people occasionally take time out from their work to learn something—often learning something that will help them in their work. Professional associations often include training sessions and tutorials in their annual meetings. Similarly in schools, there is no reason why time cannot be taken out from knowledge building, to whatever extent is judged necessary, and devoted to explicit learning activities. The more immediately relevant these are to students' knowledge building the better, of course, but there is no reason why they have to be carried out in a way that is ideologically consistent with the school's approach to knowledge building (Bereiter & Scardamalia, 1996).

6. Knowledge building provides a natural basis for involving people outside the school who are engaged in related activities—scientists, curators and librarians, experts in various trades and professions, and so on. Bringing such people into learning activities is problematic because they are too peripheral to the curriculum to have a good sense of what role they should take, and they may furthermore lack pedagogical skills that the role requires. But, contributing to other people's research is something they probably already do. This involvement of talents beyond the classroom is almost obligatory if students are free to follow a knowledge-building project wherever it leads them (Scardamalia & Bereiter, 1994).

7. The knowledge objects students produce in school will tend naturally to be ones of very basic and general applicability. This is because there is no particular job that the knowledge must serve (as there is, for instance, in the forensic chemistry laboratory); and students' questions, when freely generated, tend to be *why* questions that lead toward deep principles (Scar-

damalia & Bereiter, 1992). Consequently, the knowledge that students produce is the kind that serves broadly to overcome the limits of situated cognition.

8. The situated learning that does occur is learning how to function in a community of practice whose work is work with knowledge. The transferability of this learning to knowledge work in out-of-school situations is, of course, chancy; but it seems reasonable to assume that students who have had years of experience in explicitly working with knowledge will have an advantage over ones whose experience has been limited to the traditional kinds of scholastic learning and doing in which knowledge, as such, is seldom the object of attention.

This last point warrants elaboration, in view of the much-heralded movement toward a knowledge-based society (Drucker, 1994)—a society in which the main wealth-producing work is knowledge work. If the term has any distinctive meaning, it must imply work that is focused on knowledge objects themselves. All work, even that conventionally categorized as unskilled, involves a great deal of knowledge (Vallas, 1990). What distinguishes knowledge work is not using knowledge but creating or adding value to it.

Of course, knowledge work is situated activity and has all the characteristics of other situated activity, including tool use and leveraging off physical affordances of the environment; but it is distinctive in two respects:

1. The knowledge that is being worked with is not situated knowledge. It is knowledge that has been transformed into objects that can be treated or used in an unlimited variety of situations. Thus, knowledge is no longer bound to the situations in which it was constituted.

2. In order to work effectively with knowledge objects, people have to master the practices of nonsituated cognition. This means learning to carry out the sorts of unnatural cognitive actions performed by logic machines. This does not mean becoming less human; it means acquiring a special set of skills to use wisely or unwisely, imaginatively or ploddingly, as we do with the many other intellectual, practical, and social skills that constitute human competence.

These two characteristics mark a cultural divide. A major social issue for our time is whether the world will be run by an expert elite on one side of the divide while the bulk of humanity remains on the other. It seems to me that today's schools are on the wrong side of the divide. That bodes ill for prospects of moving much of the population to the postindustrial side.

One of the most disturbing indicators that I encounter comes from my experiences in speaking publicly about the ideas discussed in this section. People in modern businesses understand what I am talking about immediately. Educators usually do not. They think I am just talking about active learning. Educators are immersed in World 3, but they are like the proverbial fish immersed in water. They cannot see it. They do not conceive of knowledge as something that can be manufactured, modified, worked with, and in some cases even packaged and sold. Unfortunately, the rise of situated cognition theory does not help in this regard. It has contributed greatly to our understanding of the kind of knowledge that is implicit in practice, but by treating all knowledge as situated, it renders the world of knowledge objects invisible.

In a famous statement, Sir Isaac Newton likened himself to a child finding pretty stones on the shore "whilst the great ocean of truth lay all undiscovered before me." Those pretty stones, however, were the foundation of the modern world. We need schools in which students learn to work with pretty stones. As for the great ocean of truth, all we can say with confidence is that, if it ever is discovered, it will not be by fishes.

REFERENCES

Anderson, J. R. (1983). *The architecture of cognition.* Cambridge, MA: Harvard University Press.

Anderson, J. R. (1985). *Cognitive psychology and its implications* (2nd ed.). San Francisco: Freeman.

Beer, R. D. (1991). *Intelligence as adaptive behavior.* Cambridge, MA: MIT Press.

Bereiter, C. (1995). A dispositional view of transfer. In A. McKeough, J. L. Lupart, & A. Marini (Eds.), *Teaching for transfer: Fostering generalization in learning* (pp. 21–34). Hillsdale, NJ: Lawrence Erlbaum Associates.

Bereiter, C., & Scardamalia, M. (1989). Intentional learning as a goal of instruction. In L. B. Resnick (Ed.), *Knowing, learning, and instruction: Essays in honor of Robert Glaser* (pp. 361–392). Hillsdale, NJ: Lawrence Erlbaum Associates.

Bereiter, C., & Scardamalia, M. (1993). *Surpassing ourselves: An inquiry into the nature and implications of expertise.* La Salle, IL: Open Court.

Bereiter, C., & Scardamalia, M. (1996). Rethinking learning. In D. Olson & N. Torrance (Eds.), *Handbook of education and human development: New models of learning, teaching and schooling* (pp. 485–513). Cambridge, MA: Basil Blackwell.

Bereiter, C., Scardamalia, M., Cassells, C., & Hewitt, J. (in press). Postmodernism, knowledge-building, and elementary science. *Elementary School Journal.*

Brown, J. S., Collins, A., & Duguid, P. (1989). Debating the situation: A rejoinder to Palincsar and Wineburg. *Educational Researcher, 18,* 10–12, 62.

Charness, N. (1991). Expertise in chess: The balance between knowledge and search. In K. A. Ericsson & J. Smith (Eds.), *Toward a general theory of expertise: Prospects and limits* (pp. 39–63). Cambridge, UK: Cambridge University Press.

Cobb, P. (1994). Where is the mind? Constructivist and sociocultural perspectives on mathematical development. *Educational Researcher, 23*(7), 13–20.

Donaldson, M. (1978). *Children's minds.* London: Croom Helm.

Doyle, W. (1983). Academic work. *Review of Educational Research, 53,* 159–199.

Dreyfus, H. L. (1988). The Socratic and Platonic basis of cognitivism. *AI and Society, 2,* 99–112.

Dreyfus, H. L., & Dreyfus, S. E. (1986). *Mind over machine.* New York: The Free Press.

Drucker, P. F. (1994, November). The age of social transformation. *Atlantic Monthly,* pp. 53–80.

Gardner, H. (1985). *The mind's new science: A history of the cognitive revolution.* New York: Basic Books.

Greeno, J. G. (1994). Understanding concepts in activity. In C. Weaver, C. R. Fletcher, & S. Mannes (Eds.), *Discourse comprehension: Essays in honor of Walter Kintsch* (pp. 65–95). Hillsdale, NJ: Lawrence Erlbaum Associates.

Greeno, J. G., Smith, D. R., & Moore, J. L. (1993). Transfer of situated learning. In D. K. Detterman & R. J. Sternberg (Eds.), *Transfer on trial: Intelligence, cognition, and instruction* (pp. 99–167). Norwood, NJ: Ablex.

Harris, K. R., & Graham, S. (Eds.). (1994). Special issue on implications of constructivism for students with disabilities and students at risk: Issues and directions. *Journal of Special Education, 28*(3), 233–378.

Hirsch, E. D., Jr. (1987). *Cultural literacy: What every American needs to know.* Boston: Houghton Mifflin.

Inhelder, B., & Piaget, J. (1958). *The growth of logical thinking from childhood to adolescence.* New York: Basic Books.

Karmiloff-Smith, A. (1992). *Beyond modularity: A developmental perspective on cognitive science.* Cambridge, MA: MIT Press.

Kitto, H. D. F. (1954). *The Greeks.* Baltimore, MD: Penguin Books.

Luria, A. R. (1976). *Cognitive development: Its cultural and social foundations* (M. Lopez-Morillas & L. Soltaroff, Trans.). Cambridge, MA: Harvard University Press.

Margolis, H. (1987). *Patterns, thinking, and cognition.* Chicago: University of Chicago Press.

Montessori, M. (1967). *The absorbent mind.* New York: Holt, Rinehart & Winston.

Newell, A., & Simon, H. A. (1972). *Human problem solving.* Englewood Cliffs, NJ: Prentice-Hall.

Ng, E., & Bereiter, C. (1991). Three levels of goal orientation in learning. *The Journal of the Learning Sciences, 1*(3–4), 243–271.

Popper, K. R. (1972). *Objective knowledge: An evolutionary approach.* Oxford, UK: Clarendon.

Popper, K. R., & Eccles, J. C. (1977). *The self and its brain.* Berlin: Springer-Verlag.

Resnick, L. B., & Neches, R. (1984). Factors affecting individual differences in learning ability. In R. J. Sternberg (Ed.), *Advances in the psychology of human intelligence* (pp. 275–323). Hillsdale, NJ: Lawrence Erlbaum Associates.

Rumelhart, D. E. (1989). The architecture of mind: A connectionist approach. In M. I. Posner (Ed.), *Foundations of cognitive science* (pp. 133–159). Cambridge, MA: MIT Press.

Scardamalia, M., & Bereiter, C. (1992). Text-based and knowledge-based questioning by children. *Cognition and Instruction, 9*(3), 177–199.

Scardamalia, M., & Bereiter, C. (1994). Computer support for knowledge-building communities. *The Journal of the Learning Sciences, 3*(3), 265–283.

Scardamalia, M., Bereiter, C., & Lamon, M. (1994). CSILE: Trying to bring students into world 3. In K. McGilley (Ed.), *Classroom lessons: Integrating cognitive theory and classroom practice* (pp. 201–228). Cambridge, MA: MIT Press.

Schank, R. C., Collins, G. C., & Hunter, L. E. (1986). Transcending inductive category formation in learning. *Behavioral and Brain Sciences, 9*, 639–686.

Scribner, S. (1979). Modes of thinking and ways of speaking: Culture and logic reconsidered. In R. O. Freedle (Ed.), *New directions in discourse processing* (pp. 223–243). Norwood, NJ: Ablex.

Tolman, E. C. (1949). There is more than one kind of learning. *Psychological Review, 56*, 144–155.

Vallas, S. P. (1990). The concept of skill: A critical review. *Work and Occupations, 17*, 379–398.

Vera, A. H., & Simon, H. A. (1993). Situated action: A symbolic interpretation. *Cognitive Science, 17*, 7–48.

Whitehead, A. N. (1929). *The aims of education.* New York: Macmillan.

Wineburg, S. S. (1989). Remembrance of theories past. *Educational Researcher, 18*, 7–10.

Woodworth, R. S. (1958). *Dynamics of behavior.* New York: Holt.

CHAPTER TWELVE

Situated Cognition in Search of an Agenda

Yrjö Engeström
Michael Cole
University of California, San Diego

Behind the notion of situatedness lies the notion of situation. It is a deceptively simple notion: We all know what it means. But try to define it explicitly. Is a situation a moment in time? Is it a location, a place? Is it a life situation, a social situation, a configuration of relationships? Or is it perhaps more like a position, a perspective, a viewpoint of the subject?

All of these aspects play a variety of roles in the discourse on situated cognition. Yet which aspects are being focused on is seldom spelled out. Situatedness is not a black box. It is more like a Pandora's box that offers a rich variety of interpretations, possibilities, and dangers. In this sense, the notion of situatedness is a challenge, an initial push toward novel theorizing and research rather than an answer. Gee (chapter 9, this volume) states that "the word 'situated' itself takes on somewhat differently situated meanings" (p. 235). In a similar vein, Lave and Wenger (1991) wrote that situatedness "now appears to be a transitory concept, a bridge, between a view according to which cognitive processes (and thus learning) are primary and a view according to which social practice is the primary, generative phenomenon" (p. 34). So the notion of situatedness leads to the primacy of practice—a whole new landscape for the study of cognition. We sort out and discuss some of the possibilities and questions made salient by this change of scenery.

One immediately relevant set of questions concerns the units of analysis in the situated, or practice-bound, approach to cognition. Another set of issues has to do with the multiplicity of contexts of practice and the boundaries between them. A third theme concerns the role of time and the meaning of development with respect to cognition embedded in practice. Finally, our fourth topic deals with the relationship between acculturation, rebellion, and creation of new meanings and artifacts in practice-bound cognition.

Our discussion of the four themes is something like an attempt at charting the waters. Instead of presenting a singular version of what a theory of situated, practice-bound cognition should or should not be, we point out some alternative interpretations and their consequences. In so doing, we surely indicate our own favorite routes of analytical movement, without claiming exclusiveness or superiority over other routes.[1]

UNITS OF ANALYSIS

Cole (1995) recently discussed a number of current attempts to conceptualize situation and practice as units of analysis. He focused on the notions of practice, activity, context, situation, and event. Cole pointed out the pioneering role of Dewey. In his *Logic*, Dewey (1938) emphasized that a situation is not a single object or event. A situation refers to our experiencing of objects and events in connection to a contextual whole. Yet the shape and structure of that contextual whole is left ambiguous. The same can be said of Bourdieu's (1977) and Giddens' (1979) notions of practice, also discussed by Cole. Although powerful in their generality, these notions are relatively weak as tools of concrete analysis, owing to their nonspecificity.

Two additional attempts at constructing practice-based units of analysis may be mentioned. These are social world and mediated action. These two concepts help us identify a dimension along which the different practice-based units of analysis can be compared.

In symbolic interactionism, several authors have used and developed the concept of social world as a potential unit of analysis (Becker, 1982; Clarke, 1991; Strauss, 1993). Strauss (1991) defined the concept as follows:

> In each social world, at least one primary activity (along with related clusters of activity) is strikingly evident; such as climbing mountains, researching, collecting. There are sites where activities occur: hence space and shaped landscape are relevant. Technology (inherited or innovative modes of carrying out the social world's activities) is always involved. Most worlds evolve quite complex technologies. In social worlds at their outset, there may be only temporary divisions of labor, but once under way, organizations inevitably evolve to further one aspect or another of the world's activities. (p. 236)

---

[1]We have recently encountered the issue of superiority claims in theorizing cultural psychology and opted for a decidedly multivoiced, dialogical view. We feel that diversity can breed good hybrids in the related fields of cultural psychology and situated cognition. See Cole and Engeström (1995).

In a similar vein, Becker (1982) identified division of labor, cooperative links, and conventions as key elements of a social world. Thus, social world is a decidedly communitarian unit of analysis. Yet, it is not a social structure but "a recognizable forum of collective action" (Strauss, 1993, p. 223). In its collective emphasis, it stands in contrast to the concept of mediated action put forward by Wertsch and his colleagues as the unit of analysis in sociocultural research (Wertsch, del Rio, & Alvarez, 1995).

Wertsch (1995) believed that the concept of mediated action transcends the opposition between individual and society by providing "a context within which the individual and society (as well as mental functioning and sociocultural context, understood as interrelated moments" (p. 60). This claim is further clarified as follows:

> Instead of assuming that individuals, acting alone, are the agents of actions, the appropriate designation of agent is "individual-operating-with-mediational means." . . . Any insights it [the concept of mediated action] provides will derive from the fact that the mediational means that shape mental functioning and action more generally are inherent aspects of, and hence serve as indexes of, a sociocultural setting. (Wertsch, 1995, p. 64)

Mediated action as defined by Wertsch (1995) focuses on two elements, the individual and the mediational means (understood as cultural artifacts, both practical and semiotic). In this formulation, the collective, communitarian dimension is included only insofar as it is embodied in the mediating artifacts.

Wertsch (1995), conscious of the narrowness of the concept he proposed, suggested that "we must eventually expand the list of moments in the analysis of action beyond the two that have been my primary focus" (p. 71). As a remedy, he took up Burke's pentad of literary analysis, consisting of the five components of act, scene, agent, agency, and purpose. The remedy seems insufficient to meet the challenge presented by the notion of social world. The crucial factor of community and its internal relations (division of labor, conventions) are not visible in Burke's pentad, although they may hide within the vague notion of scene.[2]

Social world and mediated action represent opposite ends on a dimension that we might call horizontal. This dimension represents the width of the sociospatial scope included in the unit of analysis. Social world takes a community and its division of labor and conventions as the starting point. Mediated action takes the individual and his or her mediational means as

---

[2]In his earlier work, Wertsch (1985) saw great promise in Leont'ev's (1981) concept of activity as a way to expand the Vygotskian concept of action. Wertsch wrote: "The notion of an activity setting with its motive provides a means for relating social insitutional and individual phenomena" (p. 215).

the starting point. The functional systems analyzed by Hutchins (1995) seem to fall somewhere in between, representing relatively small but decidedly collective working groups and their artifacts focused on a shared but well-bounded task.

In concrete analyses of situated, practice-bound cognition, one wants to have both a collective and an individual perspective. Social world as a unit of analysis may easily lead to a neglect of the perspective of an individual subject, whereas mediated action obviously has difficulties in constructing the perspective of a community. Their integration is no easy task. It is this very task with which Cobb and his coauthors (chapter 8, this volume) are struggling.

Activity theory, initiated by Leont'ev (1978, 1981) and further elaborated in our own work (Cole & Engeström, 1993; Engeström, 1987), may be seen as one attempt to overcome this dualism of collectively and individually based units of analysis. One crucial aspect of this attempt is the modeling of human activity as a systemic formation (Fig. 12.1).

Figure 12.1 calls attention to both the personal perspective of the subject—any given subject involved in the collaborative activity may be selected—and its relationship to the systems perspective that views the activity from the outside. An individual artifact-mediated action may be depicted as the uppermost subtriangle in Fig. 12.1. Such individual actions are embedded in collective activity systems. This collective aspect is represented by the bottom part of the diagram, consisting of the community, its division of labor, and its rules (which include the conventions emphasized by Becker, 1982).

Several authors in this volume (Walkerdine and Gee, in particular) suggest yet another unit of analysis for situated cognition, discourse. Gee (chapter 9, this volume) summarizes the concept of discourse as follows.

> Discourses are sociohistorical coordinations of people, objects (props), ways of talking, acting, interacting, thinking, valuing, and (sometimes) writing and reading that allow for the display and recognition of socially significant iden-

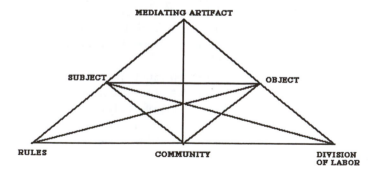

FIG. 12.1. The basic mediational triangle expanded (after Engeström, 1987) to include other people (community), social rules (rules), and the division of labor between the subject and others.

tities, like being a (certain sort of) African American, boardroom executive, feminist, lawyer, street-gang member, theoretical physicist, 18th-century mid-wife, 19th-century modernist, Soviet or Russian, schoolchild, teacher, and so on through innumerable possibilities. If you destroy a Discourse (and they do die), you also destroy its cultural models, situated meanings, and its con-comitant identities. (pp. 255, 256)

For Walkerdine (chapter 4, this volume), situated cognition is not people thinking in different practical contexts, but subjects and identities produced differently in different discourses. This shift of perspective is exciting in that it indeed promises to transcend the dichotomy of the individual and collec-tive units. The subject, such as the child, is a collective achievement, a sign created within a discursive practice. What is less promising is the fate of agency and possibility of change within this framework, as Agre (chapter 5, this volume) points out.

Development, Motives, and Agency

Kirshner (chapter 6, this volume) argues that logic and rationality serve socially to rationalize behavior, not intrapsychically to direct it. This recon-structive or retrospective nature of goals and plans has been convincingly demonstrated by Suchman (1987) and Weick (1995). A problem with this account is that it leaves unexplained—or untouched—the question of what makes development happen.

Introducing a vertical dimension into the unit of analysis, activity theory distinguishes between goal-directed individual actions and motive-driven collective activity systems. The retrospective and reconstructive view of goals and plans seems to be largely correct at the level of actions. Indeed, Leont'ev (1978) pointed out that goal formation is a "long process of appropriation of the goals by action and by their objective filling" (p. 65), which means that an individual "cannot determine the goal of his acting as long as he has not acted."

Were this the whole story, human development would indeed be a result of blind natural and cultural forces beyond the reach of human agency. However, when attention is shifted upward, to collective activity systems, the picture is radically changed. According to Leont'ev (1978), an activity is driven by its motive, and the object of an activity is its true motive. The sphere of collective motives and objects is not readily accessible to individual awareness. Harr, Clarke, and DeCarlo (1985) characterized it as both the social order and the deep structure of mind:

This accords with our understanding, and lack of understanding, of our own activity and life patterns. The parts are usually familiar: we know what we experience and what we do. What we do not always know is what are the larger-scale life patterns that these events are part of. (p. 30)

Yet this sphere is not outside of human agency. It is at this level that powerful forward-oriented and future-creating images and ideals are formed, individual dreams and collective visions merge. Such tertiary artifacts (Wartofsky, 1979) seem necessary if we want to begin to understand human development as a motivated, yet not simply goal-rational process. When Walkerdine (chapter 4, this volume) talks about "deep issues of desire, longing, need, nurturance and the ways that this is made to signify" (p. 66), she touches on the very same sphere of motives activity theory is concerned with.

A related dilemma is present in Lave and Wenger's (1991) account of situated learning in communities of practice. Legitimate peripheral participation seems to have one dominant direction of movement, namely from the periphery of the novices toward the center dominated by the well-established, competent masters. The practice itself is depicted as stable and relatively unchanging. This ignores Bronfenbrenner's (1983) famous dictum that development takes place as if in a moving train. Not only is the individual developing, the practices in which he or she is involved develop, too. The development of collective activity systems is intimately interwoven with the emergence of novel actions by individuals (Engeström, 1987). It is in this interpenetration that novel motives, cultural models, and collective movements are initiated.

TRANSFER, MULTIPLE CONTEXTS, AND BOUNDARIES

Bereiter (chapter 11, this volume) takes up the issue of transfer in situated cognition. For him, achieving transfer means overcoming situatedness. Bereiter maintains that the world of immaterial knowledge objects—Popper's World 3—is the true measure of human ability to overcome situatedness. Bereiter acknowledges that transfer is a matter of "the same kind of relationship coming into play in different situations." But this is no simple occurrence:

> People have to be looking for a relationship. And what kind of relationship is it? The word that comes to mind is *abstract*. It is a relationship based on formal, structural, or logical correspondences. . . . To discover such abstract relationships, however, one has to carry out something quite different from ordinary situated action. One has to create symbolic representations of situations and carry out operations on those symbols. (p. 288)

We see two major issues in Bereiter's argument. First, why is creating and manipulating symbolic representations not a situated action? People do that all the time in ordinary and extraordinary situations. Actions of abstraction and generalization are already evident in very early production of tools (Leont'ev, 1981) and theories of mind typical to our social intelligence

(Goody, 1995), not to speak of the creation of word meanings and language. There seems to be nothing inherently nonsituated in these actions.

Second, not all abstraction is based on formal, structural, or logical correspondences. Luria's (1976) famous early research on the cultural basis of cognition showed that along with formal-logical relations, people use functional and systemic interdependencies as bases for their abstraction and generalization. Rather than coining the latter kinds of abstraction as nonlogical or primitive, we might do well to consider it as representing rudiments of an alternative logic of evolving concrete systems. Davydov (1990) and Ilyenkov (1977) would call it dialectical logic, based on substantive, not formal abstraction (see also Falmagne, 1995). In such logic, "universality is achieved, not through abstraction, but by embracing the range of concrete particulars" (Falmagne, 1995, p. 221). The whole notion of transfer requires a thorough reexamination within this framework, a reexamination probably to a significant extent in line with the attempt of Greeno, Smith, and Moore (1993).

Lemke (chapter 3, this volume) offers the notion of networks of activities as a related route for reexamining transfer. In this view, learning does not happen only within communities of practice, but also between and across those communities:

> There is far more interpenetration of networks of different genders, sexual orientations, classes, ages, cultures, ethnicities, etc. in our ecosocial systems than our prevailing discourses and ideologies might like us to believe. . . . Individual trajectories that move between these networks also knit them together, also open them up to change due to one another's influences. (p.)

This polycontextuality of learning and cognition implies that we are a species of boundary crossers. Issues of transfer become issues of dialogical problem solving, hybridization, and formation of new concepts across boundaries in practice (see Engeström, Engeström, & Kärkkäinen, 1995). Novel notions such as the concept of third space (Gutierrez, Rymes, & Larson, 1995) are needed to capture contours of this exciting terrain.

NONCOOPERATION, CONTRADICTION, AND CREATION OF THE NEW

Agre (chapter 5, this volume), in discussing Walkerdine's work, points out a problematic feature that runs through much of situated cognition literature:

> . . . to what extent should we view the children as modeling clay that is being shaped into the discursive "child," and to what extent should we view the children as active participants in the process? This is, to be sure, a point of

instability in many theories of development. What is missing in each case is a substantive account of the children's noncooperation with the adults' plan for them.

To be sure, Lave and Wenger (1991) identified the issue. They named it the contradiction between continuity and displacement in communities of practice. However, there is still very little research on the actual dynamics and developmental potentials of noncooperation. Bateson's (1972) account of double binds remains one of the most powerful insights into the issue. It presents noncooperation as a manifestation of inner contradictions (or contraries, as Bateson would call them) of the practice in which the individual is engaged. In other words, we are not talking only about the resistance of the individual against molding and acculturation; it is more than a question of tension between the individual novice and the established collective. The developmental potential lies in the fact that the contradiction is within both the individual and the collective; it is inherent in every practice.

This insight calls attention to disturbances and discoordinations as indications of new possibilities in practices (see Engeström & Mazzocco, 1995). Taking this one step further, purposeful use of selective discoordinations becomes a tool for revealing and traversing zones of proximal development at both individual and collective levels (Cole & Engeström, 1993). Such a research stance might be characterized as situated interventionism. Its key characteristic is that it is not satisfied with observing and analyzing situated practices; it is engaged in creating new forms of practices (Cole, 1995; Engeström, 1994).

REFERENCES

Bateson, G. (1972). *Steps to an ecology of mind.* New York: Ballantine.

Becker, H. (1982). *Art worlds.* Berkeley: University of California Press.

Bourdieu, P. (1977). *Outline of a theory of practice.* New York: Cambridge University Press.

Bronfenbrenner, U. (1983). The context of development and the development of context. In R. M. Lerner (Ed.), *Developmental psychology: Historical and philosophical perspectives* (pp. 147–184). Hillsdale, NJ: Lawrence Erlbaum Associates.

Clarke, A. (1991). Social worlds/arenas theory as organizational theory. In D. Maines (Ed.), *Social organization and social process: Essays in honor of Anselm Strauss* (pp. 119–158). New York: Aldine.

Cole, M. (1995). The supra-individual envelope of development: Activity and practice; situation and context. In J. Goodnow, P. Miller, & F. Kessel (Eds.), *Cultural practices as contexts for development* (pp. 105–117). San Francisco: Jossey-Bass.

Cole, M., & Engeström, Y. (1993). A cultural-historical approach to distributed cognition. In G. Salomon (Ed.), *Distributed cognitions: Psychological and educational considerations* (pp. 1–46). Cambridge, UK: Cambridge University Press.

Cole, M., & Engeström, Y. (1995). Commentary on Joan Lucariello's "Mind, culture, person: Elements in a cultural psychology." *Human Development, 38,* 19–24.

Davydov, V. V. (1990). *Types of generalization in instruction: Logical and psychological problems in the structuring of school curricula.* Reston, VA: National Council of Teachers of Mathematics.

Dewey, J. (1938). *Logic: The theory of inquiry.* Troy, MO: Holt, Rinehart & Winston.

Engeström, Y. (1987). *Learning by expanding: An activity-theoretical approach to developmental research.* Helsinki, Finland: Orienta-Konsultit.

Engeström, Y. (1994). The working health center project: Materializing zones of proximal development in a network of organizational learning. In T. Kauppinen & M. Lahtonen (Eds.), *Action research in Finland* (pp. 233–272). Helsinki, Finland: Ministry of Labour.

Engeström, Y., Engeström, R., & Kärkkäinen, M. (1995). Polycontextuality and boundary crossing in expert cognition: Learning and problem solving in complex work activities. *Learning and Instruction, 5,* 319–336.

Engeström, Y., & Mazzocco, D. W. (1995, May). *Disturbance management and masking in a television production team: An activity-theoretical study in organizational communication.* Paper presented at the 45th Annual Conference of the International Communication Association, Albuquerque, NM.

Falmagne, R. J. (1995). The abstract and the concrete. In L. W. Martin, K. Nelson, & E. Tobach (Eds), *Sociocultural psychology: Theory and practice of doing and knowing* (pp. 205–228). New York: Cambridge University Press.

Giddens, A. (1979). *Central problems in social theory.* London: Macmillan.

Goody, E. N. (Ed.). (1995). *Social intelligence and interaction: Expressions and implications of the social bias in human intelligence.* Cambridge, UK: Cambridge University Press.

Greeno, J. G., Smith, D. R., & Moore, J. L. (1993). Transfer of situated learning. In D. K. Detterman & R. J. Sternberg (Eds.), *Transfer on trial: Intelligence, cognition, and instruction* (pp. 99–167). Norwood, NJ: Ablex.

Gutierrez, K., Rymes, B., & Larson, J. (1995). Script, counterscript, and underlife in the classroom: James Brown versus Brown v. Board of Education. *Harvard Educational Review, 65,* 445–471.

Harr, R., Clarke, D., & DeCarlo, N. (1985). *Motives and mechanisms: An introduction to the psychology of action.* London: Methuen.

Hutchins, E. (1995). *Cognition in the wild.* Cambridge, MA: MIT Press.

Ilyenkov, E. V. (1977). *Dialectical logic: Essays in its history and theory.* Moscow: Progress.

Lave, J., & Wenger, E. (1991). *Situated learning: Legitimate peripheral participation.* Cambridge, UK: Cambridge University Press.

Leont'ev, A. N. (1978). *Activity, consciousness, and personality.* Englewood Cliffs, NJ: Prentice-Hall.

Leont'ev, A. N. (1981). *Problems of the development of the mind.* Moscow: Progress.

Luria, A. R. (1976). *Cognitive development: Its cultural and social foundations.* Cambridge, MA: Harvard University Press.

Strauss, A. L. (1991). A social world perspective. In A. Strauss (Ed.), *Creating sociological awareness: Collective images and symbolic representations* (pp. 233–244). New Brunswick, NJ: Transaction Press.

Strauss, A. L. (1993). *Continual permutations of action.* New York: Aldine.

Suchman, L. A. (1987). *Plans and situated actions: The problem of human–machine communication.* Cambridge, UK: Cambridge University Press.

Wartofsky, M. (1979). *Models: Representation and scientific understanding.* Dordrecht, The Netherlands: Reidel.

Weick, K. E. (1995). *Sensemaking in organizations.* Thousand Oaks, CA: Sage.

Wertsch, J. V. (1985). *Vygotsky and the social formation of mind.* Cambridge, MA: Harvard University Press.

Wertsch, J. V. (1995). The need for action in sociocultural research. In J. V. Wertsch, P. del Rio, & A. Alvarez (Eds.), *Sociocultural studies of mind* (pp. 1–36). Cambridge, UK: Cambridge University Press.

Wertsch, J. V., del Rio, P., & Alvarez, A. (Eds.). (1995). *Sociocultural studies of mind.* Cambridge, UK: Cambridge University Press.

Author Index

Subject Index

DATE DUE

HIGHSMITH #45110